THE

GUINNESS BOOK OF SPORTS RECORDS

THE
GUINNESS BOOK OF SPORTS RECORDS

1995–1996

EDITOR

GARY M. KREBS

Facts On File®

AN INFOBASE HOLDINGS COMPANY

THE GUINNESS BOOK OF SPORTS RECORDS 1995–1996

Facts On File, Inc.
460 Park Avenue South
New York NY 10016
USA

AUG. 5 1996

This book is taken in part from *The Guinness Book of Records* © 1995

Facts On File books are available at special discounts when purchased in bulk quantities for businesses, associations, institutions or sales promotions. Please contact the Special Sales Department of our New York office at 212/683-2244 or 1-800/322-8755.

ISBN 0-8160-3262-9 (hardcover)
ISBN 0-8160-3263-7 (paperback)
ISSN 1054-4178

"Guinness" is a registered trademark of Guinness PLC for Publications

Text design by Ron Monteleone
Jacket design by Paul Agresti
Composition by Catherine Rincon Hyman/Facts On File, Inc.
Production by Jill Lazer

Printed in the United States of America

RRD FOF 10 9 8 7 6 5 4 3 2 1

This book is printed on acid-free paper.

CONTENTS

INTRODUCTION AND ACKNOWLEDGMENTS

1994: A sports year beleaguered by strikes and lockouts. One may wonder what new records could possibly be of interest to fans; surprisingly, however, there are a good many. In major league baseball, for example, which did not have a World Series for the first time in 90 years, Greg Maddux managed to win his third consecutive Cy Young Award. In the season preceding the 1994 hockey lockout, Wayne Gretzky broke the all-time goal-scoring record and the New York Rangers won their first Stanley Cup in what seemed like a millennium. World Cup Soccer was a head-banging success in terms of records, with several falling at once (including a record for most penalty flags!).

The Guinness Book of Sports Records 1995–1996 provides three all-new features: "The Record Holder Speaks" (interview profiles of record holders); "Record Quotables" (brief quotes from record holders); and "Guinness Challenge" (trivia questions). Because of popular demand, two dynamic new categories have been added: bungy jumping and inline skating (rollerblading). There is also more access to information through separate subject and name indexes.

Since this was my first opportunity to work on this book, I have had to rely on the assistance and expertise of many colleagues. I am greatly indebted to Mark Young, whose vision of this project has struck the bull's-eye since the first edition in 1991. Many thanks to my assistant, Tobey Grumet, who conducted painstaking research under deadline pressure and did an admirable job writing various "Record Holder Speaks" profiles. Jay Amster of the *Facts On File News Digest* has been a valuable source for new record information and clippings. Jill Lazer and Cathy Hyman deserve extra praise for their patience and professionalism during long waits between manuscript deliveries. Thanks also to Jo Stein, Joe Reilly, Virginia Rubens and Marjorie Bank. Of course, the entire team at Guinness Publishing Ltd. in Enfield, England—notably, Peter Matthews, Christine Heilman, Stewart Newport and Dawn Gratton—deserves a stadium-filled wave for its contributions.

Extra special thanks to the numerous sporting associations, halls of fame and museums that lent their assistance in updating records, as well as to our photo sources—all of which are credited in the captions accompanying the photos.

If you have a question about any of the records included herein—or have suggestions for including professional sports that do not appear in this edition—we'd love to hear from you. Send inquiries to:

The Guinness Book of Records
c/o Facts On File, Inc.
460 Park Avenue South
New York, N.Y. 10016

Let's hope and pray for full baseball and hockey seasons in 1995—and that it will be a banner year for record-breakers.

Gary M. Krebs
New York City

AEROBATICS

ORIGINS The first aerobatic "maneuver" is generally considered to be the sustained inverted flight in a Blériot flown by Célestin-Adolphe Pégoud (France), at Buc, France on September 21, 1913. Stunt flying became popular in the United States during the 1920s and 1930s. In the late 1950s aerobatic contests regained popularity at air shows. In 1970 the International Aerobatic Club formed standardized rules for the sport, establishing four categories of competition: unlimited, advanced, intermediate and sportsman.

WORLD CHAMPIONSHIPS First held in 1960, the world championships are a biennial event. The competition consists of three flight programs: known and unknown compulsories and a free program. The judges award scores based on a system devised by Col. José Aresti (Spain).

Most titles (team) The USSR won the men's title a record six times, 1964, 1966, 1976, 1982, 1986, and 1990.

Most titles (individual) Petr Jimus (Czechoslovakia) has won two men's world titles: 1984 and 1986. Betty Stewart (U.S.) has won two women's world titles, 1980 and 1982.

AIR RACING

Air racing, or airplane racing, consists of piloted aircraft racing a specific number of laps over a closed circuit marked by pylons. As with auto racing, the first plane to cross the finish line is the winner. Air races are divided into several categories, depending on the type of plane and engine. The top level of the sport is the unlimited class.

GUINNESS CHALLENGE

In 1994 World Cup soccer, what team finally ended its consecutive winning streak at 17 games?
See page 183 for the answer.

ORIGINS The first international airplane racing competition, the Bennett Trophy, was held at Rheims, France from August 22–28, 1909.

United States The first international air race staged in the United States was the second Bennett Trophy competition, held at Belmont Park, N.Y. in 1910. Air racing became very popular in the 1920s. Competitions, such as the National Air Races (inaugurated in 1924) and the Thompson Trophy (inaugurated in 1930), drew enormous crowds—500,000 people attended the 1929 National Air Races in Cleveland, Ohio. Following World War II the popularity of the sport declined. During the mid-1950s, enthusiasts revived the sport, racing smaller World War II military planes. In 1964 Bill Stead staged the first National Championship Air Races (NCAR) at Reno, Nev.; this is now the premier air racing event in the United States.

NATIONAL CHAMPIONSHIP AIR RACES (NCAR)

Staged annually in Reno, Nev., since 1964, the NCAR has been held at its present site, the Reno/Stead Airport, since 1986. Races are staged in four categories: Unlimited class, AT-6 class, Formula One class and Biplane class.

UNLIMITED CLASS In this class the aircraft must use piston engines, be propeller-driven and be capable of pulling six G's. The planes race over a pylon-marked 9.128 mile course.

Most titles Darryl Greenmyer has won seven unlimited NCAR titles: 1965–69, 1971 and 1977.

Fastest average speed (race) Lyle Shelton won the 1991 NCAR title recording the fastest average speed at 481.618 mph in his "Rare Bear."

Fastest qualifying speed The one-lap NCAR qualifying record is 482.892 mph, by Lyle Shelton in 1992.

AT-6 CLASS Only World War II Advanced Trainers (AT), complying to the original stock configuration, are allowed to compete. Seats can be removed and the engines stripped and reassembled, but the cubic inch displacement of the 650-horsepower 1340-R Pratt & Whitney engine cannot exceed the original level.

Most titles Eddie Van Fossen has won seven AT-6 NCAR titles: 1986–88, 1991–94.

MODEL AIRCRAFT RECORDS

Altitude

Record	Pilot	Date
26,922 feet	Maynard L. Hill (U.S.)	September 6, 1970

Speed

242.95 mph	W. Sitar (Austria)	June 10, 1977

Distance*

769.9 miles	Gianmaria Aghem (Italy)	July 26, 1986

* On a closed-circuit course

Fastest average speed (race) Eddie Van Fossen won the 1992 NCAR title recording the fastest average speed at 234.788 mph in "Miss TNT."

Fastest qualifying speed The one-lap NCAR qualifying record is 235.223 mph, by Eddie Van Fossen in 1992.

FANTASTIC FEATS

Inverted flight The duration record is 4 hours 38 minutes 10 seconds by Joann Osterud (U.S.) from Vancouver to Vanderjoof, Canada on July 24, 1991.

ARCHERY

ORIGINS The exact date of the invention of the bow is unknown, but historians agree that it was at least 50,000 years ago. The origins of archery as a competitive sport are also unclear. It is believed that the ancient Olympic Games (776 B.C. to 393 A.D.) featured archery, using tethered doves as targets. The legends

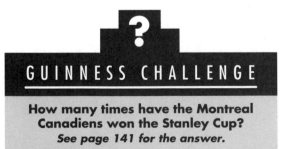

GUINNESS CHALLENGE

How many times have the Montreal Canadiens won the Stanley Cup?
See page 141 for the answer.

of Robin Hood and William Tell indicate that archery prowess was highly regarded in Europe by the 13th century. Archery became an official event in the modern Olympics in 1900. In 1931, the *Fédération Internationale de Tir à l'Arc* (FITA) was founded as the world governing body of the sport.

United States The date of the first use of the bow as a weapon in North America is unknown; however, it is believed that Native American tribes in the eastern part of North America were familiar with the bow by the 11th century. The National Archery Association was founded in 1879 in Crawfordsville, Ind. and is the oldest amateur sports organization in continuous existence in the United States.

TARGET ARCHERY

The most widely practiced discipline in archery is Olympic-style target archery (also known as FITA style). Olympic-style target archery competition is based on the Single FITA round system of scoring. A Single FITA round consists of 36 arrows shot from four distances: 90, 70, 50 and 30 meters for men; 70, 60, 50 and 30 for women, for a total of 144 arrows. Scoring ranges from 10 in the center gold circle to 1 in the outer white ring. The maximum possible score for a Single FITA round is 1,440 points. Competition varies from accumulated scores based on two or more Single FITA rounds to single elimination rounds in which each archer's score reverts to zero at each stage of the tournament.

OLYMPIC GAMES Archery made its first appearance in the 1900 Games in Paris, France. It was also featured in 1904, 1908 and 1920, but then was omitted until 1972, when enough countries had adopted FITA standardized rules to allow for a meaningful international competition.

Most gold medals Hubert van Innis (Belgium) has won six gold medals (au cordon dore—33 meters, au chapelet—33 meters, 1900; moving bird target, 28 meters, 33 meters, moving bird target [team], 33 meters, 50 meters, 1920).

Most medals Hubert van Innis has won nine medals in all: six gold (see above), and three silver (au cordon dore—50 meters, 1900; moving bird target, 50 meters, moving bird target [team] 28 meters, 1920).

FLIGHT SHOOTING WORLD RECORDS

The object in flight shooting is to fire the arrow the greatest distance possible. There are two flight shooting classifications: regular flight and broadhead flight.

Regular Flight

Men

Bow Type	Distance	Archer	Date
Crossbow	2,047 yds 0 ft 2 in	Harry Drake	July 30, 1988
Unlimited Footbow	2,028 yds 0 ft 0 in	Harry Drake	Oct. 24, 1971
Conventional Footbow	1,542 yds 2 ft 10 in	Harry Drake	Oct. 6, 1979
Unlimited Recurve Bow	1,336 yds 1 ft 3 in	Don Brown	Aug. 2, 1987
Unlimited Compound Bow	1,320 yds 1 ft 3 in	Kevin Strother	July 31, 1992
Unlimited Longbow	356 yds 1 ft 2 in	Don Brown	July 29, 1989
Unlimited Primitive Bow	521 yds 0 ft 2 in	Daniel Perry	June 18, 1993

Women

Bow Type	Distance	Archer	Date
Unlimited Recurve Bow	1,039 yds 1 ft 1 in	April Moon	Sept. 13, 1981
Conventional Footbow	1,113 yds 2 ft 6 in	Arlyne Rhode	Sept. 10, 1978
Unlimited Compound Bow	807 yds 1 ft 3 in	April Moon	Aug. 1, 1987
Unlimited Longbow	217 yds 2 ft 3 in	April Moon	July 30, 1989

Broadhead Flight

Men

Bow Type	Distance	Archer	Date
Unlimited Compound Bow	784 yds 2 ft 9 in	Bert McCune Jr.	Aug. 2, 1992
Unlimited Recurve Bow	526 yds 0 ft 5 in	Don Brown	June 26, 1988
Unlimited Longbow	332 yds 2 ft 0 in	Don Brown	Aug. 2, 1992
Unlimited Primitive Bow	244 yds 2 ft 7 in	Daniel Perry	June 24, 1990

Women

Bow Type	Distance	Archer	Date
Unlimited Compound Bow	481 yds 0 ft 7 in	April Moon	June 24, 1989
Unlimited Recurve Bow	364 yds 0 ft 4 in	April Moon	June 28, 1987
Unlimited Longbow	237 yds 2 ft 3 in	April Moon	Aug. 2, 1992
Unlimited Primitive Bow	107 yds 1 ft 5 in	Gwen Perry	June 24, 1990

Source: U.S. National Archery Association

Men

Event	Archer	Country	Points	Year
FITA	Vladimir Esheev	USSR	1,352	1990
90 m	Vladimir Esheev	USSR	330	1990
70 m	Hiroshi Yamamoto	Japan	344	1990
50 m	Rick McKinney	U.S.	345	1982
30 m	Antonio Vazquez Megldo	Spain	358	1992
Final	Vladimir Esheev	USSR	345	1989

Women

Event	Archer	Country	Points	Year
FITA	Cho Youn-Jeong	S. Korea	1,375	1992
70 m	Cho Youn-Jeong	S. Korea	338	1992
60 m	Kim Soo-nyung	S. Korea	347	1989
50 m	Cho Youn-Jeong	S. Korea	338	1992
30 m	Joanne Edens	Great Britain	357	1990
Final	Kim Soo-nyung	S. Korea	346	1990

Source: U.S. National Archery Association

WORLD CHAMPIONSHIPS Target archery world championships were first held in 1931 in Lvov, Poland. The championships are staged biennially.

Most titles (archer) The most titles won is seven, by Janina Spychajowa-Kurkowska (Poland) in 1931–34, 1936, 1939 and 1947. The most titles won by a man is four, by Hans Deutgen (Sweden) in 1947–50.

Most titles (country) The United States has a record 14 men's (1959–83) and eight women's (1952–77) team titles.

UNITED STATES NATIONAL CHAMPIONSHIPS The U.S. national championships were first held in Chicago, Ill. from August 12–14, 1879, and are staged annually.

Most titles The most archery titles won is 17, by Lida Howell between 1883 and 1907. The most men's titles is nine (three individual, six pairs), by Rick McKinney, 1977, 1979–83, and 1985–87.

WINNER TAKE AIM ■ **RICK MCKINNEY HAS WON A RECORD NINE U.S. NATIONAL TITLES.** (NATIONAL ARCHERY ASSOCIATION)

Greatest draw on a longbow Gary Sentman of Roseberg, Ore. drew a longbow weighing a record 176 lb to the maximum draw on the arrow of 28¼ inches at Forksville, Pa. on September 20, 1975.

AUSTRALIAN RULES FOOTBALL

ORIGINS A cross between soccer and rugby, Australian Rules Football was developed in the mid-19th century by Henry Harrison and Thomas Wills, who helped form the Melbourne Football Club in 1858. In 1877, the Victorian Football Association was founded, from which eight clubs broke away to form the Victorian Football League (VFL). Four more teams had been admitted by 1925, and in 1987 teams from Queensland and Western Australia joined the league, which has since been renamed the Australian Football League.

GRAND FINAL The sports premier event is the Grand Final, played annually since 1897. Staged at the Melbourne Cricket Ground, it had a record attendance of 121,696 in 1970.

Most wins Two teams have won the Grand Final on 15 occasions: Carlton, 1906–08, 1914–15, 1938, 1945, 1947, 1968, 1970, 1972, 1979, 1981–82, 1987; Essendon, 1897, 1901, 1911–12, 1923–24, 1942, 1946, 1949–50, 1962, 1965, 1984–85, 1993.

AUTO RACING

The nationality of the competitors in this section is U.S. unless noted otherwise.

ORIGINS The site of the first automobile race is open to debate. There is a claim that the first race was held in the United States in 1878, from Green Bay to Madison, Wis., won by an Oshkosh steamer. However, France discounts this, claiming that *La Velocipede*, a 19.3-mile race in Paris on April 20, 1887, was the first race. The first organized race did take place in France: 732 miles from Paris to Bordeaux and back, on June 11–14, 1895. The first closed-circuit race was held over five laps of a one-mile dirt track at Narragansett Park,

Cranston, R.I. on September 7, 1896. Grand Prix racing started in 1906, also in France. The Indianapolis 500 was first run on May 30, 1911 (see below).

INDIANAPOLIS 500

The first Indianapolis 500 was held on May 30, 1911 at the Indianapolis Motor Speedway, where the event is still run. The Speedway was opened on August 19, 1909. The original track surface was crushed stone and tar, but several accidents during its initial races convinced the owners to install a paved surface, a project that required 3.2 million bricks and was completed by December 1909. In 1937, parts of the track were resurfaced with asphalt, and the track was completely resurfaced in 1976. The race track is a 2½-mile-square oval that has two straightaways of 3,300 feet and two of 660 feet, all 50 feet wide. The four turns are each 1,320 feet, all 60 feet wide and banked 9 degrees, 12 minutes. A 36-inch strip of original brick marks the start–finish line.

VICTORY LANE

Most wins Three drivers have won the race four times: A. J. Foyt Jr., in 1961, 1964, 1967 and 1977; Al Unser, in 1970–71, 1978 and 1987; and Rick Mears, in 1979, 1984, 1988 and 1991.

Fastest win The record time is 2 hours 41 minutes 18.404 seconds (185.981 mph) by Arie Luyendyk (Netherlands) driving a 1990 Lola-Chevrolet on May 27, 1990.

Slowest win The slowest time is 6 hours 42 minutes 8 seconds (74.602 mph) by Ray Harroun in the inaugural race in 1911.

Consecutive wins Four drivers have won the race in consecutive years: Wilbur Shaw, 1939–40; Mauri Rose, 1947–48; Bill Vukovich, 1953–54; and Al Unser, 1970–71.

Oldest winner Al Unser became the oldest winner when he won the 1987 race at age 47 years 11 months.

Youngest winner Troy Ruttman became the youngest winner when he won the 1952 race at age 22 years 2 months.

Closest finish The closest margin of victory was 0.043 seconds in 1992 when Al Unser Jr. edged Scott Goodyear (Canada).

Lap leader Al Unser has led the race for a cumulative 644 laps during his 27 starts, 1965–93.

Highest earnings The record prize fund is $7,864,801 awarded in 1994. The individual prize record is $1,373,813, by Al Unser Jr. in 1994. Rick Mears leads the field in career earnings at $4,299,392 from 15 starts, 1978–92.

QUALIFYING

Official time trials are held on the two weekends prior to the race to allow entrants to qualify for the 33 starting positions. A completed trial consists of four consecutive laps around the track with the course cleared of all other traffic. Pole position is determined at the "first day" trials. Qualifiers on each subsequent day are lined up behind the qualifiers of previous days. In 1991 Rick Mears gained pole position with an average speed of 224.113 mph, but Gary Bettenhausen recorded the fastest overall average speed of 224.468 mph on the following day, yet only gained a spot on Row 5 of the starting grid. This was the 14th time that this paradox had happened since the introduction of speed time trials in 1915.

Most starts A. J. Foyt Jr. has started a record 35 races (1958–92).

Pole position Rick Mears has gained a record six poles, in 1979, 1982, 1986, 1988–89 and 1991.

Fastest qualifier The record average speed for four laps qualifying is 232.482 mph by Roberto Guerrero (Colombia) in a Lola-Buick on May 9, 1992. On the same day he set the one-lap record of 233.433 mph.

INDIANAPOLIS 500 WINNERS (1911–1954)

Year	Driver	Av. Speed (mph)	Year	Driver	Av. Speed (mph)
1911	Ray Harroun	74.602	1933	Louis Meyer	104.162
1912	Joe Dawson	78.719	1934	William Cummings	104.863
1913	Jules Goux	75.933	1935	Kelly Petillo	106.240
1914	Rene Thomas	82.474	1936	Louis Meyer	109.069
1915	Ralph DePalma	89.840	1937	Wilbur Shaw	113.580
1916	Dario Resta	84.001	1938	Floyd Roberts	117.200
1917	(not held)		1939	Wilbur Shaw	115.035
1918	(not held)		1940	Wilbur Shaw	114.277
1919	Howard Wilcox	88.050	1941	Floyd Davis & Mauri Rose	115.117
1920	Gaston Chevrolet	88.618	1942	(not held)	
1921	Tommy Milton	89.621	1943	(not held)	
1922	Jimmy Murphy	94.484	1944	(not held)	
1923	Tommy Milton	90.954	1945	(not held)	
1924	L.L. Corum & Joe Boyer	98.234	1946	George Robson	114.820
1925	Peter DePaolo	101.127	1947	Mauri Rose	116.338
1926	Frank Lockhart	95.904	1948	Mauri Rose	119.814
1927	George Souders	97.545	1949	Bill Holland	121.327
1928	Louis Meyer	99.482	1950	Johnnie Parsons	124.002
1929	Ray Keech	97.585	1951	Lee Wallard	126.244
1930	Billy Arnold	100.448	1952	Troy Ruttman	128.922
1931	Louis Schneider	96.629	1953	Bill Vukovich	128.740
1932	Fred Frame	104.144	1954	Bill Vukovich	130.840

INDY CAR RACING

The first Indy Car Championship was held in 1909 under the sponsorship of the American Automobile Association (AAA). In 1956 the United States Automobile Club (USAC) took over the running of the Indy series. Since 1979, Championship Auto Racing Teams Inc. (CART) has organized the Indy Championship, which has been called the PPG Indy Car World Series Championship since 1979.

VICTORY LANE

Most championships A.J. Foyt Jr. has won seven Indy Car National Championships: 1960–61, 1963–64, 1967, 1975 and 1979.

Most consecutive championships Ted Horn won three consecutive national titles from 1946–48.

Most wins (career) A.J. Foyt Jr. has won a career record 67 Indy car races, 1957–92. Foyt's first victory came at the DuQuoin 100 in 1960 and his last at the Pocono 500 in 1981.

Most wins (season) The record for most victories in a season is 10, shared by two drivers: A.J. Foyt Jr. in 1964 and Al Unser in 1970.

Consecutive winning seasons Bobby Unser won at least one race per season for 11 seasons from 1966–76.

Most wins (road course) Mario Andretti has won a record 21 road course races, 1964–94.

Most wins (500-mile races) A. J. Foyt Jr. has won nine 500-mile races: Indianapolis 500 in 1961, 1964, 1967 and 1977; Pocono 500 in 1973, 1975, 1979 and 1981; California 500 in 1975.

INDIANAPOLIS 500 WINNERS (1955–1994)

Year	Driver	Av. Speed (mph)	Year	Driver	Av. Speed (mph)
1955	Bob Sweikert	128.209	1975	Bobby Unser	149.213
1956	Pat Flaherty	128.490	1976	Johnny Rutherford	148.725
1957	Sam Hanks	135.601	1977	A. J. Foyt Jr.	161.331
1958	Jim Bryan	133.791	1978	Al Unser	161.363
1959	Rodger Ward	135.857	1979	Rick Mears	158.899
1960	Jim Rathmann	138.767	1980	Johnny Rutherford	142.862
1961	A. J. Foyt Jr.	139.131	1981	Bobby Unser	139.084
1962	Rodger Ward	140.293	1982	Gordon Johncock	162.029
1963	Parnelli Jones	143.137	1983	Tom Sneva	162.117
1964	A. J. Foyt Jr.	147.350	1984	Rick Mears	163.612
1965	Jim Clark[1]	150.686	1985	Danny Sullivan	152.982
1966	Graham Hill[1]	144.317	1986	Bobby Rahal	170.722
1967	A. J. Foyt Jr.	151.207	1987	Al Unser	162.175
1968	Bobby Unser	152.882	1988	Rick Mears	144.809
1969	Mario Andretti	156.867	1989	Emerson Fittipaldi[2]	167.581
1970	Al Unser	155.749	1990	Arie Luyendyk[3]	185.981
1971	Al Unser	157.735	1991	Rick Mears	176.457
1972	Mark Donohue	162.962	1992	Al Unser Jr.	134.477
1973	Gordon Johncock	159.036	1993	Emerson Fittipaldi[2]	157.207
1974	Johnny Rutherford	158.589	1994	Al Unser Jr.	160.872

1—Great Britain; 2—Brazil; 3—Netherlands

QUIETER PASTURES ■ MARIO ANDRETTI IN ONE OF HIS FINAL RACES IN 1994. (ALLSPORT/PASCAL RONDEAU)

Oldest winner On April 4, 1993 Mario Andretti won the Valvoline 200 at the Phoenix International Raceway. At 53 years 52 days Andretti became the oldest driver to win an Indy Car race. (See "The Record Holder Speaks" on page 9.)

Youngest winner Troy Ruttman's victory in the 1952 Indianapolis 500 at age 22 years 2 months is the youngest age any driver has won an Indy Car race.

Closest races The closest margin of victory in an Indy car race was 0.02 seconds on April 10, 1921 when Ralph DePalma edged Roscoe Sarles to win the Beverly Hills 25. The closest finish in a 500-mile event was Al Unser Jr.'s 0.043-second victory in the 1992 Indianapolis 500. Mario Andretti pulled off the closest finish in an Indy road race, when he won the Portland 200 by 0.07 seconds on

FASTEST INDY CAR RACES

Distance	Race	Driver	Av. Speed (mph)	Year
100 miles	Ontario 100	Wally Dallenbach	179.910	1973
150 miles	Atlanta 150	Rick Mears	182.094	1979
200 miles	Michigan 200	Rick Mears	182.325	1983
250 miles	Michigan 250	Bobby Rahal	181.701	1986
500 miles	Michigan 500	Al Unser Jr.	189.727	1990

Source: CART

ALLSPORT/PASCAL RONDEAU

MARIO ANDRETTI

The smoke, dust, burnt rubber and car smashes are now part of history. Having driven his 407th and final race on October 9, 1994, Mario Andretti can look back on a legacy of racing records and ahead to a life of retirement. "I'm just going to have to find out if there is life after driving after all," Andretti says. "And I'm sure there is."

At 54, Andretti would like to think he'll always be part of racing, through ownership, through watching his sons Michael and Jeffrey and his nephew John tearing up the track—or maybe even through continuing driving. "I don't know when to let go, you see," Andretti says, shaking his head. "It's very important to me to walk away while I'm still competitive. There are many people in

different walks of life who have been successful and are happy with it for a short stint. I'm in it truly for the love of it."

The Andretti "kids"—including Andretti's daughter Barbra Dee, who rides horses at the national level and does stunt work on the side—may earn their own spots in the record book, and that's okay by Mario. "Their eyes are wide open," he says. "I'm always concerned about the risks, but it would be hypocritical to say, it was good enough for me, but not good enough for you.

"All these records don't mean anything until you actually reach them. Part of setting records is just being able to still be around," Andretti says with a laugh. "I thank the man upstairs for looking after me."

June 15, 1986. The loser in this memorable show-down was his son, Michael.

Highest earnings (season) The single-season record is $2,575,554, set in 1993 by Emerson Fittipaldi.

Highest earnings (career) Through the 1994 season, Al Unser Jr. has the highest career earnings for Indy drivers with $15,379,906.

QUALIFYING

Most starts Mario Andretti made a record 407 starts in Indy car racing, 1964–94.

Most poles and laps led (career) Mario Andretti earned a record 66 pole positions, 1964–94. He also holds the record for laps led (7,587).

Most poles (season) A.J. Foyt Jr. earned 10 poles in 1965.

Most poles (road courses) Mario Andretti has earned 26 poles on road courses, 1964–94.

Most poles (500-mile races) Rick Mears has earned a record 16 poles in 500-mile races.

Fastest qualifiers The fastest qualifying lap ever for an Indy car race was 234.275 mph by Mario Andretti on August 1, 1993 in qualifying for the Marlboro 500.

NASCAR (NATIONAL ASSOCIATION FOR STOCK CAR AUTO RACING)

The National Association for Stock Car Racing, Inc., was founded by Bill France Sr. in 1947. The first NASCAR-sanctioned race was held on February 15, 1948 on Daytona's beach course. The first NASCAR championship, the Grand National series, was held in 1949. Since 1970, the championship series has been called the Winston Cup Championship. The Winston Cup is won by the driver who accumulates the most points during the season series.

VICTORY LANE

Most championships Richard Petty has won a record seven NASCAR titles: 1964, 1967, 1971–72, 1974–75 and 1979.

Most consecutive titles Cale Yarborough is the only driver to "threepeat" as NASCAR champion, winning in 1976–78.

Most wins (career) Richard Petty has won 200 NASCAR Winston Cup races out of 1,185 in which he competed, 1958–92.

Most wins (season) Richard Petty won a record 27 races in 1967.

Fastest average speed The fastest average speed in a Winston Cup race is 186.288 mph, set by Bill Elliott at Talladega Superspeedway, Ala. on May 5, 1985.

Highest earnings (season) Dale Earnhardt earned a record $3,353,789 in 1993.

Highest earnings (career) Dale Earnhardt also holds the career earnings mark at $20,085,061, 1975–94.

DAYTONA 500

The Daytona 500 has been held at the 2½ mile oval Daytona International Speedway in Daytona Beach, Fla. since 1959. The Daytona 500 is the most prestigious event on the NASCAR calendar.

VICTORY LANE

Most wins Richard Petty has won a record seven times: 1964, 1966, 1971, 1973–74, 1979 and 1981.

Consecutive wins Richard Petty and Cale Yarborough are the only drivers to have repeated as Daytona 500 winners in consecutive years. Petty's double was in 1973–74 and Yarborough's in 1983–84.

Oldest winner Bobby Allison became the oldest winner of the race in 1988 at age 50 years 2 months 11 days.

Youngest winner Richard Petty became the youngest winner in 1964, at age 26 years 4 months 18 days.

Fastest win The record average speed for the race is 177.602 mph, by Buddy Baker in 1980.

Slowest win The slowest average speed is 124.740 mph, by Junior Johnson in 1960.

Highest earnings The individual race earnings record is $253,275, by Sterling Marlin in 1994. The career earnings record is $1,124,256, by Dale Earnhardt in 16 races, 1979–94.

QUALIFYING

Most starts Richard Petty competed in 32 Daytona 500 races, 1959–92.

Fastest qualifying time The record average speed for qualifying for the race is 210.364 mph, set by Bill Elliott in 1987.

LIFE IN THE MONEY LANE ■ **DALE EARNHARDT, THE TOP VICTORY LANE MONEY EARNER.** (NASCAR)

Most poles Cale Yarborough has earned a record four poles at the Daytona 500, in 1968, 1970, 1978 and 1984.

FORMULA ONE (GRAND PRIX)

The World Drivers' Championship was inaugurated in 1950. Currently the championship is contested over 16 races in 14 different countries worldwide. Points are awarded to the first six finishers in each race; the driver with the most points at the end of the season is the champion.

VICTORY LANE

Most championships Juan-Manuel Fangio (Argentina) has won the drivers' championship five times, 1951 and 1954–57. He also holds the record for consecutive titles with four straight, 1954–57.

Oldest champion Juan-Manuel Fangio is the oldest world champion, winning the 1957 title at age 46 years 41 days.

DAYTONA 500 WINNERS (1959–1994)

Year	Driver	Av. Speed (mph)	Year	Driver	Av. Speed (mph)
1959	Lee Petty	135.521	1977	Cale Yarborough	153.218
1960	Junior Johnson	124.740	1978	Bobby Allison	159.730
1961	Marvin Panch	149.601	1979	Richard Petty	143.977
1962	Fireball Roberts	152.529	1980	Buddy Baker	177.602
1963	Tiny Lund	151.566	1981	Richard Petty	169.651
1964	Richard Petty	154.334	1982	Bobby Allison	153.991
1965	Fred Lorenzen	141.539	1983	Cale Yarborough	155.979
1966	Richard Petty	160.627	1984	Cale Yarborough	150.994
1967	Mario Andretti	149.926	1985	Bill Elliott	172.265
1968	Cale Yarborough	143.251	1986	Geoff Bodine	148.124
1969	LeeRoy Yarborough	157.950	1987	Bill Elliott	176.263
1970	Pete Hamilton	149.601	1988	Bobby Allison	137.531
1971	Richard Petty	144.462	1989	Darrell Waltrip	148.466
1972	A. J. Foyl Jr.	161.550	1990	Derrike Cope	165.761
1973	Richard Petty	157.205	1991	Ernie Irvan	148.148
1974	Richard Petty	140.894	1992	Davey Allison	160.256
1975	Benny Parsons	153.649	1993	Dale Jarrett	154.972
1976	David Pearson	152.181	1994	Sterling Marlin	156.931

Youngest champion Emerson Fittipaldi (Brazil) became the youngest champion in 1972, at age 25 years 273 days.

Most wins (career) Alain Prost (France) has won 51 Formula One races (from 200), between 1980–93.

Most wins (season) Nigel Mansell (Great Britain) won a record nine races in 1992. His victories came in South Africa, Mexico, Brazil, Spain, San Marino, France, Great Britain, Germany and Portugal.

Oldest winner The oldest driver to win an official race was Luigi Fagioli (Italy), who was 53 years 22 days old when he won the 1951 French Grand Prix.

Youngest winner The youngest driver to win an official race was Troy Ruttman, who was 22 years 2 months old when he won the 1952 Indianapolis 500, which counted in the World Drivers' Championship that year.

Closest finish The narrowest margin of victory in a Formula One race was when Ayrton Senna (Brazil) held off Nigel Mansell by 0.014 seconds to win the Spanish Grand Prix on April 13, 1986.

United States Two Americans have won the Formula One title—Phil Hill in 1961 and Mario Andretti in 1978.

QUALIFYING

Most starts Riccardo Patrese (Italy) has raced in a record 255 Grand Prix races from 1977–93.

Most poles Ayrton Senna earned a record 65 poles in 161 races, 1985–93.

Fastest qualifying time Keke Rosberg (Finland) set the fastest qualifying lap in Formula One history, when he qualified for the British Grand Prix at Silverstone with an average speed of 160.817 mph on July 20, 1985.

POLE POSITION ■ AYRTON SENNA, RECORD HOLDER FOR MOST QUALIFYING POLES IN FORMULA ONE RACING.
(SUTTON PHOTOGRAPHIC)

SPEEDY KEKE ■ KEKE ROSBERG'S RECORD FOR FASTEST QUALIFYING TIME IN FORMULA ONE RACING HAS HELD FOR NEARLY A DECADE. (SUTTON PHOTOGRAPHIC)

DRAG RACING

Drag racing is an acceleration contest between two cars racing from a standing start over a precisely measured, straight-line, quarter-mile course. Competition is based on two-car elimination heats culminating in a final round. The fastest elapsed time wins the race. Elapsed time is measured over the distance of the course; the top speed is a measurement of the last 66 feet of the track, where a special speed trap electronically computes the speed of the dragster. There are several classifications in drag racing, based on the engine size, type of fuel and vehicle weight limitations of the car. The most prominent drag racing organization is the National Hot Rod Association (NHRA), which was founded in 1951. The NHRA recognizes 12 categories of racers, with the three main categories being Top Fuel, Funny Car and Pro Stock.

TOP FUEL

Top Fuel dragsters are 4,000-horsepower machines that are powered by nitromethane. The engines are mounted behind the driver, and parachutes are the primary braking system.

SPEED RECORDS

Quickest elapsed time in an NHRA event The quickest elapsed time recorded by a Top Fuel dragster from a standing start for 440 yards is 4.690 seconds by Michael Brotherton at the Oopar Parts Nationals in Englishtown, NJ on May 20, 1994.

Fastest top speed in an NHRA event The fastest speed recorded in a Top Fuel race is 314.46 mph by Kenny Bernstein on October 30, 1994 at the Winston Select Finals at Pomona, CA.

VICTORIES

Most wins (career) Don Garlits has won a record 35 Top Fuel races (1975–92).

Most wins (season) Six drivers have won six Top Fuel races in a season: Don Garlits, 1985; Darrell Gwynn, 1988; Gary Ormsby, 1989; Joe Amato, 1990; Kenny Bernstein, 1991; and Eddie Hill, 1993.

FUNNY CAR

A Funny Car is a short-wheelbase version of the Top Fuel dragster. Funny Cars mount a fiberglass replica of a production car with the engine located in front of the driver.

CLOUDS OF DUST ■ IN 1994 KURT JOHNSON BROKE THE RECORD FOR QUICKEST ELAPSED TIME IN AN NHRA EVENT IN THE PRO STOCK CLASS. (NHRA PHOTOGRAPHIC)

POETRY IN MOTION ■ ON JULY 30, 1994, DARRELL ALDERMAN SMASHED WARREN JOHNSON'S TOP SPEED RECORD FOR AN NHRA EVENT IN THE PRO STOCK CLASS. (NHRA PHOTOGRAPHIC)

Quickest elapsed time in an NHRA event The quickest elapsed time recorded in the Funny Car class is 4.939 seconds, by John Force on October 1, 1994 at the Sears Craftsman Nationals at Topeka, Kan.

Fastest top speed in an NHRA event John Force was timed at 303.95 mph at the Winston Select Nationals at Topeka, Kan., on October 30, 1994.

VICTORIES

Most wins (career) John Force has won a record 42 Funny Car races (1975–94).

Most wins (season) John Force won a record 11 races in 1993.

PRO STOCK

Pro Stock dragsters look like their oval-racing counterparts, but feature extensive engine modifications. A maximum 500-cubic-inch displacement and a minimum vehicle weight of 2,350 pounds are allowed under NHRA rules.

SPEED RECORDS

Quickest elapsed time in an NHRA event The quickest elapsed time in the Pro Stock class is 6.988 seconds by Kurt Johnson on May 20, 1994 at the Oopar Parts Nationals, Englishtown, NJ.

Fastest top speed in an NHRA event The fastest speed in a Pro Stock race is 197.80 mph by Darrell Alderman on July 30, 1994 at the Auto Lite Nationals, Sonoma, CA.

VICTORIES

Most wins (career) Bob Glidden has won a record 84 races (1972–93), the most victories of any driver in NHRA events.

Most wins (season) Darrell Alderman won a record 11 races in 1991.

NHRA WINSTON DRAG RACING SERIES The NHRA World Championship Series was inaugurated in 1951. Since 1975 the series has been known as the NHRA Winston Drag Racing Series.

MOST TITLES

Top Fuel Joe Amato has won a record five national titles: 1984, 1988 and 1990–92.

Funny Car Three drivers have won a record four national titles: Don Prudhomme, 1975–78,

Kenny Bernstein, 1985–88 and John Force (1993–94).

Pro Stock Bob Glidden has won a record 10 national titles, in 1974–75, 1978–80 and 1985–89.

BADMINTON

ORIGINS Badminton is a descendant of the children's game of battledore and shuttlecock. It is believed that a similar game was played in China more than 2,000 years ago. Badminton takes its name from Badminton House in England, where the Duke of Beaufort's family and guests popularized the game in the 19th century. British army officers took the game to India in the 1870s, where the first modern rules were codified in 1876. The world governing body is the International Badminton Federation, formed in 1934.

United States The earliest known reference to badminton in the United States is a description of battledore shuttlecock in the 1864 *American Boy's Book of Sports and Games*. The first badminton club formed in the United States was the Badminton Club of New York, founded in 1878. The game was not organized at the national level until 1935, when the American Badminton Association (ABA) was founded in Boston, Mass. In 1978 the ABA was renamed the United States Badminton Association.

OLYMPIC GAMES Badminton was included in the Olympic Games as an official sport for the first time at the Barcelona Games in 1992. The game was included as a demonstration sport at the Munich Games in 1972.

Most medals No player in Barcelona won more than one medal. The four gold medals awarded were shared equally between players from Indonesia and South Korea.

WORLD CHAMPIONSHIPS The first championships were staged in Malmo, Sweden in 1977. Since 1983 the event has been held biennially.

Most titles (overall) Park Joo-bong (South Korea) has won a record five world titles: men's doubles in 1985 and 1991; mixed doubles in 1985, 1989 and 1991. Three women have won three titles: Lin Ying (China), doubles in 1983, 1987 and 1989; Li Lingwei (China), singles in 1983 and 1989,

STREAKY ■ A GROUP PHOTO OF THE MILLER PLACE HIGH SCHOOL BADMINTON SQUAD—THE TEAM THAT COULDN'T BE BEATEN. (MILLER PLACE HIGH SCHOOL)

doubles in 1985; Guan Weizhan (China), doubles in 1987, 1989 and 1991.

Most titles (singles) Yang Yang (China) is the only man to have won two world singles titles, in 1987 and 1989. Two women have won two singles titles: Li Lingwei (China), 1983 and 1989; Han Aiping (China), 1985 and 1987.

UNITED STATES NATIONAL CHAMPIONSHIPS The first competition was held in 1937.

Most titles Judy Hashman (née Devlin) has won a record 31 titles: 12 women's singles, 1954, 1956–63 and 1965–67; 12 women's doubles, 1953–55, 1957–63 and 1966–67 (10 with her sister Susan); and seven mixed doubles, 1956–59, 1961–62 and 1967. David G. Freeman has won a record seven men's singles titles: 1939–42, 1947–48 and 1953.

GUINNESS CHALLENGE

How much does Konishiki, the world's heaviest sumo wrestler, weigh?
See page 225 for the answer.

Winning streak The longest continuous winning streak by an American badminton team is 338 wins, by Miller Place High School in Miller Place, N.Y., accomplished up through June 20, 1994.

BASEBALL

ORIGINS In 1907, baseball's national commission appointed a committee to research the history of the game. The report, filed in 1908, concluded that Abner Doubleday had invented the game in 1839 at Cooperstown, N.Y. At the time, the report was viewed with some skepticism because of the friendship between Doubleday and the committee chairman, A. G. Mills; however, in 1939, major league baseball celebrated its centennial and cemented the legend of Doubleday's efforts in American folklore. Sports historians today discount the Doubleday theory, claiming that baseball in North America evolved from such English games as cricket, paddleball and rounders.

Uncontested is that Alexander Cartwright Jr. formulated the rules of the modern game in 1845, and that the first match under these rules was played on June 19, 1846 when the New York Nine defeated the New York Knickerbockers, 23–1, in four innings. On March 17, 1871 the National Association of Professional Base Ball Players was formed, the first professional league in the United States. Today there are two main professional baseball associations, the National League (organized in 1876) and the American League (organized in 1901, recognized in 1903), which together form the major leagues, along with approximately 20 associations that make up the minor leagues. The champions of the two leagues first played a World Series in 1903 and have played one continuously since 1905. (For further details on World Series history, see page 35.)

MAJOR LEAGUE RECORDS

Records listed in this section are for the all-time major league record. Where an all-time record is dated prior to 1900, the modern record (1900–present) is also listed.

GAMES PLAYED

Career 3,562, by Pete Rose, Cincinnati Reds (NL), 1963–78, 1984–86; Philadelphia Phillies (NL), 1979–83; Montreal Expos (NL), 1984.

Consecutive 2,130, by Lou Gehrig, New York Yankees (AL), June 1, 1925 through April 30, 1939.

BATTING RECORDS

BATTING AVERAGE

Career .367, by Ty Cobb, Detroit Tigers (AL), 1905–26; Philadelphia Athletics (AL), 1927–28. Cobb compiled his record from 4,191 hits in 11,429 at-bats.

Season .438, by Hugh Duffy, Boston Beaneaters (NL) in 1894. Duffy compiled 236 hits in 539 at-bats. The modern record is .424, by Rogers Hornsby, St. Louis Cardinals (NL), in 1924. Hornsby compiled 227 hits in 536 at-bats.

HITS

Career 4,256, by Pete Rose, Cincinnati Reds (NL), 1963–78, 1984–86; Philadelphia Phillies (NL), 1979–83; Montreal Expos (NL), 1984. Rose compiled his record hits total in 14,053 at-bats.

Season 257, by George Sisler, St. Louis Browns (AL), in 1920, in 631 at-bats.

Game Nine, by John Burnett, Cleveland Indians (AL), during an 18-inning game on July 10, 1932. The record for a nine-inning game is seven hits, by two players: Wilbert Robinson, Baltimore Orioles

(NL), on June 10, 1892; Rennie Stennett, Pittsburgh Pirates (NL), on September 16, 1975.

SINGLES

Career 3,215, by Pete Rose, Cincinnati Reds (NL), 1963–78, 1984–86; Philadelphia Phillies, 1979–83, Montreal Expos, 1984.

Season 206, by Wee Willie Keeler, Baltimore Orioles (NL) in 1898. The modern-day record is 198, by Lloyd Waner, Pittsburgh Pirates, in 1927.

Game Seven, by John Burnett, Cleveland Indians (AL), in an 18-inning game on July 10, 1932. In regulation play the record for both the National and American leagues is six hits by several players.

DOUBLES

Career 793, by Tris Speaker, Boston Red Sox (AL), 1907–1915; Cleveland Indians (AL), 1916–1926; Washington Senators (AL), 1927; Philadelphia Athletics (AL), 1928.

Season 67, by Earl Webb, Boston Red Sox (AL), in 1931.

Game Four, by many players in both leagues.

TRIPLES

Career 312, by Sam Crawford, Cincinnati Reds (NL), 1899–1902; Detroit Tigers (AL), 1903–17.

Season 36, by Owen Wilson, Pittsburgh Pirates (NL), in 1912.

Game Four, by two players: George A. Strief, Philadelphia Athletics (American Association) on June 25, 1885; William Joyce, New York Giants (NL) on May 18, 1897. The modern-day record for both leagues is three, achieved by several players.

HOME RUNS

Career 755, by Hank Aaron, Milwaukee/Atlanta Braves (NL), 1954–74; Milwaukee Brewers (AL), 1975–76. Aaron hit his record dingers in 12,364 at-bats.

Record Quotable

"I'm just like everybody else. I have two arms, two legs and 4,000 hits."

—Pete Rose, quoted in *The Sporting News*, on his record for most lifetime hits.

The 1994 Season: "The Year

At the beginning of the 1994 baseball season, some sportscasters dubbed 1994 "the year of the long ball"—a reaction to the statistics showing an increase in home runs over previous years. There were even those who made accusations that the ball was intentionally "juiced" by manufacturers to create a more exciting game. In any event, with a strike-shortened baseball year—and an unplayed World Series—we'll never really know what long-ball records might have been shattered had the 1994 season been played out in full.

ROGER MARIS'S HOME RUN RECORD (61)

Who had the best chance at breaking Roger Maris's home run record? Matt Williams? Ken Griffey Jr.? The following chart shows what might have happened had the top home-run-hitting players continued at the same pace.

Player	Home Runs	At-bats/Games	Pace at 162 games
Matt Williams (San Francisco/NL)	43	445/112	62
Ken Griffey Jr. (Seattle/AL)	40	433/111	58
Jeff Bagwell (Houston/NL)	39	400/110	57
Frank Thomas (Chicago/AL)	38	399/113	54
Barry Bonds (San Francisco/NL)	37	391/112	53

Note: There has never been a year when three players hit 50 or more home runs in the same season.

(ALLSPORT/OTTO GREULE)

MATT WILLIAMS

(NATIONAL BASEBALL LIBRARY)

BARRY BONDS

STRUCK DOWN!

Listed below in chronological order are all sports-related strikes and lockouts. Asterisks indicate the latter.

Sport	Dates	Cause of Strike/Lockout
Hockey*	September 30, 1994–January 11, 1995	Payroll taxes
Baseball	August 12, 1994–present	Player salary caps
Hockey	April 1, 1991–April 10, 1991	Contract renegotiation
Baseball*	February 15, 1989–March 18, 1990	Contract renegotiation
Football	September 22, 1987–October 25, 1987	Ability for a player to change teams without restriction once his contract has expired
Baseball	August 6, 1985–August 9, 1985	Player pension fund
Football	September 21, 1982–November 21, 1982	Contract renegotiation
Baseball	June 12, 1981–August 10, 1981	Compensation for free agent signings
Baseball	April 5, 1972–February 28, 1973	Player pension fund

.400 BATTING AVERAGE

No one has hit .400 since Ted Williams hit .406 in 1941. George Brett (.390 in 1980) and Rod Carew (.388 in 1977) have come the closest since then. All four players listed below flirted with .400 at one time or another during the 1994 season—and all had at least an outside chance of accomplishing the feat if the season had concluded normally.

Major League Leaders	Average
Tony Gwynn (San Diego/NL)	.394
Jeff Bagwell (Houston/NL)	.368
Paul O'Neill (New York/AL)	.359
Albert Belle (Cleveland/AL)	.357

TRIPLE CROWN

The last player to win the Triple Crown—leading the league in batting, home runs and runs batted in—was Carl Yastrzemski in 1967. With a strong September and October, any of the players below could have accomplished this rare feat.

Player	Batting	Home Runs	Runs Batted In
Frank Thomas (Chicago/AL)	3rd (.353)	2nd (38)	tied 3rd (101)
Albert Belle (Cleveland/AL)	2nd (.357)	3rd (38)	tied 3rd (101)
Jeff Bagwell (Houston/NL)	2nd (.368)	2nd (39)	1st (116)

CONSECUTIVE GAMES PLAYED

Perhaps the most revered of all baseball records is the one held by Lou Gehrig, the Iron Horse first baseman of the New York Yankees: most consecutive games played (2,130). Durable Orioles shortstop Cal Ripken is creeping up on that famed record, having reached the magic number 2,000 on August 2, 1994. Assuming the strike ends prior to the 1995 season—and that Ripken stays healthy—he should break the record by the end of August, 1995.

(NATIONAL BASEBALL LIBRARY)

CAL RIPKEN

THE SHORT END OF THE STICK?

Which of the active players listed below won't make 3,000 lifetime hits because the strike affected their career totals?

Player	Age	Hits
Eddie Murray	38	2,930
Andre Dawson	40	2,700
Paul Molitor	38	2,647
Wade Boggs	36	2,392
Ozzie Smith	39	2,365
Lou Whitaker	34	2,296
Alan Trammell	36	2,260
Cal Ripken	33	2,227
Rickey Henderson	35	2,216
Tony Gwynn	34	2,204
Harold Baines	35	2,156
Tim Raines	34	2,152
Brett Butler	37	2,089
Don Mattingly	33	2,021

(continued on page 20)

ARE BASEBALL PLAYERS OVERPAID?—YOU DECIDE

Player salaries over time

Year	Minimum Salary	Average Salary
1994	$109,000	$1,150,000
1984	$40,000	329,408
1974	$15,000	40,839
1950	$5,000	13,263

Top 12 salaries: 1994

Player	Salary
Bobby Bonilla (New York Mets)	$6,300,000
Ryne Sandberg (Chicago Cubs)	$5,975,000
Joe Carter (Toronto Blue Jays)	$5,500,000
Rafael Palmeiro (Baltimore Orioles)	$5,406,603
Cal Ripken Jr. (Baltimore Orioles)	$5,400,000
Jack McDowell (Chicago White Sox)	$5,300,000
Jimmy Key (New York Yankees)	$5,250,000
Kirby Puckett (Minnesota Twins)	$5,200,000
Roger Clemens (Chicago White Sox)	$5,155,250
Jose Canseco (Texas Rangers)	$5,100,000
Ken Griffey Jr. (Seattle Mariners)	$5,000,000
David Cone (Kansas City Royals)	$5,000,000

Source: National Baseball Hall of Fame and Museum, Inc.

Season 61, Roger Maris, New York Yankees (AL), in 1961.

Game Four, by 12 players: Bobby Lowe, Boston (NL), May 30, 1894; Ed Delahanty, Philadelphia Phillies (NL), July 13, 1896; Lou Gehrig, New York Yankees (AL), June 3, 1932; Chuck Klein, Philadelphia Phillies (NL), July 10, 1936; Pat Seerey, Chicago White Sox (AL), July 18, 1948; Gil Hodges, Brooklyn Dodgers (NL), August 31, 1950; Joe Adcock, Milwaukee Braves (NL), July 31, 1954; Rocky Colavito, Cleveland Indians (AL), June 10, 1959; Willie Mays, San Francisco Giants (NL), April 30, 1961; Mike Schmidt, Philadelphia Phillies (NL), April 17, 1976; Bob Horner, Atlanta Braves (NL), July 6, 1986; and Mark Whiten, St. Louis Cardinals (NL), September 7, 1993. Klein, Schmidt and Seerey matched the record in extra-inning games.

Grand Slams

Career 23, by Lou Gehrig, New York Yankees (AL), 1923–39.

Season Six, by Don Mattingly, New York Yankees (AL), in 1987.

Game Two, by seven players: Tony Lazzeri, New York Yankees (AL), May 24, 1936; Jim Tabor, Boston Red Sox (AL), July 4, 1939; Rudy York, Boston Red Sox (AL), July 27, 1946; Jim Gentile, Baltimore Orioles (AL), May 9, 1961; Tony Cloninger, Atlanta Braves (NL), July 3, 1966; Jim Northrup, Detroit Tigers (AL), June 24, 1968; and Frank Robinson, Baltimore Orioles (AL), June 26, 1970. Cloninger is the only player from the National League to achieve this feat, and he was a pitcher!

RUNS BATTED IN

Career 2,297, by Hank Aaron, Milwaukee/Atlanta Braves (NL), 1954–74; Milwaukee Brewers (AL), 1975–76.

Season 190, by Hack Wilson, Chicago Cubs (NL), in 1930.

Game 12, by two players: Jim Bottomley, St. Louis Cardinals (NL), on September 16, 1924; and Mark Whiten, St. Louis Cardinals (NL), on September 7, 1993.

RUNS SCORED

Career 2,245, by Ty Cobb, Detroit Tigers (AL), 1905–26; Philadelphia Athletics (AL), 1927–28.

Season 196, by Billy Hamilton, Philadelphia Phillies (NL), in 1894. The modern-day record is 177 runs, scored by Babe Ruth, New York Yankees (AL), in 1921.

Game Seven, by Guy Hecker, Louisville Colonels (American Association), on August 15, 1886. The modern-day record is six runs scored, achieved by 12 players, 10 in the National League and two in the American League.

TOTAL BASES

Career 6,856, by Hank Aaron, Milwaukee/Atlanta Braves (NL), 1954–74; Milwaukee Brewers (AL), 1975–76. Aaron's record is comprised of 2,294 singles, 624 doubles, 98 triples and 755 home runs.

Season 457, by Babe Ruth, New York Yankees (AL) in 1921. Ruth's total comprised 85 singles, 44 doubles, 16 triples and 59 home runs.

Game 18, by Joe Adcock, Milwaukee Braves (NL) on July 31, 1954. Adcock hit four home runs and a double.

WALKS

Career 2,056, by Babe Ruth, Boston Red Sox (AL), 1914–19; New York Yankees (AL), 1920–34; Boston Braves (NL), 1935.

Season 170, by Babe Ruth, New York Yankees (AL) in 1923.

STRIKEOUTS

Career 2,597, by Reggie Jackson, Kansas City/Oakland Athletics (AL), 1967–75, 1987; Baltimore Orioles (AL), 1976; New York Yankees (AL), 1977–81; California Angels (AL), 1982–86.

Season 189, by Bobby Bonds, San Francisco Giants (NL), in 1970.

HIT BY PITCH

Career 267, by Don Baylor, Baltimore Orioles (AL), 1970–75; Oakland Athletics (AL), 1976, 1988; California Angels (AL), 1977–82; New York Yankees (AL), 1983–85; Boston Red Sox (AL), 1986–87; Minnesota Twins (AL), 1987.

Season 50, by Ron Hunt, Montreal Expos (NL) in 1971.

IS ANYBODY LISTENING?

Are baseball fans mad about the 1994 baseball strike? They're as mad as hell—and at least one radio station did something about it.

WJMP 1520 AM, an Akron, Ohio sports talk radio station, played "Take Me Out to the Ball Game" continuously 57,161 times. The station began broadcasting the song at 6:20 A.M. on August 12, 1994—the day the strike began—and ended at noon on October 19, 1994.

From sunup to sundown, WJMP alternated between two versions of the song: a 70-second recording sung by Tom Chalkley with the Bruce Springstone (no, not Springsteen) band; and a 30-second instrumental. The music was recorded in 1982 for Clean Cuts Records (now distributed by Rhino); Jack Heyrman was producer and Craig Hankin the arranger. The classic "Take Me Out to the Ball Game" was written in 1908 by Jack Norworth (words) and Albert Von Tilzer (music).

In response to concerns over whether WJMP might lose sponsors as a result of the stunt, station vice president Robert A. Klaus had this to say: "On the whole we've been able to keep our advertisers. But we've also lost a few. If that's the price we have to pay, it's worth it."

Sports Radio AM 1520 WJMP

CONSECUTIVE BATTING RECORDS

Hits in a row 12, by two players: Pinky Higgins, Boston Red Sox (AL), over four games, June 19–21, 1938; and Walt (Moose) Dropo, Detroit Tigers (AL), over three games, July 14–15, 1952.

Games batted safely 56, by Joe DiMaggio, New York Yankees (AL), May 15 through July 16, 1941. During the streak, DiMaggio gained 91 hits in 223 at-bats: 56 singles, 16 doubles, 4 triples and 15 home runs.

Home runs in a row Four, by four players: Bobby Lowe, Boston (NL), May 30, 1894; Lou Gehrig, New York Yankees (AL), June 3, 1932; Rocky Colavito, Cleveland Indians (AL), June 10, 1959; and Mike Schmidt, Philadelphia Phillies (NL), April 17, 1976.

Games hitting home runs Eight, by three players: Dale Long, Pittsburgh Pirates (NL), May 19–28, 1956; Don Mattingly, New York Yankees (AL), July 8–18, 1987; and Ken Griffey Jr., Seattle Mariners (AL), July 20–28, 1993.

Walks in a row Seven, by four players: Billy Rogell, Detroit Tigers (AL), August 17–19, 1938; Mel Ott, New York Giants (NL), June 16–18, 1943; Eddie Stanky, New York Giants (NL), August 29–30, 1950; Jose Canseco, Oakland Athletics (AL), August 4–5, 1994.

Games receiving a walk 22, by Roy Cullenbine, Detroit Tigers (AL), July 2 through July 22, 1947.

PITCHING RECORDS

GAMES PLAYED

Career 1,070, by Hoyt Wilhelm, New York Giants (NL), 1952–56; St. Louis Cardinals (NL), 1957; Cleveland Indians (AL), 1957–58; Baltimore Orioles (AL), 1958–62; Chicago White Sox (AL), 1963–68; California Angels (AL), 1969; Atlanta Braves (NL), 1969–70; Chicago Cubs (NL), 1970; Atlanta Braves (NL), 1971; Los Angeles Dodgers (NL), 1971–72.

Season 106, by Mike Marshall, Los Angeles Dodgers (NL), in 1974.

VICTORIES

Career 511, by Cy Young, Cleveland Spiders (NL), 1890–98; St. Louis Cardinals (NL), 1899–1900; Boston Red Sox (AL), 1901–08; Cleveland Indians (AL), 1909–11; Boston Braves (NL), 1911.

Season 60, by "Old Hoss" Radbourn, Providence Grays (NL), in 1884. The modern-day record is 41, by Jack Chesbro, New York Yankees (AL), in 1904.

LOSSES

Career 313, by Cy Young, Cleveland Spiders (NL), 1890–98; St. Louis Cardinals (NL), 1899–1900; Boston Red Sox (AL), 1901–08; Cleveland Indians (AL), 1909–11; Boston Braves (NL), 1911.

Season 48, by John Coleman, Philadelphia Phillies (NL), in 1883. The modern-day record is 29, by Vic Willis, Boston Braves (NL), in 1905.

EARNED RUN AVERAGE (ERA)

Career (min. 2,000 innings) 1.82, by Ed Walsh, Chicago White Sox (AL), 1904–16; Boston Braves (NL), 1917.

Season (min. 200 innings) 1.01, by Dutch Leonard, Boston Red Sox (AL), in 1914.

Widest differential (min. 200 innings) In 1994, Greg Maddux (Atlanta Braves, NL) had an ERA of 1.56, 2.56 below the league's overall average.

INNINGS PITCHED

Career 7,356, by Cy Young, Cleveland Spiders (NL), 1890–98; St. Louis Cardinals (NL), 1899–1900; Boston Red Sox (AL), 1901–08; Cleveland Indians (AL), 1909–11; Boston Braves (NL), 1911.

Season 680, by Will White, Cincinnati Reds (NL), in 1879. The modern-day record is 464, by Ed Walsh, Chicago White Sox (AL), in 1908.

NO-HITTERS

On September 4, 1991, baseball's Committee for Statistical Accuracy defined a no-hit game as "one in which a pitcher or pitchers complete a game of nine innings or more without allowing a hit." All previously considered no-hit games that did not fit into this definition—such as rain-shortened games; eight-inning, complete game no-hitters hurled by losing pitchers; and games in which hits were recorded in the tenth inning or later—would be considered "notable achievements," not no-hitters.

The first officially recognized no-hitter was pitched by Joe Borden for Philadelphia of the National Association *v.* Chicago on July 28, 1875. Through the 1993 season 238 no-hitters have been pitched. The most no-hitters pitched in one season is seven, on two occasions: 1990 and 1991.

Career Seven, by Nolan Ryan: California Angels v. Kansas City Royals (3–0), on May 15, 1973; California Angels v. Detroit Tigers (6–0), on July 15, 1973; California Angels v. Minnesota Twins (4–0), on September 28, 1974; California Angels v. Baltimore Orioles (1–0), on June 1, 1975; Houston Astros v. Los Angeles Dodgers (5–0), on September 26, 1981; Texas Rangers v. Oakland Athletics (5–0), on June 11, 1990; and Texas Rangers v. Toronto Blue Jays (3–0), on May 1, 1991.

Season Two, by four players: Johnny Vander Meer, Cincinnati Reds (NL), in 1938; Allie Reynolds, New York Yankees (AL), in 1951; Virgil Trucks, Detroit Tigers (AL) in 1952; and Nolan Ryan, California Angels (AL), in 1973.

PERFECT GAMES

In a perfect game, no batter reaches base during a complete game of at least nine innings.

The first officially recognized perfect game was hurled by John Richmond on June 12, 1880 for Worcester v. Cleveland in a National League game. Through the 1994 season there have been 15 perfect games pitched: Richmond (see above); John Ward, Providence v. Buffalo (NL), June 17, 1880; Cy Young, Boston Red Sox v. Philadelphia Athletics (AL), May 5, 1904; Addie Joss, Cleveland Indians v. Chicago White Sox (AL), October 2, 1908; Ernie Shore, Boston Red Sox v. Washington Senators (AL), June 23, 1917; Charlie Robertson, Chicago White Sox v. Detroit Tigers (AL), April 30, 1922; Don Larsen, New York Yankees v. Brooklyn Dodgers (World Series game), October 8, 1956; Jim Bunning, Philadelphia Phillies v. New York Mets (NL), June 21, 1964; Sandy Koufax, Los Angeles Dodgers v. Chicago Cubs (NL), September 9, 1965; Catfish Hunter, Oakland Athletics v. Minnesota Twins (AL), May 8, 1968; Len Barker,

Cleveland Indians v. Toronto Blue Jays (AL), May 15, 1981; Mike Witt, California Angels v. Texas Rangers (AL), September 30, 1984; Tom Browning, Cincinnati Reds v. Los Angeles Dodgers (NL), September 16, 1988; Dennis Martinez, Montreal Expos v. Los Angeles Dodgers (NL), July 28, 1991; and Kenny Rogers, Texas Rangers (AL) v. California Angels (AL), July 29, 1994.

COMPLETE GAMES

Career 750, by Cy Young, Cleveland Spiders (NL), 1890–98; St. Louis Cardinals (NL), 1899–1900; Boston Red Sox (AL), 1901–08; Cleveland Indians (AL), 1909–11; Boston Braves (NL), 1911. The modern-day record is 531, by Walter Johnson, Washington Senators (AL), 1907–27.

Season 75, by Will White, Cincinnati Reds (NL) in 1879. The modern-day record is 48, by Jack Chesbro, New York Yankees (AL), in 1904.

SHUTOUTS

Career 110, by Walter Johnson, Washington Senators (AL), 1907–27.

Season 16, by two pitchers: George Bradley, St. Louis (NL), in 1876; and Grover Alexander, Philadelphia Phillies (NL), in 1916.

STRIKEOUTS

Career 5,714, by Nolan Ryan, New York Mets (NL), 1966–71; California Angels (AL), 1972–79; Houston Astros (NL), 1980–88; Texas Rangers (AL), 1989–93.

Season 513, by Matt Kilroy, Baltimore (American Association), in 1886. The modern-day record is 383, by Nolan Ryan, California Angels (AL), in 1973.

Game (extra innings) 21, by Tom Cheney, Washington Senators (AL), on September 12, 1962 in a 16-inning game.

Game (nine innings) 20, by Roger Clemens, Boston Red Sox (AL), on April 29, 1986.

WALKS

Career 2,795, by Nolan Ryan, New York Mets (NL), 1966–71; California Angels (AL), 1972–79; Houston Astros (NL), 1980–88; Texas Rangers (AL), 1989–93.

Season 218, by Amos Rusie, New York Giants (NL), in 1893. The modern-day record is 208, by Bob Feller, Cleveland Indians (AL), in 1938.

Record Quotable

"It gave me no chance. He just blew it by me. But it's an honor. I'll have another paragraph in all the baseball books. I'm already in the books three or four times."

—Rickey Henderson, quoted in *The Sporting News*, on being Nolan Ryan's 5,000th strikeout victim.

Game 16, by two pitchers: Bruno Haas, Philadelphia Athletics (AL), on June 23, 1915 in a nine-inning game; Tom Byrne, St. Louis Browns (AL) on August 22, 1951 in a 13-inning game.

SAVES

Career 434, by Lee Smith, Chicago Cubs (NL), 1980–87; Boston Red Sox (AL), 1988–90; St. Louis Cardinals (NL), 1990–93; New York Yankees (AL), 1993; the Baltimore Orioles (AL), 1994.

Season 57, by Bobby Thigpen, Chicago White Sox (AL), in 1990.

CONSECUTIVE PITCHING RECORDS

Games won 24, by Carl Hubbell, New York Giants (NL), 16 in 1936 and eight in 1937.

Starting assignments 544, by Steve Carlton, from May 15, 1971 through 1986 while playing for four teams: St. Louis Cardinals (NL), Philadelphia Phillies (NL), San Francisco Giants (NL), and Chicago White Sox (AL).

Scoreless innings 59, by Orel Hershiser, Los Angeles Dodgers (NL), from sixth inning, August 30 through tenth inning, September 28, 1988.

No-hitters Two, by Johnny Vander Meer, Cincinnati Reds (NL), on June 11 and June 15, 1938.

Shutouts Six, by Don Drysdale, Los Angeles Dodgers (NL), May 14 through June 4, 1968.

Strikeouts 10, by Tom Seaver, New York Mets (NL) on April 22, 1970.

BASERUNNING

STOLEN BASES

Career 1,117, by Rickey Henderson, Oakland Athletics (AL), 1979–84, 1989–94; New York Yankees (AL), 1985–89; Toronto Blue Jays (AL), 1993; Oakland Athletics (AL), 1994.

Season 130, by Rickey Henderson, Oakland Athletics (AL), in 1982.

Game Seven, by two players: George Gore, Chicago Cubs (NL), on June 25, 1881; Billy Hamilton, Philadelphia Phillies (NL), on August 31, 1894. The modern-day record is six, by two players: Eddie Collins, Philadelphia Athletics (AL), on September 11, 1912; Otis Nixon, Atlanta Braves (NL), on June 17, 1991.

40/40 Club The only player to steal at least 40 bases and hit at least 40 home runs in one season is Jose Canseco, Oakland Athletics (AL), in 1988, when he stole 40 bases and hit 42 home runs.

FIELDING

HIGHEST FIELDING PERCENTAGE

Career .996, by Don Mattingly, New York Yankees (AL), 1982–94.

ASSISTS

Career 8,133, by Bill Dahlen, Chicago Cubs (NL), 1891–98; Brooklyn Dodgers (NL), 1899–1903, 1910–11; New York Giants (NL), 1904–07; Boston Braves (NL), 1908–09. Dahlen played 2,132 games at shortstop, 223 at third base, 19 at second base and 58 in the outfield.

HELP IS ON THE WAY ■ LEE SMITH, BASEBALL'S PREMIER RELIEF PITCHER. (NATIONAL BASEBALL LIBRARY)

BACK WHERE HE STARTED ■ RICKEY HENDERSON, ONCE AGAIN IN AN A'S UNIFORM, CONTINUES TO ADD TO HIS CAREER RECORD FOR MOST BASES STOLEN. (NATIONAL BASEBALL LIBRARY)

Most Valuable Player Award (MVP) There have been three different MVP Awards in baseball: the Chalmers Award (1911–14), the League Award (1922–29), and the Baseball Writers' Association of America Award (1931–present).

CHALMERS AWARD (1911–1914)

	National League				American League		
Year	Player	Team	Position	Year	Player	Team	Position
1911	Wildfire Schulte	Chicago Cubs	OF	1911	Ty Cobb	Detroit Tigers	OF
1912	Larry Doyle	New York Giants	2B	1912	Tris Speaker	Boston Red Sox	OF
1913	Jake Daubert	Brooklyn Dodgers	1B	1913	Walter Johnson	Washington Senators	P
1914	Johnny Evers	Boston Braves	2B	1914	Eddie Collins	Philadelphia A's	2B

LEAGUE AWARD (1922-1929)

National League

Year	Player	Team	Position
1922	no selection		
1923	no selection		
1924	Dazzy Vance	Brooklyn Dodgers	P
1925	Rogers Hornsby	St. Louis Cardinals	2B
1926	Bob O'Farrell	St. Louis Cardinals	C
1927	Paul Waner	Pittsburgh Pirates	OF
1928	Jim Bottomley	St. Louis Cardinals	1B
1929	Rogers Hornsby	Chicago Cubs	2B

American League

Year	Player	Team	Position
1922	George Sisler	St. Louis Browns	1B
1923	Babe Ruth	New York Yankees	OF
1924	Walter Johnson	Washington Senators	P
1925	Roger Peckinpaugh	Washington Senators	SS
1926	George Burns	Cleveland Indians	1B
1927	Lou Gehrig	New York Yankees	1B
1928	Mickey Cochrane	Philadelphia A's	C
1929	no selection		

BASEBALL WRITERS' AWARD (1931-1948)

Most wins Three, by eight players: Jimmie Foxx, Philadelphia Athletics (AL), 1932–33, 1938; Joe DiMaggio, New York Yankees (AL), 1939, 1941, 1947; Stan Musial, St. Louis Cardinals (NL), 1943, 1946, 1948; Roy Campanella, Brooklyn Dodgers (NL), 1951, 1953, 1955; Yogi Berra, New York Yankees (AL), 1951, 1954–55; Mickey Mantle, New York Yankees (AL), 1956–57, 1962; Mike Schmidt, Philadelphia Phillies (NL), 1980–81, 1986; and Barry Bonds, Pittsburgh Pirates (NL), 1990, 1992, San Francisco Giants (NL), 1993.

Wins, both leagues Frank Robinson, Cincinnati Reds (NL), in 1961; Baltimore Orioles (AL), in 1966.

National League

Year	Player	Team	Position
1931	Frankie Frisch	St. Louis Cardinals	2B
1932	Chuck Klein	Philadelphia Phillies	OF
1933	Carl Hubbell	New York Giants	P
1934	Dizzy Dean	St. Louis Cardinals	P
1935	Gabby Hartnett	Chicago Cubs	C
1936	Carl Hubbell	New York Giants	P
1937	Joe Medwick	St. Louis Cardinals	OF
1938	Ernie Lombardi	Cincinnati Reds	C
1939	Bucky Walters	Cincinnati Reds	P
1940	Frank McCormick	Cincinnati Reds	1B
1941	Dolf Camilli	Brooklyn Dodgers	1B
1942	Mort Cooper	St. Louis Cardinals	P
1943	Stan Musial	St. Louis Cardinals	OF
1944	Marty Marion	St. Louis Cardinals	SS
1945	Phil Cavarretta	Chicago Cubs	1B
1946	Stan Musial	St. Louis Cardinals	1B–OF
1947	Bob Elliott	Boston Braves	3B
1948	Stan Musial	St. Louis Cardinals	OF

American League

Year	Player	Team	Position
1931	Lefty Grove	Philadelphia A's	P
1932	Jimmie Foxx	Philadelphia A's	1B
1933	Jimmie Foxx	Philadelphia A's	1B
1934	Mickey Cochrane	Detroit Tigers	C
1935	Hank Greenberg	Detroit Tigers	1B
1936	Lou Gehrig	New York Yankees	1B
1937	Charlie Gehringer	Detroit Tigers	2B
1938	Jimmie Foxx	Boston Red Sox	1B
1939	Joe DiMaggio	New York Yankees	OF
1940	Hank Greenberg	Detroit Tigers	OF
1941	Joe DiMaggio	New York Yankees	OF
1942	Joe Gordon	New York Yankees	2B
1943	Spud Chandler	New York Yankees	P
1944	Hal Newhouser	Detroit Tigers	P
1945	Hal Newhouser	Detroit Tigers	P
1946	Ted Williams	Boston Red Sox	OF
1947	Joe DiMaggio	New York Yankees	OF
1948	Lou Boudreau	Cleveland Indians	SS

BASEBALL WRITERS' AWARD (1949–1982)

National League				American League			
Year	Player	Team	Position	Year	Player	Team	Position
1949	Jackie Robinson	Brooklyn Dodgers	2B	1949	Ted Williams	Boston Red Sox	OF
1950	Jim Konstanty	Philadelphia Phillies	P	1950	Phil Rizzuto	New York Yankees	SS
1951	Roy Campanella	Brooklyn Dodgers	C	1951	Yogi Berra	New York Yankees	C
1952	Hank Sauer	Chicago Cubs	OF	1952	Bobby Shantz	Philadelphia A's	P
1953	Roy Campanella	Brooklyn Dodgers	C	1953	Al Rosen	Cleveland Indians	3B
1954	Willie Mays	New York Giants	OF	1954	Yogi Berra	New York Yankees	C
1955	Roy Campanella	Brooklyn Dodgers	C	1955	Yogi Berra	New York Yankees	C
1956	Don Newcombe	Brooklyn Dodgers	P	1956	Mickey Mantle	New York Yankees	OF
1957	Hank Aaron	Milwaukee Braves	OF	1957	Mickey Mantle	New York Yankees	OF
1958	Ernie Banks	Chicago Cubs	SS	1958	Jackie Jensen	Boston Red Sox	OF
1959	Ernie Banks	Chicago Cubs	SS	1959	Nellie Fox	Chicago White Sox	2B
1960	Dick Groat	Pittsburgh Pirates	SS	1960	Roger Maris	New York Yankees	OF
1961	Frank Robinson	Cincinnati Reds	OF	1961	Roger Maris	New York Yankees	OF
1962	Maury Wills	Los Angeles Dodgers	SS	1962	Mickey Mantle	New York Yankees	OF
1963	Sandy Koufax	Los Angeles Dodgers	P	1963	Elston Howard	New York Yankees	C
1964	Ken Boyer	St. Louis Cardinals	3B	1964	Brooks Robinson	Baltimore Orioles	3B
1965	Willie Mays	San Francisco Giants	OF	1965	Zoilo Versalles	Minnesota Twins	SS
1966	Roberto Clemente	Pittsburgh Pirates	OF	1966	Frank Robinson	Baltimore Orioles	OF
1967	Orlando Cepeda	St. Louis Cardinals	1B	1967	Carl Yastrzemski	Boston Red Sox	OF
1968	Bob Gibson	St. Louis Cardinals	P	1968	Denny McLain	Detroit Tigers	P
1969	Willie McCovey	San Francisco Giants	1B	1969	Harmon Killebrew	Minnesota Twins	1B-3B
1970	Johnny Bench	Cincinnati Reds	C	1970	Boog Powell	Baltimore Orioles	1B
1971	Joe Torre	St. Louis Cardinals	3B	1971	Vida Blue	Oakland A's	P
1972	Johnny Bench	Cincinnati Reds	C	1972	Dick Allen	Chicago White Sox	1B
1973	Pete Rose	Cincinnati Reds	OF	1973	Reggie Jackson	Oakland A's	OF
1974	Steve Garvey	Los Angeles Dodgers	1B	1974	Jeff Burroughs	Texas Rangers	OF
1975	Joe Morgan	Cincinnati Reds	2B	1975	Fred Lynn	Boston Red Sox	OF
1976	Joe Morgan	Cincinnati Reds	2B	1976	Thurman Munson	New York Yankees	C
1977	George Foster	Cincinnati Reds	OF	1977	Rod Carew	Minnesota Twins	1B
1978	Dave Parker	Pittsburgh Pirates	OF	1978	Jim Rice	Boston Red Sox	OF-DH
1979	Willie Stargell	Pittsburgh Pirates	1B*	1979	Don Baylor	California Angels	OF-DH
	Keith Hernandez	St. Louis Cardinals	1B*				
1980	Mike Schmidt	Philadelphia Phillies	3B	1980	George Brett	Kansas City Royals	3B
1981	Mike Schmidt	Philadelphia Phillies	3B	1981	Rollie Fingers	Milwaukee Brewers	P
1982	Dale Murphy	Atlanta Braves	OF	1982	Robin Yount	Milwaukee Brewers	SS

* Tied vote

BASEBALL WRITERS' AWARD (1983–1994)

	National League				American League		
Year	Player	Team	Position	Year	Player	Team	Position
1983	Dale Murphy	Atlanta Braves	OF	1983	Cal Ripken Jr.	Baltimore Orioles	SS
1984	Ryne Sandberg	Chicago Cubs	2B	1984	Willie Hernandez	Detroit Tigers	P
1985	Willie McGee	St. Louis Cardinals	OF	1985	Don Mattingly	New York Yankees	1B
1986	Mike Schmidt	Philadelphia Phillies	3B	1986	Roger Clemens	Boston Red Sox	P
1987	Andre Dawson	Chicago Cubs	OF	1987	George Bell	Toronto Blue Jays	OF
1988	Kirk Gibson	Los Angeles Dodgers	OF	1988	Jose Canseco	Oakland A's	OF
1989	Kevin Mitchell	San Francisco Giants	OF	1989	Robin Yount	Milwaukee Brewers	OF
1990	Barry Bonds	Pittsburgh Pirates	OF	1990	Rickey Henderson	Oakland A's	OF
1991	Terry Pendleton	Atlanta Braves	3B	1991	Cal Ripken Jr.	Baltimore Orioles	SS
1992	Barry Bonds	Pittsburgh Pirates	OF	1992	Dennis Eckersley	Oakland A's	P
1993	Barry Bonds	San Francisco Giants	OF	1993	Frank Thomas	Chicago White Sox	1B
1994	Jeff Bagwell	Houston Astros	1B	1994	Frank Thomas	Chicago White Sox	1B

MANAGERS

Most games managed 7,755, by Connie Mack, Pittsburgh Pirates (NL), 1894–96; Philadelphia Athletics (AL), 1901–50. Mack's career record was 3,731 wins, 3,948 losses, 75 ties and one no-decision.

Most wins 3,731, by Connie Mack, Pittsburgh Pirates (NL), 1894–96; Philadelphia Athletics (AL), 1901–50.

Most losses 3,948, by Connie Mack, Pittsburgh Pirates (NL), 1894–96; Philadelphia Athletics (AL), 1901–50.

Highest winning percentage .615, by Joe McCarthy, Chicago Cubs (NL), 1926–30; New York Yankees (AL), 1931–46; Boston Red Sox (AL), 1948–50. McCarthy's career record was 2,125 wins, 1,333 losses, 26 ties and three no-decisions.

MISCELLANEOUS

Youngest player The youngest major league player of all time was the Cincinnati Reds (AL) pitcher Joe Nuxhall, who played one game in June 1944, at age 15 years 314 days. He did not play again in the National League until 1952.

Oldest player Satchel Paige pitched for the Kansas City A's (AL) at age 59 years 80 days on September 25, 1965.

Shortest and tallest players The shortest major league player was Eddie Gaedel, a 3-foot-7-inch, 65-pound midget, who pinch-hit for the St. Louis Browns (AL) v. the Detroit Tigers (AL) on August 19, 1951. Wearing number ⅛, the batter with the smallest-ever major league strike zone walked on four pitches. Following the game, major league rules were hastily rewritten to prevent any recurrence. The tallest major leaguers of all time are two 6-foot-10-inch pitchers: Randy Johnson, who played in his first game for the Montreal Expos

GUINNESS CHALLENGE

How old was Ty Murray when he became the youngest rodeo champion?
See page 172 for the answer.

CY YOUNG AWARD WINNERS (1956–1987)

Inaugurated in 1956, this award is given to the best pitcher in baseball as judged by the Baseball Writers' Association of America. From 1967 on, separate awards have been given to the best pitcher in each league.

Most wins Four, by Steve Carlton, Philadelphia Phillies, 1972, 1977, 1980 and 1982.

Most consecutive wins Greg Maddux is the only pitcher in baseball history to win the Cy Young Award three times in a row: Chicago Cubs (NL), 1992; Atlanta Braves (NL), 1993, 1994.

Wins, both leagues The only pitcher to win the Cy Young Award in both leagues is Gaylord Perry: Cleveland Indians (AL), 1972; San Diego Padres (NL), 1978.

Year	Pitcher	Team	Year	Pitcher	Team
1956	Don Newcombe	Brooklyn Dodgers (NL)	1962	Don Drysdale	Los Angeles Dodgers (NL)
1957	Warren Spahn	Milwaukee Braves (NL)	1963	Sandy Koufax	Los Angeles Dodgers (NL)
1958	Bob Turley	New York Yankees (AL)	1964	Dean Chance	Los Angeles Angels (AL)
1959	Early Wynn	Chicago White Sox (AL)	1965	Sandy Koufax	Los Angeles Dodgers (NL)
1960	Vernon Law	Pittsburgh Pirates (NL)	1966	Sandy Koufax	Los Angeles Dodgers (NL)
1961	Whitey Ford	New York Yankees (AL)			

National League			American League		
1967	Mike McCormick	San Francisco Giants	1967	Jim Lonborg	Boston Red Sox
1968	Bob Gibson	St. Louis Cardinals	1968	Denny McLain	Detroit Tigers
1969	Tom Seaver	New York Mets	1969*	Mike Cuellar / Denny McLain	Baltimore Orioles / Detroit Tigers
1970	Bob Gibson	St. Louis Cardinals	1970	Jim Perry	Minnesota Twins
1971	Ferguson Jenkins	Chicago Cubs	1971	Vida Blue	Oakland Athletics
1972	Steve Carlton	Philadelphia Phillies	1972	Gaylord Perry	Cleveland Indians
1973	Tom Seaver	New York Mets	1973	Jim Palmer	Baltimore Orioles
1974	Mike Marshall	Los Angeles Dodgers	1974	"Catfish" Hunter	Oakland Athletics
1975	Tom Seaver	New York Mets	1975	Jim Palmer	Baltimore Orioles
1976	Randy Jones	San Diego Padres	1976	Jim Palmer	Baltimore Orioles
1977	Steve Carlton	Philadelphia Phillies	1977	Sparky Lyle	New York Yankees
1978	Gaylord Perry	San Diego Padres	1978	Ron Guidry	New York Yankees
1979	Bruce Sutter	Chicago Cubs	1979	Mike Flanagan	Baltimore Orioles
1980	Steve Carlton	Philadelphia Phillies	1980	Steve Stone	Baltimore Orioles
1981	Fernando Valenzuela	Los Angeles Dodgers	1981	Rollie Fingers	Milwaukee Brewers
1982	Steve Carlton	Philadelphia Phillies	1982	Pete Vukovich	Milwaukee Brewers
1983	John Denny	Philadelphia Phillies	1983	LaMarr Hoyt	Chicago White Sox
1984	Rick Sutcliffe	Chicago Cubs	1984	Willie Hernandez	Detroit Tigers
1985	Dwight Gooden	New York Mets	1985	Bret Saberhagen	Kansas City Royals
1986	Mike Scott	Houston Astros	1986	Roger Clemens	Boston Red Sox
1987	Steve Bedrosian	Philadelphia Phillies	1987	Roger Clemens	Boston Red Sox

* Tied vote

CY YOUNG AWARD WINNERS (1988–1994)

National League			American League		
Year	Pitcher	Team	Year	Pitcher	Team
1988	Orel Hershiser	Los Angeles Dodgers	1988	Frank Viola	Minnesota Twins
1989	Mark Davis	San Diego Padres	1989	Bret Saberhagen	Kansas City Royals
1990	Doug Drabek	Pittsburgh Pirates	1990	Bob Welch	Oakland Athletics
1991	Tom Glavine	Atlanta Braves	1991	Roger Clemens	Boston Red Sox
1992	Greg Maddux	Chicago Cubs	1992	Dennis Eckersley	Oakland Athletics
1993	Greg Maddux	Atlanta Braves	1993	Jack McDowell	Chicago White Sox
1994	Greg Maddux	Atlanta Braves	1994	David Cone	Kansas City Royals

(NL) on September 15, 1988; and Eric Hillman, who debuted for the New York Mets (NL) on May 18, 1992.

Father and son On August 31, 1990, Ken Griffey Sr. and Ken Griffey Jr., of the Seattle Mariners (AL), became the first father and son to play for the same major league team at the same time. In 1989 the Griffeys had been the first father/son combination to play in the major leagues at the same time. Griffey Sr. played for the Cincinnati Reds (NL) during that season.

Father, son and grandson On August 19, 1992, Bret Boone made his major league debut for the Seattle Mariners (AL), making the Boone family the first three-generation family in major league history. Boone's father Bob Boone played 18 seasons in the majors, 1972–89, and his grandfather Ray Boone played from 1948–60.

Record Quotable

"You always set goals, but to win a Cy Young, or to even win three of them, was never really a goal. . . . I think any time you exceed your own expectations, it's even that much more gratifying."

—Greg Maddux, at a
1994 press conference, commenting
on his third consecutive
Cy Young Award.

ERA KING ■ IN 1994, THE "YEAR OF THE LONG BALL," GREG MADDUX COULD BOAST AN INCREDIBLE 1.56 EARNED RUN AVERAGE. HERE HE WINDS UP FOR THE CHICAGO CUBS IN 1992, THE FIRST YEAR HE WON THE CY YOUNG AWARD. (BASEBALL HALL OF FAME/TV SPORTS MAILBAG)

ROOKIE OF THE YEAR (1947–1971)

The Rookie of the Year Award is voted on by the Baseball Writers Association and was first presented in 1947. From 1947–1948 only one award was given for both leagues.

MVP winner (Baseball Writers' Award): The only Rookie of the Year to win the MVP was Fred Lynn (Boston Red Sox, 1976).

Ties: Ties have only occurred twice, once in each league. In the National League, Butch Metzger (San Dieto Padres) and Pat Zachry (Cincinnati Reds) tied in 1976. In the American League, John Castino (Minnesota Twins) and Alfredo Griffin (Toronto Blue Jays) tied in 1979.

Youngest Rookie of the Year: 19—Dwight Gooden, New York Mets, 1984.

Oldest Rookie of the Year: Four players are tied at 28—Jackie Robinson, Brooklyn Dodgers, 1947; Sam Jethroe, Boston Braves, 1950; Joe Black, Brooklyn Dodgers, 1952; and Jack Sanford, Philadelphia Phillies, 1957.

Most Rookie of the Year honors by a team: 13—Los Angeles Dodgers, 1949, 1952, 1953, 1960, 1965, 1969, 1979–82, 1992–94.

Most consecutive Rookie of the Year honors by a team: 4—Los Angeles Dodgers, 1979–82.

American League and National League Combined

Year	Player	Team	Position	Year	Player	Team	Position
1947	Jackie Robinson	Brooklyn Dodgers (NL)	1B	1948	Alvin Dark	Boston Braves (NL)	SS

National League / American League

Year	Player	Team	Position	Year	Player	Team	Position
1949	Don Newcombe	Brooklyn Dodgers	P	1949	Roy Sievers	St. Louis Cardinals	OF
1950	Sam Jethroe	Boston Braves	OF	1950	Walt Dropo	Boston Red Sox	1B
1951	Willie Mays	New York Giants	OF	1951	Gil McDougald	New York Yankees	3B
1952	Joe Black	Brooklyn Dodgers	P	1952	Harry Byrd	Philadelphia Athletics	P
1953	Jim Gilliam	Brooklyn Dodgers	2B	1953	Harvey Kuenn	Detroit Tigers	SS
1954	Wally Moon	St. Louis Cardinals	OF	1954	Bob Grim	New York Yankees	P
1955	Bill Virdon	St. Louis Cardinals	OF	1955	Herb Score	Cleveland Indians	P
1956	Frank Robinson	Cincinnati Reds	OF	1956	Luis Aparicio	Chicago White Sox	SS
1957	Jack Sanford	Philadelphia Phillies	P	1957	Tony Kubek	New York Yankees	OF-INF
1958	Orlando Cepeda	San Francisco Giants	1B	1958	Albie Pearson	Washington Senators	OF
1959	Willie McCovey	San Francisco Giants	1B	1959	Bob Allison	Washington Senators	OF
1960	Frank Howard	Los Angeles Dodgers	OF	1960	Ron Hansen	Baltimore Orioles	SS
1961	Billy Williams	Chicago Cubs	OF	1961	Don Schwall	Boston Red Sox	P
1962	Ken Hubbs	Chicago Cubs	2B	1962	Tom Tresh	New York Yankees	SS-OF
1963	Pete Rose	Cincinnati Reds	2B	1963	Gary Peters	Chicago White Sox	P
1964	Richie Allen	Philadelphia Phillies	3B	1964	Tony Oliva	Minnesota Twins	OF
1965	Jim Lefebvre	Los Angeles Dodgers	2B	1965	Curt Blefary	Baltimore Orioles	OF
1966	Tommy Helms	Cincinnati Reds	3B	1966	Tommy Agee	Chicago White Sox	OF
1967	Tom Seaver	New York Mets	P	1967	Rod Carew	Minnesota Twins	2B
1968	Johnny Bench	Cincinnati Reds	C	1968	Stan Bahnsen	New York Yankees	P
1969	Ted Sizemore	Los Angeles Dodgers	2B	1969	Lou Piniella	Kansas City Royals	OF
1970	Carl Morton	Montreal Expos	P	1970	Thurman Munson	New York Yankees	C
1971	Earl Williams	Atlanta Braves	C	1971	Chris Chambliss	Cleveland Indians	1B

ROOKIE OF THE YEAR (1972–1994)

National League

Year	Player	Team	Position
1972	Jon Matlack	New York Mets	P
1973	Gary Matthews	San Francisco Giants	OF
1974	Bake McBride	St. Louis Cardinals	OF
1975	John Montefusco	San Francisco Giants	P
1976	Butch Metzger	San Diego Padres	P
	Pat Zachry	Cincinnati Reds	P
1977	Andre Dawson	Montreal Expos	OF
1978	Bob Horner	Atlanta Braves	3B
1979	Rick Sutcliffe	Los Angeles Dodgers	P
1980	Steve Howe	Los Angeles Dodgers	P
1981	Fernando Valenzuela	Los Angeles Dodgers	P
1982	Steve Sax	Los Angeles Dodgers	2B
1983	Darryl Strawberry	New York Mets	OF
1984	Dwight Gooden	New York Mets	P
1985	Vince Coleman	St. Louis Cardinals	OF
1986	Todd Worrell	St. Louis Cardinals	P
1987	Benito Santiago	San Diego Padres	C
1988	Chris Sabo	Cincinnati Reds	3B
1989	Jerome Walton	Chicago Cubs	OF
1990	David Justice	Atlanta Braves	OF
1991	Jeff Bagwell	Houston Astros	1B
1992	Eric Karros	Los Angeles Dodgers	1B
1993	Mike Piazza	Los Angeles Dodgers	C
1994	Raul Mondesi	Los Angeles Dodgers	OF

American League

Year	Player	Team	Position
1972	Carlton Fisk	Boston Red Sox	C
1973	Al Bumbry	Baltimore Orioles	OF
1974	Mike Hargrove	Texas Rangers	1B
1975	Fred Lynn	Boston Red Sox	OF
1976	Mark Fidrych	Detroit Tigers	P
1977	Eddie Murray	Baltimore Orioles	1B-DH
1978	Lou Whitaker	Detroit Tigers	2B
1979	John Castino	Minnesota Twins	3B
	Alfredo Griffin	Toronto Blue Jays	SS
1980	Joe Charboneau	Cleveland Indians	DH-OF
1981	Dave Righetti	New York Yankees	P
1982	Cal Ripken Jr.	Baltimore Orioles	SS
1983	Ron Kittle	Chicago White Sox	OF
1984	Alvin Davis	Seattle Mariners	1B
1985	Ozzie Guillen	Chicago White Sox	SS
1986	Jose Canseco	Oakland Athletics	OF
1987	Mark McGwire	Oakland Athletics	1B
1988	Walt Weiss	Oakland Athletics	SS
1989	Greg Olson	Baltimore Orioles	P
1990	Sandy Alomar Jr.	Cleveland Indians	C
1991	Chuck Knoblauch	Minnesota Twins	2B
1992	Pat Listach	Milwaukee Brewers	SS
1993	Tim Salmon	California Angels	DH
1994	Robert Hamelin	Kansas City Royals	1B

Record attendances The all-time season record for attendance for both leagues is 70,257,938, set in 1993 (33,333,365 for the 14-team American League, and 36,924,573 for the 14-team National League). The American League and National League totals were both league records. The record for home-team attendance is held by the Colorado Rockies (NL) at 4,483,350 in 1993. The American League record is held by the Toronto Blue Jays at 4,057,947 in 1993.

Shortest game The New York Giants (NL) beat the Philadelphia Phillies (NL), 6–1, in nine innings in 51 minutes on September 28, 1919.

Longest games The Brooklyn Dodgers (NL) and the Boston Braves (NL) played to a 1–1 tie after 26 innings on May 1, 1920. The Chicago White Sox (AL) played the longest ballgame in elapsed time—8 hours 6 minutes—before beating the Milwaukee Brewers, 7–6, in the 25th inning on May 9, 1984 in Chicago. The game started on a Tuesday night and was tied at 3–3 when the 1 A.M. curfew caused suspension until Wednesday night.

The actual longest game was a minor league game in 1981 that lasted 33 innings. At the end of nine innings the score was tied, 1–1, with the Rochester (N.Y.) Red Wings battling the home team Pawtucket (R.I.) Red Sox. At the end of 32 innings the score was still 2–2, when the game was suspended. Two months later, play was resumed, and 18 minutes later, Pawtucket scored one run and won.

GAMES PLAYED

Most series played 11, by Reggie Jackson, Oakland Athletics (AL), 1971–75; New York Yankees (AL), 1977–78, 1980–81; California Angels (AL), 1982, 1986.

LEAGUE CHAMPIONSHIP SERIES (1969–1994)

League Championship Series (LCS) playoffs began in 1969 when the American and National Leagues expanded to 12 teams each and created two divisions, East and West. To determine the respective league pennant winners, the division winners played a best-of-five-games series, which was expanded to best-of-seven in 1985.

National League

Year	Winner	Loser	Series
1969	New York Mets (East)	Atlanta Braves (West)	3–0
1970	Cincinnati Reds (West)	Pittsburgh Pirates (East)	3–0
1971	Pittsburgh Pirates (East)	San Francisco Giants (West)	3–1
1972	Cincinnati Reds (West)	Pittsburgh Pirates (East)	3–2
1973	New York Mets (East)	Cincinnati Reds (West)	3–2
1974	Los Angeles Dodgers (West)	Pittsburgh Pirates (East)	3–1
1975	Cincinnati Reds (West)	Pittsburgh Pirates (East)	3–0
1976	Cincinnati Reds (West)	Philadelphia Phillies (East)	3–0
1977	Los Angeles Dodgers (West)	Philadelphia Phillies (East)	3–1
1978	Los Angeles Dodgers (West)	Philadelphia Phillies (East)	3–1
1979	Pittsburgh Pirates (East)	Cincinnati Reds (West)	3–0
1980	Philadelphia Phillies (East)	Houston Astros (West)	3–2
1981	Los Angeles Dodgers (West)	Montreal Expos (East)	3–2
1982	St. Louis Cardinals (East)	Atlanta Braves (West)	3–0
1983	Philadelphia Phillies (East)	Los Angeles Dodgers (West)	3–1
1984	San Diego Padres (West)	Chicago Cubs (East)	3–2
1985	St. Louis Cardinals (East)	Los Angeles Dodgers (West)	4–2
1986	New York Mets (East)	Houston Astros (West)	4–2
1987	St. Louis Cardinals (East)	San Francisco Giants (West)	4–3
1988	Los Angeles Dodgers (West)	New York Mets (East)	4–3
1989	San Francisco Giants (West)	Chicago Cubs (East)	4–1
1990	Cincinnati Reds (West)	Pittsburgh Pirates (East)	4–2
1991	Atlanta Braves (West)	Pittsburgh Pirates (East)	4–3
1992	Atlanta Braves (West)	Pittsburgh Pirates (East)	4–3
1993	Philadelphia Phillies (East)	Atlanta Braves (West)	4–2
1994	Canceled		

Most games played 45, by Reggie Jackson, Oakland Athletics (AL), 1971–75; New York Yankees (AL), 1977–78, 1980–81; California Angels (AL), 1982, 1986.

HITTING RECORDS (CAREER)

Batting average (minimum 50 at-bats) .386, by Mickey Rivers, New York Yankees (AL), 1976–78. Rivers collected 22 hits in 57 at-bats in 14 games.

Hits 45, by Pete Rose, Cincinnati Reds (NL), 1970, 1972–73, 1975–76; Philadelphia Phillies (NL), 1980, 1983.

Home runs Nine, by George Brett, Kansas City Royals (AL), 1976–78, 1980, 1984–85.

Runs batted in (RBIs) 21, by Steve Garvey, Los Angeles Dodgers (NL), 1974, 1977–78, 1981; San Diego Padres (NL), 1984.

Runs scored 22, by George Brett, Kansas City Royals (AL), 1976–78, 1980, 1984–85.

Walks 23, by Joe Morgan, Cincinnati Reds (NL), 1972–73, 1975–76, 1979; Houston Astros (NL), 1980; Philadelphia Phillies (NL), 1983.

LEAGUE CHAMPIONSHIP SERIES (1969–1994)

American League

Year	Winner	Loser	Series
1969	Baltimore Orioles (East)	Minnesota Twins (West)	3–0
1970	Baltimore Orioles (East)	Minnesota Twins (West)	3–0
1971	Baltimore Orioles (East)	Oakland A's (West)	3–0
1972	Oakland A's (West)	Detroit Tigers (East)	3–2
1973	Oakland A's (West)	Baltimore Orioles (East)	3–2
1974	Oakland A's (West)	Baltimore Orioles (East)	3–1
1975	Boston Red Sox (East)	Oakland A's (West)	3–0
1976	New York Yankees (East)	Kansas City Royals (West)	3–2
1977	New York Yankees (East)	Kansas City Royals (West)	3–2
1978	New York Yankees (East)	Kansas City Royals (West)	3–1
1979	Baltimore Orioles (East)	California Angels (West)	3–1
1980	Kansas City Royals (West)	New York Yankees (East)	3–0
1981	New York Yankees (East)	Oakland A's (West)	3–0
1982	Milwaukee Brewers (East)	California Angels (West)	3–2
1983	Baltimore Orioles (East)	Chicago White Sox (West)	3–1
1984	Detroit Tigers (East)	Kansas City Royals (West)	3–0
1985	Kansas City Royals (West)	Toronto Blue Jays (East)	4–3
1986	Boston Red Sox (East)	California Angels (West)	4–3
1987	Minnesota Twins (West)	Detroit Tigers (East)	4–1
1988	Oakland A's (West)	Boston Red Sox (East)	4–0
1989	Oakland A's (West)	Toronto Blue Jays (East)	4–1
1990	Oakland A's (West)	Boston Red Sox (East)	4–0
1991	Minnesota Twins (West)	Toronto Blue Jays (East)	4–1
1992	Toronto Blue Jays (East)	Oakland A's (West)	4–2
1993	Toronto Blue Jays (East)	Chicago White Sox (West)	4–2
1994	Canceled		

Stolen bases 14, by Rickey Henderson, Oakland Athletics (AL), 1981, 1989–90, 1992; Toronto Blue Jays (AL), 1993.

Most series pitched Eight, by Bob Welch, Los Angeles Dodgers (NL), 1978, 1981, 1983, 1985; Oakland Athletics (AL), 1988–90, 1992.

Most games pitched 15, by two pitchers: Tug McGraw, New York Mets (NL), 1969, 1973; Philadelphia Phillies (NL), 1976–78, 1980; Dennis Eckersley, Chicago Cubs (NL), 1984; Oakland Athletics (AL), 1988–90, 1992.

Wins Eight, by Dave Stewart, Oakland Athletics (AL), 1988–90, 1992; Toronto Blue Jays (AL), 1993.

Losses Seven, by Jerry Reuss, Pittsburgh Pirates (NL), 1974–75; Los Angeles Dodgers (NL), 1981, 1983, 1985.

Innings pitched 69⅓, by Jim "Catfish" Hunter, Oakland Athletics (AL), 1971–74, New York Yankees (AL), 1976, 1978.

Complete games Five, by Jim Palmer, Baltimore Orioles (AL), 1969–71, 1973–74, 1979.

Strikeouts 46, by two players: Nolan Ryan, New York Mets (NL), 1969; California Angels (AL), 1979; Houston Astros (NL), 1980, 1986; and Jim Palmer, Baltimore Orioles (AL), 1969–71, 1973–74, 1979.

Saves 10, by Dennis Eckersley, Chicago Cubs (NL), 1984; Oakland Athletics (AL), 1988–90, 1992.

WORLD SERIES

ORIGINS Played annually between the champions of the National League and the American League, the World Series was first staged unofficially in 1903, and officially from 1905 on. On October 20, 1992 the Toronto Blue Jays hosted the first World Series game played outside the United States. The Blue Jays won the 1992 Series, thus becoming the first non-U.S. team to win the fall classic.

WORLD SERIES RECORDS

TEAM RECORDS

Most wins 22, by the New York Yankees (AL), 1923, 1927–28, 1932, 1936–39, 1941, 1943, 1947, 1949–53, 1956, 1958, 1961–62, 1977–78.

Most appearances 33, by the New York Yankees (AL), 1921–23, 1926–28, 1932, 1936–39, 1941–43, 1947, 1949–53, 1955–58, 1960–64, 1976–78, 1981.

INDIVIDUAL RECORDS

GAMES PLAYED

Most series 14, by Yogi Berra, New York Yankees (AL), 1947, 1949–53, 1955–58, 1960–63.

Most series (pitcher) 11, by Whitey Ford, New York Yankees (AL), 1950, 1953, 1955–58, 1960–64.

Most games 75, by Yogi Berra, New York Yankees (AL), 1947, 1949–53, 1955–58, 1960–63.

Most games (pitcher) 22, by Whitey Ford, New York Yankees (AL), 1950, 1953, 1955–58, 1960–64.

HITTING RECORDS

BATTING AVERAGE

Career (min. 20 games) .391, by Lou Brock, St. Louis Cardinals (NL), 1964, 1967–68. Brock collected 34 hits in 87 at-bats over 21 games.

Series (min. four games) .750, by Billy Hatcher, Cincinnati Reds (NL), in 1990. Hatcher collected nine hits in 12 at-bats in four games.

HITS

Career 71, by Yogi Berra, New York Yankees (AL), 1947–63. In 259 at-bats, Berra hit 12 home runs, 10 doubles and 49 singles.

Series 13, by three players: Bobby Richardson, New York Yankees (AL), in 1960; Lou Brock, St. Louis Cardinals (NL), in 1968; Marty Barrett, Boston Red Sox (AL), in 1986.

HOME RUNS

Career 18, by Mickey Mantle, New York Yankees (AL), 1951–53, 1955–58, 1960–64. Mantle hit his record 18 homers in 230 at-bats in 65 games.

Series Five, by Reggie Jackson, New York Yankees (AL), in 1977.

Game Three, by two players: Babe Ruth, New York Yankees (AL), who did it twice: on October 6, 1926 *v.* St. Louis Cardinals, and on October 9, 1928 *v.* St. Louis Cardinals; and Reggie Jackson, New York Yankees (AL), on October 18, 1977 *v.* Los Angeles Dodgers.

WORLD SERIES (1903–1938)

Year	Winner	Loser	Series
1903	Boston Pilgrims (AL)	Pittsburgh Pirates (NL)	5–3
1904	no series		
1905	New York Giants (NL)	Philadelphia A's (AL)	4–1
1906	Chicago White Sox (AL)	Chicago Cubs (NL)	4–2
1907	Chicago Cubs (NL)	Detroit Tigers (AL)	4–0–1*
1908	Chicago Cubs (NL)	Detroit Tigers (AL)	4–1
1909	Pittsburgh Pirates (NL)	Detroit Tigers (AL)	4–3
1910	Philadelphia A's (AL)	Chicago Cubs (NL)	4–1
1911	Philadelphia A's (AL)	New York Giants (NL)	4–2
1912	Boston Red Sox (AL)	New York Giants (NL)	4–3–1*
1913	Philadelphia A's (AL)	New York Giants (NL)	4–1
1914	Boston Braves (NL)	Philadelphia A's (AL)	4–0
1915	Boston Red Sox (AL)	Philadelphia Phillies (NL)	4–1
1916	Boston Red Sox (AL)	Brooklyn Robins (NL)	4–1
1917	Chicago White Sox (AL)	New York Giants (NL)	4–2
1918	Boston Red Sox (AL)	Chicago Cubs (NL)	4–2
1919	Cincinnati Reds (NL)	Chicago White Sox (AL)	5–3
1920	Cleveland Indians (AL)	Brooklyn Robins (NL)	5–2
1921	New York Giants (NL)	New York Yankees (AL)	5–3
1922	New York Giants (NL)	New York Yankees (AL)	4–0–1*
1923	New York Yankees (AL)	New York Giants (NL)	4–2
1924	Washington Senators (AL)	New York Giants (NL)	4–3
1925	Pittsburgh Pirates (NL)	Washington Senators (AL)	4–3
1926	St. Louis Cardinals(NL)	New York Yankees (AL)	4–3
1927	New York Yankees (AL)	Pittsburgh Pirates (NL)	4–0
1928	New York Yankees (AL)	St. Louis Cardinals (NL)	4–0
1929	Philadelphia A's (AL)	Chicago Cubs (NL)	4–1
1930	Philadelphia A's (AL)	St. Louis Cardinals (NL)	4–2
1931	St. Louis Cardinals (NL)	Philadelphia A's (AL)	4–3
1932	New York Yankees (AL)	Chicago Cubs (NL)	4–0
1933	New York Giants (NL)	Washington Senators (AL)	4–1
1934	St. Louis Cardinals (NL)	Detroit Tigers (AL)	4–3
1935	Detroit Tigers (AL)	Chicago Cubs (NL)	4–2
1936	New York Yankees (AL)	New York Giants (NL)	4–2
1937	New York Yankees (AL)	New York Giants (NL)	4–1
1938	New York Yankees (AL)	Chicago Cubs (NL)	4–0

* Tied game

WORLD SERIES (1939–1975)

Year	Winner	Loser	Series
1939	New York Yankees (AL)	Cincinnati Reds (NL)	4–0
1940	Cincinnati Reds (NL)	Detroit Tigers (AL)	4–3
1941	New York Yankees (AL)	Brooklyn Dodgers (NL)	4–1
1942	St. Louis Cardinals (NL)	New York Yankees (AL)	4–1
1943	New York Yankees (AL)	St. Louis Cardinals (NL)	4–1
1944	St. Louis Cardinals (NL)	St. Louis Browns (AL)	4–2
1945	Detroit Tigers (AL)	Chicago Cubs (NL)	4–3
1946	St. Louis Cardinals (NL)	Boston Red Sox (AL)	4–3
1947	New York Yankees (AL)	Brooklyn Dodgers (NL)	4–3
1948	Cleveland Indians (AL)	Boston Braves (NL)	4–2
1949	New York Yankees (AL)	Brooklyn Dodgers (NL)	4–1
1950	New York Yankees (AL)	Philadelphia Phillies (NL)	4–0
1951	New York Yankees (AL)	New York Giants (NL)	4–2
1952	New York Yankees (AL)	Brooklyn Dodgers (NL)	4–3
1953	New York Yankees (AL)	Brooklyn Dodgers (NL)	4–2
1954	New York Giants (NL)	Cleveland Indians (AL)	4–0
1955	Brooklyn Dodgers (NL)	New York Yankees (AL)	4–3
1956	New York Yankees (AL)	Brooklyn Dodgers (NL)	4–3
1957	Milwaukee Braves (NL)	New York Yankees (AL)	4–3
1958	New York Yankees (AL)	Milwaukee Braves (NL)	4–3
1959	Los Angeles Dodgers (NL)	Chicago White Sox (AL)	4–2
1960	Pittsburgh Pirates (NL)	New York Yankees (AL)	4–3
1961	New York Yankees (AL)	Cincinnati Reds (NL)	4–1
1962	New York Yankees (AL)	San Francisco Giants (NL)	4–3
1963	Los Angeles Dodgers (NL)	New York Yankees (AL)	4–0
1964	St. Louis Cardinals (NL)	New York Yankees (AL)	4–3
1965	Los Angeles Dodgers (NL)	Minnesota Twins (AL)	4–3
1966	Baltimore Orioles (AL)	Los Angeles Dodgers (NL)	4–0
1967	St. Louis Cardinals (NL)	Boston Red Sox (AL)	4–3
1968	Detroit Tigers (AL)	St. Louis Cardinals (NL)	4–3
1969	New York Mets (NL)	Baltimore Orioles (AL)	4–1
1970	Baltimore Orioles (AL)	Cincinnati Reds (NL)	4–1
1971	Pittsburgh Pirates (NL)	Baltimore Orioles (AL)	4–3
1972	Oakland A's (AL)	Cincinnati Reds (NL)	4–3
1973	Oakland A's (AL)	New York Mets (NL)	4–3
1974	Oakland A's (AL)	Los Angeles Dodgers (NL)	4–1
1975	Cincinnati Reds (NL)	Boston Red Sox (AL)	4–3

WORLD SERIES (1976–1994)

Year	Winner	Loser	Series
1976	Cincinnati Reds (NL)	New York Yankees (AL)	4–0
1977	New York Yankees (AL)	Los Angeles Dodgers (NL)	4–2
1978	New York Yankees (AL)	Los Angeles Dodgers (NL)	4–2
1979	Pittsburgh Pirates(NL)	Baltimore Orioles (AL)	4–3
1980	Philadelphia Phillies (NL)	Kansas City Royals (AL)	4–2
1981	Los Angeles Dodgers (NL)	New York Yankees (AL)	4–2
1982	St. Louis Cardinals (NL)	Milwaukee Brewers (AL)	4–3
1983	Baltimore Orioles (AL)	Philadelphia Phillies (NL)	4–1
1984	Detroit Tigers (AL)	San Diego Padres (NL)	4–1
1985	Kansas City Royals (AL)	St. Louis Cardinals (NL)	4–3
1986	New York Mets (NL)	Boston Red Sox (AL)	4–3
1987	Minnesota Twins (AL)	St. Louis Cardinals (NL)	4–3
1988	Los Angeles Dodgers (NL)	Oakland A's (AL)	4–1
1989	Oakland A's (AL)	San Francisco Giants (NL)	4–0
1990	Cincinnati Reds (NL)	Oakland A's (AL)	4–0
1991	Minnesota Twins (AL)	Atlanta Braves (NL)	4–3
1992	Toronto Blue Jays (AL)	Atlanta Braves (NL)	4–2
1993	Toronto Blue Jays (AL)	Philadelphia Phillies (NL)	4–2
1994	Canceled		

RUNS BATTED IN (RBIs)

Career 40, by Mickey Mantle, New York Yankees (AL), 1951–53, 1955–58, 1960–64.

Series 12, by Bobby Richardson, New York Yankees (AL), in 1960.

Game Six, by Bobby Richardson, New York Yankees (AL), on October 8, 1960 *v*. Pittsburgh Pirates.

PITCHING RECORDS

WINS

Career 10, by Whitey Ford, New York Yankees (AL), in 11 series, 1950–64. Ford's career record was 10 wins, 8 losses in 22 games.

Series Three, by 12 pitchers. Only two pitchers have won three games in a five-game series: Christy Mathewson, New York Giants (NL) in 1905; Jack Coombs, Philadelphia Athletics (AL) in 1910.

STRIKEOUTS

Career 94, by Whitey Ford, New York Yankees (AL), in 11 series, 1950–64.

Series 35, by Bob Gibson, St. Louis Cardinals (NL) in 1968, from seven games.

Game 17, by Bob Gibson, St. Louis Cardinals (NL), on October 2, 1968 *v*. Detroit Tigers.

INNINGS PITCHED

Career 146, by Whitey Ford, New York Yankees (AL), in 11 series, 1950, 1953, 1955–58, 1960–64.

Series 44, by Deacon Phillippe, Pittsburgh Pirates (NL), in 1903 in an eight-game series.

Game 14, by Babe Ruth, Boston Red Sox (AL), on October 9, 1916 *v*. Brooklyn Dodgers.

SAVES

Career Six, by Rollie Fingers, Oakland Athletics (AL), 1972–74.

SULTAN OF STRIKEOUTS? ■ BABE RUTH WAS A FEARED PITCHER ON THE BOSTON RED SOX BEFORE HE WAS A FEARED SLUGGER FOR THE NEW YORK YANKEES. HE POSTED A LIFETIME RECORD OF 94–46 WITH 488 STRIKEOUTS AND AN ERA OF 2.28.
(NATIONAL BASEBALL LIBRARY)

Record Quotable

"The Yankees don't pay me to win every day—just two out of three."

—Casey Stengel, widely attributed.

Series Three, by Kent Tekulve, Pittsburgh Pirates (NL), in 1979 in a seven-game series.

PERFECT GAME The only perfect game in World Series history was hurled by Don Larsen, New York Yankees (AL), on October 8, 1956 *v.* Brooklyn Dodgers.

MOST VALUABLE PLAYER AWARD The World Series MVP award has been won a record two times by three players: Sandy Koufax, Los Angeles Dodgers (NL), 1963 and 1965; Bob Gibson, St. Louis Cardinals (NL), 1964 and 1967; and Reggie Jackson, Oakland Athletics (AL), 1973, New York Yankees (AL), 1977.

MANAGERS

Most series 10, by Casey Stengel, New York Yankees (AL), 1949–53, 1955–58, 1960. Stengel's record was seven wins, three losses.

Most wins Seven, by two managers: Joe McCarthy, New York Yankees (AL), 1932, 1936–39, 1941, 1943; and Casey Stengel, New York Yankees (AL), 1949–53, 1956, 1958.

WORLD SERIES WIZARD ■ CASEY STENGEL HAD A REMARKABLE FLAIR FOR WORDS AND FOR LEADING THE NEW YORK YANKEES TO THE WORLD SERIES.
(NATIONAL BASEBALL LIBRARY)

COLLEGE WORLD SERIES (1947–1994)

Year	Winner	Loser	Score	Year	Winner	Loser	Score
1947	California	Yale	2–0 *	1971	Southern Cal.	Southern Ill.	7–2
1948	Southern Cal.	Yale	2–1 *	1972	Southern Cal.	Arizona St.	1–0
1949	Texas	Wake Forest	10–3	1973	Southern Cal.	Arizona St.	4–3
1950	Texas	Washington St.	3–0	1974	Southern Cal.	Miami (Fla.)	7–3
1951	Oklahoma	Tennessee	3–2	1975	Texas	South Carolina	5–1
1952	Holy Cross	Missouri	8–4	1976	Arizona	Eastern Mich.	7–1
1953	Michigan	Texas	7–5	1977	Arizona St.	South Carolina	2–1
1954	Missouri	Rollins	4–1	1978	Southern Cal.	Arizona St.	10–3
1955	Wake Forest	Western Mich.	7–6	1979	Cal. St. Fullerton	Arkansas	2–1
1956	Minnesota	Arizona	12–1	1980	Arizona	Hawaii	5–3
1957	California	Penn State	1–0	1981	Arizona St.	Oklahoma St.	7–4
1958	Southern Cal.	Missouri	8–7	1982	Miami (Fla.)	Wichita St.	9–3
1959	Oklahoma St.	Arizona	5–3	1983	Texas	Alabama	4–3
1960	Minnesota	Southern Cal.	2–1	1984	Cal. St. Fullerton	Texas	3–1
1961	Southern Cal.	Oklahoma St.	1–0	1985	Miami (Fla.)	Texas	10–6
1962	Michigan	Santa Clara	5–4	1986	Arizona	Florida St.	10–2
1963	Southern Cal.	Arizona	5–2	1987	Stanford	Oklahoma St.	9–5
1964	Minnesota	Missouri	5–1	1988	Stanford	Arizona St.	9–4
1965	Arizona St.	Ohio St.	2–1	1989	Wichita St.	Texas	5–3
1966	Ohio St.	Oklahoma St.	8–2	1990	Georgia	Oklahoma St.	2–1
1967	Arizona St.	Houston	11–2	1991	Louisiana St.	Wichita St.	6–3
1968	Southern Cal.	Southern Ill.	4–3	1992	Pepperdine	Cal. State Fullerton	3–2
1969	Arizona St.	Tulsa	10–1	1993	Louisiana St.	Wichita St.	8–0
1970	Southern Cal.	Florida St.	2–1	1994	Oklahoma	Georgia Tech.	13–5

* Series score

Most losses Six, by John McGraw, New York Giants (NL), 1911–13, 1917, 1923–24.

Wins, both leagues The only manager to lead a team from each league to a World Series title is Sparky Anderson, who skippered the Cincinnati Reds (NL) to championships in 1975–76, and the Detroit Tigers (AL) in 1984.

COLLEGE BASEBALL

ORIGINS Various forms of college baseball have been played throughout the 20th century; how-ever, the NCAA did not organize a championship until 1947 and did not begin to keep statistical records until 1957.

NCAA DIVISION I

HITTING RECORDS (CAREER)

Home runs 100, by Pete Incaviglia, Oklahoma State, 1983–85.

Hits 418, by Phil Stephenson, Wichita State, 1979–82.

PITCHING RECORDS (CAREER)

Wins 51, by Don Heinkel, Wichita State, 1979–82.

LITTLE LEAGUE BASEBALL WORLD CHAMPIONSHIP (1947–1983)

Year	Winner	Loser	Score
1947	Maynard, Pa.	Lock Haven, Pa.	16–7
1948	Lock Haven, Pa.	St. Petersburg, Fla.	6–5
1949	Hammonton, N.J.	Pensacola, Fla.	5–0
1950	Houston, Tex.	Bridgeport, Conn.	2–1
1951	Stamford, Conn.	North Austin Lions, Tex.	3–0
1952	Norwalk, Conn.	Monongahela, Pa.	4–3
1953	Birmingham, Ala.	Schenectady, N.Y.	1–0
1954	Schenectady, N.Y.	Colton Lions, Calif.	7–5
1955	Morrisville, Pa.	Delaware/Merchantville, N.J.	4–3
1956	Rosewell Lions Hondo, N.M.	Delaware Township, N.J.	3–1
1957	Monterrey, Mexico	La Mesa Northern, Calif.	4–0
1958	Monterrey, Mexico	Kankakee, Ill.	10–1
1959	Hamtramck, Mich.	West Auburn, Calif.	12–0
1960	Levittown, Pa.	Fort Worth, Tex.	5–0
1961	El Cajon, Calif.	El Campo, Tex.	4–2
1962	San Jose, Calif.	Kankakee, Ill.	3–0
1963	Granada Hills, Calif.	Stamford, Conn.	2–1
1964	Staten Island, N.Y.	Monterrey, Mexico	4–0
1965	Windsor Locks, Conn.	Stoney Creek, Canada	3–1
1966	Houston, Tex.	West New York, N.J.	8–2
1967	Tokyo, Japan	North Roseland, Ill.	4–1
1968	Wakayama, Japan	Tuckahoe, Va.	1–0
1969	Taipei, Taiwan	Briarwood of Santa Clara, Calif.	5–0
1970	Wayne, N.J.	Campbell, Calif.	2–0
1971	Tainan, Taiwan	Anderson, Ind.	12–3
1972	Taipei, Taiwan	Edison, Ind.	6–0
1973	Tainan City, Taiwan	Cactus of Tucson, Ariz.	12–0
1974	Kao Hsiung, Taiwan	Red Bluff, Calif.	12–1
1975	Lakewood, N.J.	Belmont Heights, Fla.	4–3
1976	Chofu, Japan	Campbell, Calif.	10–3
1977	Li-Teh, Taiwan	El Cajon, Calif.	7–2
1978	Pin-Kuang, Taiwan	Danville, Calif.	11–1
1979	Pu-Tzu Town, Taiwan	Campbell, Calif.	2–1
1980	Iong Kuong, Taiwan	Belmont Heights, Fla.	4–3
1981	Tai-Ping, Taiwan	Belmont Heights, Fla.	4–2
1982	Kirkland, Wash.	Pu-Tzu Town, Taiwan	6–0
1983	Marietta, Ga.	Liquito Hernandez, Dom. Rep.	3–1

LITTLE LEAGUE BASEBALL WORLD CHAMPIONSHIP (1984–1994)

Year	Winner	Loser	Score
1984	Seoul, South Korea	Altamonte Springs, Fla.	6–2
1985	Seoul, South Korea	Mexicali, Baja Calif., Mexico	7–1
1986	Tainan Park, Taiwan	Tucson, Ariz.	12–0
1987	Hua Lian, Taiwan	Northwood, Irvine, Calif.	21–1
1988	Tai Ping, Taiwan	Pearl City, Hawaii	10–0
1989	Trumbull, Conn.	Kang-Tu, Taiwan	5–2
1990	San-Hua, Taiwan	Shippensburg, Pa.	9–0
1991	Hsi Nan, Tai Chung, Taiwan	Danville, Calif.	11–0
1992	Long Beach, Calif.	Zamboanga City, Philippines	6–0*
1993	Long Beach, Calif.	Chiriqui, Panama	3–2
1994	Venezuela	Western Region, North. Calif.	4–3

*Zamboanga won the game 15–4, but was subsequently disqualified for fielding overage players. The game was declared a 6–0 forfeit.

Strikeouts 602, by John Powell, Auburn University, 1990–94.

COLLEGE WORLD SERIES The first College World Series was played in 1947 at Kalamazoo, Mich. The University of California at Berkeley defeated Yale University in a best-of-three-game series, 2–0. In 1949 the series format was changed to a championship game. Since 1950 the College World Series has been played at Rosenblatt Stadium, Omaha, Neb.

Most championships The most wins is 11, by Southern Cal., in 1948, 1958, 1961, 1963, 1968, 1970–74 and 1978.

HITTING RECORDS (CAREER)

Home runs Four, by five players: Bud Hollowell, Southern Cal., 1963; Pete Incaviglia, Oklahoma State, 1983–85; Ed Sprague, Stanford, 1987–88; Gary Hymel, Louisiana State, 1990–91; and Lyle Mewton, Louisiana State, 1990–91.

Hits 23, by Keith Moreland, Texas, 1973–75.

PITCHING RECORDS (CAREER)

Wins Four, by nine players: Bruce Gardner, Southern Cal., 1958, 1960; Steve Arlin, Ohio State, 1965–66; Bert Hooten, Texas at Austin, 1969–70; Steve Rogers, Tulsa, 1969, 1971; Russ McQueen, Southern Cal., 1972–73; Mark Bull, Southern Cal., 1973–74; Greg Swindell, Texas, 1984–85; Kevin Sheary, Miami (Fla.), 1984–85; Greg Brummett, Wichita State, 1988–89.

Strikeouts 64, by Carl Thomas, Arizona, 1954–56.

BASKETBALL

ORIGINS Basketball was invented by the Canadian-born Dr. James Naismith at the Training School of the International YMCA College at Springfield, Mass. in mid-December 1891. The first game played under modified rules was on January 20, 1892. The International Amateur Basketball Federation (FIBA) was founded in 1932; it has now dropped the word Amateur from its title.

NATIONAL BASKETBALL ASSOCIATION (NBA)

ORIGINS The Amateur Athletic Union (AAU) organized the first national tournament in the United States in 1897. The first professional league was the National Basketball League (NBL), founded in 1898, but this league lasted only two seasons. The American Basketball League was formed in 1925, but declined, and the NBL was refounded in 1937. This organization merged with the Basketball Associa-

NBA INDIVIDUAL RECORDS

Games Played

		Player(s)	Team(s)	Date(s)
Season	88	Walt Bellamy	New York Knicks, Detroit Pistons	1968–69
Career	1,560	Kareem Abdul-Jabbar	Milwaukee Bucks, Los Angeles Lakers	1969–89

Minutes Played

Game	69	Dale Ellis	Seattle SuperSonics v. Milwaukee Bucks	Nov. 9, 1989 (5 OT)
Season	3,882	Wilt Chamberlain	Philadelphia Warriors	1961–62
Career	57,446	Kareem Abdul-Jabbar	Milwaukee Bucks, Los Angeles Lakers	1969–89

Points

Game	100	Wilt Chamberlain	Philadelphia Warriors v. New York Knicks	March 2, 1962
Season	4,029	Wilt Chamberlain	Philadelphia Warriors	1961–62
Career	38,387	Kareem Abdul-Jabbar	Milwaukee Bucks, Los Angeles Lakers	1969–89

Field Goals

Game	36	Wilt Chamberlain	Philadelphia Warriors v. New York Knicks	March 2, 1962
Season	1,597	Wilt Chamberlain	Philadelphia Warriors	1961–62
Career	15,837	Kareem Abdul-Jabbar	Milwaukee Bucks, Los Angeles Lakers	1969–89

Three-Point Field Goals

Game	10	Brian Shaw	Miami Heat v. Milwaukee Bucks	April 8, 1993
	10	Joe Dumars	Detroit Pistons v. Minnesota Timberwolves	Nov. 8, 1994
Season	172	Vernon Maxwell	Houston Rockets	1990–91
Career	1,042	Dale Ellis	Dallas Mavericks, Seattle SuperSonics, Milwaukee Bucks, San Antonio Spurs	1983–95*

Free Throws

Game	28	Wilt Chamberlain	Philadelphia Warriors v. New York Knicks	March 2, 1962
		Adrian Dantley	Utah Jazz v. Houston Rockets	Jan. 4, 1984
Season	840	Jerry West	Los Angeles Lakers	1965–66
Career	8,509	Moses Malone	Buffalo Braves, Houston Rockets, Philadelphia 76ers, Washington Bullets, Atlanta Hawks, Milwaukee Bucks	1976–95*

* As of January 11, 1995

Source: NBA

NBA INDIVIDUAL RECORDS

Assists

		Player(s)	Team(s)	Date(s)
Game	30	Scott Skiles	Orlando Magic v. Denver Nuggets	December 30, 1990
Season	1,164	John Stockton	Utah Jazz	1990–91
Career	9,921	Magic Johnson	Los Angeles Lakers	1979–91

Rebounds

Game	55	Wilt Chamberlain	Philadelphia Warriors v. Boston Celtics	November 24, 1960
Season	2,149	Wilt Chamberlain	Philadelphia Warriors	1960–61
Career	23,924	Wilt Chamberlain	Philadelphia/San Francisco Warriors, Philadelphia 76ers, Los Angeles Lakers	1959–73

Steals

Game	11	Larry Kenon	San Antonio Spurs v. Kansas City Kings	December 26, 1976
Season	301	Alvin Robertson	San Antonio Spurs	1985–86
Career	2,310	Maurice Cheeks	Philadelphia 76ers, San Antonio Spurs, New York Knicks, Atlanta Hawks, New Jersey Nets	1978–94

Blocked Shots †

Game	17	Elmore Smith	Los Angeles Lakers v. Portland Trail Blazers	October 28, 1973
Season	456	Mark Eaton	Utah Jazz	1984–85
Career	3,189	Kareem Abdul-Jabbar	Milwaukee Bucks, Los Angeles Lakers	1973–89

Personal Fouls

Game	8	Don Otten	Tri-Cities v. Sheboygan	November 24, 1949
Season	386	Darryl Dawkins	New Jersey Nets	1983–84
Career	4,657	Kareem Abdul-Jabbar	Milwaukee Bucks, Los Angeles Lakers	1969–89

Disqualifications ††

Season	26	Don Meineke	Fort Wayne Pistons	1952–53
Career	127	Vern Mikkelsen	Minneapolis Lakers	1950–59

---

† Compiled since 1973–74 season.

†† Through January 11, 1995, Moses Malone (Houston Rockets, Philadelphia 76ers, Washington Bullets, Atlanta Hawks, Milwaukee Bucks) has played 1,165 consecutive games without fouling out.

tion of America in 1949 to form the National Basketball Association (NBA).

NBA TEAM RECORDS

SCORING

Most points (one team) 186, by the Detroit Pistons, defeating the Denver Nuggets, 186–184, at Denver, on December 13, 1983 after three overtimes.

Most points, regulation (one team) 173, by two teams: Boston Celtics *v.* Minneapolis Lakers (139 points), at Boston, on February 27, 1959; Phoenix Suns *v.* Denver Nuggets (143 points), at Phoenix, on November 10, 1990.

Highest-scoring game (aggregate) 370 points, Detroit Pistons defeated the Denver Nuggets, 186–184, at Denver, on December 13, 1983 after three overtimes.

Highest-scoring game (aggregatc), regulation 320 points, Golden State Warriors defeated the

BASKETS FOR FREE ■ MOSES MALONE, RECORD HOLDER FOR MOST CAREER FREE THROWS. (ALLSPORT/ BRIAN DRAKE)

Denver Nuggets, 162–158, at Denver, on November 2, 1990.

Lowest-scoring game (aggregate) 37 points, Fort Wayne Pistons defeated the Minneapolis Lakers, 19–18, at Minneapolis, on November 22, 1950.

Greatest margin of victory 68 points, by the Cleveland Cavaliers, defeating the Miami Heat, 148–80, on December 17, 1991.

WINS AND LOSSES

Most wins (season) 69, by the Los Angeles Lakers in 1971–72.

Most consecutive wins 33, by the Los Angeles Lakers. The Lakers' streak began with a 110–106 victory over the Baltimore Bullets on November 5, 1971 in Los Angeles, and ended on January 9, 1972 when they were beaten 120–104 by the Milwaukee Bucks in Milwaukee.

TIED AT 10 ■ JOE DUMARS, SEEN HERE DRIBBLING UPCOURT, TIED BRIAN SHAW'S THREE-POINT FIELD GOAL RECORD IN 1994. (ALLSPORT/J.D. CUBAN)

NBA MOST VALUABLE PLAYER AWARD (1956–1994)

The Maurice Podoloff Trophy was instituted in 1956 to be awarded to the NBA's most valuable player. From 1956 to 1980 the award was decided by a vote of eligible NBA players; since 1980 the winner has been decided by a vote of eligible writers and broadcasters.

Most wins Six, by Kareem Abdul-Jabbar, Milwaukee Bucks, 1971–72, 1974; Los Angeles Lakers, 1976–77, 1980.

Year	Player	Team	Year	Player	Team
1956	Bob Pettit	St. Louis Hawks	1976	Kareem Abdul-Jabbar	Los Angeles Lakers
1957	Bob Cousy	Boston Celtics	1977	Kareem Abdul-Jabbar	Los Angeles Lakers
1958	Bill Russell	Boston Celtics	1978	Bill Walton	Portland Trail Blazers
1959	Bob Pettit	St. Louis Hawks	1979	Moses Malone	Houston Rockets
1960	Wilt Chamberlain	Philadelphia Warriors	1980	Kareem Abdul-Jabbar	Los Angeles Lakers
1961	Bill Russell	Boston Celtics	1981	Julius Erving	Philadelphia 76ers
1962	Bill Russell	Boston Celtics	1982	Moses Malone	Houston Rockets
1963	Bill Russell	Boston Celtics	1983	Moses Malone	Philadelphia 76ers
1964	Oscar Robertson	Cincinnati Royals	1984	Larry Bird	Boston Celtics
1965	Bill Russell	Boston Celtics	1985	Larry Bird	Boston Celtics
1966	Wilt Chamberlain	Philadelphia 76ers	1986	Larry Bird	Boston Celtics
1967	Wilt Chamberlain	Philadelphia 76ers	1987	Magic Johnson	Los Angeles Lakers
1968	Wilt Chamberlain	Philadelphia 76ers	1988	Michael Jordan	Chicago Bulls
1969	Wes Unseld	Baltimore Bullets	1989	Magic Johnson	Los Angeles Lakers
1970	Willis Reed	New York Knicks	1990	Magic Johnson	Los Angeles Lakers
1971	Kareem Abdul-Jabbar	Milwaukee Bucks	1991	Michael Jordan	Chicago Bulls
1972	Kareem Abdul-Jabbar	Milwaukee Bucks	1992	Michael Jordan	Chicago Bulls
1973	Dave Cowens	Boston Celtics	1993	Charles Barkley	Phoenix Suns
1974	Kareem Abdul-Jabbar	Milwaukee Bucks	1994	Hakeem Olajuwon	Houston Rockets
1975	Bob McAdoo	Buffalo Braves			

Most losses (season) 73, by the Philadelphia 76ers in 1972–73.

Most consecutive losses 24, by the Cleveland Cavaliers. The Cavs' undesirable roll started on March 19, 1982 when they lost to the Milwaukee Bucks, 119–97, in Milwaukee, and ended on November 10, 1982 when they defeated the Golden State Warriors 132–120 in overtime on November 10, 1982. During the streak the Cavs lost the last 19 games of the 1981– 82 season, and the first five of the 1982–83 season.

INDIVIDUAL RECORDS (GENERAL)

Youngest player The youngest NBA player was Bill Willoughby, who made his debut for the At-

MVP ■ HAKEEM OLAJUWON SHOWING UP NEW YORK KNICKS STAR PATRICK EWING IN THE 1994 NBA FINALS. (ALLSPORT)

OLD MEN CAN JUMP ■ KAREEM ABDUL-JABBAR, THE OLDEST PLAYER EVER ON AN NBA COURT, BACK IN 1988. (ALLSPORT/MIKE POWELL)

lanta Hawks on October 23, 1975 at 18 years 156 days.

Oldest player The oldest NBA player was Kareem Abdul-Jabbar, who made his last appearance for the Los Angeles Lakers at 42 years 59 days in 1989.

Tallest basketball player Gheorge Muresan, 7 feet 7 inches, is the tallest player in NBA history.

Record Quotable

"Nobody roots for Goliath."
—Wilt Chamberlain, quoted in *Sports Quotes* by
Bob Abel and Michael Valenti.

He made his pro debut for the Washington Bullets in 1994.

CONSECUTIVE RECORDS (INDIVIDUAL)

Games played 906, by Randy Smith, from February 18, 1972 to March 13, 1983. During his streak, Smith played for the Buffalo Braves, San Diego Clippers (twice), Cleveland Cavaliers, and New York Knicks.

Games scoring 50+ points Seven, by Wilt Chamberlain, Philadelphia Warriors, December 16–29, 1961.

Games scoring 10+ points 787, by Kareem Abdul-Jabbar, Los Angeles Lakers, from December 4, 1977 through December 2, 1987.

BY GHEORGE! ■ OPPONENTS WILL HAVE A DIFFICULT TIME REACHING OVER 7 FOOT 7 INCH GHEORGE MURESAN, THE TALLEST PLAYER IN BASKETBALL HISTORY. (ALLSPORT/J.D. CUBAN)

Free throws 97, by Micheal Williams, Minnesota Timberwolves, from March 24 through November 9, 1993.

Free throws (game) 23, by Dominique Wilkins, Atlanta Hawks, on December 8, 1992.

COACHES

Most wins 939, by Lenny Wilkens as of January 7, 1995. Wilkens coached coached for the Seattle SuperSonics (1969–72), the Portland Trail Blazers (1974–76), the Seattle SuperSonics (1977–85), the Cleveland Cavaliers (1986–93) and the Atlanta Hawks (1994–95).

Most wins (playoffs) Pat Riley has won a record 131 playoff games, 102 with the Los Angeles Lakers (1981–90) and 29 with the New York Knicks (1992–94), to set the all-time NBA mark.

Highest winning percentage .719, by Pat Riley, Los Angeles Lakers, 1981–90, New York Knicks, 1991–January 11, 1995. Riley's record is 665 wins, 260 losses.

Most games 1,722, by Bill Fitch, Cleveland Cavaliers, 1970–79; Boston Celtics, 1979–83; Houston Rockets, 1983–88; New Jersey Nets, 1989–92. Fitch's career totals are 845 wins, 877 losses.

NBA CHAMPIONSHIP

The NBA recognizes the 1946–47 season as its first championship; however, at that time the league was known as the Basketball Association of America (BAA).

Most titles 16, by the Boston Celtics, 1957, 1959–66, 1968–69, 1974, 1976, 1981, 1984, 1986.

Consecutive titles Eight, by the Boston Celtics, 1959–66.

Most titles (coach) Nine, by Red Auerbach, Boston Celtics, 1957, 1959–66.

Record Quotable

"The games might not get high marks for artistic impression, but you can't complain about the intensity of the competition."

—Pat Riley, quoted in *Sports Illustrated*, referring to the 1994 Finals against the Houston Rockets.

PATIENCE AND POISE ■ PAT RILEY, THE COACH WITH THE HIGHEST WINNING PERCENTAGE IN BASKETBALL HISTORY. (ALLSPORT/JONATHAN DANIEL)

NBA CHAMPIONSHIP RECORDS (FINALS SERIES)

INDIVIDUAL RECORDS (GAME)

Most minutes played 62, by Kevin Johnson, Phoenix Suns *v.* Chicago Bulls on June 13, 1993. The game went to three overtimes.

Most points scored 61, by Elgin Baylor, Los Angeles Lakers *v.* Boston Celtics on April 14, 1962 in Boston.

Most field goals made 22, by two players: Elgin Baylor, Los Angeles Lakers *v.* Boston Celtics on April 14, 1962 in Boston; Rick Barry, San Francisco Warriors *v.* Philadelphia 76ers on April 18, 1967 in San Francisco.

Most free throws made 19, by Bob Pettit, St. Louis Hawks *v.* Boston Celtics on April 9, 1958 in Boston.

Most rebounds 40, by Bill Russell, Boston Celtics, who has performed this feat twice: *v.* St. Louis

Hawks on March 29, 1960; *v.* Los Angeles Lakers on April 18, 1962, in an overtime game.

Most assists 21, by Magic Johnson, Los Angeles Lakers *v.* Boston Celtics on June 3, 1984.

Most steals Six, by four players: John Havlicek, Boston Celtics *v.* Milwaukee Bucks, May 3, 1974; Steve Mix, Philadelphia 76ers *v.* Portland Trail Blazers, May 22, 1977; Maurice Cheeks, Philadelphia 76ers *v.* Los Angeles Lakers, May 7, 1980; Isiah Thomas, Detroit Pistons *v.* Los Angeles Lakers, June 19, 1988.

Most blocked shots Eight, by two players: Bill Walton, Portland Trail Blazers *v.* Philadelphia 76ers, June 5, 1977; Hakeem Olajuwon, Houston Rockets *v.* Boston Celtics, June 5, 1986.

TEAM RECORDS (GAME)

Most points (one team) 148, by the Boston Celtics *v.* Los Angeles Lakers (114 points) on May 27, 1985.

Highest-scoring game (aggregate) 276 points, Philadelphia 76ers defeated the San Francisco Warriors, 141–135, in overtime, on April 14, 1967.

Highest-scoring game, regulation (aggregate) 263 points, Los Angeles Lakers defeated the Boston Celtics, 141–122, on June 4, 1987.

Greatest margin of victory 35 points, Washington Bullets shot down the Seattle SuperSonics, 117–82, on June 4, 1978.

NBA CHAMPIONSHIP FINALS (1947–1994)

Year	Winner	Loser	Series	Year	Winner	Loser	Series
1947	Philadelphia Warriors	Chicago Stags	4–1	1971	Milwaukee Bucks	Baltimore Bullets	4–0
1948	Baltimore Bullets	Philadelphia Warriors	4–2	1972	Los Angeles Lakers	New York Knicks	4–1
1949	Minneapolis Lakers	Washington Capitols	4–2	1973	New York Knicks	Los Angeles Lakers	4–1
1950	Minneapolis Lakers	Syracuse Nationals	4–2	1974	Boston Celtics	Milwaukee Bucks	4–3
1951	Rochester Royals	New York Knicks	4–3	1975	Golden State Warriors	Washington Bullets	4–0
1952	Minneapolis Lakers	New York Knicks	4–3	1976	Boston Celtics	Phoenix Suns	4–2
1953	Minneapolis Lakers	New York Knicks	4–1	1977	Portland Trail Blazers	Philadelphia 76ers	4–2
1954	Minneapolis Lakers	Syracuse Nationals	4–3	1978	Washington Bullets	Seattle SuperSonics	4–3
1955	Syracuse Nationals	Fort Wayne Pistons	4–3	1979	Seattle SuperSonics	Washington Bullets	4–1
1956	Philadelphia Warriors	Fort Wayne Pistons	4–1	1980	Los Angeles Lakers	Philadelphia 76ers	4–2
1957	Boston Celtics	St. Louis Hawks	4–3	1981	Boston Celtics	Houston Rockets	4–2
1958	St. Louis Hawks	Boston Celtics	4–2	1982	Los Angeles Lakers	Philadelphia 76ers	4–2
1959	Boston Celtics	Minneapolis Lakers	4–0	1983	Philadelphia 76ers	Los Angeles Lakers	4–0
1960	Boston Celtics	St. Louis Hawks	4–3	1984	Boston Celtics	Los Angeles Lakers	4–3
1961	Boston Celtics	St. Louis Hawks	4–1	1985	Los Angeles Lakers	Boston Celtics	4–2
1962	Boston Celtics	Los Angeles Lakers	4–3	1986	Boston Celtics	Houston Rockets	4–2
1963	Boston Celtics	Los Angeles Lakers	4–2	1987	Los Angeles Lakers	Boston Celtics	4–2
1964	Boston Celtics	San Francisco Warriors	4–1	1988	Los Angeles Lakers	Detroit Pistons	4–3
1965	Boston Celtics	Los Angeles Lakers	4–1	1989	Detroit Pistons	Los Angeles Lakers	4–0
1966	Boston Celtics	Los Angeles Lakers	4–3	1990	Detroit Pistons	Portland Trail Blazers	4–1
1967	Philadelphia 76ers	San Francisco Warriors	4–2	1991	Chicago Bulls	Los Angeles Lakers	4–1
1968	Boston Celtics	Los Angeles Lakers	4–2	1992	Chicago Bulls	Portland Trail Blazers	4–2
1969	Boston Celtics	Los Angeles Lakers	4–3	1993	Chicago Bulls	Phoenix Suns	4–2
1970	New York Knicks	Los Angeles Lakers	4–3	1994	Houston Rockets	New York Knicks	4–3

NBA PLAYOFF RECORDS

Points

		Player(s)	Team(s)	Date(s)
Game	63	Michael Jordan	Chicago Bulls v. Boston Celtics	April 20, 1986 (2 OT)
	61	Elgin Baylor	Los Angeles Lakers v. Boston Celtics	April 14, 1962*
Series	284	Elgin Baylor	Los Angeles Lakers v. Boston Celtics	1962
Career	5,762	Kareem Abdul-Jabbar	Milwaukee Bucks, Los Angeles Lakers	1969–89

Field Goals

		Player(s)	Team(s)	Date(s)
Game	24	Wilt Chamberlain	Philadelphia Warriors v. Syracuse Nationals	March 14, 1960
		John Havlicek	Boston Celtics v. Atlanta Hawks	April 1, 1973
		Michael Jordan	Chicago Bulls v. Cleveland Cavaliers	May 1, 1988
Series	113	Wilt Chamberlain	San Francisco Warriors v. St. Louis	1964
Career	2,356	Kareem Abdul-Jabbar	Milwaukee Bucks, Los Angeles Lakers	1970–89

Free Throws

		Player(s)	Team(s)	Date(s)
Game	30	Bob Cousy	Boston Celtics v. Syracuse Nationals	March 21, 1953 (4 OT)
	23	Michael Jordan	Chiacgo Bulls v. New York Knicks	May 14, 1989*
Series	86	Jerry West	Los Angeles Lakers v. Baltimore Bullets	1965
Career	1,213	Jerry West	Los Angeles Lakers	1960–74

Assists

		Player(s)	Team(s)	Date(s)
Game	24	Magic Johnson	Los Angeles Lakers v. Phoenix Suns	May 15, 1984
		John Stockton	Utah Jazz v. Los Angeles Lakers	May 17, 1988
Series	115	John Stockton	Utah Jazz v. Los Angeles Lakers	1988
Career	2,320	Magic Johnson	Los Angeles Lakers	1979–91

Rebounds

		Player(s)	Team(s)	Date(s)
Game	41	Wilt Chamberlain	Philadelphia 76ers v. Boston Celtics	April 5, 1967
Series	220	Wilt Chamberlain	Philadelphia 76ers v. Boston Celtics	1965
Career	4,104	Bill Russell	Boston Celtics	1956–69

Steals

		Player(s)	Team(s)	Date(s)
Game	8	Rick Barry	Golden State Warriors v. Seattle SuperSonics	April 14, 1975
		Lionel Hollins	Portland Trail Blazers v. Los Angeles Lakers	May 8, 1977
		Maurice Cheeks	Philadelphia 76ers v. New Jersey Nets	April 11, 1979
		Craig Hodges	Milwaukee Bucks v. Philadelphia 76ers	May 9, 1986
		Tim Hardaway	Golden State Warriors v. Los Angeles Lakers	May 8, 1991
		Tim Hardaway	Golden State Warriors v. Seattle SuperSonics	April 30, 1992
Series	28	John Stockton	Utah Jazz v. Los Angeles Lakers	1988
Career	358	Magic Johnson	Los Angeles Lakers	1979–91

* Regulation play
Source: NBA

NCAA College Basketball

Men's Basketball (NCAA)

The National Collegiate Athletic Association (NCAA) has compiled statistics for its men's basketball competitions since the 1937–38 season. NCAA men's basketball is classified by three divisions: I, II and III.

NCAA Individual Records (Divisions I, II, III)

Points Scored

Game 113, by Clarence "Bevo" Francis, Rio Grande (Division II), *v*. Hillsdale on February 2, 1954.

Season 1,381, by Pete Maravich, Louisiana State (Division I) in 1970. Pistol Pete hit 522 field goals and 337 free throws in 31 games.

Career 4,045, by Travis Grant, Kentucky State (Division II), 1969–72.

Field Goals Made

Game 41, by Frank Selvy, Furman (Division I), *v*. Newberry on February 13, 1954. Selvy amassed his record total from 66 attempts.

Season 539, by Travis Grant, Kentucky State (Division II) in 1972. Grant's season record was gained from 869 attempts.

Career 1,760, by Travis Grant, Kentucky State (Division II), 1969–72. Grant achieved his career record from 2,759 attempts.

Assists

Game 26, by Robert James, Kean (Division III), *v*. New Jersey Tech on March 11, 1989.

Season 406, by Mark Wade, UNLV (Division I) in 1987. Wade played in 38 games.

Career 1,076, by Bobby Hurley, Duke (Division I), 1990–93. During his record-setting career Hurley played in 140 games.

Rebounds

Game 51, by Bill Chambers, William & Mary (Division I), *v*. Virginia on February 14, 1953.

Season 799, by Elmore Smith, Kentucky State (Division II) in 1971. Smith played in 33 games.

Career 2,334, by Jim Smith, Steubenville (Division II), 1955–58. Smith amassed his record total from 112 games.

NCAA Team Records (Division I)

Most points scored (one team) 186, by Loyola Marymount (Cal.) *v*. U.S. International (140 points), on January 5, 1991.

Highest-scoring game (aggregate) 331 points, Loyola Marymount (Cal.) defeating U.S. International, 181–150, on January 31, 1989.

Fewest points scored (team) Six, by two teams: Temple *v*. Tennessee (11 points), on December 15, 1973; Arkansas State *v*. Kentucky (75 points), on January 8, 1945.

Lowest-scoring game (aggregate) 17 points, Tennessee defeating Temple, 11–6, on December 15, 1973.

Widest margin of victory 97 points, Southern-Baton Rouge defeating Patten, 154–57, on November 26, 1993.

Greatest deficit overcome 32 points, Duke defeating Tulane, 74–72, on December 30, 1950, after trailing 22–54 with two minutes left in the first half.

Most wins (season) 37, by two teams: Duke in 1986 (37 wins, 3 losses); UNLV in 1987 (37 wins, 2 losses).

Most losses (season) 28, by Prairie View in 1992 (0 wins, 28 losses).

Consecutive Records (Individual, Division I)

Games scoring 10+ points 115, by Lionel Simmons, La Salle, 1987–90.

Games scoring 50+ points Three, by Pete Maravich, Louisiana State, February 10 to February 15, 1969.

Field goals 25, by Ray Voelkel, American, over nine games from November 24 through December 16, 1978.

Field goals (game) 16, by Doug Grayson, Kent *v*. North Carolina on December 6, 1967.

Three-point field goals 15, by Todd Leslie, Northwestern, over four games from December 15 through December 28, 1990.

Three-point field goals (game) 11, by Gary Bossert, Niagara *v*. Siena, January 7, 1987.

Free throws 64, by Joe Dykstra, Western Illinois, over eight games, December 1, 1981 through January 4, 1982.

NCAA DIVISION I MEN'S RECORDS
Points

		Player(s)	Team(s)	Date(s)
Game	100	Frank Selvy	Furman v. Newberry	February 13, 1954
	72	Kevin Bradshaw	U.S. International v. Loyola-Marymount	January 5, 1991*
Season	1,381	Pete Maravich	Louisiana State	1970
Career	3,667	Pete Maravich	Lousiana State	1968–70

Field Goals

Game	41	Frank Selvy	Furman v. Newberry	February 13, 1954
Season	522	Pete Maravich	Lousiana State	1970
Career	1,387	Pete Maravich	Lousiana State	1968–70

Three-point Goals

Game	14	Dave Jamerson	Ohio v. Charleston	December 21, 1989
		Askia Jones	Kansas State v. Fresno State	March 24, 1994

Free Throws

Game	30	Pete Maravich	Louisiana State v. Oregon State	December 22, 1969
Season	355	Frank Selvy	Furman	1954
Career	905	Dickie Hemric	Wake Forest	1952–55

Assists

Game	22	Tony Fairly	Baptist CS v. Armstrong State	February 9, 1987
		Avery Johnson	Southern-B.R. v. Texas Southern	January 25, 1988
		Sherman Douglas	Syracuse v. Providence	January 28, 1989
Season	406	Mark Wade	UNLV	1987
Career	1,076	Bobby Hurley	Duke	1990–93

Rebounds

Game	51	Bill Chambers	William & Mary v. Virginia	February 14, 1953
Season	734	Walt Dukes	Seton Hall	1953
Career	2,201	Tom Gola	La Salle	1952–55

Blocked Shots

Game	14	David Robinson	Navy v. N.C.–Wilmington	January 4, 1986
		Shawn Bradley	BYU v. Eastern Kentucky	December 7, 1990
Season	207	David Robinson	Navy	1986
Career	453	Alonzo Mourning	Georgetown	1989–92

Steals

Game	13	Mookie Blaylock	Oklahoma v. Centenary	December 12, 1987
		Mookie Blaylock	Oklahoma v. Loyola–Marymount	December 17, 1988
Season	150	Mookie Blaylock	Oklahoma	1988
Career	376	Eric Murdock	Providence	1988–91

* Game between two Division I teams
Source: NCAA

Free throws (game) 24, by Arlen Clark, Oklahoma State *v.* Colorado, March 7, 1959.

CONSECUTIVE RECORDS (TEAM, DIVISION I)

Wins (regular season) 76, by UCLA, from January 30, 1971 through January 17, 1974. The streak

ASKIA'S THE LIMIT ■ ON MARCH 24, 1994, ASKIA JONES TIED THE NCAA DIVISION I RECORD FOR THREE-POINT GOALS. (KANSAS STATE UNIVERSITY)

was ended on January 19, 1974 when the Bruins were defeated by Notre Dame, 71–70.

Wins (regular season and playoffs) 88, by UCLA, from January 30, 1971 through January 17, 1974.

Losses 37, by Citadel, from January 16, 1954 through December 12, 1955.

Winning seasons 46, by Louisville, 1945–90.

COACHES (DIVISION I)

Most wins 876, by Adolph Rupp, Kentucky, 1931–72.

Highest winning percentage .837, by Jerry Tarkanian, Long Beach State, 1969–73; UNLV, 1974–92. The shark's career record was 625 wins, 122 losses.

Most games 1,105, by Henry Iba, Northwest Missouri State, 1930–33; Colorado, 1934; Oklahoma State, 1935–70. Iba's career record was 767 wins, 338 losses.

Most years 48, by Phog Allen, Baker, 1906–08; Kansas, 1908–09; Haskell, 1909, Central Missouri State, 1913–19, Kansas, 1920–56.

NCAA CHAMPIONSHIP TOURNAMENT

The NCAA finals were first contested in 1939 at Northwestern University, Evanston, Ill. The University of Oregon, University of Oklahoma, Villanova University and Ohio State University were the first "final four." Oregon defeated Ohio State 46–33 to win the first NCAA title.

Most wins (team) 10, by UCLA, 1964–65, 1967–73, 1975.

Most wins (coach) 10, by John Wooden. Wooden coached UCLA to each of its NCAA titles.

CHAMPIONSHIP GAME RECORDS (INDIVIDUAL, 1939–1994)

Most points 44, by Bill Walton, UCLA *v.* Memphis State in 1973.

Most field goals 21, by Bill Walton, UCLA *v.* Memphis State in 1973.

Most rebounds 27, by Bill Russell, San Francisco *v.* Iowa in 1956.

Most assists 11, by Rumeal Robinson, Michigan *v.* Seton Hall, 1989.

NCAA DIVISION I MEN'S CHAMPIONS (1939–1994)

Year	Winner	Runner-Up	Score	Year	Winner	Runner-Up	Score
1939	Oregon	Ohio State	46–33	1967	UCLA	Dayton	79–64
1940	Indiana	Kansas	60–42	1968	UCLA	North Carolina	78–55
1941	Wisconsin	Washington State	39–34	1969	UCLA	Purdue	92–72
1942	Stanford	Dartmouth	53–38	1970	UCLA	Jacksonville	80–69
1943	Wyoming	Georgetown	46–34	1971	UCLA	Villanova*	68–62
1944	Utah	Dartmouth	42–40†	1972	UCLA	Florida State	81–76
1945	Oklahoma State	NYU	49–45	1973	UCLA	Memphis State	87–66
1946	Oklahoma State	North Carolina	43–40	1974	N. Carolina State	Marquette	76–64
1947	Holy Cross	Oklahoma	58–47	1975	UCLA	Kentucky	92–85
1948	Kentucky	Baylor	58–42	1976	Indiana	Michigan	86–68
1949	Kentucky	Oklahoma State	46–36	1977	Marquette	North Carolina	67–59
1950	CCNY	Bradley	71–68	1978	Kentucky	Duke	94–88
1951	Kentucky	Kansas State	68–58	1979	Michigan State	Indiana State	75–64
1952	Kansas	St. John's	80–63	1980	Louisville	UCLA*	59–54
1953	Indiana	Kansas	69–68	1981	Indiana	North Carolina	63–50
1954	LaSalle	Bradley	92–76	1982	North Carolina	Georgetown	63–62
1955	San Francisco	LaSalle	77–63	1983	N. Carolina State	Houston	54–52
1956	San Francisco	Iowa	83–71	1984	Georgetown	Houston	84–75
1957	North Carolina	Kansas	54–53‡	1985	Villanova	Georgetown	66–64
1958	Kentucky	Seattle	84–72	1986	Louisville	Duke	72–69
1959	California	West Virginia	71–70	1987	Indiana	Syracuse	74–73
1960	Ohio State	California	75–55	1988	Kansas	Oklahoma	83–79
1961	Cincinnati	Ohio State	70–65†	1989	Michigan	Seton Hall	80–79†
1962	Cincinnati	Ohio State	71–59	1990	UNLV	Duke	103–73
1963	Loyola (Ill.)	Cincinnati	60–58†	1991	Duke	Kansas	72–65
1964	UCLA	Duke	98–83	1992	Duke	Michigan	71–51
1965	UCLA	Michigan	91–80	1993	North Carolina	Michigan	77–71
1966	UTEP	Kentucky	72–65	1994	Arkansas	Duke	76–72

* These teams were disqualified by the NCAA for rules violations uncovered following the completion of the tournament.
† Overtime
‡ Triple overtime

WOMEN'S BASKETBALL

ORIGINS Senda Berenson and Clara Baer are generally credited as the pioneers of women's basketball. In 1892, Berenson, a physical education instructor at Smith College, adapted James Naismith's rules of basketball to create a "divided-court" version, which required the players to remain in their assigned sections of the court, making the game less physically demanding and thus, presumably, more suitable for women. Clara Baer introduced women's basketball to Sophie New-

NCAA DIVISION I WOMEN'S RECORDS

Points

		Player(s)	Team(s)	Date(s)
Game	60	Cindy Brown	Long Beach State *v.* San Jose State	February 16, 1987
Season	974	Cindy Brown	Long Beach State	1987
Career	3,122	Patricia Hoskins	Mississippi Valley	1985–89

Field Goals

Game	27	Lorri Bauman	Drake *v.* Southwest Missouri State	January 6, 1984
Season	392	Barbara Kennedy	Clemson	1982
Career	1,259	Joyce Walker	Louisiana State	1981–84

Free Throws

Game	23	Shaunda Greene	Washington *v.* Illinois	November 30, 1991
Season	275	Lorri Bauman	Drake	1982
Career	907	Lorri Bauman	Drake	1981–84

Assists

Game	23	Michelle Burden	Kent *v.* Ball State	February 6, 1991
Season	355	Suzie McConnell	Penn State	1987
Career	1,307	Suzie McConnell	Penn State	1984–88

Rebounds

Game	40	Deborah Temple	Delta State *v.* Alabama– Birmingham	February 14, 1983
Season	534	Wanda Ford	Drake	1985
Career	1,887	Wanda Ford	Drake	1983–86

Blocked Shots

Game	15	Amy Lundquist	Loyola (Cal.) *v.* Western Illinois	December 20, 1992
Season	151	Michelle Wilson	Texas Southern	1989
Career	428	Genia Miller	Cal. St. Fullerton	1987–91

Steals

Game	14	Natalie White	Florida A&M *v.* South Alabama	December 13, 1991
		Heidi Caruso	Lafayette *v.* Kansas St.	December 5, 1992
Season	172	Natalie White	Florida A&M	1994
Career	532	Heidi Caruso	Lafayette	1990–94

Source: NCAA

comb Memorial College in her native New Orleans, La., in 1893. Baer also adapted the style of Naismith's game, and published her own set of rules in 1895; these became known as the Newcomb College rules.

The game spread rapidly in the late 19th century, with the first women's collegiate game being played between California and Stanford on April 4, 1896. Women's basketball was unable to sustain its growth in the 20th century, however, due to controversy over whether it was safe for women to play the game. It wasn't until after World War II that attitudes changed and women's basketball began to organize itself on a national level and bring its rules into line with the men's game.

In 1969, Carol Eckman, coach at West Chester University, Pa., organized the first national invitation tournament. Under the auspices of the Association for Intercollegiate Athletics for Women (AIAW) the national tournament was expanded, and in 1982 the NCAA was invited to take over the tournament.

NCAA INDIVIDUAL RECORDS (DIVISIONS I, II, III)

POINTS SCORED

Game 67, by Jackie Givens, Fort Valley State (Division II), v. Knoxville on February 22, 1991. Givens hit 19 field goals, six three-point field goals, and 11 free throws.

Season 1,075, by Jackie Givens, Fort Valley State (Division II), in 1991. Givens' record-setting season consisted of 249 field goals, 120 three-point field goals, and 217 free throws in 28 games.

Career 3,171, by Jeannie Demers, Buena Vista (Division III), 1983–87. Demers' career totals are 1,386 field goals and 399 free throws in 105 games.

FIELD GOALS MADE

Game 28, by Ann Gilbert, Oberlin (Division III), v. Allegheny on February 6, 1991.

Season 392, by Barbara Kennedy, Clemson (Division I) in 1982. Kennedy set her record total from 760 attempts.

Career 1,386, by Jeannie Demers, Buena Vista (Division III), 1983–87. Demers made her record total from 2,838 attempts.

ASSISTS

Game 23, by two players: Michelle Burden, Kent (Division I), v. Ball State on February 6, 1991; and Selina Bynum, Albany State (Ga.) (Division II), v. Moyne-Owen on January 13, 1993.

Season 355, by Suzie McConnell, Penn State (Division I), in 1987.

NCAA WOMEN'S CHAMPIONS (1982–1994)

Year	Winner	Runner-Up	Score
1982	Louisiana Tech.	Cheyney	76–62
1983	Southern Cal.	Louisiana Tech.	69–67
1984	Southern Cal.	Tennessee	72–61
1985	Old Dominion	Georgia	70–65
1986	Texas	Southern Cal.	97–81
1987	Tennessee	Louisiana Tech.	67–44
1988	Louisiana Tech.	Auburn	56–54
1989	Tennessee	Auburn	76–60
1990	Stanford	Auburn	88–81
1991	Tennessee	Virginia	70–67*
1992	Stanford	Western Kentucky	78–62
1993	Texas Tech.	Ohio State	84–82
1994	North Carolina	Louisiana Tech.	60–59

* Overtime

Career 1,307, by Suzie McConnell, Penn State (Division I), 1984–88.

REBOUNDS

Game 40, by Deborah Temple, Delta State (Division I), *v.* Alabama–Birmingham, on February 14, 1983.

Season 635, by Francine Perry, Quinnipiac (Division II), in 1982.

Career 1,887, by Wanda Ford, Drake (Division I), 1983–86.

NCAA TEAM RECORDS (DIVISION I)

Most points scored (one team) 149, by Long Beach State *v.* San Jose State (69 points), on February 16, 1987.

Highest-scoring game (aggregate) 243 points, Virginia defeating North Carolina State, 123–120, after three overtimes on January 12, 1991.

Fewest points scored (one team) 12, by Bennett *v.* North Carolina A&T (85 points), on November 21, 1990.

Lowest-scoring game (aggregate) 72 points, Virginia defeating San Diego State, 38–34, on December 29, 1981.

Most wins (season) 35, by three teams: Texas, 1982; Louisiana Tech., 1982; Tennessee, 1989.

Most losses (season) 28, by Charleston Southern in 1991.

COACHES (DIVISION I)

Most wins 647, by Jody Conradt, Texas, 1970–January 17, 1995. (See "The Record Holder Speaks" on p. 58.)

Highest winning percentage .859, by Leon Barmore, Louisiana Tech., 1983–January 17, 1995. Barmore's career record through the 1993–94 season is 352 wins, 58 losses.

LOOKING FOR AN OPENING ■ VICKIE JOHNSON OF LOUISIANA TECH. JOHNSON'S COACH, LEON BARMORE, HOLDS THE RECORD FOR HIGHEST WINNING PERCENTAGE IN NCAA WOMEN'S DIVISION I BASKETBALL. (LOUISIANA TECH)

UNIVERSITY OF TEXAS

JODY CONRADT

Of Jody Conradt's many basketball coaching victories, one stands out: the National Conference championship win in 1986, the year the University of Texas at Austin's women's basketball team was undefeated. "But each and every win is a thrill," she is quick to point out. "Each game has its own distinctive personality."

Conradt's involvement with basketball began when she played on her high school basketball team in Goldthwait, Texas. After she graduated from Baylor College in Waco, Texas—where she also played basketball— she taught for a couple of years until she became a coach's assistant at Midway High School in Waco. She subsequently coached full-time at Sam Houston State University and then at the University of Texas, Arling-

ton. She began coaching at the University of Texas, Austin in 1976, where her enthusiasm and diligence have created a contagious environment for success.

The wins have piled up over the years and now Conradt can lay claim to being the all-time NCAA division record holder with a total of 647 victories. "No, I didn't keep track of the record, even though a lot of attention was paid to it," Conradt says with a laugh. "There was a celebration afterward—which was fun, but if I'd known beforehand I never would have agreed to it." Conradt, who has devoted her entire life to coaching, has a simple but effective philosophy: "I consider myself a disciplinarian. But I have the ability to be flexible. I always keep in mind that the game must be played by the players—not the coach."

NCAA CHAMPIONSHIP TOURNAMENT

The NCAA instituted a women's basketball championship in 1982.

Most wins (team) Three, by Tennessee, 1987, 1989 and 1991.

Most wins (coach) Three, by Pat Summitt. Summitt coached Tennessee to all three NCAA titles.

CHAMPIONSHIP GAME RECORDS (INDIVIDUAL)

Most points 47, by Sheryl Swoopes, Texas Tech *v.* Ohio State in 1993.

Most field goals 16, by Sheryl Swoopes, Texas Tech *v.* Ohio State, in 1993.

Most rebounds 23, by Charlotte Smith, North Carolina *v.* Louisiana Tech, in 1994.

Most assists 10, by two players: Kamie Ethridge, Texas *v.* Southern Cal, in 1986; Melissa McCray, Tennessee *v.* Auburn, in 1989.

OLYMPIC GAMES The men's basketball competition was introduced at the Berlin Olympics in

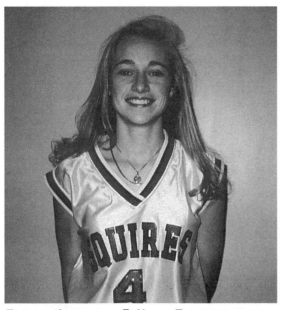

FIERSTOS'S FINEST ■ NIKKI FIERSTOS, PLAYER ON THE NORTH MANCHESTER, IND. VARSITY BASKETBALL TEAM. HER 79-FOOT FIELD GOAL GAVE FIERSTOS AND HER TEAM SOMETHING TO SMILE ABOUT, EVEN THOUGH THEY WERE DOWN SOME 55 POINTS. (DAN FIERSTOS)

1936. In April 1989, the International Olympic Committee voted to allow professional players to compete in the Games. The women's basketball competition was introduced at the Montreal Olympics in 1976.

Most gold medals (men) The United States has won 10 gold medals in Olympic basketball competition: 1936, 1948, 1952, 1956, 1960, 1964, 1968, 1976, 1984 and 1992.

Most gold medals (women) In the women's basketball tournament the gold medal has been won three times by the USSR/Unified Teams: 1976, 1980 and 1992.

WORLD CHAMPIONSHIPS An official men's world championship was first staged in 1950 in Buenos Aires, Argentina, and has been held quadrennially since. A women's world championship was first staged in 1953 and is now also staged as a quadrennial event.

Most titles (men) Two countries have won the men's title three times: USSR, 1967, 1974 and 1982; Yugoslavia, 1970, 1978 and 1990.

Most titles (women) The USSR has won the women's event a record six times: 1959, 1964, 1967, 1971, 1975 and 1983.

United States The United States has won the women's title five times: 1953, 1957, 1979, 1986 and 1990; and the men's title twice: 1954 and 1986.

FANTASTIC FEATS

Basketball-spinning On November 18, 1993, Bruce Crevier balanced and spun 17 balls across his body.

Dribbling (total distance) Jamie Borges (U.S.) dribbled a basketball, without traveling, from Barrington to Boston, Mass., a distance of 284.9 miles, from October 21–28, 1993.

Dribbing (24 hours) Ashrita Furman (U.S.) dribbled a basketball a distance of 83 miles in 24 hours on January 6–7, 1994.

Longest goal (men) Christopher Eddy scored a field goal measured at 90 feet 2¾ inches for Fairview High School in Erie, Pa. on February 25, 1989.

Longest goal (women) Nikki Fierstos scored a field goal of approximately 79 feet on January 2, 1993 at Huntington North High School, Huntington, Ind.

Most valuable basket Don Calhoun, a spectator randomly picked from the stands at a Chicago Bulls home game on April 14, 1993, sank a basket from the opposite foul line—a distance of 75 feet—and won $1 million.

Vertical dunk height Joey Johnson of San Pedro, CA successfully dunked a basketball at a rim height of 11 feet 7 inches at the One-on-One Collegiate Challenge on June 25, 1990 at Trump Plaza Hotel and Casino in Atlantic City, New Jersey.

BIATHLON

The biathlon is a composite test of cross-country skiing and rifle marksmanship. Competitors ski over a prepared course carrying a small-bore rifle; at designated ranges the skiers stop and complete the shooting assignment for the race. Time penalties are assessed for missed shots; the winner of the event is the one with the fastest time.

ORIGINS The sport reflects one of the earliest techniques of human survival; rock carvings in Roedoey, Norway dating to 3000 B.C. seem to depict hunters stalking their prey on skis. Biathlon as a modern sport evolved from military ski patrol maneuvers, which tested the soldier's ability as a fast skier and accurate marksman. In 1958 the *Union Internationale de Pentathlon Moderne et Biathlon* (UIPMB) was formed as the international governing body of biathlon and modern pentathlon. Biathlon was included in the Olympic Games for the first time in 1960.

United States The 1960 Olympic Games at Squaw Valley, Calif. introduced biathlon to this country. National championships were first held in 1965. The current governing body of the sport is the United States Biathlon Association, founded in 1980 and based in Essex Junction, Vt.

OLYMPIC GAMES "Military patrol," the forerunner to biathlon, was included in the Games of 1924, 1928, 1936 and 1948. Biathlon was included in the Winter Games for the first time at Squaw Valley, Calif. in 1960. Women's events were included for the first time at the 1992 Games at Albertville, France.

Most gold medals Aleksandr Tikhonov (USSR) has won four gold medals as a member of the Soviet relay team that won the 4 x 7,500 meter races in 1968, 1972, 1976 and 1980. Magnar Solberg (Norway) and Franz-Peter Rotsch (East Germany) have both won two gold medals in individual events. Solberg won the 20,000 meters in 1968 and 1972; Rotsch won the 10,000 meters and 20,000 meters in 1988.

Most medals Aleksandr Tikhonov has won a record five medals in Olympic competition. In addition to his four gold medals (see above), he won the silver medal in the 20,000 meters in 1968.

WORLD CHAMPIONSHIPS First held in 1958 for men and in 1984 for women, the world championships are an annual event. In Olympic years, the Games are considered the world championships; therefore, records in this section include results from the Games.

Most titles (overall) Aleksandr Tikhonov (USSR) has won 14 world titles: 10 in the 4 x 7,500 meter relay, 1968–74, 1976–77 and 1980; four individual events, 10,000 meter in 1977 and 20,000 meter in 1969–70 and 1973. In women's events, Kaya Parve (USSR) has won a record six gold medals: four in the 3 x 5,000 meter relay, 1984–86, 1988; two individual titles, the 5,000 meter in 1986 and the 10,000 meter in 1985.

Most titles (individual) Frank Ullrich (East Germany) has won a record six individual titles: 10,000 meter, 1978–81; 20,000 meter, 1982–83.

UNITED STATES NATIONAL CHAMPIONSHIPS In this competition, first held in 1965 in Rosendale, N.Y., men's events have been staged annually. Women's events were included in 1985.

Most titles Lyle Nelson has won seven national championships: five in the 10,000 meter, 1976, 1979, 1981, 1985 and 1987; two in the 20,000 meter, 1977 and 1985. Anna Sonnerup holds the women's record with five titles: two in the 10,000 meter, 1986–87; two in the 15,000 meter, 1989 and 1991; and one in the 7,500 meter in 1989.

BOBSLED AND LUGE

BOBSLED

ORIGINS The earliest known sled is dated c. 6500 B.C. and was found at Heinola, Finland. There are references to sled racing in Norwegian folklore dating from the 15th century. The first tracks built for sled racing were constructed in the mid-18th century in St. Petersburg, Russia. The modern sport of bobsled dates to the late

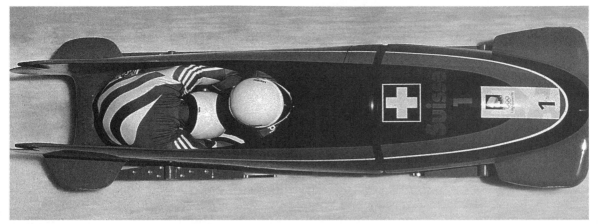

CAREENING ■ SWITZERLAND'S TWO-MAN BOB TEAM IS GAINING ON THE SWISS FOUR-MAN BOB FOR MOST TOTAL TITLES. (ALLSPORT/PASCAL RONDEAU)

19th century, when British enthusiasts organized competitions in Switzerland. The first run built for bobsled racing was constructed in St. Moritz, Switzerland in 1902. The *Federation Internationale de Bobsleigh de Tobagganing* (FIBT) was founded in 1923 and is the world governing body of bobsled racing.

United States The United States Bobsled & Skeleton Federation was founded in 1941 and is still the governing body for the sport in this country.

OLYMPIC GAMES A four-man bob competition was included in the first Winter Games in 1924 at Chamonix, France. Bobsled events have been included in every Games except 1960, when the Squaw Valley organizing committee refused to build a bobsled track.

Four-man bob Switzerland has won a record five Olympic titles: 1924, 1936, 1956, 1972 and 1988.

Two-man bob Switzerland has won a record four Olympic titles: 1948, 1980, 1992 and 1994.

Most gold medals Meinhard Nehmer and Bernhard Germeshausen (both East Germany) have both won a record three gold medals. They were both members of the 1976 two-man and four-man winning crews and the 1980 four-man winning crews.

Most medals Eugenio Monti (Italy) has won six medals: two gold, two silver and two bronze, 1956–68.

WORLD CHAMPIONSHIPS A world championship staged independently of the Olympic Games was first held in 1930 for four-man bob, and from 1931 for two-man bob. In Olympic years the Games are considered the world championship; therefore, records in this section include the Games of 1924 and 1928.

Four-man bob Switzerland has won the world title a record 20 times: 1924, 1936, 1939, 1947, 1954–57, 1971–73, 1975, 1982–83, 1986–90 and 1993.

Two-man bob Italy has won the world title 14 times: 1954, 1956–63, 1966, 1968–69, 1971 and 1975.

Most titles Eugenio Monti (Italy) has won 11 bobsled world championships: eight in the two-man, 1957–1961, 1963, 1966 and 1968; three in the four-man, 1960–61 and 1968.

LUGE

In luge the rider adopts a supine as opposed to a sitting position.

ORIGINS The first international luge race took place in 1883. Organized by the hotel keepers of Davos, Switzerland to promote their town, the race attracted 21 entrants from seven countries, including the United States. The course was 2½ miles, from St. Wolfgang to Klosters. The FIBT governed luge racing until 1957, when the *Fédération Internationale de Luge* (FIL) was formed.

United States The United States has participated in all Olympic luge events since the sport was sanctioned for the 1964 Games, but there was no organized governing body for the sport in this country until 1979, when the United States Luge Association was formed. The only luge run in the

United States accredited for international competition is the refrigerated run used for the Lake Placid Olympics in 1980.

OLYMPIC GAMES One-man skeleton races were included in the 1928 and 1948 Games; however, in skeleton races riders race face down rather than lying on their backs as in luge. Luge was included in the Games for the first time in 1964 in Innsbruck, Austria.

Most gold medals Thomas Kohler, Hans Rinn, Norbert Hahn and Steffi Martin-Walter (all East Germany) have each won two Olympic titles: Kohler won the single-seater in 1964 and the two-seater in 1968; Rinn and Hahn won the two-seater in 1976 and 1980; Martin-Walter won the women's single-seater in 1984 and 1988.

United States No American luger has won a medal at the Olympic Games. In the skeleton sled races held in 1928 and 1948, the United States won one gold and two silvers out of six races. Jennison Heaton was the winner of the 1928 single skeleton sled event.

WORLD CHAMPIONSHIPS First held in 1955, the world championships have been staged biennially since 1981. In Olympic years the Games are considered the world championships; therefore, records in this section include results from the Games.

Most titles Thomas Kohler and Hans Rinn (both East Germany) have both won six world titles: Kohler won the single-seater in 1962, 1964 and 1966–67, and the two-seater in 1967–68; Rinn won the single-seater in 1973 and 1977, and the two-seater in 1976–77 and 1980 (two world championships were held in 1980, with Rinn winning each time).

Margit Schumann (East Germany) holds the women's mark with five world titles, 1973–77.

UNITED STATES NATIONAL CHAMPIONSHIPS This competition was inaugurated in 1974.

Most titles Frank Masley has won a record six men's championships: 1979, 1981–83 and 1987–88. Two people have won a record five women's titles: Bonny Warner, 1983–84, 1987–88, 1990; and Cammy Myler, 1985, 1989, 1991–93.

BOWLING

ORIGINS The ancient German game of nine-pins (*Heidenwerfen*—"knock down pagans") was exported to the United States in the early 17th century. In 1841, the Connecticut state legislature prohibited the game, and other states followed. Eventually a tenth pin was added to evade the ban. The first body to standardize rules was the American Bowling Congress (ABC), established in New York City on September 9, 1895.

PROFESSIONAL BOWLERS ASSOCIATION (PBA)

The PBA was founded in 1958 by Eddie Elias and is based in Akron, Ohio.

Most titles (career) Earl Anthony of Dublin, Calif. has won a career record 41 PBA titles, 1970–83.

Most titles (season) The record number of titles won in one PBA season is eight, by Mark Roth of North Arlington, N.J., in 1978.

PBA TOUR SCORING RECORDS

Games	Score	Bowler	Site	Year
6	1,635	Norm Duke	Peoria, Ill.	1994
8	2,165	Billy Hardwick	Tokyo, Japan	1968
12	3,061	Norm Duke	Peoria, Ill.	1994
16	4,015	Carmen Salvino	Sterling Heights, Mich.	1980
18	4,696	Norm Duke	Peoria, Ill.	1994
24	5,826	Kelly Coffman	Riverside, Calif.	1993

Source: PBA Tour

TRIPLE CROWN The United States Open, the PBA National Championship and the Tournament of Champions comprise the Triple Crown of men's professional bowling. No bowler has won all three titles in the same year, and only three have managed to win all three during a career. The first bowler to accumulate the three legs of the triple crown was Billy Hardwick: National Championship (1963); Tournament of Champions (1965); U.S. Open (1969). Hardwick's feat was matched by Johnny Petraglia: Tournament of Champions (1971); U.S. Open (1977); National (1980); and by Pete Weber: Tournament of Champions (1987); U.S. Open (1988 and 1991); National (1989).

U.S. OPEN In this tournament, inaugurated in 1942, the most wins is four, by two bowlers: Don Carter in 1953–54 and 1957–58, and Dick Weber in 1962–63 and 1965–66.

PBA NATIONAL CHAMPIONSHIP In this contest, inaugurated in 1960, the most wins is six, by Earl Anthony in 1973–75 and 1981–83.

TOURNAMENT OF CHAMPIONS In this tournament, inaugurated in 1965, the most wins is three, by Mike Durbin in 1972, 1982 and 1984.

PERFECT GAMES

A total of 210 perfect (300 score) games were bowled in PBA tournaments in 1993, the most ever for one year.

1994 RECORD BREAKER ■ **PETE WEBER, THE NEW RECORD HOLDER FOR CAREER PBA EARNINGS.** (PBA)

CONSISTENCY ■ **KELLY COFFMAN HOLDS THE RE-CORD FOR HIGHEST BOWLING SCORE IN 24 GAMES.** (PBA)

Most perfect games (career) Since 1977, when the PBA began to keep statistics on perfect games, Wayne Webb has bowled 35 in tournament play.

Most perfect games (season) Three bowlers have bowled seven perfect games in one season: Amleto Monaccelli, 1989; Walter Ray Williams, Jr., 1993; and Dave Arnold, 1993.

Perfect games (tournament) Walter Ray Williams Jr. bowled four perfect games in one tournament, in Mechanicsburg, Pa. in 1993. He also rolled seven perfect games on the 1993 tour, tying Amleto Monacelli's record, set in 1989.

Highest earnings Pete Weber has won a career record $1,820,987 in PBA competitions through 1994. Mike Aulby of Indianapolis, Ind. set a single-season earnings mark of $298,237 in 1989.

TIM MORRISSEY

EVELYN CULBERT

"I didn't get nervous until the ninth strike," Evelyn Culbert recalls about her 300 game, which she bowled on April 4, 1993 at Echo Lanes Bowling Alley in Austin, Minnesota. "My teammates were quiet the entire time. I noticed people had crowded around and were watching, but they were also quiet."

At 66 years of age, Evelyn Culbert became the oldest woman to bowl a perfect game. Culbert, a mailroom worker for the *Austin Daily Herald*, accomplished the feat while bowling in the six-team Women's City Bowling League.

Culbert, who uses a 12 lb. ball, has been bowling since 1962. She usually bowls in the 150–160 range, and her previous high score had been 234; she says she had never even come close to a perfect game before.

What does she think is the best part of her record? "Setting the record was even better than winning a championship. . . . I'm very proud of it. Especially when I hear my grandkids going around telling people, 'My grandma bowled a 300.'"

Will Evelyn Culbert ever retire? Not on your life, she says: "I'm gonna keep going 'til I can't bowl any more."

BOWLING FOR TITLES ■ IN ADDITION TO BEING THE RECORD HOLDER FOR MOST BOWLING TITLES, LISA WAGNER ALSO HOLDS THE FOLLOWING HONORS: 1980 ROOKIE OF THE YEAR, 1980'S BOWLER OF THE DECADE, THREE-TIME LIND SHOES PLAYER OF THE YEAR, SEVEN-TIME BOWLERS JOURNAL ALL-AMERICAN AND THREE-TIME BOWLER OF THE YEAR FROM THE BOWLING WRITERS' ASSOCIATION OF AMERICA. (LPBA)

LADIES PROFESSIONAL BOWLERS TOUR (LPBT)

Founded in 1981, the LPBT is based in Rockford, Ill.

Most titles (career) Lisa Wagner has won 28 tournaments in her 13-year career, 1980–94.

Most titles (season) Patty Costello won a season record seven tournaments in 1976.

PERFECT GAMES

Most bowled (career) Two bowlers have bowled an LPBT-approved record 21 perfect games: Jeanne Naccarato (née Maiden) and Trish Johnson.

Most bowled (season) The record for most perfect games in a season is seven, by Trish Johnson in 1993.

Highest earnings Aleta Fill has won a career record $656,931 in prize money through 1994. She also had the season high record in 1994, with $126,325 in earnings.

AMERICAN BOWLING CONGRESS (ABC)

SCORING RECORDS

Highest individual score (three games) The highest individual score for three games is 899, by Thomas Jordan at Union, N.J. on March 7, 1989.

Highest team score (one game) The all-time ABC-sanctioned two-man single-game record is 600, held jointly by five teams: John Cotta and Steve Larson, May 1, 1981 at Manteca, Calif.; Jeff Mraz and Dave Roney, November 8, 1987 at Canton, Ohio; William Gruner and Dave Conway, February 27, 1990 at Oceanside, Calif.; Scott Williams and Willie Hammar, June 7, 1990 at Utica, N.Y; Darrell Guertin and George Tignor, February 20, 1993 at Rutland, Vt.

Highest team score (three games) The highest three-game team score is 3,868, by Hurst Bowling Supplies, of Luzerne, Pa. on February 23, 1994.

PERFECTION ■ JEANNE NACCARATO'S CAREER 21 PERFECT GAMES TIE HER FOR THE LPBT RECORD. "ALL I CAN DO IS BOWL MY GAME," NACCARATO SAYS. (LPBA)

Highest season average The highest season average attained in sanctioned competition is 247.89, by Jeff Phipps of Salem, Ore., in the 1992–93 season.

Juniors Brentt Arcement, at age 16, bowled a three-game series of 888, the highest ever bowled in a league or tournament sanctioned by the Young American Bowling Alliance, which is the national organization serving junior bowlers (age 21 and under). The highest score by a girl is 824 by Cindy Shipman of Endicott, N.Y. during the 1985–86 season.

Consecutive strikes The record for consecutive strikes in sanctioned play is 33, by two bowlers: John Pezzin at Toledo, Ohio on March 4, 1976, and Fred Dusseau at Yuma, Ariz., on March 3, 1992.

PERFECT GAMES

Most bowled (career) The highest number of sanctioned 300 games is 43, by Bob Learn Jr. of Erie, Pa.

Oldest The oldest person to bowl a perfect game is Jerry Wehman of Port St. Lucie, Fla. He performed the feat at St. Lucie Lanes on April 15, 1992 when aged 81 years old.

Youngest The youngest person to bowl a perfect game is Matthew Gilman of Davie, Fla. He achieved perfection on July 17, 1993, aged 11 years 2 months.

Consecutive Two perfect games were rolled back-to-back *twice* by two bowlers: Al Spotts of West Reading, Pa. on March 14, 1982 and again on February 1, 1985, and Jerry Wright of Idaho Falls, Idaho on January 9, 1992 and again on February 26, 1992.

WOMEN'S INTERNATIONAL BOWLING CONGRESS (WIBC)

SCORING RECORDS

Highest individual score (three games) The highest individual score for three games is 865, by Anne Marie Duggan at Dallas, Tex., on July 18, 1993.

Highest team score (one game) Pamela Beach and Cindy Fry bowled the all-time two-woman single-game highest score of 578 in Lansing, Mich., on November 21, 1992.

Highest team score (three games) The highest three-game team score is 3,446, by Drug Package Inc. of St. Louis, Mo., on January 5, 1993.

Highest season average The highest season average attained in sanctioned WIBC competition is 234, by Elizabeth Johnson of Niagara Falls, N.Y. in the 1993–94 season.

Consecutive strikes Jeanne Naccarato bowled a record 40 consecutive strikes on November 23, 1986 at Sodon, Ohio.

PERFECT GAMES

Most bowled (career) The highest number of WIBC-sanctioned perfect games (300) is 21, by Jeanne Naccarato.

Oldest The oldest woman to bowl a perfect game is Evelyn Culbert of Austin, Minn. She performed the feat at Eden Lanes, Austin, Minn., on April 4, 1993 when aged 66 years old. (See "The Record Holder Speaks" on p. 64.)

Bowled, lowest average Of all the women who have rolled a perfect game, the one with the lowest average was Diane Ponza of Santa Cruz, Calif., who had a 112 average in the 1977–78 season.

FANTASTIC FEATS

Consecutive strikes, spares and splits The record for the most consecutive strikes is 40, by Jeanne Naccarato. Mabel Henry of Winchester, Ky. had 30 consecutive spares in the 1986–87 season. Shirley Tophigh of Las Vegas, Nev. holds the record of rolling 14 consecutive splits.

Highest score in 24 hours A team of six scored 217,969 at Strykers Pleasure Bowl, Bushbury, Great Britain on October 15–16, 1993. During this attempt a member of the team, Dan Steeles, set an individual record of 48,969.

BOXING

The nationality of the competitors in this section is U.S. unless stated otherwise.

ORIGINS Boxing with gloves is depicted on a fresco from the Isle of Thera, Greece that has been dated to 1520 B.C. The earliest prize-ring code of rules was formulated in England on August 16, 1743 by the champion pugilist Jack Broughton, who reigned from 1734 to 1750. In 1867, boxing came under the Queensberry Rules, formulated for John Sholto Douglas, 8th Marquess of Queensberry.

United States New York was the first state to legalize boxing, in 1896. Today professional boxing is regulated in each state by athletic or boxing commissions.

Longest fights The longest recorded fight with gloves was between Andy Bowen and Jack Burke at New Orleans, La. on April 6–7, 1893. It lasted 110 rounds, 7 hours 19 minutes (9:15 P.M.–4:34 A.M.) and was declared a no contest (later changed to a draw). The longest bare-knuckle fight was 6 hours 15 minutes between James Kelly and Jack Smith at Fiery Creek, Dalesford, Victoria, Australia on December 3, 1855.

The greatest number of rounds was 276 in 4 hours 30 minutes when Jack Jones beat Patsy Tunney in Cheshire, England in 1825.

Shortest fights The shortest fight on record appears to be one in a Golden Gloves tournament at Minneapolis, Minn. on November 4, 1947, when Mike Collins floored Pat Brownson with the first punch and the contest was stopped, without a count, 4 seconds after the bell. The World Boxing Council reports that the shortest fight in the history of professional boxing occured on June 19, 1991, when Paul Rees (Australia) scored a technical knockout over Charlie Hansen (Australia) in five seconds in a junior-middleweight bout in Brisbane, Australia.

The shortest world title fight was 20 seconds, when Gerald McClellan beat Jay Bell in a WBC middleweight bout at Bayamon, Puerto Rico on August 7, 1993.

Most fights without loss Of boxers with complete records, Packey McFarland had 97 fights (five draws) from 1905 to 1915 without a defeat.

Consecutive wins Pedro Carrasco (Spain) won 83 consecutive fights from April 22, 1964 to September 3, 1970.

Most knockouts The greatest number of finishes classified as "knockouts" in a career is 145 (129 in professional bouts), by Archie Moore.

Record Quotable

"He can run, but he can't hide."
—Joe Louis, taunting boxer Billy Conn, quoted in *Sports Quotes*, by Bob Abel and Michael Valenti.

Consecutive knockouts The record for consecutive knockouts is 44, by Lamar Clark from 1958 to January 11, 1960.

Most knock-downs in a title fight Vic Toweel (South Africa) floored Danny O'Sullivan 14 times in 10 rounds in winning the bantamweight bout on December 2, 1950 at Johannesburg, South Africa.

Attendance The largest paid attendance at any boxing event is 132,274, at the Aztec Stadium, Mexico City on February 20, 1993. The card featured four world title bouts headed by the Julio César Chavez (Mexico) *v.* Greg Haugen WBC super light-welterweight title fight. Chavez knocked out Haugen in the fifth round.

The largest nonpaying attendance is 135,132, at the Tony Zale *v.* Billy Pryor bout at Juneau Park, Milwaukee, Wis., on August 16, 1941.

Lowest attendance The smallest crowd at a world heavyweight title fight was 2,434, at the Cassius Clay (Muhammad Ali) *v.* Sonny Liston fight at Lewiston, Me., on May 25, 1965. Clay knocked out Liston in the first round.

HEAVYWEIGHT DIVISION

Long accepted as the first world heavyweight title fight, with gloves and three-minute rounds, was that between John L. Sullivan and James J. "Gentleman Jim" Corbett in New Orleans, La. on September 7, 1892. Corbett won in 21 rounds.

Longest reign Joe Louis was champion for 11 years 252 days, from June 22, 1937, when he knocked out James J. Braddock in the eighth round at Chicago, Ill., until announcing his retirement on March 1, 1949. During his reign, Louis defended his title a record 25 times.

Shortest reign The shortest reign was 64 days for IBF champion Tony Tucker, May 30–August 1, 1987.

Most recaptures Muhammad Ali is the only man to have regained the heavyweight championship twice. Ali first won the title on February 25, 1964, defeating Sonny Liston. He defeated George Foreman on October 30, 1974, having been stripped of the title by the world boxing authorities on April 28, 1967. He won the WBA title from Leon Spinks on September 15, 1978, having previously lost to him on February 15, 1978.

JUST ONE PUNCH ■ **GEORGE FOREMAN HAD LOST THE FIRST NINE ROUNDS OF HIS TITLE BOUT WITH MICHAEL MOORER BEFORE SENDING THE CHAMP DOWN FOR THE COUNT IN THE TENTH.** (AP/LENNOX McLENDON)

Undefeated Rocky Marciano is the only world champion at any weight to have won every fight of his entire professional career (1947–56); 43 of his 49 fights were by knockouts or stoppages.

Oldest champion The oldest heavyweight boxing champion is George Foreman, age 45. The heavyweight knocked out former WBA/IBF champion Michael Moorer in the tenth round on November 5, 1994. Foreman was Moorer's senior by 19 years, and he outweighed him by 28 pounds. It had been 21 years since Foreman had lost the crown; he defeated Joe Frazier for the title in 1973, but lost it the following year to Muhammad Ali.

Youngest champion Mike Tyson was 20 years 144 days when he beat Trevor Berbeck to win the WBC title at Las Vegas, Nev., on Nov. 22, 1986. He became the youngest undisputed champion on August 1, 1987 when he defeated Tony Tucker for the IBF title.

Lightest champion Bob Fitzsimmons (Great Britain) weighed 167 pounds when he won the title by knocking out James J. Corbett at Carson City, Nev. on March 17, 1897.

Heaviest champion Primo Carnera (Italy) weighed in at 270 pounds for the defense of his title *v.* Tommy Loughran on March 1, 1934. Carnera won a unanimous point decision.

Quickest knockout The quickest knockout in a heavyweight title fight was 55 seconds, by James J. Jeffries over Jack Finnegan at Detroit, Mich. on April 6, 1900.

WORLD CHAMPIONS (ANY WEIGHT)

Reign (longest) Joe Louis's heavyweight duration record of 11 years 252 days stands for all divisions.

Reign (shortest) Tony Canzoneri was world light welterweight champion for 33 days, May 21 to June 23, 1933, the shortest period for a boxer to have won and lost the world title in the ring.

Most recaptures The only boxer to win a world title five times at one weight is Sugar Ray Robinson, who beat Carmen Basilio in Chicago Stadium, Ill. on March 25, 1958 to regain the world middleweight title for the fourth time.

Greatest weight difference Primo Carnera (Italy) outweighed his opponent, Tommy Loughran, by 86

pounds (270 pounds to 184 pounds) when they fought for the heavyweight title on March 1, 1934 in Miami, Fla. Surprisingly, the bout went the distance, with Carnera winning on points.

Greatest tonnage The greatest tonnage recorded in any fight is 700 pounds, when Claude "Humphrey" McBride, 340 pounds, knocked out Jimmy Black, 360 pounds, in the third round of their bout at Oklahoma City, Okla. on June 1, 1971. The greatest combined weight for a world title fight is 488¾ pounds, when Primo Carnera (Italy), 259½ pounds, fought Paolino Uzcudun (Spain), 229¼ pounds, in Rome, Italy on October 22, 1933.

AMATEUR

OLYMPIC GAMES Boxing contests were included in the ancient games, and were first included in the modern Games in 1904.

Most gold medals Two boxers have won three gold medals: Laszlo Papp (Hungary) won the middleweight title in 1948, and the light middleweight in 1952 and 1956; Teofilo Stevenson (Cuba) won the heavyweight division in 1972, 1976 and 1980. The only man to win two titles at the same Games was Oliver L. Kirk, who won both the bantamweight and featherweight titles in 1904. It should be noted that Kirk only had to fight one bout in each class.

WORLD CHAMPIONSHIPS The world championships were first staged in 1974, and are held quadrennially.

Most titles Félix Savon (Cuba) has won a record four world titles. Savon won the heavyweight division in 1986, 1989, 1991 and 1993.

UNITED STATES NATIONAL CHAMPIONSHIPS U.S. amateur championships were first staged in 1888.

Most titles The most titles won is five, by middleweight W. Rodenbach, 1900–04.

BUNGY JUMPING

ORIGINS Bungy jumping (also commonly spelled "bungee"; possibly derived from the British slang word "bung," meaning "to toss" or "throw") most likely dates back to a 1,500-year-old tradition that continues to this day on Pentacost Island, part of the Republic of Vanatu in the South Pacific. As part of tradition, islanders build a rickety 80-foot

Record Quotable

"On this planet we will always know that the athlete of all athletes is between 45 and 55."
—George Foreman to reporters, after his age-barrier-breaking title win in 1994.

WHAT A HANGOVER! ■ CHRIS ALLUM MAKING HIS RECORD-BREAKING BUNGY LEAP OFF NEW RIVER GORGE BRIDGE IN WEST VIRGINIA ON OCTOBER 17, 1992. (CHRIS ALLUM)

tower of sticks lashed together with vines. "Land divers" tie long vines from their ankles to the top of the tower and jump off. A successful, injury-free leap symbolizes a young man's reaching manhood, and is said to ensure a bountiful yam crop.

Since the mid-1980s, bungy jumping has caught on as a worldwide craze. Professional bungy jumpers tie 100% pure latex rubber cords to their feet and jump off high fixed structures, such as buildings, bridges, viaducts, cranes and cliff hangings. In addition to fixed structures, bungy daredevils jump off moving craft, such as hot air balloons, airplanes, helicopters, etc. (such jumps cannot be legitimately measured).

The North American Bungy Association has the largest professional bungy membership in the world. It has organized over 130,000 incident-free jumps since 1985.

Longest jump from a fixed structure According to the North American Bungy Association, Chris Allum holds the record for longest bungy jump at 822 feet. Allum made the death-defying leap off New River Gorge Bridge in West Virginia on October 17, 1982.

CANOEING

ORIGINS The most influential pioneer of canoeing as a sport was John MacGregor, a British attorney, who founded the Canoe Club in Surrey, England in 1866. The sport's world governing body is the International Canoe Federation, founded in 1924.

United States The New York Canoe Club, founded in Staten Island, N.Y., in 1871, is the oldest in the United States. The American Canoe Association was formed on August 3, 1880.

OLYMPIC GAMES Canoeing was first included in the Games as a demonstration sport in 1924. At the 1936 Games, canoeing was included as an official Olympic sport for the first time.

Most gold medals Gert Fredriksson (Sweden) won a record six Olympic gold medals: 1,000 meter Kayak Singles (K1), 1948, 1952 and 1956; 10,000 meter K1, 1948 and 1956; 1,000 meter Kayak Pairs (K2), 1960. In women's competition, Birgit Schmidt (née Fischer; East Germany/Germany) has won four golds: 500 meter K1, 1980 and 1992; 500 meter K2, 1988; 500 meter K4, 1988.

WORLD CHAMPIONSHIPS In Olympic years, the Games also serve as the world championship.

Most titles Birgit Schmidt (East Germany/Germany) has won a record 27 titles, 1978–94. The men's record is 13, by three canoeists: Gert Fredriksson (Sweden), 1948–60; Rudiger Helm (East Germany), 1976–83; and Ivan Patzaichin (Romania), 1968–84.

UNITED STATES NATIONAL CHAMPIONSHIPS

Most titles Marcia Smoke won 35 national titles from 1962–81. The men's record is 33, by Ernest Riedel from 1930–48.

CRICKET

ORIGINS Cricket originated in England in the Middle Ages. It is impossible to pinpoint its exact origin; however, historians believe that the modern game developed in the mid-16th century. The earliest surviving scorecard is from a match played between England and Kent on June 18, 1744. The Marylebone Cricket Club (MCC) was founded in 1787 and, until 1968, was the world governing body for the sport. The International Cricket Conference (ICC) is responsible for international (Test) cricket, while the MCC remains responsible for the laws of cricket.

INTERNATIONAL (TEST) CRICKET

Test match cricket is the highest level of the sport. The Test-playing nations are Australia, England, India, New Zealand, Zimbabwe, Pakistan, South Africa, Sri Lanka and the West Indies. Test matches are generally played over five days. The result is decided by which team scores the most runs in two full innings (one inning sees all 11 members of a team come to bat; their opponents must achieve 10 outs to end the inning). If, at the end of the allotted time period, one or either team has not completed two full innings, the game is declared a tie. The first Test match was played at Melbourne, Australia on March 15–19, 1877 between Australia and England.

TEST MATCH RECORDS (TEAM)

Most runs (innings) England scored 903 runs (for 7 declared) *v.* Australia at The Oval, London on August 20–22, 1938.

Most runs (total aggregate) In a 10-day match played from March 3–14, 1939 in Durban, South Africa, England and South Africa scored 1,981 runs. South Africa scored 530 runs in the first innings and 481 in the second. England scored 316 runs in the first innings and 654 for 5 in the second. The record for a five-day match (standard for current Test matches) is 1,764 runs, Australia (533, 339 for 9) *v.* West Indies (276, 616) at Adelaide, Australia on January 24–29, 1969. Both games ended in stalemate and were declared ties as time ran out.

Fewest runs (innings) New Zealand scored 26 runs *v.* England at Auckland on March 28, 1955.

Fewest runs (two innings) South Africa scored a combined 81 runs (36, 45) *v.* Australia at Melbourne, Australia on February 12–15, 1932. Australia scored 153 runs and won the match by an inning and 72 runs.

Greatest margin of victory England defeated Australia by an inning and 579 runs at The Oval on August 20–24, 1938. Australia scored 201 in its first innings and 123 in the second. In each innings they played with only nine players, two short of a full team.

Tied score matches There have been two tied score matches (both teams' aggregate scores the same at the end of play on the final day) in Test cricket history: Australia *v.* West Indies in Brisbane, Australia, December 9–14, 1960; India *v.* Australia, in Madras, India, September 18–22, 1986.

TEST MATCH RECORDS (INDIVIDUAL)

Most runs (game) 375 not out, by Brian Lara, West Indies *v.* England at St. Johns, Antigua on April 16–18, 1994.

Most runs (career) 11,174 runs, by Allan Border, Australia, 1978–94. Border has played in 156 Tests for an average of 50.56 runs.

Highest average (career) 99.94 runs, by Donald Bradman, Australia, 1928–48. "The Don" played in 52 Tests scoring 6,996 runs.

Most wickets (game) 19, by Jim Laker for England *v.* Australia at Old Trafford, Manchester, from July 27–31, 1956.

Most wickets (career) 434, by Kapil Dev, India. As of February 8, 1994, Kapil has played in 131 Tests.

Record Quotable

"He might have done just as well playing with a stick of celery."

—The *Sydney Morning Herald*, remarking on Brian Lara's racking up 277 runs in one at bat.

Australia The premier event in Australia is the Sheffield Shield, an interstate competition contested since 1891–94. New South Wales has won the title a record 42 times.

England The major championship in England is the County Championship, an intercounty competition officially recognized since 1890. Yorkshire has won the title a record 30 times.

India The Ranji Trophy is India's premier cricket competition. Established in 1934 in memory of K. S. Ranjitsinhji, it is contested on a zonal basis, culminating in a playoff competition. Bombay has won the tournament a record 30 times.

New Zealand Since 1975, the major championship in New Zealand has been the Shell Trophy. Otago, Wellington and Auckland have each won the competition four times.

Pakistan Pakistan's national championship is the Quaid-e-Azam Trophy, established in 1953. Karachi has won the trophy a record eight times.

South Africa The Currie Cup, donated by Sir Donald Currie, was first contested in 1889. Transvaal has won the competition a record 28 times.

West Indies The Red Stripe Cup, established in 1966, is the premier prize played for by the association of Caribbean islands (plus Guyana) that form the West Indies Cricket League. Barbados has won the competion a record 13 times.

CROQUET

ORIGINS Its exact beginnings are unknown; however, it is believed that croquet developed from the French game *jeu de mail*. A game resembling croquet was played in Ireland in the 1830s and introduced to England 20 years later. Although croquet was played in the United States for a number of years, a national body was not established until the formation of the United States Croquet Association (USCA) in 1976. The first United States championship was played in 1977.

WORLD CHAMPIONSHIPS The first World Championships were held at the Hurlington Club in Great Britain in 1989. Robert Fulford (Great Britain) has won a record four times: 1990, 1992–94.

FOUR-TIME CROQUET CHAMP ■ ROBERT FULFORD HOLDING UP HIS 1992 CHAMPIONSHIP TROPHY, THE SECOND OF HIS FOUR PRIZES. (ANNE C. FROST)

USCA NATIONAL CHAMPIONSHIPS J. Archie Peck has won the singles title a record four times (1977, 1979–80, 1982). Ted Prentis has won the doubles title four times with three different partners (1978, 1980–81, 1988). The teams of Ted Prentis and Ned Prentis (1980–81), Dana Dribben and Ray Bell (1985–86) and Reid Fleming and Debbie Cornelius (1990–91) have each won the doubles title twice. The New York Croquet Club has won a record six National Club Championships (1980–83, 1986, 1988).

CROSS-COUNTRY RUNNING

ORIGINS The earliest recorded international cross-country race took place on March 20, 1898 between England and France. The race was staged at Ville d'Avray, near Paris, France over a course 9 miles 18 yards long.

WORLD CHAMPIONSHIPS The first international cross-country championships were staged in Glasgow, Scotland on March 28, 1903. Since 1973 the event has been an official world championship organized by the International Amateur Athletic Federation.

Most titles England has won the men's team event a record 45 times, 1903–14, 1920–21, 1924–25, 1930–38, 1951, 1953–55, 1958–60, 1962, 1964–72, 1976, 1979–80. The women's competition has been won eight times by two countries: United States, 1968–69, 1975, 1979, 1983–85, 1987; USSR, 1976–77, 1980–82, 1988–90.

Most titles (individual) Two women have won five titles: Doris Brown (U.S.), 1967–71, and Grete Waitz (Norway), 1978–81 and 1983. John Ngugi (Kenya) has won the men's title a record five times, 1986–89 and 1992.

UNITED STATES NATIONAL CHAMPIONSHIPS This competition was first staged in 1890 for men, and in 1972 for women.

Most titles Pat Porter has won the men's event a record eight times, 1982–89. Lynn Jennings has won the women's event seven times, 1985, 1987–90 and 1992–93.

NCAA CHAMPIONSHIPS The first NCAA cross-country championship was held in 1938, and was open only to men's teams. A women's event was not staged until 1981.

Most titles (team) In men's competition, Michigan State has won the team title a record eight times: 1939, 1948–49, 1952, 1955–56, 1958–59.

Most titles (individuals) Three athletes have won the men's individual title three times: Gerry Lindgren (Washington State), 1966–67 and 1969; Steve Prefontaine (Oregon), 1970–71 and 1973; Henry Rono (Washington State), 1976–77 and 1979.

Most titles (team) In women's competition, Villanova has won the team title five times, 1989–93.

Most titles (individual) Three runners have won the title twice: Betty Springs (North Carolina State), 1981 and 1983; Sonia O'Sullivan (Villanova), 1990 and 1991; Carole Zajac (Villanova), 1992–93.

CURLING

ORIGINS The traditional home of curling is Scotland; some historians, however, believe that the sport originated in the Netherlands in the 15th century. There is evidence of a curling club in Kilsyth, Scotland in 1716, but the earliest recorded club is the Muthill Curling Club, Tayside, Scotland, formed in 1739, which produced the first known written rules of the game on November 17, 1739. The Grand (later Royal) Caledonian Curling Club was founded in 1838 and was the international governing body of the sport until 1966, when the International Curling Federation was formed; this was renamed the World Curling Federation in 1991.

United States and Canada Scottish immigrants introduced curling to North America in the 18th century. The earliest known club was the Royal Montreal Curling Club, founded in 1807. The first international game was between Canada and the United States in 1884—the inaugural Gordon International Medal series. In 1832, Orchard Lake Curling Club, Mich., was founded, the first in the United States. The oldest club in continuous existence in the U.S. is the Milwaukee Curling Club, Wis., formed *c.* 1850. Regional curling associations governed the sport in the U.S. until 1947, when the United States Women's Curling Association was formed, followed in 1958 by the Men's Curling Association. In 1986, the United States Curling Association was formed and is the current governing body for the sport. In Canada, the Dominion Curling Association was formed in 1935, renamed the Canadian Curling Association in 1968.

OLYMPIC GAMES Curling has been a demonstration sport at the Olympic Games of 1924, 1932, 1964, 1988 and 1992.

WORLD CHAMPIONSHIPS First held in 1959, these championships are held annually. Women's competition was introduced in 1979.

Most titles (men) Canada has dominated this event, winning 22 titles: 1959–64, 1966, 1968–72, 1980, 1982–83, 1985–87, 1989–90, and 1993–94. Ernie Richardson (Canada) has been winning skip a record four times, 1959–60, 1962–63.

Most titles (women) Canada has won eight championships, in 1980, 1984–87, 1989, and 1993–94. Djordy Nordby (Norway) has been skip of two winning teams, 1990–91.

UNITED STATES NATIONAL CHAMPIONSHIPS A men's tournament was first held in 1957. A women's event was introduced in 1977.

Men Two curlers have been skips on five championship teams: Bud Somerville (Superior Curling

Club, Wis. in 1965, 1968–69, 1974 and 1981), and Bruce Roberts (Hibbing Curling Club, Minn. in 1966–67, 1976–77 and 1984).

Women In this competition, Nancy Langley of Seattle, Wash. has been the skip of a record four championship teams: 1979, 1981, 1983 and 1988.

THE LABATT BRIER (FORMERLY THE MACDONALD BRIER 1927–79) The Brier is the Canadian men's curling championship. The competition was first held at the Granite Club, Toronto in 1927. Sponsored by Macdonald Tobacco Inc., it had been known as the Macdonald Brier; since 1980 Labatt Brewery has sponsored the event.

Most titles The most wins is 23, by Manitoba (1928–32, 1934, 1936, 1938, 1940, 1942, 1947, 1949, 1952–53, 1956, 1965, 1970–72, 1979, 1981, 1984 and 1992). Ernie Richardson (Saskatchewan) has been winning skip a record four times (1959–60 and 1962–63).

Perfect game Stu Beagle, of Calgary, Alberta, played a perfect game (48 points) against Nova Scotia in the Canadian Championships (Brier) at Fort William (now Thunder Bay), Ontario on March 8, 1960. Andrew McQuiston skipped the Scotland team to a perfect game v. Switzerland at the Uniroyal Junior Men's World Championship at Kitchener, Ontario, Canada in 1980.

Bernice Fekete, of Edmonton, Alberta, Canada, skipped her rink to two consecutive eight-enders on the same ice at the Derrick Club, Edmonton on January 10 and February 6, 1973.

Two eight-enders in one bonspiel were scored at the Parry Sound Curling Club, Ontario, Canada from January 6–8, 1983.

CYCLING

ORIGINS The forerunner of the bicycle, the *celerifere*, was demonstrated in the garden of the Palais Royale, Paris, France in 1791. The velocipede, the first practical pedal-propelled vehicle, was built in March 1861 by Pierre Michaux and his son Ernest and demonstrated in Paris. The first velocipede race occurred on May 31, 1868 at the Parc St. Cloud, Paris, over a distance of 1.24 miles. The first international organization was the International Cyclist Association (ICA), founded in 1892, which launched the first world championships in 1893. The current governing body, the *Union Cycliste Internationale* (UCI), was founded in 1900.

TRANSCONTINENTAL CYCLING RECORDS

Men's Records (United States Crossing)

Event	Rider(s)	Start/Finish	Days: Hrs: Min	Av. mph	Year
Solo (time)	Michael Secrest	HB–NYC	7:23:16	15.24	1990
Solo (av. mph)	Pete Penseyres	HB–AC	8:09:47	15.40	1986
Tandem	Lon Haldeman & Pete Penseyres	HB–AC	7:14:15	15.97	1987

Men's Records (Canada Crossing)

Event	Rider(s)	Start/Finish	Days: Hrs: Min	Av. mph	Year
Solo	William Narasnek	Van–Hal	13:09:06	11.68	1991

Women's Records (United States Crossing)

Event	Rider(s)	Start/Finish	Days: Hrs: Min	Av. mph	Year
Solo	Susan Notorangelo	CM–NYC	9:09:09	12.93	1989
Tandem	Estelle Grey & Cheryl Marek	SM–NYC	10:22:48	11.32	1984

HB: Huntington Beach Calif.; NYC: New York City; AC: Atlantic City N.J.; Van: Vancouver; Hal: Halifax, Nova Scotia; CM: Costa Mesa, Calif.; SM: Santa Monica, Calif.

Source: Ultra Marathon Cycling Association (UMCA), The Guinness Book of Records, 1993

TOUR DE FRANCE CHAMPIONS (1903–1948)

Year	Winner	Country	Year	Winner	Country
1903	Maurice Garin	France	1926	Lucien Buysse	Belgium
1904	Henri Cornet	France	1927	Nicholas Frantz	Luxembourg
1905	Louis Trousselier	France	1928	Nicholas Frantz	Luxembourg
1906	Rene Pottier	France	1929	Maurice Dewaele	Belgium
1907	Lucien Petit-Breton	France	1930	Andre Leducq	France
1908	Lucien Petit-Breton	France	1931	Antonin Magne	France
1909	Francois Faber	Luxembourg	1932	Andre Leducq	France
1910	Octave Lapize	France	1933	Georges Speicher	France
1911	Gustave Garrigou	France	1934	Antonin Magne	France
1912	Odile Defraye	Belgium	1935	Romain Maes	Belgium
1913	Philippe Thys	Belgium	1936	Sylvere Maes	Belgium
1914	Philippe Thys	Belgium	1937	Roger Lapebie	France
1915	not held		1938	Gino Bartali	Italy
1916	not held		1939	Sylvere Maes	Belgium
1917	not held		1940	not held	
1918	not held		1941	not held	
1919	Firmin Labot	Belgium	1942	not held	
1920	Philippe Thys	Belgium	1943	not held	
1921	Leon Scieur	Belgium	1944	not held	
1922	Firmin Labot	Belgium	1945	not held	
1923	Henri Pelissier	France	1946	Jean Lazarides	France
1924	Ottavio Bottecchia	Italy	1947	Jean Robic	France
1925	Ottavio Bottecchia	Italy	1948	Gino Bartali	Italy

OLYMPIC GAMES Cycling was included in the first modern Games held in 1896, and has been part of every Games since, with the exception of 1904. Women's events were first staged in 1984.

Most gold medals Four men have won three gold medals: Paul Masson (France), 1,000 meter time-trial, 1,000 meter sprint, 10,000 meter track in 1896; Francesco Verri (Italy), 1,000 meter time-trial, 1,000 meter sprint, 5,000 meter track in 1906; Robert Charpentier (France), individual road race, team road race, 4,000 meter team pursuit in 1936; Daniel Morelon (France), 1,000 meter sprint in 1968 and 1972, 2,000 meter tandem in 1968.

Most medals Daniel Morelon (France) has won five Olympic medals: three gold (see above); one silver, 1,000 meter sprint in 1972; one bronze, 1,000 meter sprint in 1964.

WORLD CHAMPIONSHIPS World championships are contested annually. They were first staged for amateurs in 1893 and for professionals in 1895.

Most titles (one event) The most wins in one event is 10, by Koichi Nakano (Japan), professional sprint 1977–86. The most wins in a men's amateur event is seven, by two cyclists: Daniel Morelon (France), sprint, 1966–67, 1969–71, 1973, 1975; and Leon Meredith (Great Britain), 100 kilometer motor-paced, 1904–05, 1907–09, 1911 and 1913.

The most women's titles is eight, by Jeannie Longo (France), pursuit 1986 and 1988–89 and road 1985–87 and 1989–90.

TOUR DE FRANCE CHAMPIONS (1949–1994)

Year	Winner	Country	Year	Winner	Country
1949	Fausto Coppi	Italy	1972	Eddy Merckx	Belgium
1950	Ferdinand Kubler	Switzerland	1973	Luis Ocana	Spain
1951	Hugo Koblet	Switzerland	1974	Eddy Merckx	Belgium
1952	Fausto Coppi	Italy	1975	Bernard Thevenet	France
1953	Louison Bobet	France	1976	Lucien van Impe	Belgium
1954	Louison Bobet	France	1977	Bernard Thevenet	France
1955	Louison Bobet	France	1978	Bernard Hinault	France
1956	Roger Walkowiak	France	1979	Bernard Hinault	France
1957	Jacques Anquetil	France	1980	Joop Zoetemilk	Netherlands
1958	Charly Gaul	Luxembourg	1981	Bernard Hinault	France
1959	Federico Bahamontes	Spain	1982	Bernard Hinault	France
1960	Gastone Nencini	Italy	1983	Laurent Fignon	France
1961	Jacques Anquetil	France	1984	Laurent Fignon	France
1962	Jacques Anquetil	France	1985	Bernard Hinault	France
1963	Jacques Anquetil	France	1986	Greg LeMond	U.S.
1964	Jacques Anquetil	France	1987	Stephen Roche	Ireland
1965	Felice Gimondi	Italy	1988	Pedro Delgado	Spain
1966	Lucien Aimar	France	1989	Greg LeMond	U.S.
1967	Roger Pingeon	France	1990	Greg LeMond	U.S.
1968	Jan Janssen	Netherlands	1991	Miguel Indurain	Spain
1969	Eddy Merckx	Belgium	1992	Miguel Indurain	Spain
1970	Eddy Merckx	Belgium	1993	Miguel Indurain	Spain
1971	Eddy Merckx	Belgium	1994	Miguel Indurain	Spain

United States The most world titles won by a U.S. cyclist is five, in women's 3 kilometer pursuit by Rebecca Twigg, 1982, 1984–85, 1987, and 1993. The most successful man has been Greg LeMond, winner of the individual road race in 1983 and 1989.

UNITED STATES NATIONAL CHAMPIONSHIPS National cycling championships have been held annually since 1899. Women's events were first included in 1937.

Most titles Leonard Nitz has won 16 titles: five pursuit (1976 and 1980–83); eight team pursuit (1980–84, 1986 and 1988–89); two 1 kilometer time-trial (1982 and 1984); one criterium (1986). Connie Carpenter has won 11 titles in women's

events: four road race (1976–77, 1979 and 1981); three pursuit (1976–77 and 1979); two criterium (1982–83); two points (1981–82).

TOUR DE FRANCE

First staged in 1903, the Tour meanders throughout France and sometimes neighboring countries over a four-week period.

Most wins Three riders have each won the event five times: Jacques Anquetil (France), 1957, 1961–64; Eddy Merckx (Belgium), 1969–72, 1974; Bernard Hinault (France), 1978–79, 1981–82, 1985.

Longest race The longest race held was 3,569 miles in 1926.

CATCHING UP ■ **WITH HIS FOURTH CONSECUTIVE TOUR DE FRANCE WIN IN 1994, MIGUEL INDURAIN IS ONLY ONE VICTORY SHORT OF TYING THE ALL-TIME RECORD. WILL 1995 AGAIN BE HIS YEAR?**
(ALLSPORT/F. MONS)

Closest race The closest race ever was in 1989, when after 2,030 miles over 23 days (July 1–23) Greg LeMond (U.S.), who completed the Tour in 87 hours 38 minutes 35 seconds, beat Laurent Fignon (France) in Paris by only 8 seconds.

Fastest speed The fastest average speed was 24.547 mph, by Miguel Indurain (Spain) in 1992.

Longest stage The longest-ever stage was the 486 kilometers (302 miles) from Les Sables d'Olonne to Bayonne in 1919.

Most participants The most participants was 210 starters in 1986.

Most finishers A record 151 riders finished the 1988 race.

Most races Joop Zoetemilk (Netherlands) participated in a record 16 tours, 1970–86. He won the race in 1980 and finished second a record six times.

Most stage wins Eddy Merckx (Belgium) won a record 35 individual stages in just seven races, 1969–75.

United States Greg LeMond became the first American winner in 1986; he returned from serious injury to win again in 1989 and 1990.

RACE ACROSS AMERICA

ORIGINS An annual nonstop transcontinental crossing of the United States from west to east, the Race Across AMerica was first staged in 1982. A women's division was introduced in 1984. The start and finish lines have varied, but currently the race starts in Irvine, Calif., and finishes in Savannah, Ga. The race must travel a minimum distance of 2,900 miles.

Most wins Three cyclists have won two men's titles: Lon Haldeman, 1982–83; Pete Penseyres, 1984, 1986; Bob Fourney, 1990–91. In the women's division two riders have won two titles: Susan Notorangelo, 1985 and 1989; Seana Hogan, 1992–93.

DARTS

ORIGINS Darts, or dartes (heavily weighted 10-inch throwing arrows) were first used in Ireland in the 16th century, as a weapon for self-defense. The Pilgrims played darts for recreation aboard the *Mayflower* in 1620. The modern game dates to 1896, when Brian Gamlin of Bury, England devised the present board numbering system. The first recorded score of 180, the maximum with three darts, was by John Reader at the Highbury Tavern, Sussex, England in 1902.

WORLD CHAMPIONSHIP This competition was instituted in 1978.

Most titles Eric Bristow of England has won the title a record five times (1980–81, 1984–86).

SCORING RECORDS (HIGHEST SCORES)

10-HOURS SCORES

Individual The pair of Jon Archer and Neil Rankin (Great Britain) scored 465,919, while retriev-

DARTS SCORING RECORDS (FEWEST THROWN)

Scores of 201 in four darts, 301 in six darts, 401 in seven darts and 501 in nine darts have been achieved on many occasions.

Score	Darts Thrown	Player(s)	Date
1,001	19	Cliff Inglis (England)	Nov. 11, 1975
	19	Jocky Wilson (Scotland)	March 23, 1989
2,001	52	Alan Evans (Wales)	Sept. 3, 1976
3,001	73	Tony Benson (England)	July 12, 1986
100,001	3,732	Alan Downie (Scotland)	Nov. 21, 1986
1,000,001	36,583	Eight-man team (U.S.)*	Oct. 19–20, 1991

* An eight-man team set the record at Buzzy's Pub and Grub in Lynn, Mass.

ing their own darts, at the Royal Oak, Cossington, England on November 17, 1990.

Bulls Johnny "Darts" Mielcarek (U.S.) hit 1,200 bulls in 10 hours at the Pete Rose Ballpark Cafe, Boca Raton, Fla., on May 27, 1993.

24-HOURS SCORES

Individual Davy Richardson-Page (Great Britain) scored 518,060 points at Blucher Social Club, Newcastle, England on July 6–7, 1991.

Team (8-man) The Broken Hill Darts Club of New South Wales, Australia scored 1,722,249 points in 24 hours from September 28–29, 1985.

Team (8-woman) A team representing the Lord Clyde Pub of London, England scored 744,439 points on October 13–14, 1990.

Bulls and 25s (8-man team) The Kent and Canterbury Hospital Sports and Social Club of Canturbury, England hit 510,625 bulls and 25s on October 20–21, 1989.

DIVING

ORIGINS Diving as an organized sport traces its roots to the gymnastics movement that developed in Germany and Sweden in the 17th century. During the summer, gymnasts would train at the beach, and acrobatic techniques would be performed over water as a safety measure. From this activity the sport of diving developed. The world governing body for diving is the *Fédération Internationale de Natation Amateur* (FINA), founded in 1980. FINA is also the governing body for swimming, water polo and synchronized swimming.

United States Ernst Bransten and Mike Peppe are considered the two main pioneers of diving in the United States. Bransten, a Swede, came to the United States following World War I. He introduced Swedish training methods and diving techniques, which revolutionized the sport in this country. Peppe's highly successful program at Ohio State University, 1931–63, produced several Olympic medalists and helped promote the sport here.

OLYMPIC GAMES Men's diving events were introduced at the 1904 Games, and women's events in 1912.

Most gold medals Two divers have won four gold medals: Pat McCormick (U.S.), who won both the women's springboard and the highboard events in 1952 and 1956; and Greg Louganis (U.S.), who performed the highboard/springboard double in 1984 and 1988.

Most medals Two divers have won five medals: Klaus Dibiasi (Italy), three golds, highboard in 1968, 1972 and 1976, and two silver, highboard in 1964 and springboard in 1968; and Greg Louganis, four golds (see above) and one silver, highboard in 1976.

World Championships Diving events were included in the first world aquatic championships staged in 1973.

Most titles Greg Louganis (U.S.) won a record five world titles—highboard in 1978 and the highboard/springboard double in 1982 and 1986. Philip Boggs (U.S.) is the only diver to win three gold medals at one event, springboard, in 1973, 1975 and 1978.

United States National Championships The Amateur Athletic Union (AAU) organized the first national diving championships in 1909. Since 1981, United States Diving has been the governing body of the sport in this country, and thus responsible for the national championships.

Most titles Greg Louganis has won a record 47 national titles: 17, one-meter springboard; 17, three-meter springboard; 13, platform. In women's competition, Cynthia Potter has won a record 28 titles.

EQUESTRIAN SPORTS

Origins Evidence of horseback riding dates from a Persian engraving dated *c.* 3000 B.C. The three separate equestrian competitions recognized at the Olympic level are show jumping, the three-day event and dressage. The earliest known show jumping competition was in Ireland, when the Royal Dublin Society held its first "Horse Show" on April 15, 1864. Dressage competition derived from the exercises taught at 16th century Italian and French horsemanship academies, while the three-day event developed from cavalry endurance rides. The world governing body for all three disciplines is the *Fédération Equestre Internationale* (FEI), founded in Brussels, Belgium in 1921.

GUINNESS CHALLENGE

Who made the most rebounds in a single NBA game?
See page 44 for the answer.

Olympic Games In the ancient games, chariot races featured horses, and later riding contests were included. Show jumping was included in the 1900 Games; the three-day event and dressage disciplines were not added until 1912. In 1956 the equestrian events were held in Stockholm, Sweden, separate from the main Games in Melbourne, Australia, because of the strict Australian quarantine laws.

Most medals (all events) Germany has dominated the equestrian events, winning 64 medals overall: 27 gold, 17 silver and 20 bronze.

SHOW JUMPING

OLYMPIC GAMES

Most gold medals (rider) Hans-Gunther Winkler (West Germany) has won five titles, 1956, 1960, 1964 and 1972 in the team competition, and the individual championship in 1956. The only rider to win two individual titles is Pierre Jonqueres d'Oriola (France), in 1952 and 1964.

Most gold medals (horse) The most successful horse is Halla, ridden by Hans-Gunther Winkler during his individual and team wins in 1956, and during the team win in 1960.

Most medals Hans-Gunther Winkler has won a record seven medals: five gold (see above), one silver and one bronze in the team competition in 1976 and 1968.

United States Two American riders have won the individual event: Bill Steinkraus in 1968, and Joe Fargis in 1984. The United States won the team event in 1984.

World Championships The men's world championship was inaugurated in 1953. In 1965, 1970 and 1974 separate women's championships were held. An integrated championship was first held in 1978 and is now held every four years.

Most titles Two riders share the record for most men's championships with two victories: Hans-Gunther Winkler (West Germany), 1954–55, and Raimondo d'Inzeo (Italy), 1956 and 1960. The women's title was won twice by Janou Tissot (née Lefebvre) of France, in 1970 and 1974. No rider has won the integrated competition more than once.

THREE-DAY EVENT

OLYMPIC GAMES

Most gold medals Charles Pahud de Mortanges (Netherlands) has won four gold medals—the individual title in 1928 and 1932, and the team event in 1924 and 1928. Mark Todd (New Zealand) is the only other rider to have won the individual title twice, in 1984 and 1988.

Most medals (rider) Charles Pahud de Mortanges has won five medals: four gold (see above) and one silver in the 1932 team event.

Most gold medals (horse) Marcroix was ridden by Charles Pahud de Mortanges in three of his four medal rounds, 1928–32.

United States The most medals won for the U.S. is six, by J. Michael Plumb: team gold, 1976 and 1984, and four silver medals, team 1964, 1968 and 1972, and individual 1976. Tad Coffin is the only U.S. rider to have won both team and individual gold medals, in 1976.

WORLD CHAMPIONSHIP First held in 1966, the event is held quadrenially and is open to both men and women.

Most titles (rider) Two riders have won three world titles: Bruce Davidson (U.S.), individual title in 1974 and 1978, team title in 1974; and Virginia Leng (Great Britain), individual 1986 and team in 1982 and 1986. Davidson is the only rider to have won two individual championships.

Most titles (country) Great Britain has won the team title a record three times, 1970, 1982 and 1986. The United States won the team event in 1974.

DRESSAGE

OLYMPIC GAMES

Most gold medals (rider) Reiner Klimke (West Germany) has won six gold medals: one individual in 1984, and five team in 1964, 1968, 1976, 1984 and 1988. Henri St. Cyr (Sweden) is the only rider to have won two individual titles, in 1952 and 1956. Two riders have won the individual title on two occasions: Henri St. Cyr (Sweden), 1952 and 1956; and Nicole Uphoff (Germany), 1988 and 1992.

Most gold medals (horse) Rembrandt was ridden by Nicole Uphoff in all four of her medal-winning rounds—two individual titles and two team titles, both in 1988 and 1992.

Most medals Reiner Klimke won eight medals: six gold (see above), and two bronze in the individual event in 1968 and 1976.

United States The United States has never won a gold medal in dressage. In the team event the United States has won one silver, 1948, and three bronze, in 1932, 1976, and 1992. Hiram Tuttle is the only rider to have won an individual medal, earning the bronze in 1932.

WORLD CHAMPIONSHIPS This competition was instituted in 1966.

Most titles (country) West Germany has won a record six times: 1966, 1974, 1978, 1982, 1986 and 1990.

Most titles (rider) Reiner Klimke (West Germany) is the only rider to have won two individual titles, on Mehmed in 1974 and on Ahlerich in 1982.

FENCING

ORIGINS Evidence of swordsmanship can be traced back to Egypt as early as *c.* 1360 B.C., where it was demonstrated during religious ceremonies. Fencing, "fighting with sticks," gained popularity as a sport in Europe in the 16th century.

The modern foil, a light court sword, was introduced in France in the mid-17th century; in the late 19th century, the fencing "arsenal" was expanded to include the épée, a heavier dueling weapon, and the saber, a light cutting sword.

The *Fédération Internationale d'Escrime* (FIE), the world governing body, was founded in Paris, France in 1913. The first European championships were held in 1921 and were expanded into world championships in 1935.

United States In the United States, the Amateur Fencers League of America (AFLA) was founded on April 22, 1891 in New York City. This group

GUINNESS CHALLENGE

Who was the oldest driver to win an Indy car race?
See page 8 for the answer.

assumed supervision of the sport in the U.S., staging the first national championship in 1892. In June 1981, the AFLA changed its name to the United States Fencing Association (USFA).

OLYMPIC GAMES Fencing was included in the first Olympic Games of the modern era at Athens in 1896, and is one of only six sports to be featured in every Olympiad.

Most gold medals Aladar Gerevich (Hungary) has won a record seven gold medals, all in saber: individual, 1948; team, 1932, 1936, 1948, 1952, 1956 and 1960. In individual events, two fencers have won three titles: Ramon Fonst (cuba), épée, 1900 and 1904, and foil, 1904; Nedo Nadi (Italy), foil, 1912 and 1920, and saber, 1920. The most golds won by a woman is four, by Yelena Novikova (née Belova; USSR), all in foil: individual, 1968; team, 1968, 1972 and 1976.

Most medals Edoardo Mangiarotti (Italy) has won a record 13 medals in fencing: six gold, five

silver and two bronze in foil and épée events from 1936 to 1960.

United States Albertson Van Zo Post is the only American to have won an Olympic title. He won the single sticks competition and teamed with two Cubans to win the team foil title in 1904. In overall competition the United States has won 19 medals (both Cuba and the United States are credited with a gold medal for the 1904 team foil): two gold, six silver and 11 bronze—all in men's events.

WORLD CHAMPIONSHIPS The first world championships were staged in Paris, France in 1937. Foil, épée and saber events were held for men and just foil for women. In 1989, a women's épée event was added. The tournament is staged annually.

Most titles The greatest number of individual world titles won is five, by Aleksandr Romankov (USSR), at foil, 1974, 1977, 1979, 1982 and 1983. Five women foilists have won three world titles: Hélène Mayer (Germany), 1929, 1931 and 1937; Ilona

TOUCHÉ! ■ ERIC "NICK" BRAVIN DEFEATING AL CARLAY IN THE 1994 NATIONAL CHAMPIONSHIP. BRAVIN HAD ELIMINATED EIGHT-TIME U.S. CHAMPION MICHAEL MARX IN THE PREVIOUS ROUND. (UNITED STATES FENCING ASSOCIATION)

Schacherer-Elek (Hungary), 1934–35, 1951; Ellen Müller-Preis (Austria), 1947, 1949–50; Cornelia Hanisch (West Germany), 1979, 1981 and 1985; and Anja Fichtel (West Germany), 1986, 1988 and 1990.

UNITED STATES NATIONAL CHAMPIONSHIPS

Most titles The most U.S. titles won at one weapon is 12 at saber, by Peter Westbrook, in 1974, 1975, 1979–86, 1988 and 1989. The women's record is 10 at foil, by Janice Romary in 1950–51, 1956–57, 1960–61, 1964–66 and 1968.

The most individual foil championships won is eight, by Michael Marx in 1977, 1979, 1982, 1985–87, 1990 and 1993. L. G. Nunes won the most épée championships, with six—1917, 1922, 1924, 1926, 1928 and 1932. Vincent Bradford won a record number of women's épée championships with four in 1982–84 and 1986.

NCAA CHAMPIONSHIP DIVISION I (TEAM) A men's championship was first staged in 1941. A women's championship was not introduced until 1982. In 1990 these two tournaments were replaced by a combined team event. In the now-defunct separate events, New York University won the men's title 12 times, 1947–76; and Wayne State (Mich.), won the women's event three times, 1982, 1988–89.

Most wins Two teams have won two titles: Penn State, 1990–91; and Columbia–Barnard, 1992–93.

Most titles (fencer) Michael Lofton, New York University, has won the most titles in a career, with four victories in saber, 1984–87. In women's competition, Caitlin Bilodeaux, Columbia–Barnard, and Molly Sullivan, Notre Dame, have both won the individual title twice: Bilodeaux in 1985 and 1987, and Sullivan in 1986 and 1988.

FIELD HOCKEY

ORIGINS Hitting a ball with a stick is a game that dates back to the origins of the human race. Bas-reliefs and frescoes discovered in Egypt and Greece depict hockey-like games. A drawing of a "bully" on the walls of a tomb at Beni Hassan in the Nile Valley has been dated to *c.* 2050 B.C. The birthplace of modern hockey is Great Britain, where the first definitive code of rules was established in 1886. The *Fédération Internationale de Hockey* (FIH), the world governing body, was founded on January 7, 1924.

United States The sport was introduced to this country in 1921 by a British teacher, Constance M. K. Applebee. The Field Hockey Association of America (FHAA) was founded in 1928 by Henry Greer. The first game was staged between the Germantown Cricket Club and the Westchester Field Hockey Club, also in 1928.

OLYMPIC GAMES Field hockey was added to the Olympic Games in 1908 and became a permanent feature in 1928; a women's tournament was added in 1980.

Most gold medals (team) In the men's competition, India has won eight gold medals: 1928, 1932, 1936, 1948, 1952, 1956, 1964 and 1980. In the women's competition, no team has won the event more than once.

United States The United States has never won either the men's or women's events; the best result has been a bronze in 1932 (men), and in 1984 (women).

Most international appearances Alison Ramsay has made a record 234 international appearances, 127 for Scotland and 107 for Great Britain, 1982–94.

Most appearances (U.S.) Sheryl Johnson made a U.S. record 137 appearances from 1978–89.

NCAA DIVISION I (WOMEN) The women's championship was inaugurated in 1981.

Most titles Old Dominion has won the most championships, with seven titles: 1982–84, 1988 and 1990–92.

SCORING RECORDS

Highest score The highest score in an international game was India's 24–1 defeat of the United States at Los Angeles, Calif., in the 1932 Olympic Games. In women's competition, England hammered France 23–0 at Merton, England on February 3, 1923.

Most goals Paul Litjens (Netherlands) holds the record for most goals by one player in international play. He scored 267 goals in 177 games.

Fastest goal The fastest goal scored in an international game was netted only seven seconds after the bully by John French for England *v.* West Germany at Nottingham, England on April 25, 1971.

FIGURE SKATING

ORIGINS The earliest reference to ice skating is in Scandinavian literature dating to the second century A.D. Jackson Haines, a New Yorker, is regarded as the pioneer of the modern concept of figure skating, a composite of skating and dancing. Although his ideas were not initially favored in the United States, Haines moved to Europe in the mid-1860s, where his "International Style of Figure Skating" was warmly received and promoted. The first artificial rink was opened in London, England on January 7, 1876. The world governing body is the International Skating Union (ISU), founded in 1892. The sport functioned informally in the United States until 1921, when the United States Figure Skating Association (USFSA) was formed to oversee skating in this country—a role it still performs.

OLYMPIC GAMES Figure skating was first included in the 1908 Summer Games in London, and has been featured in every Games since 1920. Uniquely, both men's and women's events have been included in the Games from the first introduction of the sport.

Most gold medals Three skaters have won three gold medals: Gillis Grafstrom (Sweden) in 1920, 1924 and 1928; Sonja Henie (Norway) in 1928, 1932 and 1936; Irina Rodnina (USSR), with two different partners, in the pairs in 1972, 1976 and 1980.

United States Dick Button is the only American skater to win two gold medals, in 1948 and 1952. American skaters have won the men's title six times and the women's five. No American team has won either the pairs or dance titles.

WORLD CHAMPIONSHIPS This competition was first staged in 1896.

Most titles (individual) The greatest number of men's individual world figure skating titles is 10, by Ulrich Salchow (Sweden), in 1901–05 and 1907–11. The women's record (instituted 1906) is also 10 individual titles, by Sonja Henie (Norway) between 1927 and 1936.

Most titles (pairs) Irina Rodnina (USSR) has won 10 pairs titles (instituted 1908), four with Aleksey Ulanov, 1969–72, and six with her husband, Aleksandr Zaitsev, 1973–78.

Most titles (ice dance) The most ice dance titles (instituted 1952) won is six, by Lyudmila Pakhomova and her husband, Aleksandr Gorshkov (USSR), 1970–74 and 1976.

United States Dick Button won five world titles, 1948–52. Five women's world titles were won by Carol Heise, 1956–60.

UNITED STATES NATIONAL CHAMPIONSHIPS The U.S. championships were first held in 1914.

Most titles The most titles won by an individual is nine, by Maribel Y. Vinson, 1928–33 and 1935–37. She also won six pairs titles, and her aggregate of 15 titles is equaled by Therese Blanchard (née Weld), who won six individual and nine pairs titles between 1914 and 1927. The men's individual record is seven, by Roger Turner, 1928–34, and by Dick Button, 1946–52.

HIGHEST MARKS The highest tally of maximum six marks awarded in an international championship was 29, to Jayne Torvill and Christopher Dean (Great Britain) in the World Ice Dance Championships at Ottawa, Canada on March 22–24, 1984. They previously gained a perfect set of nine sixes for artistic presentation in the free dance at the 1983 World Championships in Helsinki, Finland and at the 1984 Winter Olympic Games in Sarajevo, Yugoslavia. In their career, Torvill and Dean received a record total of 136 sixes.

The highest tally by a soloist is seven, by Donald Jackson (Canada) in the World Men's Championship at Prague, Czechoslovakia in 1962; and by Midori Ito (Japan) in the World Ladies' Championships at Paris, France in 1989.

FANTASTIC FEATS

Barrel jumping At Terrebonne, Quebec, Canada, Yvon Jolin cleared 18 barrels on January 25, 1981. The distance of 29 feet 5 inches was a record for a jumper wearing ice skates.

GUINNESS CHALLENGE

How many consecutive strikes did Jeanne Naccarato bowl?
See page 66 for the answer.

FISHING

Oldest existing club The Ellem fishing club was formed by a number of Edinburgh and Berwickshire gentlemen in Scotland in 1829. Its first annual general meeting was held on April 29, 1830.

Largest single catch The largest officially ratified fish ever caught on a rod was a man-eating great white shark (*Carcharodon carcharias*) weighing 2,664 lb and measuring 16 ft 10 in long, caught on a 130-lb test line by Alf Dean at Denial Bay, near Ceduna, South Australia on April 21, 1959. A great white shark weighing 3,388 lb was caught by Clive

FRESHWATER AND SALT WATER ALL-TACKLE CLASS WORLD RECORDS

A selection of records ratified by the International Game Fish Association to January 1, 1995.

Species	Weight	Caught By	Location	Date
Arawana	10 lb 2 oz	Gilberto Fernandes	Brazil	Feb. 3, 1990
Barracuda, great	83 lb 0 oz	K. Hackett	Nigeria	Jan. 13, 1952
Bass, kelp	14 lb 2 oz	Wes Worthing	Catalina Island, Calif.	Nov. 17, 1992
Bass, largemouth	22 lb 4 oz	George W. Perry	Montgomery Lake, Ga.	June 2, 1932
Bass, smallmouth	11 lb 15 oz	David L. Hayes	Dale Hollow Lake, Ky.	July 9, 1955
Bass, striped	78 lb 8 oz	Albert Reynolds	Atlantic City, N.J.	Sept. 21, 1982
Bluefish	31 lb 12 oz	James M. Hussey	Hatteras, N.C.	Jan. 30, 1972
Carp, common	75 lb 11 oz	Leo van der Gugten	France	May 21, 1987
Carp, grass	62 lb 0 oz	Craig Bass	Pinson, Ala.	May 13, 1991
Catfish, blue	109 lb 4 oz	George A. Lijewski	Moncks Corner, S.C.	March 14, 1991
Chub, Bermuda	11 lb 2 oz	Herman Cross	Fort Pierce, Fla.	Jan. 18, 1993
Cod, Atlantic	98 lb 12 oz	Alphonse Bielevich	Isle of Shoals, N.H.	June 8, 1969
Conger	110 lb 8 oz	Hans Clausen	English Channel	Aug. 20, 1991
Eel, American	8 lb 8 oz	Gerald Lapierre	Brewster, Mass.	May 17, 1992
Flounder, summer	22 lb 7 oz	Charles Nappi	Montauk, N.Y.	Sept. 15, 1975
Geelbek	16 lb 15 oz	Ellen Saunders	South Africa	Oct. 5, 1992
Goldfish	3 lb 0 oz	Kenneth Kinsey	Livingston, Tex.	May 8, 1988
Grouper, black	113 lb 6 oz	Donald Bone	Dry Tortugas, Fla.	Jan. 27, 1990
Grouper, broomtail	83 lb 0 oz	Enrique Weisson	Ecuador	June 28, 1992
Haddock	11 lb 11 oz	Jim Mailea	Ogunquit, Me.	Sept. 12, 1991
Halibut, Atlantic	255 lb 4 oz	Sonny Manley	Gloucester, Mass.	July 28, 1989
Halibut, Pacific	368 lb 0 oz	Celia Dueitt	Gustavus, Alaska	July 5, 1991
Houndfish	14 lb 0 oz	Deborah Dunaway	Costa Rica	July 18, 1992
Mackerel, broad barred	17 lb 10 oz	Glen Walker	Australia	Aug. 6, 1992
Marlin, black	1,560 lb 0 oz	Alfred Glassell Jr.	Peru	Aug. 4, 1953
Marlin, blue (Atlantic)	1,402 lb 2 oz	Roberto A. Amorim	Brazil	Feb. 29, 1992
Marlin, blue (Pacific)	1,376 lb 0 oz	Jay de Beaubien	Kona, Hawaii	May 31, 1982
Perch, Nile	191 lb 8 oz	Andy Davison	Kenya	Sept. 5, 1991
Pike, northern	55 lb 1 oz	Lothar Louis	Germany	Oct. 16, 1986

Green off Albany, Western Australia on April 26, 1976 but will remain unratified, as whale meat was used as bait.

In June 1978, a great white shark measuring 20 ft 4 in in length and weighing more than 5,000 lb was harpooned and landed by fishermen in the harbor of San Miguel, Azores.

The largest marine animal killed by hand harpoon was a blue whale 97 ft in length, by Archer Davidson in Twofold Bay, New South Wales, Australia in 1910. Its tail flukes measured 20 ft across and its jawbone 23 ft 4 in.

FRESHWATER AND SALT WATER ALL-TACKLE CLASS WORLD RECORDS

A selection of records ratified by the International Game Fish Association to January 1, 1995.

Species	Weight	Caught By	Location	Date
Piranha, black	3 lb 0 oz	Doug Olander	Brazil	Nov. 23, 1991
Quilback	6 lb 8 oz	Mike Berg	Lake Michigan, Ind.	Jan. 15, 1993
Ray, black	82 lb 10 oz	Peter Blondell	Australia	Jan. 20, 1993
Roosterfish	114 lb 0 oz	Abe Sackheim	Mexico	June 1, 1960
Sailfish, Atlantic	135 lb 5 oz	Ron King	Nigeria	Nov. 10, 1991
Sailfish, Pacific	221 lb 0 oz	C.W. Stewart	Ecuador	Feb. 12, 1947
Salmon, Atlantic	79 lb 2 oz	Henrik Henriksen	Norway	1928
Salmon, chinook	97 lb 4 oz	Les Anderson	Kenai River, Alaska	May 17, 1985
Salmon, pink	13 lb 1 oz	Ray Higaki	Canada	Sept. 23, 1992
Samson fish	80 lb 7 oz	Terry Coote	Australia	Jan. 3, 1993
Shad, American	11 lb 4 oz	Bob Thibodo	S. Hadley, Mass.	May 19, 1986
Shark, blue	437 lb 0 oz	Peter Hyde	Australia	Oct. 2, 1976
Shark, Greenland	1,708 lb 9 oz	Terje Nordtvedt	Norway	Oct. 18, 1987
Shark, hammerhead	991 lb 0 oz	Allen Ogle	Sarasota, Fla.	May 30, 1982
Shark, mako	1,115 lb 0 oz	Patrick Guillanton	Mauritius	Nov. 16, 1988
Shark, narrow tooth	533 lb 8 oz	Gaye Harrison-Armstrong	New Zealand	Jan. 9, 1993
Shark, tiger	1,780 lb 0 oz	Walter Maxwell	Cherry Grove, S.C.	June 14, 1964
Shark, white	2,664 lb 0 oz	Alfred Dean	Australia	April 21, 1959
Snapper, red	46 lb 8 oz	E. Lane Nichols	Destin, Fla.	Oct. 1, 1985
Stingray, southern	229 lb 0 oz	David Anderson	Galveston Bay, Tex.	June 2, 1991
Sturgeon, lake	92 lb 4 oz	James DeOtis	Kettle River, Minn.	Sept. 11, 1986
Sturgeon, white	468 lb 0 oz	Joey Pallotta III	Benica, Calif.	July 9, 1983
Swordfish	1,182 lb 0 oz	L. Marron	Chile	May 7, 1953
Tarpon	283 lb 4 oz	Yvon Sebag	Sierra Leone	April 16, 1991
Trout, brook	14 lb 8 oz	W.J. Cook	Canada	July, 1916
Trout, brown	40 lb 4 oz	Howard L. Collins	Heber Springs, Ark.	May 9, 1992
Trout, rainbow	42 lb 2 oz	David White	Bell Island, Alaska	June 22, 1970
Tuna, bluefin	1,496 lb 0 oz	Ken Fraser	Canada	Oct. 26, 1979
Wahoo	155 lb 8 oz	William Bourne	Bahamas	April 3, 1990

Casting The longest freshwater cast ratified under ICF (International Casting Federation) rules is 574 ft 2 in, by Walter Kummerow (West Germany), for the Bait Distance Double-Handed 30 g event held at Lenzerheide, Switzerland in the 1968 Championships.

At the currently contested weight of 17.7 g, the longest Double-Handed cast is 457 ft ½ in by Kevin Carriero (U.S.) at Toronto, Canada on July 24, 1984.

The longest Fly Distance Double-Handed cast is 319 ft 1 in by Wolfgang Feige (West Germany) at Toronto, Canada on July 23, 1984.

WORLD CHAMPIONSHIP (FRESHWATER) The first freshwater world championships were held in 1957. The event is staged annually.

Most wins (team) France has won the team event 12 times, 1959, 1963–64, 1966, 1968, 1972, 1974–75, 1978–79, 1981 and 1990.

Most wins (individual) Robert Tesse (France) has won the individual title three times, 1959–60 and 1965.

WORLD CHAMPIONSHIP (FLY FISHING) First staged in 1981, this event is held annually.

Most wins (team) Italy has won the team event five times, 1982–84, 1985 and 1992.

Most wins (individual) No fisherman has won the title more than once.

FOOTBAG

A footbag (also sometimes known by the brand names Hackeysack or Sipa Sipa) is a small, pliable, pellet-filled ball-like object with little or no bounce. The concept of the game is to keep the footbag in the air for the longest possible time. Both the time and the number of consecutive kicks are recorded.

ORIGINS The sport of footbag was invented by Mike Marshall and John Stalberger (U.S.) in 1972. The governing body for the sport is the World Footbag Association, based in Golden, Colo.

CONSECUTIVE RECORDS

Men's singles 51,155 kicks by Ted Martin (U.S.) on May 29, 1993 in Mount Prospect, Ill. Martin kept the footbag aloft for 7 hours 1 minute 37 seconds.

Women's singles 15,458 kicks by Francine Beaudry (Canada) on July 28, 1987 in Golden, Colo. Beaudry kept the footbag aloft for 2 hours 35 minutes 13 seconds.

Men's doubles 100,001 kicks by Andy Linder and Ted Martin (both U.S.) on April 9, 1994 in Mount Prospect, Ill. The pair kept the footbag aloft for 15 hours 38 minutes 40 seconds.

FOOT FEAT ■ IN 1994 TED MARTIN CLAIMED YET ANOTHER FOOTBAG RECORD. (HANS MARTIN)

Women's doubles 21,025 kicks by Constance Reed and Marie Elsner (both U.S.) on July 31, 1986. The pair kept the footbag aloft for 3 hours 6 minutes 37 seconds.

FOOTBALL

ORIGINS On November 6, 1869, Princeton and Rutgers staged what is generally regarded as the first intercollegiate football game at New Brunswick, N.J. In October 1873 the Intercollegiate Football Association was formed (Columbia, Princeton, Rutgers and Yale), with the purpose of standardizing rules. At this point football was a modified version of soccer. The first significant move toward today's style of play came when Harvard accepted an invitation to play McGill Univer-

Record Quotable

\ "It's a lonesome walk to the sidelines, especially when thousands of people are cheering your replacement."

—Fran Tarkenton, quoted in
The Sports Curmudgeon by George Sullivan

sity (Montreal, Canada) in a series of three challenge matches, the first being in May 1874, under modified rugby rules. Walter Camp is credited with organizing the basic format of the current game. Between 1880 and 1906, Camp sponsored the concepts of scrimmage lines, 11-man teams, reduction in field size, "downs" and "yards to gain" and a new scoring system.

NATIONAL FOOTBALL LEAGUE (NFL)

ORIGINS William (Pudge) Heffelfinger became the first professional player on November 12, 1892, when he was paid $500 by the Allegheny Athletic Association (AAA) to play for them against the Pittsburgh Athletic Club (PAC). In 1893, PAC signed one of its players, believed to have been Grant Dibert, to the first known professional contract. The first game to be played with admitted professionals participating was played at Latrobe, Pa., on August 31, 1895, with Latrobe YMCA defeating the Jeanette Athletic Club 12–0. Professional leagues existed in Pennsylvania and Ohio at the turn of the 20th century; however, the major breakthrough for professional football was the formation of the American Professional Football Association (APFA), founded in Canton, Ohio on September 17, 1920. Reorganized a number of times, the APFA was renamed the National Football League (NFL) on June 24, 1922. Since 1922, several rival leagues have challenged the NFL, the most significant being the All-America Football Conference (AAFL) and the American Football League (AFL). The AAFL began play in 1946 but after four seasons merged with the NFL for the 1950 season. The AFL challenge was stronger and more acrimonious. Formed in 1959, it had its inaugural season in 1960. The AFL–NFL "war" was halted on June 4, 1966, when an agreement to merge the leagues was announced. The leagues finally merged for the 1970 season, but an AFL–NFL championship game, the Super Bowl, was first played in January 1967.

NFL INDIVIDUAL RECORDS (1922–1994)

ENDURANCE

Most games played (career) George Blanda played in a record 340 games in a record 26 seasons in the NFL, for the Chicago Bears (1949, 1950–

58), the Baltimore Colts (1950), the Houston Oilers (1960–66), and the Oakland Raiders (1967–75).

Most consecutive games played Jim Marshall played 282 consecutive games from 1960–79 for two teams: the Cleveland Browns, 1960, and the Minnesota Vikings, 1961–79.

LONGEST PLAYS

Run from scrimmage Tony Dorsett, Dallas Cowboys, ran through the Minnesota Vikings defense for a 99-yard touchdown on January 3, 1983.

Pass completion The longest pass completion, all for touchdowns, is 99 yards, performed by six quarterbacks: Frank Filchock (to Andy Farkas), Washington Redskins *v.* Pittsburgh Steelers, October 15, 1939; George Izo (to Bobby Mitchell), Washington Redskins *v.* Cleveland Browns, September 15, 1963; Karl Sweetan (to Pat Studstill), Detroit Lions *v.* Baltimore Colts, October 16, 1966; Sonny Jurgensen (to Gerry Allen), Washington Redskins *v.* Chicago Bears, September 15, 1968; Jim Plunkett (to Cliff Branch), Los Angeles Raiders *v.* Washington Redskins, October 2, 1983; Ron Jaworski (to Mike Quick), Philadelphia Eagles *v.* Atlanta Falcons, November 10, 1985.

Pass completion (playoffs) On January 8, 1995, Cowboys quarterback Troy Aikman and receiver Alvin Harper combined for a 94-yard pass play against the Green Bay Packers.

THE SCRAMBLER ■ CONTEMPORARY VETERANS SUCH AS DAN MARINO AND JOE MONTANA STILL HAVEN'T POSED MUCH OF A THREAT TO FRAN TARKENTON'S NUMEROUS CAREER PASSING RECORDS. (ALLSPORT/S. CUNNINGHAM)

Field goal The longest was 63 yards, by Tom Dempsey, New Orleans Saints *v.* Detroit Lions, on November 8, 1970.

Punt Steve O'Neal, New York Jets, boomed a 98-yard punt on September 21, 1969 *v.* Denver Broncos.

Interception return The longest interception return, both for touchdowns, is 103 yards, by two players: Vencie Glenn, San Diego Chargers *v.* Denver Broncos, November 29, 1987; and Louis Oliver, Miami Dolphins *v.* Buffalo Bills, October 4, 1992.

Kickoff return Three players share the record for a kickoff return at 106 yards: Al Carmichael, Green Bay Packers *v.* Chicago Bears, October 7, 1956; Noland Smith, Kansas City Chiefs *v.* Denver Broncos, December 17, 1967; and Roy Green, St. Louis Cardinals *v.* Dallas Cowboys, October 21, 1979. All three players scored touchdowns.

Kickoff return yardage (game) Tyrone Hughes, New Orleans Saints, combined punt and kickoff

TY-RUN ■ ON OCTOBER 23, 1994, TYRONE HUGHES BROKE MARKS FOR PUNT AND KICKOFF RETURNS. (ALLSPORT/JONATHAN DANIEL)

NFL INDIVIDUAL RECORDS

POINTS SCORED

		Player(s)	Team(s)	Date(s)
Game	40	Ernie Nevers	Chicago Cardinals v. Chicago Bears	Nov. 18, 1929
Season	176	Paul Hornung	Green Bay Packers	1960
Career	2,002	George Blanda	Chicago Bears, Baltimore Colts, Houston Oilers, Oakland Raiders	1949–75

TOUCHDOWNS SCORED

Game	6	Ernie Nevers	Chicago Cardinals v. Chicago Bears	Nov. 28, 1929
		Dub Jones	Cleveland Browns v. Chicago Bears	Nov. 25, 1951
		Gale Sayers	Chicago Bears v. San Francisco 49ers	Dec. 12, 1965
Season	24	John Riggins	Washington Redskins	1983
Career	126	Jim Brown	Cleveland Browns	1957–65

PASSING

Yards Gained

Game	554	Norm Van Brocklin	Los Angeles Rams v. New York Yankees	Sept. 28, 1951
Season	5,084	Dan Marino	Miami Dolphins	1984
Career	47,003	Fran Tarkenton	Minnesota Vikings, New York Giants	1961–78

Completions

Game	42	Richard Todd	New York Jets v. San Francisco 49ers	Sept. 21, 1980
Season	404	Warren Moon	Houston Oilers	1991
Career	3,686	Fran Tarkenton	Minnesota Vikings, New York Giants	1961–78

Attempts

Game	68	George Blanda	Houston Oilers v. Buffalo Bills	Nov. 1, 1964
Season	655	Warren Moon	Houston Oilers	1991
Career	6,467	Fran Tarkenton	Minnesota Vikings, New York Giants	1961–78

Touchdowns Thrown

Game	7	Sid Luckman	Chicago Bears v. New York Giants	Nov. 14, 1943
		Adrian Burk	Philadelphia Eagles v. Washington Redskins	Oct. 17, 1954
		George Blanda	Houston Oilers v. New York Titans	Nov. 19, 1961
		Y. A. Tittle	New York Giants v. Washington Redskins	Oct. 28, 1962
		Joe Kapp	Minnesota Vikings v. Baltimore Colts	Sept. 28, 1969
Season	48	Dan Marino	Miami Dolphins	1984
Career	342	Fran Tarkenton	Minnesota Vikings, New York Giants	1961–78

NFL INDIVIDUAL RECORDS

PASSING (cont.)

Average Yards Gained

		Player(s)	Team(s)	Date(s)
Game (min. 20 attempts)	18.58	Sammy Baugh	Washington Redskins v. Boston Yanks (24–446)	Oct. 31, 1948
Season (qualifiers)	11.17	Tommy O'Connell	Cleveland Browns (110–1,229)	1957
Career (min. 1,500 attempts)	8.63	Otto Graham	Cleveland Browns (1,565–13,499)	1950–55

PASS RECEIVING

Receptions

Game	18	Tom Fears	Los Angeles Rams v. Green Bay Packers	Dec. 3, 1950
Season	112	Sterling Sharpe	Green Bay Packers	1993
Career	934	Art Monk	Washington Redskins, New York Jets	1980–95

Yards Gained

Game	336	Willie Anderson	Los Angeles Rams v. New Orleans Saints	Nov. 26, 1989*
Season	1,746	Charley Hennigan	Houston Oilers	1961
Career	14,004	James Lofton	Green Bay Packers, Los Angeles Raiders, Buffalo Bills, Los Angeles Rams, Philadelphia Eagles	1978–95

Touchdown Receptions

Game	5	Bob Shaw	Chicago Cardinals v. Baltimore Colts	Oct. 2, 1950
		Kellen Winslow	San Diego Chargers v. Oakland Raiders	Nov. 22, 1981
		Jerry Rice	San Francisco 49ers v. Atlanta Falcons	Oct. 14, 1990
Season	22	Jerry Rice	San Francisco 49ers	1987
Career	131	Jerry Rice	San Francisco 49ers	1985–95

Average Yards Gained

Game (min. 3 catches)	60.67	Bill Groman	Houston Oilers v. Denver Broncos (3–182)	Nov. 20, 1960
		Homer Jones	New York Giants v. Washington Redskins (3–182)	Dec. 12, 1965
Season (min. 24 catches)	32.58	Don Currivan	Boston Yanks (24–782)	1947
Career (min. 200 catches)	22.26	Homer Jones	New York Giants, Cleveland Browns (224–4,986)	1964–70

---

* Overtime

returns for a record total 347 yards against the Los Angeles Rams on October 23, 1994. In the same game, Hughes also set the mark for kickoff return yardage with 304.

Missed field goal return   Al Nelson, Philadelphia Eagles, returned a Dallas Cowboys' missed field goal 101 yards for a touchdown on September 26, 1971.

Punt return   Four players share the record for the longest punt return at 98 yards: Gil LeFebvre, Cincinnati Reds v. Brooklyn Dodgers, December 3, 1933; Charlie West, Minnesota Vikings v. Washington Redskins, November 3, 1968; Dennis Morgan, Dallas Cowboys v. St. Louis Cardinals, October 13, 1974; Terance Mathis, New York Jets v. Dallas Cowboys, November 4, 1990. All four players scored touchdowns.

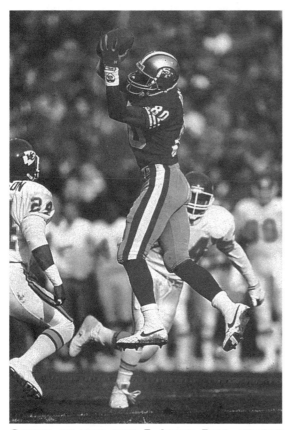

CATCH OF THE DAY ■ JERRY RICE, RECORD HOLDER FOR MOST TOUCHDOWN RECEPTIONS IN A SEASON AND LIFETIME, DISPLAYING HIS FLAIR FOR ACROBATICS. (ALLSPORT/O. GREULE, JR.)

Fumble return   Jack Tatum, Oakland Raiders, returned a Green Bay Packers fumble 104 yards for a touchdown on September 24, 1972.

CONSECUTIVE RECORDS

Scoring (games) 186, Jim Breech, Oakland Raiders, 1979; Cincinnati Bengals, 1980–92.

Scoring touchdowns (games) 18, Lenny Moore, Baltimore Colts, 1963–65.

Points after touchdown (PATs), consecutive kicked 234, Tommy Davis, San Francisco 49ers, 1959–65.

Field goals, consecutive kicked 29, John Carney, San Diego Chargers, 1992–93.

Field goals (games) 31, Fred Cox, Minnesota Vikings, 1968–70.

100+ yards rushing (games) 11, Marcus Allen, Los Angeles Raiders, 1985–86.

200+ yards rushing (games) 2, by two players: O.J. Simpson, Buffalo Bills, 1973, 1976; Earl Campbell, Houston Oilers, 1980.

Touchdown passes (games) 47, Johnny Unitas, Baltimore Colts, 1956–60.

Touchdown rushes (games) 13, by two players: John Riggins, Washington Redskins, 1982–83; George Rogers, Washington Redskins, 1985–86.

Touchdown receptions (games) 13, Jerry Rice, San Francisco 49ers, 1986–87.

Passes completed (consecutive) 22, Joe Montana, San Francisco 49ers v. Cleveland Browns, November 29, 1987 (5); v. Green Bay Packers, December 6, 1987 (17).

300+ yards passing (games) 5, Joe Montana, San Francisco 49ers, 1982.

Four or more touchdown passes (games) 4, Dan Marino, Miami Dolphins, 1984.

Pass receptions (games) 180, by Art Monk, Washington Redskins, 1980–93 and New York Jets, 1994.

NFL TEAM RECORDS

WINS AND LOSSES

Most consecutive games won The Chicago Bears won 17 straight regular-season games, covering the 1933–34 seasons.

ALLSPORT/SCOTT HALLERAN

ART MONK

I still enjoy the game—I've always loved it," Art Monk of the New York Jets says. "As long as I can contribute to the team, I'll keep playing." Monk attributes his prosperity to determination. "I don't really think about my accomplishments, I just go out there and do the best I can. Never let anyone say you can't achieve your dreams."

Thought by many to be the most accomplished receiver ever to grace the football field, Monk holds the NFL record for most career pass receptions with 934. He is also the new record holder for most consecutive games with a reception. "Faith is the key to success. Discipline and sacrifice, it's the little things that give you the edge."

Although his reception record is impressive, Monk does not rest on his laurels. "I never let it all go to my head," he says. "I always aim to give 100% in every game. I've done all I can to use the talents I was given to make myself the best I can be."

Monk's passion since childhood has always been football. "When I was a kid we used to play all different sports in the neighborhood . . . stickball, basketball . . . but football was always my love. I knew early on that this was what I wanted to do.

"There is one thing that I'd like to achieve," Monk admits. "I don't know if it will happen, but I'd really like to catch 1,000 balls." With his talent and determination, Art Monk's dream just might come true.

NFL INDIVIDUAL RECORDS

RUSHING

Yards Gained

		Player(s)	Team(s)	Date(s)
Game	275	Walter Payton	Chicago Bears v. Minnesota Vikings	Nov. 20, 1977
Season	2,105	Eric Dickerson	Los Angeles Rams	1984
Career	16,726	Walter Payton	Chicago Bears	1975–87

Attempts

Game	45	Jamie Morris	Washington Redskins v. Cincinnati Bengals	Dec. 17, 1988*
Season	407	James Wilder	Tampa Bay Buccaneers	1984
Career	3,838	Walter Payton	Chicago Bears	1975–87

Touchdowns Scored

Game	6	Ernie Nevers	Chicago Cardinals v. Chicago Bears	Nov. 28, 1929
Season	24	John Riggins	Washington Redskins	1983
Career	110	Walter Payton	Chicago Bears	1975–87

Average Yards Gained

Game (min. 10 attempts)	17.09	Marion Mottley	Cleveland Browns v. Pittsburgh Steelers (11–188)	Oct. 29, 1950
Season (qualifiers)	8.44	Beattie Feathers	Chicago Bears (119–1,004)	1934
Career (min. 700 attempts)	5.22	Jim Brown	Cleveland Browns (2,359–12,312)	1957–65

INTERCEPTIONS

Game	4	16 players have achieved this feat.		
Season	14	Dick "Night Train" Lane	Los Angeles Rams	1952
Career	81	Paul Krause	Washington Redskins, Minnesota Vikings	1964–79

Interceptions Returned for Touchdowns

Game	2	18 players have achieved this feat.		
Season	4	Ken Houston	Houston Oilers	1971
		Jim Kearney	Kansas City Chiefs	1972
		Eric Allen	Philadelphia Eagles	1993
Career	9	Ken Houston	Houston Oilers, Washington Redskins	1967–80

---

* Overtime

NFL INDIVIDUAL RECORDS

SACKS
(compiled since 1982)

		Player(s)	Team(s)	Date(s)
Game	7	Derrick Thomas	Kansas City v. Seattle Seahawks	Nov. 11, 1990
Season	22	Mark Gastineau	New York Jets	1984
Career	145	Reggie White	Philadelphia Eagles, Green Bay Packers	1985–95

KICKING

Field Goals

Game	7	Jim Bakken	St. Louis Cardinals v. Pittsburgh Steelers	Sept. 24, 1967
		Rich Karlis	Minnesota Vikings v. Los Angeles Rams	Nov. 5, 1989*
Season	35	Ali Haji-Sheikh	New York Giants	1983
Career	373	Jan Stenerud	Kansas City Chiefs, Green Bay Packers, Minnesota Vikings	1967–85

Highest Percentage

Game	100.00	This has been achieved by many kickers. The most field goals kicked with no misses is 7, by Rich Karlis, Minnesota Vikings v. Los Angeles Rams on Nov. 5, 1989 in an overtime game.		
Season (qualifiers)	100.00	Tony Zendejas	Los Angeles Rams (17–17)	1991
Career (min. 100 field goals)	80.41	Nick Lowery	New England Patriots, Kansas City Chiefs (349–434)	1978, 1980–94

Field Goals 50 or More Yards

Game	2	This record has been achieved 24 times; Nick Lowery, Kansas City Chiefs, is the only kicker to have done it 3 times.		
Season	6	Dean Biasucci	Indianapolis Colts	1988
Career	21	Morten Andersen	New Orleans Saints	1982–92

Points After Touchdown (PATs)

Game	9	Pat Harder	Chicago Cardinals v. New York Giants	Oct. 17, 1948
		Bob Waterfield	Los Angeles Rams v. Baltimore Colts	Oct. 22, 1950
		Charlie Gogolak	Washington Redskins v. New York Giants	Nov. 27, 1966
Season	66	Uwe von Schamann	Miami Dolphins	1984
Career	943	George Blanda	Chicago Bears, Baltimore Colts, Houston Oilers, Oakland Raiders	1949–75

* Overtime

Most consecutive games unbeaten The Canton Bulldogs played 25 regular-season games without a defeat, covering the 1921–23 seasons. The Bulldogs won 22 games and tied three.

Most games won in a season Two teams have compiled 15-win seasons: the San Francisco 49ers in 1984, and the Chicago Bears in 1985.

Perfect season The only team to win all its games in one season was the 1972 Miami Dolphins. The

Dolphins won 14 regular-season games and then won three playoff games, including Super Bowl VII, to complete the only perfect season in NFL history.

Most consecutive games lost This most undesirable of records is held by the Tampa Bay Buccaneers, who lost 26 straight games from 1976–77.

Most games lost in a season Four teams hold the dubious honor of having lost 15 games in one

NFL INDIVIDUAL RECORDS

PUNTING

Punts

		Player(s)	Team(s)	Date(s)
Game	15	John Teltschik	Philadelphia Eagles v. New York Giants	Dec. 6, 1987*
Season	114	Bob Parsons	Chicago Bears	1981
Career	1,154	Dave Jennings	New York Giants, New York Jets	1974–87

Average Yards Gained

Game (min. 4 punts)	61.75	Bob Cifers	Detroit Lions v. Chicago Bears (4–247)	Nov. 24, 1946
Season (qualifiers)	51.40	Sammy Baugh	Washington Redskins (35–1,799)	1940
Career (min. 300 punts)	45.10	Sammy Baugh	Washington Redskins (338–15,245)	1937–52

SPECIAL TEAMS

Punt Returns for Touchdowns

Game	2	Jack Christiansen	Detroit Lions v. Los Angeles Rams	Oct. 14, 1951
		Jack Christiansen	Detroit Lions v. Green Bay Packers	Nov. 22, 1951
		Dick Christy	New York Titans v. Denver Broncos	Sept. 24, 1961
		Rick Upchurch	Denver Broncos v. Cleveland Browns	Sept. 26, 1976
		LeRoy Irvin	Los Angeles Rams v. Atlanta Falcons	Oct. 11, 1981
		Vai Sikahema	St. Louis Cardinals v. Tampa Bay Buccaneers	Dec. 21, 1986
		Todd Kinchen	Los Angeles Rams v. Atlanta Falcons	Dec. 27, 1992
		Eric Metcalf	Cleveland Browns v. Pittsburgh Steelers	Oct. 24, 1993
Season	4	Jack Christiansen	Detroit Lions	1951
		Rick Upchurch	Denver Broncos	1976
Career	8	Jack Christiansen	Detroit Lions	1951–58
		Rick Upchurch	Denver Broncos	1975–83

Kickoff Returns for Touchdowns

Game	2	Timmy Brown	Philadelphia Eagles v. Dallas Cowboys	Nov. 6, 1966
		Travis Williams	Green Bay Packers v. Cleveland Browns	Nov. 12, 1967
		Ron Brown	Los Angeles Rams v. Green Bay Packers	Nov. 24, 1985
		Tyrone Hughes	New Orleans Saints v. Los Angeles Rams	Oct. 23, 1994
Season	4	Travis Williams	Green Bay Packers	1967
		Cecil Turner	Chicago Bears	1970
Career	6	Ollie Matson	Chicago Cardinals, Los Angeles Rams, Detroit Lions, Philadelphia Eagles	1952–64
		Gale Sayers	Chicago Bears	1965–71
		Travis Williams	Green Bay Packers, Los Angeles Rams	1967–71

* Overtime
Source: NFL

season: the New Orleans Saints in 1980, the Dallas Cowboys in 1989, the New England Patriots in 1990 and the Indianapolis Colts in 1991.

SCORING

Most points scored, game The Washington Redskins scored 72 points *v.* the New York Giants on November 27, 1966 to set the single-game NFL regular-season record for most points scored by one team.

Highest aggregate score On November 27, 1966, the Washington Redskins defeated the New York Giants 72–41 in Washington, D.C. The Redskins' total was an NFL record for most points (see above).

Largest deficit overcome On January 3, 1993, the Buffalo Bills, playing at home in the AFC Wild Card game, trailed the Houston Oilers 35-3 with 28 minutes remaining. The Bills rallied to score 35 unanswered points and take the lead with 3:08 left. The Bills eventually won the game in overtime, overcoming a deficit of 32 points—the largest in NFL history.

TRADES

Largest in NFL history Based on the number of players and/or draft choices involved, the largest trade in NFL history is 15, which has happened twice. On March 26, 1953 the Baltimore Colts and the Cleveland Browns exchanged 15 players; and on January 28, 1971, the Washington Redskins and the Los Angeles Rams completed the transfer of seven players and eight draft choices.

COACHES

Most seasons 40, George Halas, Decatur/Chicago Staleys/Chicago Bears: 1920–29, 1933–42, 1946–55, 1958–67.

Most wins (including playoffs) 337, by Don Shula, Baltimore Colts, 1963–69; Miami Dolphins, 1970–94.

NFL CHAMPIONSHIP

The first NFL championship was awarded in 1920 to the Akron Pros, as the team with the best record. From 1920 to 1931, the championship was based on regular-season records. The first championship game was played in 1932.

In 1966, the National Football League (NFL) and the American Football League (AFL) agreed to merge their competing leagues to form an expanded NFL. Regular-season play would not begin

until 1970, but the two leagues agreed to stage an annual AFL–NFL world championship game beginning in January 1967. The proposed championship game was dubbed the Super Bowl, and in 1969 the NFL officially recognized the title.

Most NFL titles The Green Bay Packers have won 11 NFL championships: 1929–31, 1936, 1939, 1944, 1961–62, 1965, and Super Bowls I and II (1966 and 1967 seasons).

THE SUPER BOWL

Super Bowl I was played on January 15, 1967, with the Green Bay Packers (NFL) defeating the Kansas City Chiefs (AFL), 35–10.

Most wins In 1995, the San Francisco 49ers won their fifth Super Bowl. The 49ers won Super Bowls XVI, XIX, XXIII, XXIV and XXIX.

Consecutive wins Five teams have won Super Bowls in successive years: the Green Bay Packers, I and II; the Miami Dolphins, VII and VIII; the Pittsburgh Steelers (twice), IX and X, and XIII and XIV; the San Francisco 49ers, XXIII and XXIV; and the Dallas Cowboys, XXVII and XXVIII.

Most appearances The Dallas Cowboys have played in seven Super Bowls: V, VI, X, XII, XIII, XXVII and XXVIII. The Cowboys have won four games and lost three.

SCORING RECORDS

Most points scored The San Francisco 49ers scored 55 points *v.* the Denver Broncos in Super Bowl XXIV.

Highest aggregate score The highest aggregate score is 75 points, set when the San Francisco 49ers beat the San Diego Chargers 49–26 in Super Bowl XXIX.

Greatest margin of victory The greatest margin of victory is 45 points, set by the San Francisco 49ers when they defeated the Denver Broncos 55–10 in Super Bowl XXIV.

Most MVP awards Joe Montana, quarterback of the San Francisco 49ers, has been voted the Super Bowl MVP on a record three occasions, XVI, XIX and XXIV.

COACHES

Most wins Chuck Noll led the Pittsburgh Steelers to four Super Bowl titles, IX, X, XIII and XIV.

NFL CHAMPIONS (1920–1957)

Season	Winner	Loser	Score
1920	Akron Pros	—	—
1921	Chicago Staleys	—	—
1922	Canton Bulldogs	—	—
1923	Canton Bulldogs	—	—
1924	Cleveland Bulldogs	—	—
1925	Chicago Cardinals	—	—
1926	Frankford Yellowjackets	—	—
1927	New York Giants	—	—
1928	Providence Steam Roller	—	—
1929	Green Bay Packers	—	—
1930	Green Bay Packers	—	—
1931	Green Bay Packers	—	—
1932	Chicago Bears	Portsmouth Spartans	9–0
1933	Chicago Bears	New York Giants	23–21
1934	New York Giants	Chicago Bears	30–13
1935	Detroit Lions	New York Giants	26–7
1936	Green Bay Packers	Boston Redskins	21–6
1937	Washington Redskins	Chicago Bears	28–21
1938	New York Giants	Green Bay Packers	23–17
1939	Green Bay Packers	New York Giants	27–0
1940	Chicago Bears	Washington Redskins	73–0
1941	Chicago Bears	New York Giants	37–9
1942	Washington Redskins	Chicago Bears	14–6
1943	Chicago Bears	Washington Redskins	41–21
1944	Green Bay Packers	New York Giants	14–7
1945	Cleveland Rams	Washington Redskins	15–14
1946	Chicago Bears	New York Giants	24–14
1947	Chicago Cardinals	Philadelphia Eagles	28–21
1948	Philadelphia Eagles	Chicago Cardinals	7–0
1949	Philadelphia Eagles	Los Angeles Rams	14–0
1950	Cleveland Browns	Los Angeles Rams	30–28
1951	Los Angeles Rams	Cleveland Browns	24–17
1952	Detroit Lions	Cleveland Browns	17–7
1953	Detroit Lions	Cleveland Browns	17–16
1954	Cleveland Browns	Detroit Lions	56–10
1955	Cleveland Browns	Los Angeles Rams	38–14
1956	New York Giants	Chicago Bears	47–7
1957	Detroit Lions	Cleveland Browns	59–14

NFL CHAMPIONS (1958–1965)

Season	Winner	Loser	Score
1958	Baltimore Colts	New York Giants	23–17*
1959	Baltimore Colts	New York Giants	31–16
1960	Philadelphia Eagles	Green Bay Packers	17–13
1961	Green Bay Packers	New York Giants	37–0
1962	Green Bay Packers	New York Giants	16–7
1963	Chicago Bears	New York Giants	14–10
1964	Cleveland Browns	Baltimore Colts	27–0
1965	Green Bay Packers	Cleveland Browns	23–12

* Overtime

SUPER BOWL RESULTS (1967–1995)

Bowl	Date	Winner	Loser	Score	Site
I	Jan. 15, 1967	Green Bay Packers	Kansas City Chiefs	35–10	Los Angeles, Calif.
II	Jan. 14, 1968	Green Bay Packers	Oakland Raiders	33–14	Miami, Fla.
III	Jan. 12, 1969	New York Jets	Baltimore Colts	16–7	Miami, Fla.
IV	Jan. 11, 1970	Kansas City Chiefs	Minnesota Vikings	23–7	New Orleans, La.
V	Jan. 17, 1971	Baltimore Colts	Dallas Cowboys	16–13	Miami, Fla.
VI	Jan. 16, 1972	Dallas Cowboys	Miami Dolphins	24–3	New Orleans, La.
VII	Jan. 14, 1973	Miami Dolphins	Washington Redskins	14–7	Los Angeles, Calif.
VIII	Jan. 13, 1974	Miami Dolphins	Minnesota Vikings	24–7	Houston, Tex.
IX	Jan. 12, 1975	Pittsburgh Steelers	Minnesota Vikings	16–6	New Orleans, La.
X	Jan. 18, 1976	Pittsburgh Steelers	Dallas Cowboys	21–17	Miami, Fla.
XI	Jan. 9, 1977	Oakland Raiders	Minnesota Vikings	32–14	Pasadena, Calif.
XII	Jan. 15, 1978	Dallas Cowboys	Denver Broncos	27–10	New Orleans, La.
XIII	Jan. 21, 1979	Pittsburgh Steelers	Dallas Cowboys	35–31	Miami, Fla.
XIV	Jan. 20, 1980	Pittsburgh Steelers	Los Angeles Rams	31–19	Pasadena, Calif.
XV	Jan. 25, 1981	Oakland Raiders	Philadelphia Eagles	27–10	New Orleans, La.
XVI	Jan. 24, 1982	San Francisco 49ers	Cincinnati Bengals	26–21	Pontiac, Mich.
XVII	Jan. 30, 1983	Washington Redskins	Miami Dolphins	27–17	Pasadena, Calif.
XVIII	Jan. 22, 1984	Los Angeles Raiders	Washington Redskins	38–9	Tampa, Fla.
XIX	Jan. 20, 1985	San Francisco 49ers	Miami Dolphins	38–16	Stanford. Calif.
XX	Jan. 26, 1986	Chicago Bears	New England Patriots	46–10	New Orleans, La.
XXI	Jan. 25, 1987	New York Giants	Denver Broncos	39–20	Pasadena, Calif.
XXII	Jan. 31, 1988	Washington Redskins	Denver Broncos	42–10	San Diego, Calif.
XXIII	Jan. 22, 1989	San Francisco 49ers	Cincinnati Bengals	20–16	Miami, Fla.
XXIV	Jan. 28, 1990	San Francisco 49ers	Denver Broncos	55–10	New Orleans, La.
XXV	Jan. 27, 1991	New York Giants	Buffalo Bills	20–19	Tampa, Fla.
XXVI	Jan. 25, 1992	Washington Redskins	Buffalo Bills	37–24	Minneapolis, Minn.
XXVII	Jan. 31, 1993	Dallas Cowboys	Buffalo Bills	52–17	Pasadena, Calif.
XXVIII	Jan. 30, 1994	Dallas Cowboys	Buffalo Bills	30–13	Atlanta, Ga.
XXIX	Jan. 29, 1995	San Francisco 49ers	San Diego Chargers	49–26	Miami, Fla.

SUPER BOWL RECORDS

POINTS SCORED

		Player(s)	Team(s)	Super Bowl
Game	18	Roger Craig	San Francisco 49ers	XIX
		Jerry Rice	San Francisco 49ers	XXIV, XXIX
Career	42	Jerry Rice	San Francisco 49ers	XXIII, XXIV, XXIX

TOUCHDOWNS SCORED

Game	3	Roger Craig	San Francisco 49ers	XIX
		Jerry Rice	San Francisco 49ers	XXIV, XXIX
		Ricky Watters	San Francisco 49ers	XXIX
Career	7	Jerry Rice	San Francisco 49ers	XXIII, XXIV, XXIX

PASSING

Yards Gained

Game	357	Joe Montana	San Francisco 49ers	XXIII
Career	1,142	Joe Montana	San Francisco 49ers	XVI, XIX, XXIII, XXIV

Completions

Game	29	Dan Marino	Miami Dolphins	XIX
Career	83	Joe Montana	San Francisco 49ers	XVI, XIX, XXIII, XXIV

Touchdowns Thrown

Game	6	Steve Young	San Francisco 49ers	XXIX
Career	11	Joe Montana	San Francisco 49ers	XVI, XIX, XXIII, XXIV

Highest Completion Percentage

Game (min. 20 attempts)	88.0	Phil Simms	New York Giants (22–25)	XXI
Career (min. 40 attempts)	68.0	Joe Montana	San Francisco 49ers (83–122)	XVI, XIX, XXIII, XXIV

PASS RECEIVING

Receptions

Game	11	Dan Ross	Cincinnati Bengals	XVI
		Jerry Rice	San Francisco 49ers	XXIII
Career	28	Jerry Rice	San Francisco 49ers	XXIII, XXIV, XXIX

SUPER BOWL RECORDS

PASS RECEIVING (cont.)

		Player(s)	Team(s)	Super Bowl
		Yards Gained		
Game	215	Jerry Rice	San Francisco 49ers	XXIII
Career	512	Jerry Rice	San Francisco 49ers	XXIII, XXIV, XXIX
		Touchdown Receptions		
Game	3	Jerry Rice	San Francisco 49ers	XXIV, XXIX
Career	7	Jerry Rice	San Francisco 49ers	XXIII, XXIV, XXIX

RUSHING
Yards Gained

Game	204	Timmy Smith	Washington Redskins	XXII
Career	354	Franco Harris	Pittsburgh Steelers	IX, X, XIII, XIV

Touchdowns Scored

Game	2	This feat has been achieved by 10 players		
Career	4	Franco Harris	Pittsburgh Steelers	IX, X, XIII, XIV
		Thurman Thomas	Buffalo Bills	XXV–XXVIII

Interceptions

Game	3	Rod Martin	Oakland Raiders	XV
Career	3	Chuck Howley	Dallas Cowboys	V, VI
		Rod Martin	Oakland/Los Angeles Raiders	XV, XVIII

FIELD GOALS KICKED

Game	4	Don Chandler	Green Bay Packers	II
		Ray Wersching	San Francisco 49ers	XVI
Career	5	Ray Wersching	San Francisco 49ers	XVI, XIX

LONGEST PLAYS

Run from Scrimmage	74 yards	Marcus Allen	Los Angeles Raiders	XVIII
Pass Completion	80 yards	Jim Plunkett	(to Kenny King) Oakland Raiders	XV
		Doug Williams	(to Ricky Sanders) Washington Redskins	XXII
Field Goal	54 yards	Steve Christie	Buffalo Bills	XXVIII
Kickoff Return	98 yards	Fulton Walker	Miami Dolphins	XVII
		Andre Coleman	San Diego Chargers	XXIX
Punt	63 yards	Lee Johnson	Cincinnati Bengals	XXIII

Source: NFL

Most appearances Don Shula has been the head coach of six Super Bowl teams: the Baltimore Colts, III; the Miami Dolphins, VI, VII, VIII, XVII and XIX. He won two games and lost four.

COLLEGE FOOTBALL (NCAA)

ORIGINS At the turn of the 20th century, football's popularity was rising rapidly; however, with the increased participation came a rise in serious injuries and even some deaths. Many institutions, alarmed at the violent nature of the game, called for controls to be established.

In December 1905, 13 universities, led by Chancellor Henry M. MacCracken of New York University, outlined a plan to establish an organization to standardize playing rules. On December 28, the Intercollegiate Athletic Association of the United States (IAAUS) was founded in New York City with 62 charter members. The IAAUS was officially constituted on March 31, 1906, and was renamed the National Collegiate Athletic Association (NCAA) in 1910.

The NCAA first began to keep statistics on football in 1937, and the records in this section date from that time. In 1973, the NCAA introduced a classification system creating Divisions I, II, and III to identify levels of college play. In 1978, Division I was subdivided into I-A and I-AA.

INDIVIDUAL RECORDS

NCAA OVERALL CAREER RECORDS (DIVISIONS I-A, I-AA, II AND III)

POINTS SCORED

Game Three players have scored 48 points in an NCAA game: Junior Wolf, Panhandle State (Div.

II), set the mark on November 8, 1958 v. St. Mary's (Kans.); Paul Zaeske, North Park (Div. II), tied the record on October 12, 1968 v. North Central; Howard Griffith, Illinois (Div I-A), created a triumvirate on September 22, 1990.

Season The most points scored in a season is 234, by Barry Sanders, Oklahoma State (Div. I-A) in 1988, all from touchdowns, 37 rushing and two receptions.

Career The career record for most points scored is 474, by Joe Dudek, Plymouth State (Div. III), 1982–85. Dudek scored 79 touchdowns, 76 rushing and three receptions.

RUSHING (YARDS GAINED)

Game Carey Bender, Coe College (Div. III) rushed for an NCAA single-game record 417 yards v. Grinnell on October 9, 1993.

Season The most yards gained in a season is 2,628, by Barry Sanders, Oklahoma State (Div. I-A), in 1988. Sanders played in 11 games and carried the ball 344 times for an average gain of 7.64 yards per carry.

Career The career record for most yards gained is 6,320, by Johnny Bailey, Texas A&I (Div. II), 1986–89. Bailey carried the ball 885 times for an average gain of 7.14 yards per carry.

PASSING (YARDS GAINED)

Game David Klingler, Houston (Div. I-A) threw for an NCAA single-game record 716 yards v. Arizona State on December 2, 1990.

Season The single-season NCAA mark is held by Ty Detmer, BYU, who threw for 5,188 yards in 1990.

Career The career passing record is 15,031 yards, set by Ty Detmer, BYU (Div. I-A).

RECEIVING (YARDS GAINED)

Game The most yards gained from pass receptions in a single game is 370, by two players: Barry Wagner, Alabama A&M (Div. II), v. Clark Atlanta on November 4, 1989; Michael Lerch, Princeton (Div. 1-AA), v. Brown on October 12, 1991.

Season The single-season NCAA record is 1,876 yards, by Chris George, Glenville State (Div. II). George caught 117 passes for an average gain of 16.03 yards.

Career The all-time NCAA mark is held by Jerry Rice, Mississippi Valley (Div. I-AA), 1981–84. He gained 4,693 yards on 301 catches (also an NCAA career record), for an average gain of 15.6 yards.

FIELD GOALS (MOST MADE)

Game Goran Lingmerth, Northern Arizona (Div. I-AA) booted 8 out of 8 field goals v. Idaho on October 25, 1986. The distances were 39, 18, 20, 33, 46, 27, 22 and 35 yards each.

Season The most kicks made in a season is 29, by John Lee, UCLA (Div. I-A) from 33 attempts in 1984.

Career The NCAA all-time career record is 80, by Jeff Jaeger, Washington (Div. I-A) from 99 attempts, 1983–86.

LONGEST PLAYS (DIVISION I-A)

Run from scrimmage 99 yards, by four players: Gale Sayers (Kansas v. Nebraska), 1963; Max Anderson (Arizona State v. Wyoming), 1967; Ralph

OFFENSIVE POWER ■ DAVID KLINGLER, UNIVERSITY OF HOUSTON, FADING BACK TO PASS. (UNIVERSITY OF HOUSTON)

NCAA DIVISION I–A RECORDS

SCORING

Points Scored

		Player(s)	Team(s)	Date(s)
Game	48	Howard Griffith	Illinois v. Southern Illinois (8 TDs)	Sept. 22, 1990
Season	234	Barry Sanders	Oklahoma State (39 TDs)	1988
Career	423	Roman Anderson	Houston (70 FGs, 213 PATs)	1988–91

Touchdowns Scored

Game	8	Howard Griffith	Illinois v. Southern Illinois (all rushing)	Sept. 22, 1990
Season	39	Barry Sanders	Oklahoma State	1988
Career	65	Anthony Thompson	Indiana (64 rushing, 1 reception)	1986–89

2-Point Conversions

Game	6	Jim Pilot	New Mexico State v. Hardin-Simmons	Nov. 25, 1961
Season	6	Pat McCarthy	Holy Cross	1960
		Jim Pilot	New Mexico State	1961
		Howard Twilley	Tulsa	1964
Career	13	Pat McCarthy	Holy Cross	1960–62

PASSING

Touchdown Passes

Game	11	David Klingler	Houston v. Eastern Washington	Nov. 17, 1990
Season	54	David Klingler	Houston	1990
Career	121	Ty Detmer	BYU	1988–91

Yards Gained

Game	716	David Klingler	Houston v. Arizona State	Dec. 1, 1990
Season	5,188	Ty Detmer	BYU	1990
Career	15,049	Steve McNair	Alcorn State	1991–94

Completions

Game	48	David Klingler	Houston v. SMU	Oct. 20, 1990
Season	374	David Klingler	Houston	1990
Career	958	Ty Detmer	BYU	1988–91

Attempts

Game	79	Matt Vogler	TCU v. Houston	Nov. 3, 1990
Season	643	David Klingler	Houston	1990
Career	1,530	Ty Detmer	BYU	1988–91

NCAA DIVISION I–A RECORDS

PASSING (cont.)

Average Yards Gained per Attempt

		Player(s)	Team(s)	Date(s)
Game (min. 40 attempts)	14.07	John Walsh	BYU v. Utah State (44 for 619 yards)	Oct. 30, 1993
Season (min. 400 attempts)	11.07	Ty Detmer	BYU (412 for 4,560 yards)	1989
Career (min. 1,000 attempts)	9.82	Ty Detmer	BYU (1,530 for 15,031 yards)	1988–91

PASS RECEIVING

Touchdown Receptions

Game	6	Tim Delaney	San Diego State v. New Mexico State	Nov. 15, 1969
Season	22	Emmanuel Hazard	Houston	1989
Career	43	Aaron Turner	Pacific (Cal.)	1989–92

Receptions

Game	22	Jay Miller	BYU v. New Mexico	Nov. 3, 1973
Season	142	Emmanuel Hazard	Houston	1989
Career	266	Aaron Turner	Pacific (Cal.)	1989–92

Yards Gained

Game	349	Chuck Hughes	UTEP v. North Texas	Sept. 18, 1965
Season	1,779	Howard Twilley	Tulsa	1965
Career	4,345	Aaron Turner	Pacific (Cal.)	1989–92

Average Yards Gained per Reception

Game (min. 5 catches)	52.6	Alexander Wright	Auburn v. Pacific (5 for 263 yards)	Sept. 9, 1989
Season (min. 50 catches)	24.4	Henry Ellard	Fresno State (62 for 1,510 yards)	1982
Career (min. 105 catches)	22.0	Herman Moore	Virginia (114 for 2,504 yards)	1988–90

NCAA DIVISION I–A RECORDS

RUSHING

Yards Gained

		Player(s)	Team(s)	Date(s)
Game	396	Tony Sands	Kansas v. Missouri	Nov. 23, 1991
Season	2,628	Barry Sanders	Oklahoma State	1988
Career	6,082	Tony Dorsett	Pittsburgh	1973–76

Attempts

Game	58	Tony Sands	Kansas v. Missouri	Nov. 23, 1991
Season	403	Marcus Allen	Southern Cal.	1981
Career	1,215	Steve Bartalo	Colorado State	1983–86

Average Yards Gained per Attempt

Game (min. 15 rushes)	21.40	Tony Jeffery	TCU v. Tulane (16 for 343 yards)	Sept. 13, 1986
Season (min. 250 rushes)	7.81	Mike Rozier	Nebraska (275 for 2,148 yards)	1983
Career (min. 600 rushes)	7.16	Mike Rozier	Nebraska (668 for 4,780 yards)	1981–83

Touchdowns Scored

Game	8	Howard Griffith	Illinois v. Southern Illinois	Sept. 22, 1990
Season	37	Barry Sanders	Oklahoma State	1988
Career	64	Anthony Thompson	Indiana	1986–89

TOTAL OFFENSE (Rushing plus Passing)

Yards Gained

Game	732	David Klingler	Houston v. Arizona State (716 passing, 16 rushing)	Dec. 2, 1990
Season	5,221	David Klingler	Houston (81 rushing, 5,140 passing)	1990
Career	14,665	Ty Detmer	BYU (–366 rushing, 15,031 passing)	1988–91

Interceptions

Game	5	Lee Cook	Oklahoma State v. Detroit	Nov. 28, 1942
		Walt Pastuszak	Brown v. Rhode Island	Oct. 8, 1949
		Byron Beaver	Houston v. Baylor	Sept. 22, 1962
		Dan Rebsch	Miami (Ohio) v. Western Michigan	Nov. 4, 1972
Season	14	Al Worley	Washington	1968
Career	29	Al Brosky	Illinois	1950–52

NCAA DIVISION I-A RECORDS

KICKING

Field Goals Kicked

		Player(s)	Team(s)	Date(s)
Game	7	Mike Prindle	Western Michigan v. Marshall	Sept. 29, 1984
		Dale Klein	Nebraska v. Missouri	Oct. 19, 1985
Season	29	John Lee	UCLA	1984
Career	80	Jeff Jaeger	Washington	1983–86

Points Scored

Game	24	Mike Prindle	Western Michigan v. Marshall (7 FGs, 3 PATSs)	Sept. 29, 1984
Season	131	Roman Anderson	Houston (22 FGs, 65 PATs)	1989
Career	423	Roman Anderson	Houston (70 FGs, 213 PATs)	1988–91

Points After Touchdown (PATs)

Game	13	Terry Leiweke	Houston v. Tulsa	Nov. 23, 1968
		Derek Mahoney	Fresno State v. New Mexico	Oct. 5, 1991
Season	67	Cary Blanchard	Oklahoma State	1988
Career	216	Derek Mahoney	Fresno State	1990–93

PUNTING

Most Punts

Game	36	Charlie Calhoun	Texas Tech v. Centenary	Nov. 11, 1939
Season	101	Jim Bailey	Virginia Military	1969
Career	320	Cameron Young	TCU	1976–79

Average Yards Gained

Game (min. 5 punts)	60.4	Lee Johnson	BYU v. Wyoming (5 for 302 yds)	Oct. 8, 1983
Season (min. 50 punts)	48.2	Ricky Anderson	Vanderbilt (58 for 2,793)	1984
Career (min. 200 punts)	44.7	Ray Guy	Southern Mississippi (200 for 8,934)	1970–72

Yards Gained

Game	1,318	Charlie Calhoun	Texas Tech v. Centenary	Nov. 11, 1939
Season	4,138	Johnny Pingel	Michigan State	1938
Career	12,947	Cameron Young	TCU	1976–79

Source: NCAA

Thompson (West Texas State v. Wichita State), 1970; Kelsey Finch (Tennessee v. Florida), 1977.

Pass completion 99 yards, on eight occasions, performed by seven players (Terry Peel and Robert Ford did it twice): Fred Owens (to Jack Ford), Portland v. St. Mary's, Calif., 1947; Bo Burris (to Warren McVea), Houston v. Washington State, 1966; Colin Clapton (to Eddie Jenkins), Holy Cross v. Boston U, 1970; Terry Peel (to Robert Ford), Houston v. Syracuse, 1970; Terry Peel (to Robert Ford), Houston v. San Diego State, 1972; Cris Collingsworth (to Derrick Gaffney), Florida v. Rice, 1977; Scott Ankrom (to James Maness), TCU v. Rice, 1984; Gino Torretta (to Horace Copeland), Miami v. Arkansas, 1991.

Field goal 67 yards, by three players: Russell Erxleben (Texas v. Rice), 1977; Steve Little (Arkansas v. Texas), 1977; Joe Williams (Wichita State v. Southern Illinois), 1978.

Punt 99 yards, by Pat Brady, Nevada–Reno v. Loyola, Calif. in 1950.

CONSECUTIVE RECORDS

REGULAR SEASON (INDIVIDUAL—DIVISION I-A)

Scoring touchdowns (games) 23, by Bill Burnett, Arkansas. Burnett amassed 47 touchdowns during his 23-game streak, which ran from October 5, 1968–October 31, 1970.

Touchdown passes (games) 35, Ty Detmer, BYU, September 7, 1989–November 23, 1991.

Touchdown passes (consecutive) 6, by Brooks Dawson, UTEP v. New Mexico, October 28, 1967. Dawson completed his first 6 passes for touchdowns, which must rank as the greatest start to a game ever!

Passes completed 22, shared by two players: Steve Young, BYU v. Utah State, October 30, 1982,

---

NCAA DIVISION I–A NATIONAL CHAMPIONS (1936–1963)

In 1936 the Associated Press introduced the AP poll, a ranking of college teams by a vote of sportswriters and broadcasters. In 1950 the United Press, later UPI, introduced a coaches' poll. The AP and UPI polls were still used as the basis for declaring the national college football champion until 1991. In 1992 the CNN/USA Today poll joined the AP as the main arbitrator of the National Championship. The polls have chosen different champions on nine occasions: 1954, 1957, 1965, 1970, 1973, 1974, 1978, 1990, and 1991. Notre Dame has been voted national champion a record eight times: 1943, 1946–47, 1949, 1966, 1973, 1977 and 1988.

Year	Team	Record	Year	Team	Record
1936	Minnesota	7–1–0	1951	Tennessee	10–0–0
1937	Pittsburgh	9–0–1	1952	Michigan State	9–0–0
1938	TCU	11–0–0	1953	Maryland	10–1–0
1939	Texas A&M	11–0–0	1954	Ohio State (AP)	10–0–0
1940	Minnesota	8–0–0		UCLA (UPI)	9–0–0
1941	Minnesota	8–0–0	1955	Oklahoma	11–0–0
1942	Ohio State	9–1–0	1956	Oklahoma	10–0–0
1943	Notre Dame	9–1–0	1957	Auburn (AP)	10–0–0
1944	Army	9–0–0		Ohio State (UPI)	9–1–0
1945	Army	9–0–0	1958	LSU	11–0–0
1946	Notre Dame	8–0–1	1959	Syracuse	11–0–0
1947	Notre Dame	9–0–0	1960	Minnesota	8–2–0
1948	Michigan	9–0–0	1961	Alabama	11–0–0
1949	Notre Dame	10–0–0	1962	Southern Cal.	11–0–0
1950	Oklahoma	10–1–0	1963	Texas	11–0–0

v. Wyoming, November 6, 1982; Chuck Long, Iowa v. Indiana, October 27, 1984.

100 yards+ rushing (games) 31, by Archie Griffin, Ohio State, September 15, 1973–November 22, 1975.

200 yards+ rushing (games) 5, shared by two players: Marcus Allen, Southern Calif., 1981; Barry Sanders, Oklahoma State, 1988.

Touchdown receptions (games) 12, by two players: Desmond Howard, Michigan, 1990–91; Aaron Turner, Pacific (Cal.), 1990–91.

Pass receptions (caught for touchdowns) 6, by two players: Carlos Carson, Louisiana State, 1977— Carlson scored touchdowns on his last five receptions v. Rice on September 24, 1977, and from his first reception v. Florida on October 1, 1977 (amazingly, these were the first six receptions of his collegiate career!)—and Gerald Armstrong, Nebraska, 1992. Armstrong caught six touchdown passes over five games, September 5–November 7.

Pass receptions (games) 46, by Carl Winston, New Mexico, 1990–93.

Field goals (consecutive) 30, by Chuck Nelson, Washington, 1981–82. Nelson converted his last five kicks of the season v. Southern Cal. on Novem-

Record Quotable

"It's not the size of the dog in the fight, but the size of the fight in the dog."

—Archie Griffin, quoted in
The Greatest Sports Excuses, Alibis and Explanations by Jeff Parietti.

NCAA DIVISION I-A NATIONAL CHAMPIONS (1964–1994)

Year	Team	Record	Year	Team	Record
1964	Alabama	10–1–0		Southern Cal. (UPI)	12–1–0
1965	Alabama (AP)	9–1–1	1979	Alabama	12–0–0
	Michigan State (UPI)	10–1–0	1980	Georgia	12–0–0
1966	Notre Dame	9–0–1	1981	Clemson	12–0–0
1967	Southern Cal.	10–1–0	1982	Penn State	11–1–0
1968	Ohio State	10–0–0	1983	Miami, Fla.	11–1–0
1969	Texas	11–0–0	1984	BYU	13–0–0
1970	Nebraska (AP)	11–0–1	1985	Oklahoma	11–1–0
	Texas (UPI)	10–1–0	1986	Penn State	12–0–0
1971	Nebraska	13–0–0	1987	Miami, Fla.	12–0–0
1972	Southern Cal.	12–0–0	1988	Notre Dame	12–0–0
1973	Notre Dame (AP)	11–0–0	1989	Miami, Fla.	11–1–0
	Alabama (UPI)	11–1–0	1990	Colorado (AP)	11–1–1
1974	Oklahoma (AP)	11–0–0		Georgia Tech (UPI)	11–0–1
	Southern Cal. (UPI)	10–1–1	1991	Miami, Fla. (AP)	12–0–0
1975	Oklahoma	11–1–0		Washington (UPI)	12–0–0
1976	Pittsburgh	12–0–0	1992	Alabama	13–0–0
1977	Notre Dame	11–1–0	1993	Florida State	12–1–0
1978	Alabama (AP)	11–1–0	1994	Nebraska	13–0–0

ber 14, 1981, and then booted the first 25 of the 1982 season, missing an attempt *v*. Washington State on November 20, 1982.

Field goals (games) 19, shared by two players: Larry Roach, Oklahoma State (1983–84); Gary Gussman, Miami (Ohio) (1986–87).

TEAM RECORDS (DIVISION I-A)

Most wins Michigan has won 739 games out of 1,017 played, 1879–1993.

Highest winning percentage The highest winning percentage in college football history is .762 by Notre Dame. The Fighting Irish have won 723, lost 211 and tied 41 out of 975 games played, 1887–1993.

Longest winning streak The longest winning streak in Division I-A football, including bowl games, is 47 games by Oklahoma from 1953–57. Oklahoma's streak was stopped on November 16, 1957, when Notre Dame defeated them 7–0 in Norman.

Longest home winning streak 57, by Alabama. The Crimson Tide defeated all visitors from 1963–82.

Longest undefeated streak Including bowl games, Washington played 63 games, 1907–17, without losing a game. California ended the streak with a 27–0 victory on November 3, 1917. Washington's record during the streak was 59 wins and 4 ties.

Longest losing streak The most consecutive losses in Division I-A football is 34 games, by Northwestern. This undesirable streak started on September 22, 1979 and was finally snapped three years later on September 25, 1982 when Northern Illinois succumbed to the Wildcats 31–6.

Most points scored Wyoming crushed Northern Colorado 103–0 on November 5, 1949 to set the Division I-A mark for most points scored by one team in a single game. The Cowboys scored 15 touchdowns and converted 13 PATs.

Highest-scoring game The most points scored in a Division I-A game is 124, when Oklahoma defeated Colorado 82–42 on October 4, 1980.

Highest-scoring tie game BYU and San Diego State played a 52–52 tie on November 16, 1991.

HEISMAN TROPHY WINNERS (1935–1960)

Awarded annually since 1935 by the Downtown Athletic Club of New York to the top college football player as determined by a poll of journalists. Most wins (player), 2, Archie Griffin, Ohio State, 1974–75. Most wins (college), 7, Notre Dame, 1943, 1947, 1949, 1953, 1956, 1964, 1987.

Year	Player	Team	Year	Player	Team
1935	Jay Berwanger	Chicago	1948	Doak Walker	SMU
1936	Larry Kelley	Yale	1949	Leon Hart	Notre Dame
1937	Clint Frank	Yale	1950	Vic Janowicz	Ohio State
1938	Davey O'Brien	TCU	1951	Dick Kazmaier	Princeton
1939	Nile Kinnick	Iowa	1952	Billy Vessels	Oklahoma
1940	Tom Harmon	Michigan	1953	Johnny Lattner	Notre Dame
1941	Bruce Smith	Minnesota	1954	Alan Ameche	Wisconsin
1942	Frank Sinkwich	Georgia	1955	Howard Cassady	Ohio State
1943	Angelo Bertelli	Notre Dame	1956	Paul Hornung	Notre Dame
1944	Les Horvath	Ohio State	1957	John David Crow	Texas A&M
1945	Doc Blanchard	Army	1958	Pete Dawkins	Army
1946	Glenn Davis	Army	1959	Billy Cannon	LSU
1947	Johnny Lujack	Notre Dame	1960	Joe Bellino	Navy

BOWL GAMES

The oldest college bowl game is the Rose Bowl. It was first played on January 1, 1902 at Tournament Park, Pasadena, Calif., where Michigan defeated Stanford 49–0. The other three bowl games that make up the "big four" are the Orange Bowl, initiated in 1935; the Sugar Bowl, 1935; and the Cotton Bowl, 1937.

ROSE BOWL In the first game, played on January 1, 1902, Michigan blanked Stanford 49–0.

Most wins Southern Cal. has won the Rose Bowl 19 times: 1923, 1930, 1932–33, 1939–40, 1944–45, 1953, 1963, 1968, 1970, 1973, 1975, 1977, 1979–80, 1985, 1990.

Most appearances Southern Cal. has played in the Rose Bowl 27 times, with a record of 19 wins and 8 losses.

ORANGE BOWL In the first game, played on January 1, 1935, Bucknell shut out Miami (Fla.) 26–0.

Most wins Oklahoma has won the Orange Bowl 11 times: 1954, 1956, 1958–59, 1968, 1976, 1979–81, 1986–87.

Most appearances Oklahoma has played in the Orange Bowl 16 times, with a record of 11 wins and 5 losses.

SUGAR BOWL In the first game, played on January 1, 1935, Tulane defeated Temple 20–14.

Most wins Alabama has won the Sugar Bowl eight times: 1962, 1964, 1967, 1975, 1978–80, 1992.

Most appearances Alabama has played in the Sugar Bowl 12 times, with a record of 8 wins and 4 losses.

COTTON BOWL In the first game, played on January 1, 1937, Texas Christian defeated Marquette 16–6.

Most wins Texas has won the Cotton Bowl nine times: 1943, 1946, 1953, 1962, 1964, 1969–70, 1973, 1982.

Most appearances Texas has played in the Cotton Bowl 18 times, with a record of 9 wins, 8 losses and 1 tie.

BOWL GAME RECORDS Alabama, Georgia, Georgia Tech and Notre Dame are the only four teams to have won each of the "big four" bowl games.

HEISMAN TROPHY WINNERS (1961–1994)

Year	Player	Team	Year	Player	Team
1961	Ernie Davis	Syracuse	1978	Billy Sims	Oklahoma
1962	Terry Baker	Oregon State	1979	Charles White	Southern Cal.
1963	Roger Staubach	Navy	1980	George Rogers	South Carolina
1964	John Huarte	Notre Dame	1981	Marcus Allen	Southern Cal.
1965	Mike Garrett	Southern Cal.	1982	Herschel Walker	Georgia
1966	Steve Spurrier	Florida	1983	Mike Rozier	Nebraska
1967	Gary Beban	UCLA	1984	Doug Flutie	Boston College
1968	O. J. Simpson	Southern Cal.	1985	Bo Jackson	Auburn
1969	Steve Owens	Oklahoma	1986	Vinny Testaverde	Miami, Fla.
1970	Jim Plunkett	Stanford	1987	Tim Brown	Notre Dame
1971	Pat Sullivan	Auburn	1988	Barry Sanders	Oklahoma State
1972	Johnny Rodgers	Nebraska	1989	Andre Ware	Houston
1973	John Cappelletti	Penn State	1990	Ty Detmer	BYU
1974	Archie Griffin	Ohio State	1991	Desmond Howard	Michigan
1975	Archie Griffin	Ohio State	1992	Gino Torretta	Miami, Fla.
1976	Tony Dorsett	Pittsburgh	1993	Charlie Ward	Florida State
1977	Earl Campbell	Texas	1994	Rashaan Salaam	Colorado

Most wins Alabama has won a record 26 bowl games: Sugar Bowl, eight times, 1962, 1964, 1967, 1975, 1978–80, 1992; Rose Bowl, four times, 1926, 1931, 1935, 1946; Orange Bowl, four times, 1943, 1953, 1963, 1966; Sun Bowl (now John Hancock Bowl), three times, 1983, 1986, 1988; Cotton Bowl, twice, 1942, 1981; Liberty Bowl, twice, 1976, 1982; Aloha Bowl, once, 1985; Blockbuster Bowl, once, 1991; Gator Bowl, once, 1993.

Consecutive seasons UCLA won a bowl game for seven consecutive seasons: Rose Bowl, 1983–84; Fiesta Bowl, 1985; Rose Bowl, 1986; Freedom Bowl, 1986; Aloha Bowl, 1987; Cotton Bowl, 1989.

Bowl game appearances Alabama has played in 46 bowl games.

COACHES

Wins (Division I-A) In Division I-A competition, Paul "Bear" Bryant has won more games than any other coach, with 323 victories over 38 years. Bryant coached four teams: Maryland, 1945 (6–2–1); Kentucky, 1956–53 (60–23–5); Texas A&M, 1954–57 (25–14–2); and Alabama, 1958–82 (232–46–9). His completed record was 323 wins–85 losses–17 ties, for a .780 winning percentage.

Wins (all divisions) In overall NCAA competition, Eddie Robinson, Grambling (Division I-AA) holds the mark for most victories with 388.

Highest winning percentage (Division I-A) The highest winning percentage in Division I-A competition is .881, held by Knute Rockne of Notre Dame. Rockne coached the Irish from 1918 to 1930, for a record of 105 wins–12 losses–5 tied.

ATTENDANCES

Single game It has been estimated that crowds of 120,000 were present for two Notre Dame games played at Soldier Field, Chicago, Ill.: *v.* Southern Cal. (November 26, 1927); *v.* Navy (October 13, 1928). Official attendance records have been kept by the NCAA since 1948. The highest official crowd for a regular-season NCAA game was 106,851 Wolverine fans at Michigan Football Stadium, Ann Arbor, Mich., on September 11, 1993 for the Michigan *v.* Notre Dame game. As Michigan lost 27–23, a record may have been set for the greatest number of depressed people at a football game!

Bowl game The record attendance for a bowl game is 106,869 people at the 1973 Rose Bowl, where Southern Cal. defeated Ohio State 42–17.

Season average The highest average attendance for home games is 105,651 for the six games played by Michigan in 1993.

CANADIAN FOOTBALL LEAGUE (CFL)

ORIGINS The earliest recorded football game in Canada was an intramural contest between students of the University of Toronto on November 9, 1861. As with football in the U.S., the development of the game in Canada dates from a contest between two universities—McGill and Harvard, played in May 1874.

Canadian football differs in many ways from its counterpart in the U.S. The major distinctions are the number of players (CFL–12, NFL–11); size of field (CFL–110 yards x 65 yards, NFL–100 yards x 53 yards); number of downs (CFL–3, NFL–4); and a completely different system for scoring and penalties.

The current CFL is comprised of nine teams in two divisions, the Western and Eastern. The divisional playoff champions meet in the Grey Cup to decide the CFL champion.

CFL TEAM RECORDS

Longest winning streak The Calgary Stampeders won 22 consecutive games between August 25, 1948 and October 22, 1949 to set the CFL mark.

Longest winless streak The Hamilton Tiger-Cats hold the dubious distinction of being the CFL's most futile team, amassing a 20-game winless streak (0–19–1), from September 28, 1948 to September 2, 1950.

Highest-scoring game The Toronto Argonauts defeated the B.C. Lions 68–43 on September 1, 1990 to set a CFL combined score record of 111 points.

Highest score by one team The Montreal Alouettes rolled over the Hamilton Tiger-Cats 82–14 on October 20, 1956 to set the CFL highest-score mark.

THE GREY CUP

In 1909, Lord Earl Grey, the governor general of Canada, donated a trophy that was to be awarded to the Canadian Rugby Football champion. The competition for the Grey Cup evolved during the first half of the 20th century from an open compe-

CFL INDIVIDUAL RECORDS

Games Played

		Player(s)	Team(s)	Date(s)
Most	300	Lui Passaglia	B.C. Lions	1976–94
Consecutive	253	Dave Cutler	Edmonton Eskimos	1969–84

Points Scored

Game	36	Bob McNamara	Winnipeg Blue Bombers v. B.C. Lions	Oct. 13, 1956
Season	236	Lance Chomyc	Toronto Argonauts	1991
Career	2,966	Lui Passaglia	B.C. Lions	1976–94

Touchdowns Scored

Game	6	Eddie James	Winnipegs v. Winnipeg St. Johns	Sept. 28, 1932
		Bob McNamara	Winnipeg Blue Bombers v. B.C. Lions	Oct. 13, 1956
Season	21	Allen Pitts	Calgary Stampeders	1994
Career	137	George Reed	Saskatchewan Roughriders	1963–75

PASSING

Yards Gained

Game	713	Matt Dunigan	Edmonton Eskimos v. Winnipeg Blue Bombers	July 14, 1994
Season	6,619	Doug Flutie	B.C. Lions	1991
Career	50,535	Ron Lancaster	Ottawa Roughriders/Saskatchewan Roughriders	1960–78

Touchdowns Thrown

Game	8	Joe Zuger	Hamilton Tiger-Cats	Oct. 15, 1962
Season	48	Doug Flutie	Calgary Stampeders	1994
Career	333	Ron Lancaster	Ottawa/Saskatchewan Roughriders	1960–78

Completions

Game	41	Dieter Brock	Winnipeg Blue Bombers v. Ottawa Roughriders	Oct. 3, 1981
		Kent Austin	Saskatchewan Roughriders v. Toronto Argonauts	Oct. 31, 1993
Season	466	Doug Flutie	B.C. Lions	1991
Career	3,384	Ron Lancaster	Ottawa Roughriders/Saskatchewan Roughriders	1960–78

CFL INDIVIDUAL RECORDS

PASS RECEIVING

Receptions

		Player(s)	Team(s)	Date(s)
Game	16	Terry Greer	Toronto Argonauts v. Ottawa Roughriders	Aug. 19, 1983
		Brian Wiggins	Calgary Stampeders v. Saskatchewan Roughriders	Oct. 23, 1993
Season	126	Allen Pitts	Calgary Stampeders	1994
Career	765	Roy Elgaard	Saskatchewan Roughriders	1983–94

Yards Gained

Game	338	Hal Patterson	Montreal Alouettes v. Hamilton Tiger-Cats	Sept. 29, 1956
Season	2,036	Allen Pitts	Calgary Stempeders	1984
Career	12,353	Ray Elgaard	Saskatchewan Roughriders	1983–94

Touchdown Receptions

Game	5	Ernie Pitts	Winnipeg Blue Bombers v. Saskatchewan Roughriders	Aug. 29, 1959
Season	21	Allen Pitts	Calgary Stampeders	1994
Career	97	Brian Kelly	Edmonton Eskimos	1979–87

RUSHING

Yards Gained

Game	287	Ron Stewart	Ottawa Roughriders v. Montreal Alouettes	Oct. 10, 1960
Season	1,972	Mike Pringle	Baltimore	1994
Career	16,116	George Reed	Saskatchewan Roughriders	1963–75

Touchdowns Scored

Game	5	Earl Lunsford	Calgary Stampeders v. Edmonton Eskimos	Sept. 3, 1962
Season	18	Gerry James	Winnipeg Blue Bombers	1957
		Jim Germany	Edmonton Eskimos	1981
Career	134	George Reed	Saskatchewan Roughriders	1963–75

Longest Plays (Yards)

Rushing	109	George Dixon	Montreal Alouettes	Sept. 2, 1963
		Willie Fleming	B.C. Lions	Oct. 17, 1964
Pass Completion	109	Sam Etcheverry to Hal Patterson	Montreal Alouettes	Sept. 22, 1956
		Jerry Keeling to Terry Evanshen	Calgary Stampeders	Sept. 27, 1966
Field Goal	60	Dave Ridgway	Saskatchewan Roughriders	Sept. 6, 1987
Punt	108	Zenon Andrusyshyn	Toronto Argonauts	Oct. 23, 1977

Source: CFL

GREY CUP RESULTS (1909–1944)

Year	Winner	Loser	Score
1909	University of Toronto	Toronto Parkdale	26–6
1910	University of Toronto	Hamilton Tigers	16–7
1911	University of Toronto	Toronto Argonauts	14–7
1912	Hamilton Alerts	Toronto Argonauts	11–4
1913	Hamilton Tigers	Toronto Parkdale	44–2
1914	Toronto Argonauts	University of Toronto	14–2
1915	Hamilton Tigers	Toronto Rowing	13–7
1916	not held		
1917	not held		
1918	not held		
1919	not held		
1920	University of Toronto	Toronto Argonauts	16–3
1921	Toronto Argonauts	Edmonton Eskimos	23–0
1922	Queen's University	Edmonton Elks	13–1
1923	Queen's University	Regina Roughriders	54–0
1924	Queen's University	Toronto Balmy Beach	11–3
1925	Ottawa Senators	Winnipeg Tammany Tigers	24–1
1926	Ottawa Senators	University of Toronto	10–7
1927	Toronto Balmy Beach	Hamilton Tigers	9–6
1928	Hamilton Tigers	Regina Roughriders	30–0
1929	Hamilton Tigers	Regina Roughriders	14–3
1930	Toronto Balmy Beach	Regina Roughriders	11–6
1931	Montreal AAA Winged Wheelers	Regina Roughriders	22–0
1932	Hamilton Tigers	Regina Roughriders	25–6
1933	Toronto Argonauts	Sarnia Imperials	4–3
1934	Sarnia Imperials	Regina Roughriders	20–12
1935	Winnipeg	Hamilton Tigers	18–12
1936	Sarnia Imperials	Ottawa Rough Riders	26–20
1937	Toronto Argonauts	Winnipeg Blue Bombers	4–3
1938	Toronto Argonauts	Winnipeg Blue Bombers	30–7
1939	Winnipeg Blue Bombers	Ottawa Rough Riders	8–7
1940 (Nov.)	Ottawa Rough Riders	Toronto Balmy Beach	8–2
1940 (Dec.)	Ottawa Rough Riders	Toronto Balmy Beach	12–5
1941	Winnipeg Blue Bombers	Ottawa Rough Riders	18–16
1942	Toronto Hurricanes	Winnipeg Bombers	8–5
1943	Hamilton Flying Wildcats	Winnipeg Bombers	23–14
1944	St. Hyacinthe-Donnacona Navy	Hamilton Wildcats	7–6

GREY CUP RESULTS (1945–1980)

Year	Winner	Loser	Score
1945	Toronto Argonauts	Winnipeg Blue Bombers	35–0
1946	Toronto Argonauts	Winnipeg Blue Bombers	28–6
1947	Toronto Argonauts	Winnipeg Blue Bombers	10–9
1948	Calgary Stampeders	Ottawa Rough Riders	12–7
1949	Montreal Alouettes	Calgary Stampeders	28–15
1950	Toronto Argonauts	Winnipeg Blue Bombers	13–0
1951	Ottawa Rough Riders	Saskatchewan Roughriders	21–14
1952	Toronto Argonauts	Edmonton Eskimos	21–11
1953	Hamilton Tiger-Cats	Winnipeg Blue Bombers	12–6
1954	Edmonton Eskimos	Montreal Alouettes	26–25
1955	Edmonton Eskimos	Montreal Alouettes	34–19
1956	Edmonton Eskimos	Montreal Alouettes	50–27
1957	Hamilton Tiger-Cats	Winnipeg Blue Bombers	32–7
1958	Winnipeg Blue Bombers	Hamilton Tiger-Cats	35–28
1959	Winnipeg Blue Bombers	Hamilton Tiger-Cats	21–7
1960	Ottawa Senators	Edmonton Eskimos	16–6
1961	Winnipeg Blue Bombers	Hamilton Tiger-Cats	21–14*
1962	Winnipeg Blue Bombers	Hamilton Tiger-Cats	28–27†
1963	Hamilton Tiger-Cats	B.C. Lions	21–10
1964	B.C. Lions	Hamilton Tiger-Cats	34–24
1965	Hamilton Tiger-Cats	Winnipeg Blue Bombers	22–16
1966	Saskatchewan Roughriders	Ottawa Senators	29–14
1967	Hamilton Tiger-Cats	Saskatchewan Roughriders	24–1
1968	Ottawa Rough Riders	Calgary Stampeders	24–21
1969	Ottawa Rough Riders	Saskatchewan Roughriders	29–11
1970	Montreal Alouettes	Calgary Stampeders	23–10
1971	Calgary Stampeders	Toronto Argonauts	14–11
1972	Hamilton Tiger-Cats	Saskatchewan Roughriders	13–10
1973	Ottawa Rough Riders	Edmonton Eskimos	22–18
1974	Montreal Alouettes	Edmonton Eskimos	20–7
1975	Edmonton Eskimos	Montreal Alouettes	9–8
1976	Ottawa Rough Riders	Saskatchewan Roughriders	23–20
1977	Montreal Alouettes	Edmonton Eskimos	41–6
1978	Edmonton Eskimos	Montreal Alouettes	20–13
1979	Edmonton Eskimos	Montreal Alouettes	17–9
1980	Edmonton Eskimos	Hamilton Tiger-Cats	48–10

* Overtime. † Halted by fog. The remaining 9:29 was played the following day.

GREY CUP RESULTS (1981–1994)

Year	Winner	Loser	Score
1981	Edmonton Eskimos	Ottawa Senators	26–23
1982	Edmonton Eskimos	Toronto Argonauts	32–16
1983	Toronto Argonauts	B.C. Lions	18–17
1984	Winnipeg Blue Bombers	Hamilton Tiger-Cats	47–17
1985	B.C. Lions	Hamilton Tiger-Cats	37–24
1986	Hamilton Tiger-Cats	Edmonton Eskimos	39–15
1987	Edmonton Eskimos	Toronto Argonauts	38–36
1988	Winnipeg Blue Bombers	B.C. Lions	22–21
1989	Saskatchewan Roughriders	Hamilton Tiger-Cats	43–40
1990	Winnipeg Blue Bombers	Edmonton Eskimos	50–11
1991	Toronto Argonauts	Calgary Stampeders	36–21
1992	Calgary Stampeders	Winnipeg Blue Bombers	24–10
1993	Edmonton Eskimos	Winnipeg Blue Bombers	33–23
1994	B.C. Lions	Baltimore	26–23

tition for amateurs, college teams and hybrid rugby teams to the championship of the professional Canadian Football League that was formed in 1958.

Most wins 12, Toronto Argonauts: 1914, 1921, 1933, 1937–38, 1945–47, 1950, 1952, 1983, 1991.

Most consecutive wins 5, Edmonton Eskimos: 1978–83.

FRISBEE (FLYING DISC THROWING)

ORIGINS The design of a carved plastic flying disc was patented in the United States by Fred Morrison in 1948. In 1957 Wham-O Inc. of San Gabriel, Calif. bought Morrison's patent and trademarked the name Frisbee in 1958. In 1968 Wham-O helped form the International Frisbee Association (IFA) as a vehicle for organizing the Frisbee craze that had swept across the United States. The IFA folded in 1982 and it wasn't until 1986 that the World Flying Disc Federation was formed to organize and standardize rules for the sport.

FLYING DISC RECORDS

Distance thrown Sam Ferrans (U.S.) set the flying disc distance record at 623 feet 7 inches on July 2, 1988 at La Habra, Calif. The women's record is 426 feet 9½ inches by Amy Bekken (U.S.) on June 25, 1990 at La Habra, Calif.

Throw, run, catch Hiroshi Oshima (Japan) set the throw, run, catch distance record at 303 feet 11 inches on July 20, 1988 at San Francisco, Calif. The women's record is 196 feet 11 inches by Judy Horowitz (U.S.) on June 29, 1985 at La Mirada, Calif.

Time aloft The record for maximum time aloft is 16.72 seconds, by Don Cain (U.S.) on May 26, 1984 at Philadelphia, Pa. The women's record is 11.81 seconds, by Amy Bekken (U.S.) on August 1, 1991.

24-hour distance (pairs) Leonard Muise and Gabe Ontiveros (both U.S.) threw a Frisbee 362.40 miles on September 20–21, 1988 at Carson, Calif. The women's record is 115.65 miles by Jo Cahow and Amy Berard (both U.S.) on December 30–31, 1979 at Pasadena, Calif.

GOLF

The nationality of the competitors in this section is U.S. unless stated otherwise.

ORIGINS The Chinese Nationalist Golf Association claims that golf (*ch'ui wan*—"the ball-hitting game") was played in China in the 3rd or 2nd century B.C. There is evidence that a game resembling golf was played in the Low Countries (present-day Belgium, Holland and northern France) in the Middle Ages. Scotland, however, is generally regarded as the home of the modern game. The oldest club of which there is written evidence is the Honourable Company of Edinburgh Golfers, Scotland, founded in 1744. The Royal & Ancient Club of St. Andrews (R&A) has been in existence since 1754. The R&A is credited with formulating the rules of golf upon which the modern game is based. Gutta percha balls succeeded feather balls in 1848. In 1899 Coburn Haskell (U.S.) invented rubber-cored balls. Steel shafts were authorized in the United States in 1925.

United States There are claims that golf was played in this country as early as the 18th century in North Carolina and Virginia. The oldest recognized club in North America is the Royal Montreal Golf Club, Canada, formed on November 4, 1873. Two clubs claim to be the first established in the U.S.: the Foxberg Golf Club, Clarion County, Pa. (1887), and St. Andrews Golf Club of Yonkers, N.Y. (1888). The United States Golf Association

(USGA) was founded in 1894 as the governing body of golf in the United States.

PROFESSIONAL GOLF (MEN)

GRAND SLAM CHAMPIONSHIPS (THE MAJORS)

GRAND SLAM In 1930, Bobby Jones won the U.S. and British Open Championships and the U.S. and British Amateur Championships. This feat was christened the "Grand Slam." In 1960, the professional Grand Slam (the Masters, U.S. Open, British Open, and Professional Golfers Association [PGA] Championships) gained recognition when Arnold Palmer won the first two legs, the Masters and the U.S. Open. However, he did not complete the set of titles, and the Grand Slam has still not been attained. Ben Hogan came the closest in 1951, when he won the first three legs, but didn't return to the U.S. from Great Britain in time for the PGA Championship.

Most grand slam titles Jack Nicklaus has won the most majors, with 18 professional titles (six

MASTERS CHAMPIONS (1934–1994)

Year	Champion	Year	Champion	Year	Champion	Year	Champion
1934	Horton Smith	1950	Jimmy Demaret	1966	Jack Nicklaus	1982	Craig Stadler
1935	Gene Sarazen	1951	Ben Hogan	1967	Gay Brewer	1983	Seve Ballesteros
1936	Horton Smith	1952	Sam Snead	1968	Bob Goalby	1984	Ben Crenshaw
1937	Byron Nelson	1953	Ben Hogan	1969	George Archer	1985	Bernhard Langer[3]
1938	Henry Picard	1954	Sam Snead	1970	Billy Casper	1986	Jack Nicklaus
1939	Ralph Guldahl	1955	Cary Middlecoff	1971	Charles Coody	1987	Larry Mize
1940	Jimmy Demaret	1956	Jack Burke Jr.	1972	Jack Nicklaus	1988	Sandy Lyle[4]
1941	Craig Wood	1957	Doug Ford	1973	Tommy Aaron	1989	Nick Faldo[4]
1942	Byron Nelson	1958	Arnold Palmer	1974	Gary Player	1990	Nick Faldo
1943	not held	1959	Art Wall Jr.	1975	Jack Nicklaus	1991	Ian Woosnam[4]
1944	not held	1960	Arnold Palmer	1976	Raymond Floyd	1992	Fred Couples
1945	not held	1961	Gary Player[1]	1977	Tom Watson	1993	Bernhard Langer
1946	Herman Keiser	1962	Arnold Palmer	1978	Gary Player	1994	José Maria Olazabal
1947	Jimmy Demaret	1963	Jack Nicklaus	1979	Fuzzy Zoeller		
1948	Claude Harmon	1964	Arnold Palmer	1980	Seve Ballesteros[2]		
1949	Sam Snead	1965	Jack Nicklaus	1981	Tom Watson		

Nationalities: 1—South Africa, 2—Spain, 3—Germany, 4—Great Britain

Masters, four U.S. Opens, three British Opens, five PGA Championships).

THE MASTERS Inaugurated in 1934, this event is held annually at the 6,980-yd Augusta National Golf Club, Augusta, Ga.

Most wins Jack Nicklaus has won the coveted green jacket a record six times (1963, 1965–66, 1972, 1975, 1986).

Consecutive wins Jack Nicklaus (1965–66) and Nick Faldo (1989–90) are the only two players to have won back-to-back Masters.

Record Quotable

"The longer you play, the better the chance the better player has of winning."
—Jack Nicklaus, quoted in *Sports Quotes* by Bob Abel and Michael Valenti.

Lowest 18-hole total (any round) 63, by Nick Price (Zimbabwe) in 1986.

U.S. OPEN CHAMPIONS (1895–1994)

Year	Champion	Year	Champion	Year	Champion	Year	Champion
1895	Horace Rawlins	1920	Edward Ray[1]	1945	not held	1970	Tony Jacklin[1]
1896	James Foulis	1921	Jim Barnes	1946	Lloyd Mangrum	1971	Lee Trevino
1897	Joe Lloyd	1922	Gene Sarazen	1947	Lew Worsham	1972	Jack Nicklaus
1898	Fred Herd	1923	Bobby Jones	1948	Ben Hogan	1973	Johnny Miller
1899	Willie Smith	1924	Cyril Walker	1949	Cary Middlecoff	1974	Hale Irwin
1900	Harry Vardon[1]	1925	Willie MacFarlane	1950	Ben Hogan	1975	Lou Graham
1901	Willie Anderson	1926	Bobby Jones	1951	Ben Hogan	1976	Jerry Pate
1902	Laurie Auchterlonie	1927	Tommy Armour	1952	Julius Boros	1977	Hubert Green
1903	Willie Anderson	1928	Johnny Farrell	1953	Ben Hogan	1978	Andy North
1904	Willie Anderson	1929	Bobby Jones	1954	Ed Furgol	1979	Hale Irwin
1905	Willie Anderson	1930	Bobby Jones	1955	Jack Fleck	1980	Jack Nicklaus
1906	Alex Smith	1931	Billy Burke	1956	Cary Middlecoff	1981	David Graham[3]
1907	Alex Ross	1932	Gene Sarazen	1957	Dick Mayer	1982	Tom Watson
1908	Fred McLeod	1933	Johnny Goodman	1958	Tommy Bolt	1983	Larry Nelson
1909	George Sargent	1934	Olin Dutra	1959	Billy Casper	1984	Fuzzy Zoeller
1910	Alex Smith	1935	Sam Parks Jr.	1960	Arnold Palmer	1985	Andy North
1911	John McDermott	1936	Tony Manero	1961	Gene Littler	1986	Raymond Floyd
1912	John McDermott	1937	Ralph Guldahl	1962	Jack Nicklaus	1987	Scott Simpson
1913	Francis Ouimet	1938	Ralph Guldahl	1963	Julius Boros	1988	Curtis Strange
1914	Walter Hagen	1939	Byron Nelson	1964	Ken Venturi	1989	Curtis Strange
1915	Jerome Travers	1940	Lawson Little	1965	Gary Player[2]	1990	Hale Irwin
1916	Charles Evans Jr.	1941	Craig Wood	1966	Billy Casper	1991	Payne Stewart
1917	not held	1942	not held	1967	Jack Nicklaus	1992	Tom Kite
1918	not held	1943	not held	1968	Lee Trevino	1993	Lee Janzen
1919	Walter Hagen	1944	not held	1969	Orville Moody	1994	Ernie Els

Nationalities: 1—Great Britain, 2—South Africa, 3—Australia

PUTT-ING IT AWAY ■ ERNIE ELS AFTER SINKING A SUCCESSFUL PUTT IN THE FINAL ROUND OF THE 1994 U.S. OPEN. (ALLSPORT/STEPHEN MUNDAY)

Lowest 72-hole total 271, by Jack Nicklaus (67, 71, 64, 69) in 1965; and Raymond Floyd (65, 66, 70, 70) in 1976.

Oldest champion 46 years 81 days, Jack Nicklaus (1986).

Youngest champion 23 years 2 days, Severiano Ballesteros (1980).

THE UNITED STATES OPEN Inaugurated in 1895, this event is held on a different course each year. The Open was expanded from a three-day, 36-hole Saturday finish to four days of 18 holes of play in 1965.

Most wins Four players have won the title four times: Willie Anderson (1901, 1903–05); Bobby Jones (1923, 1926, 1929–30); Ben Hogan (1948, 1950–51, 1953); Jack Nicklaus (1962, 1967, 1972, 1980).

Most consecutive wins Three, by Willie Anderson (1903–05).

Lowest 18-hole total (any round) 63, by three players: Johnny Miller at Oakmont Country Club,

Pa., on June 17, 1973; Jack Nicklaus and Tom Weiskopf, both at Baltusrol Country Club, Springfield, N.J., on June 12, 1980.

Lowest 72-hole total 272, by two players: Jack Nicklaus (63, 71, 70, 68), at Baltusrol Country Club, Springfield, N.J., in 1980; and Lee Janzen (67, 67, 69, 69), also at Baltusrol, in 1993.

Oldest champion 45 years 15 days, Hale Irwin (1990).

Youngest champion 19 years 317 days, John J. McDermott (1911).

THE BRITISH OPEN In this event, inaugurated in 1860, the first dozen tournaments were staged at Prestwick, Scotland. Since 1873, the locations have varied, but all venues are coastal links courses.

Most wins Harry Vardon won a record six titles, in 1896, 1898–99, 1903, 1911, 1914.

Most consecutive wins Four, by Tom Morris Jr. (1868–70, 1872; the event was not held in 1871).

Lowest 18-hole total (any round) 63, by six players: Mark Hayes at Turnberry, Scotland, on July 7, 1977; Isao Aoki (Japan) at Muirfield, Scotland, on July 19, 1980; Greg Norman (Australia) at Turnberry, Scotland, on July 18, 1986; Paul Broadhurst (Great Britain) at St. Andrews, Scotland, on July 21, 1990; Jodie Mudd at Royal Birkdale, England, on July 21, 1991; and Nick Faldo (Great Britain) on July 16, 1993 at Royal St. Georges.

Lowest 72-hole total 267 (66, 68, 69, 64) by Greg Norman (Australia) at Royal St. George's, England in 1993.

Oldest champion 46 years 99 days, Tom Morris Sr. (Great Britain) (1867).

Youngest champion 17 years 249 days, Tom Morris Jr. (Great Britain) (1868).

THE PROFESSIONAL GOLFERS ASSOCIATION (PGA) CHAMPIONSHIP Inaugurated in 1916, the tournament was a match-play event, but switched to a 72-hole stroke-play event in 1958.

Most wins Two players have won the title five times: Walter Hagen (1921, 1924–27); and Jack Nicklaus (1963, 1971, 1973, 1975, 1980).

Most consecutive wins Four, by Walter Hagen (1924–27).

Lowest 18-hole total (any round) 63, by four players: Bruce Crampton (Australia) at Fire-

BRITISH OPEN CHAMPIONS (1860–1967)

Year	Champion	Year	Champion	Year	Champion
1860	Willie Park Sr.[1]	1896	Harry Vardon[1]	1932	Gene Sarazen
1861	Tom Morris Sr.[1]	1897	Harold H. Hilton	1933	Densmore Shute
1862	Tom Morris Sr.	1898	Harry Vardon	1934	Henry Cotton[1]
1863	Willie Park Sr.	1899	Harry Vardon	1935	Alfred Perry[1]
1864	Tom Morris Sr.	1900	John H. Taylor	1936	Alfred Padgham[1]
1865	Andrew Strath[1]	1901	James Braid[1]	1937	Henry Cotton
1866	Willie Park Sr.	1902	Sandy Herd[1]	1938	Reg Whitcombe[1]
1867	Tom Morris Sr.	1903	Harry Vardon	1939	Dick Burton[1]
1868	Tom Morris Jr.[1]	1904	Jack White[1]	1940	not held
1869	Tom Morris Jr.	1905	James Braid	1941	not held
1870	Tom Morris Jr.	1906	James Braid	1942	not held
1871	not held	1907	Arnaud Massy[2]	1943	not held
1872	Tom Morris Jr	1908	James Braid	1944	not held
1873	Tom Kidd[1]	1909	John H. Taylor	1945	not held
1874	Mungo Park[1]	1910	James Braid	1946	Sam Snead
1875	Willie Park Sr.	1911	Harry Vardon	1947	Fred Daly[1]
1876	Bob Martin[1]	1912	Edward Ray[1]	1948	Henry Cotton
1877	Jamie Anderson[1]	1913	John H. Taylor	1949	Bobby Locke[3]
1878	Jamie Anderson	1914	Harry Vardon	1950	Bobby Locke
1879	Jamie Anderson	1915	not held	1951	Max Faulkner[1]
1880	Robert Ferguson[1]	1916	not held	1952	Bobby Locke
1881	Robert Ferguson	1917	not held	1953	Ben Hogan
1882	Robert Ferguson	1918	not held	1954	Peter Thomson[4]
1883	Willie Fernie[1]	1919	not held	1955	Peter Thomson
1884	Jack Simpson[1]	1920	George Duncan[1]	1956	Peter Thomson
1885	Bob Martin[1]	1921	Jock Hutchinson	1957	Bobby Locke
1886	David Brown[1]	1922	Walter Hagen	1958	Peter Thomson
1887	Willie Park Jr.[1]	1923	Arthur Havers[1]	1959	Gary Player[3]
1888	Jack Burns[1]	1924	Walter Hagen	1960	Kel Nagle[4]
1889	Willie Park Jr.	1925	Jim Barnes	1961	Arnold Palmer
1890	John Ball[1]	1926	Bobby Jones	1962	Arnold Palmer
1891	Hugh Kirkaldy[1]	1927	Bobby Jones	1963	Bob Charles[5]
1892	Harold H. Hilton[1]	1928	Walter Hagen	1964	Tony Loma
1893	William Auchterlonie[1]	1929	Walter Hagen	1965	Peter Thomson
1894	John H. Taylor[1]	1930	Bobby Jones	1966	Jack Nicklaus
1895	John H. Taylor	1931	Tommy Armour	1967	Roberto de Vicenzo[6]

Nationalities: 1—Great Britain, 2—France, 3—South Africa, 4—Australia, 5—New Zealand, 6—Argentina

BRITISH OPEN CHAMPIONS (1968–1994)

Year	Champion	Year	Champion	Year	Champion
1968	Gary Player	1977	Tom Watson	1986	Greg Norman[4]
1969	Tony Jacklin[1]	1978	Jack Nicklaus	1987	Nick Faldo[1]
1970	Jack Nicklaus	1979	Seve Ballesteros[7]	1988	Seve Ballesteros
1971	Lee Trevino	1980	Tom Watson	1989	Mark Calcavecchia
1972	Lee Trevino	1981	Bill Rogers	1990	Nick Faldo
1973	Tom Weiskopf	1982	Tom Watson	1991	Ian Baker-Finch[4]
1974	Gary Player	1983	Tom Watson	1992	Nick Faldo
1975	Tom Watson	1984	Seve Ballesteros	1993	Greg Norman
1976	Johnny Miller	1985	Sandy Lyle[1]	1994	Nick Price

Nationalities: 7—Spain

VICTORY KISS ■ NICK PRICE SHOWS AFFECTION TO HIS TROPHY AFTER WINNING THE 1994 BRITISH OPEN. (ALLSPORT/DAVID CANNON)

stone Country Club, Akron, Ohio, in 1975; Ray Floyd at Southern Hills, Tulsa, Okla., in 1982; Vijay Singh (Fiji) at the Inverness Club, Toledo, Ohio in 1993; and Gary Player (South Africa) at Shoalcreek Country Club, Birmingham, Ala. in 1993.

Lowest 72-hole total 271 (64, 71, 69, 67), by Bobby Nichols at Columbus Country Club, Ohio in 1964.

Oldest champion 48 years 140 days, Julius Boros (1968).

Youngest champion 20 years 173 days, Gene Sarazen (1922).

PROFESSIONAL GOLFERS ASSOCIATION (PGA) TOUR RECORDS

Most wins (season) Byron Nelson won a record 18 tournaments in 1945.

Most wins (career) Sam Snead won 81 official PGA tour events from 1936–65.

Most consecutive wins 11, Byron Nelson, 1945.

Most wins (same event) Sam Snead won the Greater Greensboro Open eight times to set the individual tournament win mark. His victories came in 1938, 1946, 1949–50, 1955–56, 1960, 1965.

Most consecutive wins (same event) Four, by Walter Hagen, PGA Championship, 1924–27.

Oldest winner 52 years 10 months, Sam Snead, 1965 Greater Greensboro Open.

Youngest winner 19 years 10 months, Johnny McDermott, 1911 U.S. Open.

Widest winning margin 16 strokes, by Bobby Locke (South Africa), 1948 Chicago Victory National Championship.

LOWEST SCORES

Nine holes 27, by two players: Mike Souchak at the Brackenridge Park Golf Course, San Antonio, Tex., on the back nine of the first round of the 1955 Texas Open; Andy North at the En-Joie Golf Club, Endicott, N.Y., on the back nine of the first round of the 1975 B.C. Open.

18 holes 59, by two players: Al Geiberger at the Colonial Country Club, Memphis, Tenn., during the second round of the 1977 Danny Thomas Memphis Classic; Chip Beck at the Sunrise Golf Club, Las Vegas, Nev., during the third round of the 1991 Las Vegas Invitational.

PGA CHAMPIONS (1916–1994)

Year	Champion	Year	Champion	Year	Champion
1916	Jim Barnes	1943	not held	1970	Dave Stockton
1917	not held	1944	Bob Hamilton	1971	Jack Nicklaus
1918	not held	1945	Byron Nelson	1972	Gary Player[1]
1919	Jim Barnes	1946	Ben Hogan	1973	Jack Nicklaus
1920	Jock Hutchinson	1947	Jim Ferrier	1974	Lee Trevino
1921	Walter Hagen	1948	Ben Hogan	1975	Jack Nicklaus
1922	Gene Sarazen	1949	Sam Snead	1976	Dave Stockton
1923	Gene Sarazen	1950	Chandler Harper	1977	Lanny Wadkins
1924	Walter Hagen	1951	Sam Snead	1978	John Mahaffey
1925	Walter Hagen	1952	Jim Turnesa	1979	David Graham[2]
1926	Walter Hagen	1953	Walter Burkemo	1980	Jack Nicklaus
1927	Walter Hagen	1954	Chick Harbert	1981	Larry Nelson
1928	Leo Diegel	1955	Doug Ford	1982	Raymond Floyd
1929	Leo Diegel	1956	Jack Burke Jr.	1983	Hal Sutton
1930	Tommy Armour	1957	Lionel Hebert	1984	Lee Trevino
1931	Tom Creavy	1958	Dow Finsterwald	1985	Hubert Green
1932	Olin Dutra	1959	Bob Rosburg	1986	Bob Tway
1933	Gene Sarazen	1960	Jay Herbert	1987	Larry Nelson
1934	Paul Runyan	1961	Jerry Barber	1988	Jeff Sluman
1935	Johnny Revolta	1962	Gary Player[1]	1989	Payne Stewart
1936	Densmore Shute	1963	Jack Nicklaus	1990	Wayne Grady[2]
1937	Densmore Shute	1964	Bobby Nichols	1991	John Daly
1938	Paul Runyan	1965	Dave Marr	1992	Nick Price[3]
1939	Henry Picard	1966	Al Geiberger	1993	Paul Azinger
1940	Byron Nelson	1967	Don January	1994	Ernie Els
1941	Vic Chezzi	1968	Julius Boros		
1942	Sam Snead	1969	Raymond Floyd		

Nationalities: 1—South Africa, 2—Australia, 3—Zimbabwe

36 holes 125, by three players: Gay Brewer at the Pensacola Country Club, Pensacola, Fla., during the second and third rounds of the 1967 Pensacola Open; Ron Streck at the Oak Hills Country Club, San Antonio, Tex., during the third and fourth rounds of the 1978 Texas Open; Blaine McCallister at the Oakwood Country Club, Coal Valley, Ill., during the second and third rounds of the 1988 Hardee's Golf Classic.

54 holes 189, by Chandler Harper at the Brackenridge Park Golf Course, San Antonio, Tex., during the last three rounds of the 1954 Texas Open.

72 holes 257, by Mike Souchak at the Brackenridge Park Golf Course, San Antonio, Tex., at the 1955 Texas Open.

90 holes 325, by Tom Kite at four courses, La Quinta, Calif., at the 1993 Bob Hope Chrysler Classic.

Most shots under par 35, by Tom Kite at the 90-hole 1993 Bob Hope Chrysler Classic. The most shots under par in a 72-hole tournament is 27, shared by two players: Mike Souchak, at the 1955 Texas Open; and Ben Hogan, at the 1945 Portland Invitational.

HIGHEST EARNINGS

Season Nick Price (Zimbabwe), $1,499,927 in 1994.

Career As of January 11, 1995 Tom Kite has career earnings of $9,159,419.

Most times leading money winner Eight, Jack Nicklaus, 1964–65, 1967, 1971–73, 1975–76.

SENIOR PGA TOUR

The Senior PGA tour was established in 1982. Players 50 years and older are eligible to compete on the tour. Tournaments vary between 54- and 72-hole stroke-play.

Most wins 24, by Miller Barber (1981–92).

Most wins (season) Nine, by Peter Thomson, 1985.

Most consecutive wins Three, by two players: Bob Charles and Chi Chi Rodriguez, both in 1987.

Senior Tour / Regular Tour win Ray Floyd (U.S.) is the only player to win a Senior Tour event and a PGA Tour event in the same year. He won the Doral Open PGA event in March 1992, and won his first Senior event, the GTE Northern, in September 1992.

HIGHEST EARNINGS

Season $1,190,518, Lee Trevino in 1990.

Career As of January 18, 1995 Bob Charles (New Zealand) has career earnings of $5,201,105.

THE PGA EUROPEAN TOUR

Most wins (season) Seven, by two players: Norman von Nida (Australia), 1947; and Flory van Donck (Belgium), 1953.

Most wins (career) 53, by Severiano Ballesteros (Spain), 1976–94.

HIGHEST EARNINGS

Season £1,220,540, by Nick Faldo (Great Britain) in 1992.

Career £4,745,741, by Nick Faldo, 1976–94.

Most times leading money winner Six, Severiano Ballesteros, 1976–78, 1986, 1988, 1991.

RYDER CUP A biennial match-play competition between professional representative teams of the United States and Europe (Great Britain and Ireland prior to 1979), this event was launched in 1927. The U.S. leads the series 23–5, with two ties.

Most individual wins Arnold Palmer has won the most matches in Ryder Cup competition with 22 victories out of 32 played.

Most selections Christy O'Connor Sr. (Great Britain and Ireland) has played in the most contests, with 10 selections 1955–73. The record in the United States is eight, held by three players: Billy Casper, 1961–75; Ray Floyd, 1969–93; and Lanny Wadkins, 1977–93.

PROFESSIONAL GOLF (WOMEN)

GRAND SLAM CHAMPIONSHIPS

GRAND SLAM A Grand Slam in ladies' professional golf has been recognized since 1955. From 1955–66, the United States Open, Ladies Professional Golf Association (LPGA) Championship, Western Open and Titleholders Championship served as the "majors." From 1967–82 the Grand Slam events changed, as first the Western Open (1967) and then the Titleholders Championship (1972) were discontinued. Since 1983, the U.S. Open, LPGA Championship, du Maurier Classic and Nabisco Dinah Shore have comprised the Grand Slam events.

Most grand slam titles Patty Berg has won the most majors, with 15 titles (one U.S. Open, seven Titleholders, seven Western Open).

THE UNITED STATES OPEN In this competition, inaugurated in 1946, the first event was played as a match-play tournament; however, since 1947, the 72-hole stroke-play format has been used.

Most wins Two players have won the title four times: Betsy Rawls (1951, 1953, 1957, 1960); Mickey Wright (1958–59, 1961, 1964).

Most consecutive wins Two, by five players: Mickey Wright (1958–59); Donna Caponi (1969–70); Susie Berning (1972–73); Hollis Stacy (1977–78); Betsy King (1989–90).

Lowest 18-hole total 65, by three players: Sally Little at Country Club of Indianapolis, Ind., in 1978; Judy Dickinson at Baltusrol Golf Club, Springfield, N.J., in 1985; Ayako Okamoto (Japan) at Indian Wood Golf and Country Club, Lake Orion, Mich., in 1989.

Lowest 72-hole total 277, by Liselotte Neumann (Sweden) at Baltimore Country Club, Md., in 1988.

Oldest champion 40 years 11 months, Fay Crocker (1955).

Youngest champion 22 years 5 days, Catherine Lacoste (France; 1967).

LPGA CHAMPIONSHIP This event was inaugurated in 1955; since 1987, it has been officially called the Mazda LPGA Championship.

Most wins Mickey Wright has won the LPGA a record four times: 1958, 1960–61, 1963.

Most consecutive wins Two, by two players: Mickey Wright (1960–61); Patty Sheehan (1983–84).

Lowest 18-hole total 64, by Patty Sheehan at the Jack Nicklaus Sports Center, Kings Island, Ohio, in 1984.

Lowest 72-hole total 267, by Betsy King at the Bethesda Country Club, Md., in 1992.

NABISCO DINAH SHORE Inaugurated in 1972, this event was formerly called the Colgate–Dinah Shore (1972–82). The event was designated a "major" in 1983. Mission Hills Country Club, Rancho Mirage, Calif. is the permanent site.

U.S. OPEN CHAMPIONS (1946–1994)

Year	Champion	Year	Champion	Year	Champion
1946	Patty Berg	1963	Mary Mills	1980	Amy Alcott
1947	Betty Jameson	1964	Mickey Wright	1981	Pat Bradley
1948	Babe Zaharias	1965	Carol Mann	1982	Janet Anderson
1949	Louise Suggs	1966	Sandra Spuzich	1983	Jan Stephenson
1950	Babe Zaharias	1967	Catherine Lacoste[1]	1984	Hollis Stacy
1951	Betsy Rawls	1968	Susie Berning	1985	Kathy Baker
1952	Louise Suggs	1969	Donna Caponi	1986	Jane Geddes
1953	Betsy Rawls	1970	Donna Caponi	1987	Laura Davies[2]
1954	Babe Zaharias	1971	JoAnne Carner	1988	Liselotte Neumann[3]
1955	Fay Crocker	1972	Susie Berning	1989	Betsy King
1956	Kathy Cornelius	1973	Susie Berning	1990	Betsy King
1957	Betsy Rawls	1974	Sandra Haynie	1991	Meg Mallon
1958	Mickey Wright	1975	Sandra Palmer	1992	Patty Sheehan
1959	Mickey Wright	1976	JoAnne Carner	1993	Laurie Merten
1960	Betsy Rawls	1977	Hollis Stacy	1994	Patty Sheehan
1961	Mickey Wright	1978	Hollis Stacy		
1962	Murle Lindstrom	1979	Jerilyn Britz		

1—France, 2—Great Britain, 3—Sweden

NABISCO DINAH SHORE CHAMPIONS (1972–1994)

Year	Champion	Year	Champion
1972	Jane Blalock	1984	Juli Inkster
1973	Mickey Wright	1985	Alice Miller
1974	Jo Ann Prentice	1986	Pat Bradley
1975	Sandra Palmer	1987	Betsy King
1976	Judy Rankin	1988	Amy Alcott
1977	Kathy Whitworth	1989	Juli Inkster
1978	Sandra Post	1990	Betsy King
1979	Sandra Post	1991	Amy Alcott
1980	Donna Caponi	1992	Dottie Mochrie
1981	Nancy Lopez	1993	Helen Alfredsson[1]
1982	Sally Little	1994	Donna Andrews
1983	Amy Alcott		

1—Sweden

Most wins Amy Alcott has won the title three times: 1983, 1988 and 1991.

Most consecutive wins Two, by Sandra Post (1978–79).

Lowest 18-hole total 64, by two players: Nancy Lopez in 1981; Sally Little in 1982.

Lowest 72-hole total 273, by Amy Alcott in 1991.

DU MAURIER CLASSIC Inaugurated in 1973, this event was formerly known as La Canadienne (1973) and the Peter Jackson Classic (1974–82). Granted "major" status in 1979, the tournament is held annually at different sites in Canada.

Most wins Pat Bradley has won this event a record three times, 1980, 1985–86.

Most consecutive wins Two, by Pat Bradley (1985–86).

Lowest 18-hole total 64, by three players: Jo-Anne Carner at St. George's Country Club, Toronto in 1978; Jane Geddes at Beaconsfield Country Club, Montreal, Canada in 1985; Dawn Coe-Jones at London Hunt and Country Club, Ontario in 1993.

Lowest 72-hole total 276, by three players. Pat Bradley and Ayako Okamoto (Japan) tied in regulation play in 1986 at the Board of Trade Country Club, Toronto. Bradley defeated Okamoto for the title in a sudden-death playoff. Cathy Johnston matched Bradley and Okamato in 1990 at Westmont Golf and Country Club, Kitchener, Ontario.

LADIES PROFESSIONAL GOLF ASSOCIATION (LPGA) TOUR

ORIGINS In 1944, three women golfers, Hope Seignious, Betty Hicks and Ellen Griffin, launched the Women's Professional Golf Association (WPGA). By 1947 the WPGA was unable to sustain the tour at the level that was hoped, and it seemed certain that women's professional golf would fade away. However, Wilson Sporting Goods stepped in, overhauled the tour and called it the Ladies Profes-

DU MAURIER CLASSIC CHAMPIONS (1973–1994)

Year	Champion	Year	Champion	Year	Champion
1973	Jocelyne Bourassa	1981	Jan Stephenson	1989	Tammie Green
1974	Carole Jo Skala	1982	Sandra Haynie	1990	Cathy Johnston
1975	JoAnne Carner	1983	Hollis Stacy	1991	Nancy Scranton
1976	Donna Caponi	1984	Juli Inkster	1992	Sherri Steinhauer
1977	Judy Rankin	1985	Pat Bradley	1993	Brandie Burton
1978	JoAnne Carner	1986	Pat Bradley	1994	Martha Nause
1979	Amy Alcott	1987	Jody Rosenthal		
1980	Pat Bradley	1988	Sally Little		

LPGA CHAMPIONS (1955–1994)

Year	Champion	Year	Champion	Year	Champion
1955	Beverly Hanson	1969	Betsy Rawls	1983	Patty Sheehan
1956	Marlene Hagge	1970	Shirley Englehorn	1984	Patty Sheehan
1957	Louise Suggs	1971	Kathy Whitworth	1985	Nancy Lopez
1958	Mickey Wright	1972	Kathy Ahem	1986	Pat Bradley
1959	Betsy Rawls	1973	Mary Mills	1987	Jane Geddes
1960	Mickey Wright	1974	Sandra Haynie	1988	Sherri Turner
1961	Mickey Wright	1975	Kathy Whitworth	1989	Nancy Lopez
1962	Judy Kimball	1976	Betty Burfeindt	1990	Beth Daniel
1963	Mickey Wright	1977	Chako Higuchi	1991	Meg Mallon
1964	Mary Mills	1978	Nancy Lopez	1992	Betsy King
1965	Sandra Haynie	1979	Donna Caponi	1993	Patty Sheehan
1966	Gloria Ehret	1980	Sally Little	1994	Laura Davies
1967	Kathy Whitworth	1981	Donna Caponi		
1968	Sandra Post	1982	Jan Stephenson		

CHIPPING ■ NANCY LOPEZ, WINNER OF FIVE CONSECUTIVE LPGA EVENTS. (LPGA/DEE DARDEN)

sional Golf Association. In 1950, the LPGA received its official charter.

Most wins (career) 88, by Kathy Whitworth, 1962–85.

Most wins (season) 13, by Mickey Wright, in 1963.

Most consecutive wins (scheduled events) Four, by two players: Mickey Wright, on two occasions, 1962, 1963; Kathy Whitworth, 1969.

Most consecutive wins (in events participated in) Five, by Nancy Lopez between May and June 1978.

Most wins (same event) Seven, by Patty Berg, who won two tournaments, the Titleholders Championship and the Western Open, both now defunct, on seven occasions during her illustrious career. She won the Titleholders in 1937–39, 1948, 1953, 1955, 1957; and the Western in 1941, 1943, 1948, 1951, 1955, 1957–58.

Oldest winner 46 years 5 months 9 days, JoAnne Carner at the 1985 Safeco Classic.

Youngest winner 18 years 14 days, Marlene Hagge at the 1952 Sarasota Open.

Widest margin of victory 14 strokes, by two players: Louise Suggs in the 1949 U.S. Open; Cindy Mackey in the 1986 Mastercard International.

HIGHEST EARNINGS

Season $863,578, by Beth Daniel in 1990.

Career As of January 18, 1995 Pat Bradley has earned $4,818,865.

Most times leading money winner Eight, Kathy Whitworth, 1965–68, 1970–73.

LOWEST SCORES

Nine holes 28, by four players: Mary Beth Zimmerman at the Rail Golf Club, Springfield, Ill., during the 1984 Rail Charity Golf Classic; Pat Bradley at the Green Gables Country Club, Denver, Colo., during the 1984 Columbia Savings Classic; Muffin Spencer-Devlin at the Knollwood Country Club, Elmsford, N.Y., during the 1985 MasterCard International Pro-Am; Peggy Kirsch at the Squaw-Creek Country Club, Vienna, Ohio during the 1991 Phar-Mar in Youngstown.

18 holes 62, by four players: Mickey Wright at Hogan Park Golf Club, Midland, Tex., in the first round of the 1964 Tall City Open; Vicki Fergon at Alamaden Golf & Country Club, San Jose, Calif., in the second round of the 1984 San Jose Classic; Laura Davies (Great Britain) at the Rail Golf Club, Springfield, Ill., during the 1991 Rail Charity Golf Classic; and Hollis Stacy at the Meridian Valley Country Club, Seattle, Wash., during the 1992 Safeco Classic.

36 holes 129, by Judy Dickinson at Pasadena Yacht & Country Club, St. Petersburg, Fla., during the 1985 S&H Golf Classic.

54 holes 197, by Pat Bradley at the Rail Golf Club, Springfield, Ill., in the 1991 Rail Charity Golf Classic.

72 holes 267, by Betsy King at the Bethesda Country Club, Md., in the 1992 Mazda LPGA Championship.

AMATEUR GOLF

UNITED STATES AMATEUR CHAMPIONSHIP Inaugurated in 1895, the initial format was match-play competition. In 1965, the format was changed to stroke-play; however, since 1972, the event has been played under the original match-play format.

Most wins (men) Five, by Bobby Jones, 1924–25, 1927–28, 1930.

Most wins (women) Anne Sander has won a total of seven amateur championships, 1958, 1961 and 1963 and in senior play, 1987, 1989–90, 1993.

PAT ON THE BACK ■ IN 1994 PAT BRADLEY ADDED MORE THAN $100,000 TO HER RECORD CAREER EARNINGS. (LPGA/JEFF HORNBACK)

Lowest score (stroke-play) 279, Lanny Wadkins, 1970.

Biggest winning margin (match-play: final) 12 & 11, Charles Macdonald, 1895.

NCAA CHAMPIONSHIP The men's championship was initiated in 1897 as a match-play championship. In 1967 the format was switched to stroke-play.

Most titles (team) Yale has won the most team championships with 21 victories (1897–98, 1902, 1905–13, 1915, 1924–26, 1931–33, 1936, 1943).

Most titles (individual) Two golfers have won three individual titles: Ben Crenshaw (Texas), 1971–73; Phil Mickelson (Arizona State), 1989–90, 1992.

FANTASTIC FEATS

Consecutive birdies The official PGA record for consecutive birdies is 8, recorded by three players: Bob Goalby, during the fourth round of the 1961 St. Petersburg Open; Fuzzy Zoeller, during the opening round of the 1976 Quad Cities Open; and Dewey Arnette, during the opening round of the 1987 Buick Open. Goalby was the only one to win his event.

Longest drive (standard course) Michael Hoke Austin holds the record for longest recorded drive on a standard course. On September 25, 1974, Austin hit a golf ball 515 yards in the U.S. National Seniors Open Championship in Las Vegas, Nev.

Longest drive (general) Niles Lied (Australia) drove a golf ball 2,640 yards (1½ miles) across an ice cap at Mawson Base, Antarctica in 1962.

Longest putt (tournament) The longest recorded holed putt in a professional tournament is 110 feet, by Jack Nicklaus in the 1964 Tournament of Champions; and by Nick Price in the 1992 United States PGA Championship.

Longest putt (general) Bob Cook (U.S.) sank a putt measured 140 feet 2¾ inches at St. Andrews, Great Britain in the International Fourball Pro Am Tournament on October 1, 1976.

Most balls hit in one hour The most balls driven in one hour—at least 100 yards and into a target area—is 1,536, by Noel Hunt at Shrigley Hall, Pott Shrigley, Great Britain on May 2, 1990.

Most holds (on foot) Ian Colston, 35, played 22 rounds plus five holes (401 holes in all) at Bendigo Gold Club, Victoria, Australia (par-73, 6,061 yards) on November 27–28, 1971.

Most holes (using golf cart) David Cavalier played 846 holes at Arrowhead Country Club, North Canton, Ohio (9 holes, 3,013 yards) on August 6–7, 1990.

Oldest hole in one Otto Bucher (Switzerland) was 99 years 244 days old when he sank the 130-yard 12th hole at La Manga Golf Club, Spain on January 13, 1985.

GYMNASTICS

ORIGINS The ancient Greeks and Romans were exponents of gymnastics, as shown by demonstration programs in the ancient Olympic Games (776 B.C. to A.D. 393). Modern training techniques were developed in Germany toward the end of the 18th century. Johann Friedrich Simon was the first teacher of the modern methods, at Basedow's

School, Dessau, Germany in 1776. Friedrich Jahn, who founded the Turnverein in Berlin, Germany in 1811, is regarded as the most influential of the gymnastics pioneers. The International Gymnastics Federation (FIG) was formed in 1891.

United States Gymnastics was introduced to the United States in the 19th century. With the advent of the modern Olympic Games, interest in the sport grew in this country, and in 1920 the United States entered its first gymnastics team in the Games. The sport was governed by the Amateur Athletic Union (AAU) and then by the National Collegiate Athletic Association (NCAA) until 1963, when the United States Gymnastics Federation (USGF) was formed. The USGF is still the governing body for the sport, and has its headquarters in Indianapolis, Ind.

OLYMPIC GAMES Gymnastics was included in the first modern Olympic Games in 1896; however, women's competition was not included until 1928.

Most gold medals Larissa Latynina (USSR) has won nine gold medals: six individual—all-around title, 1956 and 1960; floor exercise, 1956, 1960 and 1964; vault, 1956; and three team titles—1956, 1960 and 1964. In men's competition, Sawao Kato (Japan) has won eight gold medals: five individual—all-around title, 1968 and 1972; floor exercise, 1968; and parallel bars, 1972 and 1976; and three team titles—1968, 1972 and 1976.

Vera Caslavska (Czechoslovakia) has won a record seven individual gold medals: all-around title, 1964 and 1968; uneven bars, 1968; beam, 1964; floor exercise, 1968; and vault, 1964 and 1968. In men's competition, Boris Shakhlin and Nikolai Andrianov (both USSR) have each won six individual titles. Shakhlin won the all-around title, 1960; parallel bars, 1960; pommel horse, 1956, 1960; horizontal bar, 1964; vault, 1960. Andrianov won the all-around title, 1976; floor exercise, 1972, 1976; pommel horse, 1976; and vault, 1976 and 1980.

Most medals Larissa Latynina (USSR) has won 18 medals, the most of any athlete in any sport. She has won nine gold (six in individual events [see above] and one team event, 1980); five silver—all-around title, 1964; uneven bars, 1956 and 1960; beam, 1960; vault, 1964; and four bronze—uneven bars, 1964; beam, 1964; vault, 1964; and the portable apparatus team event (now discontinued) in 1956. Nikolai Andrianov holds the men's record at 15, which is the most by any male athlete in any sport. He won seven gold (six in individual events [see above] and one team event, 1980); five silver—team event, 1972 and 1976; all-around title, 1980; floor exercise, 1980; parallel bars, 1976; and three bronze—pommel horse, 1976; horizontal bar, 1980; and vault, 1972.

WORLD CHAMPIONSHIPS First held in Antwerp, Belgium in 1903, the championships were discontinued in 1913. Reintroduced in 1922, the event was held quadrenially until 1979, when the format became biennial. Until 1979 the Olympic Games served as the world championships, and results from Olympic competition are included in world championship statistics.

SURE NOT TO FALL ■ RECORD GOLD MEDALIST SHANNON MILLER ON THE BALANCE BEAM AT THE 1994 GOODWILL GAMES. (ALLSPORT/CLIVE BRUNSKILL)

Most titles Larissa Latynina (USSR) won 17 world titles: five team and 12 individual, 1956–64. In men's competition, Boris Shakhlin (USSR) has won 13 titles: three team and 10 individual, 1954–64.

United States Shannon Miller won a record five gold medals in 1994 at all-around and balance beam.

UNITED STATES NATIONAL CHAMPIONSHIPS

Most titles Alfred A. Jochim won a record seven men's all-around U.S. titles, 1925–30 and 1933, and a total of 34 at all exercises between 1923 and 1934. The women's record is six all-around, 1945–46 and 1949–52, and 39 at all exercises, including 11 in succession at balance beam, 1941–51, by Clara Marie Schroth Lomady.

NCAA CHAMPIONSHIPS (MEN) The men's competition was first held in 1932.

Most team titles The most team championships won is nine, by two colleges: Illinois, 1939–42, 1950, 1955–56, 1958, 1989; Penn State, 1948, 1953–54, 1957, 1959–61, 1965, 1976.

INDIVIDUAL RECORDS

Most titles (one year) Four, by two gymnasts: Jean Cronstedt, Penn State, won the all-around title, parallel bar, horizontal bar and floor exercise in 1954; Robert Lynn, Southern Cal., won the all-around title, parallel bar, horizontal bar and floor exercise in 1962.

Most titles (career) Seven, by two gymnasts: Joe Giallombardo, Illinois, won the tumbling, 1938–40; all-around title, 1938–40; and floor exercise, 1938; Jim Hartung, Nebraska, won the all-around title, 1980–81; rings, 1980–82; and parallel bar, 1981–82.

NCAA CHAMPIONSHIPS (WOMEN) The women's competition was first held in 1982.

Most team titles The most team championships won is seven, by Utah, 1982–86, 1990, 1992.

INDIVIDUAL RECORDS

Most titles (one year) Four, by Missy Marlowe, Utah, who won the all-around, balance beam, uneven bars and floor exercise in 1992.

Most titles (career) Five, by Missy Marlowe, Utah. She won the balance beam, 1991–92, all-around, 1992, uneven bars, 1992, and floor exercise, 1992.

GYMNASTICS EXERCISES

Exercise	Total	Gymnast	Date
Chins—consecutive	370	Lee Chin-Yong (South Korea)	May 14, 1988
Chins—consecutive (one arm, from a ring)	22	Robert Chrisnall (Canada)	Dec. 3, 1982
Parallel bar dips—one hour	3,726	Kim Yang-ki (South Korea)	Nov. 28, 1991
Sit-ups—24 hours	70,715	Lou Scripa Jr. (U.S.)	Dec. 1–2, 1992
Push-ups—24 hours	46,001	Charles Servizio (U.S.)	Apr. 24–25, 1993
Push-ups—five hours (one arm)	8,151	Alan Rumbell (Great Britain)	June 26, 1993
Push-ups—five hours (fingertip)	7,011	Kim Yang-ki (South Korea)	Aug. 30, 1990
Push-ups—consecutive (one finger)	124	Paul Lynch (Great Britain)	Apr. 21, 1992
Push-ups—one year	1,500,230	Paddy Doyle (Great Britain)	Oct. 1988–Oct. 1989
Leg lifts—12 hours	41,788	Lou Scripa Jr. (U.S.)	Dec. 2, 1988
Somersaults—consecutive	8,341 (over 12 miles 390 yards)	Ashrita Furman (U.S.)	April 20, 1986
Somersaults—backwards	54.68 yards in 10.8 seconds	Shigeru Iwasaki	March 30, 1980
Squats—one hour	4,289	Paul Wai Man Chung (Hong Kong)	Apr. 5, 1993
Squat thrusts—one hour	3,552	Paul Wai Man Chung (Hong Kong)	Apr. 21, 1992
Burpees—one hour	1,840	Paddy Doyle (Great Britain)	Feb. 6, 1994
Pummel horse double circles—consecutive	97	Tyler Farstad (Great Britain)	Nov. 27, 1993

ROLLING AROUND ■ ASHRITA FURMAN, HOLDER OF NINE RECORDS IN THE GUINNESS BOOK OF RECORDS, SOMERSAULTING 8,341 TIMES CONSECUTIVELY . (ASHRITA FURMAN)

RHYTHMIC SPORTIVE GYMNASTICS

Modern rhythmic gymnastics involves complex body movements combined with handling of apparatus such as ropes, hoops, balls, clubs and ribbons. The performance must include required elements, and the choreography must cover the entire floor area and include elements such as jumps, flash leaps, balances, flexibility and pivots.

ORIGINS In 1962 the International Gymnastics Federation (FIG) officially recognized rhythmic gymnastics as a distinct sport. The first world championships were held in 1963 and the sport was included in the Olympic Games in 1984.

OLYMPIC GAMES Marina Lobach (USSR) won the 1988 Olympic title with a perfect score of 60.00 points in each of her events.

WORLD CHAMPIONSHIPS

Most titles (individual) Maria Gigova (Bulgaria) has won three individual world championships in 1969, 1971 and 1973 (tied).

Most titles (country) Bulgaria has won eight team championships: 1969, 1971, 1973, 1981, 1983, 1985, 1987 and 1989 (tie).

HANG GLIDING

See also SOARING.

ORIGINS In the 11th century the monk Eilmer is reported to have flown from the 60-foot tower of Malmesbury Abbey, Wiltshire, England. The earliest modern pioneer was Otto Lilienthal (Germany), with about 2,500 flights in gliders of his own construction between 1891 and 1896. In the 1950s, Professor Francis Rogallo of the National Space Agency developed a flexible "wing" from his space capsule reentry research.

WORLD RECORDS The *Fédération Aéronautique Internationale* recognizes world records for flexible-wing, rigid-wing, and multiplace flexible-wing.

UNITED STATES The United States Hang Gliding Association (USGA), located in Colorado Springs, Colo., is the national governing body for the sport. Founded in 1971 as the Southern California Hang Gliding Association (SCHGA), it became the USGA in 1973.

FLEXIBLE WING—SINGLE PLACE DISTANCE RECORDS (MEN)

Straight line Larry Tudor (U.S.) piloted a Ram-Air 154 for a straight-line distance of 307.696 miles from Rock Springs, Wyo. to outside Stoneham, Colo. on June 30, 1994.

Single turnpoint Larry Tudor (U.S.) piloted his RamAir 154 a single turnpoint (dogleg) record 307.773 miles from Rock Springs, Wyo. to outside Stoneham, Colo. on June 30, 1994.

Triangular course James Lee Jr. (U.S.) piloted a Willis Wing HPAT 158 for a triangular course record 121.79 miles over Wild Horse Mesa, Colo. on July 4, 1991.

Out and return The out and return goal distance record is 192.818 miles, set by two pilots on the same day, July 26, 1988, over Lone Pine, Calif.: Larry Tudor, Wills Wing HPAT 158; Geoffrey Loyns (Great Britain), Enterprise Wings.

Altitude gain Larry Tudor set a height gain record of 14,250.69 feet flying a G2-155 over Horseshoe Meadows, Calif. on August 4, 1985.

FLEXIBLE WING—SINGLE PLACE DISTANCE RECORDS (WOMEN)

Straight line Kari Castle (U.S.) piloted a Wills Wing AT 145 a straight-line distance of 208.63 miles over Lone Pine, Calif. on July 22, 1991.

Single turnpoint Kari Castle piloted a Pacific Airwave Magic Kiss a single-turnpoint distance of 181.47 miles over Hobbs, N.Mex. on July 1, 1990.

Triangular course Judy Leden (Great Britain) flew a triangular course record 70.173 miles over Austria on June 22, 1991.

Out and return The out and return goal distance record is 81.99 miles, set by Tover Buas-Hansen (Norway), piloting an International Axis over Owens Valley, Calif. on July 6, 1989.

Altitude gain The record for height gain is 13,025 feet by Judy Leden, Great Britain, flying over Kuruman, South Africa on December 1, 1992.

RIGID WING—SINGLE PLACE DISTANCE RECORDS (MEN)

Straight line The straight-line distance record is 139.07 miles, set by William Reynolds (U.S), piloting a Wills Wing over Lone Pine, Calif. on June 27, 1988.

Out and return The out and return goal distance is 47.46 miles, set by Randy Bergum (U.S.), piloting an Easy Riser over Big Pine, Calif. on July 12, 1988.

Altitude gain Rainer Scholl (South Africa) set an altitude gain record of 12,532.80 feet on May 8, 1985.

FLEXIBLE WING—MULTIPLACE DISTANCE RECORDS (MEN)

Straight line The straight line distance record is 100.60 miles, set by Larry Tudor and Eri Fujita, flying a Comet II-185 on July 12, 1985.

Out and return The out and return goal distance record is 81.99 miles, set by Kevin and Tom Klinefelter (U.S.) on July 6, 1989.

Altitude gain Tom and Kevin Klinefelter set an altitude record of 10,997.30 feet on July 6, 1989 over Bishop Airport, Calif. flying a Moyes Delta Glider.

LARRY TUDOR

LARRY TUDOR

He's hovered on his hang glider at a record altitude of 14,250.69 feet; he's traveled a record 307.696 miles hang gliding in a straight line; and he's the new hang gliding distance champion via a single turnpoint (dogleg) at 307.773 miles. Did Larry Tudor laugh in the face of danger when he first set forth into the skies over 20 years ago? Not quite. "I was scared to death the first time I tried it. In fact, I was just plain scared for several *years* after the first time."

Today, however, hang gliding at high altitudes and over long distances is a breeze for Tudor. "There's no fear anymore because once you've done it for a while it becomes second nature," he says. "It's like riding a bicycle except you have to get used to seeing clouds."

Tudor—who works as a test pilot and sales rep for Wills Wing, the company that manufactured his white RamAir 154 hang glider—enjoys the freedom of being in the air without traffic congestion and boundaries. "Being up in the air is like a feeling of release. You're not bound by limitations of the ground. There are no highways, you can just go anywhere you want to go."

With his incredible skill and, of course, a little bit of luck, Tudor has managed to avoid serious injuries over the years. When Tudor hang glides, the only things that come crashing down are the records. "I like to be on the cutting edge of the sport," Tudor says with pride. "Trying for the record is my chance to explore what's possible."

HARNESS RACING

Harness racing involves two styles of racing: trotting and pacing. The distinction between trotters and pacers is in the gait of the horses. The trotting gait requires the simultaneous use of the diagonally opposite legs, while pacers thrust out their fore and hind legs simultaneously on one side.

ORIGINS Trotting races are known to have been held in Valkenburg, the Netherlands in 1554. There is also evidence of trotting races in England in the late 16th century.

United States Harness racing became popular in the United States in the mid-19th century. The National Trotting Association was founded, originally as the National Association for the Promotion of the Interests of the Trotting Turf, in 1870, and is still the governing body for the sport in the United States.

TROTTING

HORSES' RECORDS

VICTORIES

Career Goldsmith Maid won an all-time record 350 races (including dashes and heats) from 1864 through 1877.

Season Make Believe won a record 53 races in 1949.

HIGHEST EARNINGS

Career The greatest career earnings for any harness horse is $4,907,307, by Peace Corps, 1988–93.

Season The single-season earnings record for a trotter is $1,610,608, by Prakas in 1985.

Race The richest race in the trotting calendar is the Hambletonian. The richest Hambletonian was the 1992 event, with a total purse of $1,380,000. The record first-place prize was $673,000 for the 1990 race, won by Harmonious.

INDIVIDUAL RACES

THE TRIPLE CROWN The Triple Crown for trotters consists of three races: Hambletonian, Kentucky Futurity and Yonkers Trot. Six trotters have won the Triple Crown.

TRIPLE CROWN WINNERS—TROTTERS

Year	Horse	Driver
1955	Scott Frost	Joe O'Brien
1963	Speedy Scot	Ralph Baldwin
1964	Ayres	John Simpson Sr.
1968	Nevele Pride	Stanley Dancer
1969	Lindy's Pride	Howard Beissinger
1972	Super Bowl	Stanley Dancer

HAMBLETONIAN The most famous race in North American harness racing, the Hambletonian, was first run in 1926. The Hambletonian has been run at six venues: New York State Fairgrounds, Syracuse, N.Y. (1926 and 1928); The Red Mile, Lexington, Ky. (1927 and 1929); Good Time Park, Goshen, N.Y. (1930–42, 1944–56); Empire City, Yonkers, N.Y. (1943); Du Quoin State Fair, Du Quoin, Ill. (1957–80); and The Meadowlands, N.J. (1981–present). The Hambletonian is open to three-year-olds and is run over one mile.

Fastest time The fastest time is 1 minute 53⅖ seconds, by American Winner, driven by Ron Pierce, in 1993.

Most wins (driver) Three drivers have won the Hambletonian four times: Ben White, 1933, 1936, 1942 and 1943; Stanley Dancer, 1968, 1972, 1975 and 1983; William Haughton, 1974, 1976–77 and 1980.

KENTUCKY FUTURITY First held in 1893, the Kentucky Futurity is a one-mile race for three-year-olds, raced at The Red Mile, Lexington, Ky.

Fastest time The fastest time is 1 minute 52⅗ seconds, by Pine Chip, driven by John Campbell, in 1993.

Most wins (driver) Ben White has driven the winning trotter seven times: 1916, 1922, 1924–25, 1933, 1936–37.

YONKERS TROT First run in 1955, when it was known as "The Yonkers," this race has been known since 1975 as the Yonkers Trot. Run over one mile for three-year-olds, the race is currently staged at Yonkers Raceway, N.Y.

Fastest time The fastest time is 1 minute 56⅖ seconds, by American Winner, driven by Ron Pierce, in 1993.

GO AMERICA ■ AMERICAN WINNER, DRIVEN BY RON PIERCE, SET THE MARK FOR FASTEST TIME IN THE YONKERS TROT IN 1993. (U.S. TROTTING ASSOCIATION)

Most wins (driver) Stanley Dancer has driven the winning trotter six times: 1959, 1965, 1968, 1971–72 and 1975.

PACERS

HORSES' RECORDS

VICTORIES

Career Single G won 262 races (including dashes and heats), 1918–26.

Career (modern record) Symbol Allen won 241 races from 1943 through 1958.

Season Victory Hy won a record 65 races in 1950.

Consecutive wins Carty Nagle won 41 consecutive races from 1937 through 1938.

HIGHEST EARNINGS

Career The all-time earnings record for a pacer is $3,225,653, by Nihilator, 1984–85.

Season The single-season record for a pacer is $2,264,714, by Cam's Card Shark in 1994.

Race The richest race in harness racing history was the 1984 Woodrow Wilson, which carried a total purse of $2,161,000. The winner, Nihilator, earned a record $1,080,500.

INDIVIDUAL RACES

THE TRIPLE CROWN The Triple Crown for pacers consists of three races: Cane Pace, Little Brown Jug and Messenger Stakes. Seven horses have won the Triple Crown.

TRIPLE CROWN WINNERS—PACERS

Year	Horse	Driver
1959	Adios Butler	Clint Hodgins
1965	Bret Hanover	Frank Ervin
1966	Romeo Hanover	Jerry Silverman
1968	Rum Customer	William Haughton
1970	Most Happy Fella	Stanley Dancer
1980	Niatross	Clint Galbraith
1983	Ralph Hanover	Ron Waples

CANE PACE First run in 1955, this race was originally known as the Cane Futurity. Since 1975, it has been called the Cane Pace. Run over one mile, the race is open to three-year-olds, and is run at Yonkers Raceway, N.Y.

Fastest time The fastest time is 1 minute 51²/₅ seconds, by Riyadh, driven by Jim Morrill Jr., in 1993.

Most wins (driver) Stanley Dancer has driven the winning pacer four times: 1964, 1970–71 and 1976.

LITTLE BROWN JUG First run in 1946, the Jug is raced annually at Delaware County Fair, Delaware, Ohio. The race is for three-year-olds and is run over one mile.

Fastest time The fastest time is 1 minute 52 seconds, by Life Sign, driven by John Campbell, in 1993.

Most wins (driver) William Haughton has driven five winning pacers, in 1955, 1964, 1968–69 and 1974.

MESSENGER STAKES First run in 1956, this race has been staged at various locations during its history. The race is run over one mile and is open to three-year-olds only.

Fastest time The fastest time is 1 minute 51 seconds, by Cam's Card Shark, driven by John Campbell in 1994.

Most wins (drivers) William Haughton has driven the winning pacer seven times, in 1956, 1967–68, 1972 and 1974–76.

DRIVERS' RECORDS

Most wins (career) Herve Filion (Canada) has won 14,539 harness races as of January 18, 1995.

Most wins (season) Walter Case won a record 843 races in 1992.

Most wins (day) Mike Lachance won 12 races at Yonkers Raceway, N.Y. on June 23, 1987.

HIGHEST EARNINGS

Career John Campbell has won a career record $129,011,804 in prize money, 1972–January 18, 1995.

Season John Campbell won a season record $11,620,878 in 1990, when he won 543 races.

FANTASTIC FEATS

Oldest driver Eighty-three-year-old George McCandless of Vineland, N.J. guided Kehm's Scooter to victory at Freehold Raceway in 1994.

HOCKEY

The 1994–95 season was interrupted by a preseason management lockout from September 30, 1994–January 11, 1995. For further information on sports strikes, refer to page 18.

ORIGINS There is pictorial evidence that a hockey-like game (*kalv*) was played on ice in the early 16th century in the Netherlands. The game was probably first played in North America on December 25, 1855 at Kingston, Ontario, Canada, but Halifax also lays claim to priority. The International Ice Hockey Federation was founded in 1908.

NATIONAL HOCKEY LEAGUE (NHL)

ORIGINS The National Hockey League (NHL) was founded on November 22, 1917 in Montreal, Canada. The formation of the NHL was precipitated by the collapse of the National Hockey Association of Canada (NHA). Four teams formed the original league: the Montreal Canadiens, Montreal Wanderers, Ottawa Senators and Quebec Bulldogs. The Toronto Arenas were admitted as a fifth team, but the Bulldogs were unable to operate, and the league began as a four-team competition. The first NHL game was played on December 19, 1917. The NHL is now comprised of 26 teams, eight from Canada and 18 from the United States, divided into two divisions within two conferences: Northeast and Atlantic Divisions in the Eastern Conference; Pacific and Central Division in the Western Conference. At the end of the regular season, 16 teams compete in the Stanley Cup playoffs to decide the NHL Championship. (For further details of the Stanley Cup, see pages 141–148.)

TEAM RECORDS

Most wins (season) The Montreal Canadiens won 60 games during the 1976–77 season. In 80 games, "the Habs" won 60, lost 8 and tied 12.

Highest winning percentage (season) The 1929–30 Boston Bruins set an NHL record .875 winning percentage. The Bruins' record was 38 wins, 5 losses and 1 tie.

Most points (season) The Montreal Canadiens accumulated 132 points during their record-setting campaign of 1976–77, when they won a record 60 games.

Most losses (season) The Washington Capitals hold the unenviable record of having lost the most games in one season. During the 1974–75 season, the first for the franchise, the Capitals lost 67 of 80 games played.

Most goals (game) The NHL record for goals in one game is 21, which has occurred on two occasions. The mark was set on January 10, 1920, when the Montreal Canadiens defeated the Toronto St. Patricks, 14–7, at Montreal. This record was matched on December 11, 1985, when the Edmonton Oilers beat the Chicago Blackhawks, 12–9, at Chicago.

Most goals (game—one team) The Montreal Canadiens pounded the Quebec Bulldogs 16–3 on March 3, 1920 to set the single-game scoring record. To make matters worse for Quebec, it was on home ice!

Most goals (season) The Edmonton Oilers scored 446 goals in 80 games during the 1983–84 season.

Most assists (season) The Edmonton Oilers recorded 737 assists during the 1985–86 season.

Most points (season) The Edmonton Oilers amassed 1,182 points (446 goals, 736 assists) during the 1983–84 season.

Most power-play goals scored (season) The Pittsburgh Penguins scored 119 power-play goals during the 1988–89 season.

Most shorthand goals scored (season) The Edmonton Oilers scored 36 shorthand goals during the 1983–84 season.

Most penalty minutes in one game At the Boston Garden on February 26, 1981, the Boston Bruins and the Minnesota North Stars received a combined 406 penalty minutes, a record for one game. The Bruins received 20 minors, 13 majors, three 10-minute misconducts and six game misconducts for a total of 195 penalty minutes; the North Stars received 18 minors, 13 majors, four 10-minute misconducts and seven game misconducts for a total of 211 penalty minutes. It is also reported that a hockey game broke out between the fights, which the Bruins won 5–1.

Longest winning streak The Pittsburgh Penguins won 17 consecutive games from March 9–April 10, 1993.

Longest undefeated streak The longest undefeated streak in one season is 35 games by the Philadelphia Flyers. The Flyers won 25 games and tied 10 from October 14, 1979–January 6, 1980.

Longest losing streak Two teams share the unwanted honor of losing 17 consecutive games: Washington Capitals from February 18–March 26, 1975; San Jose Sharks from January 4–February 12, 1993.

Longest winless streak The Winnipeg Jets set the mark for the longest winless streak at 30 games. From October 19 to December 20, 1980, the Jets lost 23 games and tied seven.

Longest game The longest game was played between the Detroit Red Wings and the Montreal Maroons at the Forum Montreal and lasted 2 hours 56 minutes 30 seconds. The Red Wings won when Mud Bruneteau scored the only goal of the game in the sixth period of overtime at 2:25 A.M. on March 25, 1936. Norm Smith, the Red Wings goaltender, turned aside 92 shots for the NHL's longest shutout.

INDIVIDUAL RECORDS

Most games played Gordie Howe played 1,767 games over a record 26 seasons for the Detroit Red Wings (1946–71) and Hartford Whalers (1979–80). The most games played by a goaltender is 971, by Terry Sawchuk, who played 21 seasons for five teams: Detroit Red Wings, Boston Bruins, Toronto Maple Leafs, Los Angeles Kings and New York Rangers (1949–70).

Most consecutive games played Doug Jarvis played 964 consecutive games from October 8,

NATIONAL HOCKEY LEAGUE RECORDS

Goals

		Player(s)	Team(s)	Date(s)
Period	4	Busher Jackson	Toronto Maple Leafs *v.* St. Louis Eagles	November 20, 1934
		Max Bentley	Chicago Blackhawks *v.* New York Rangers	January 28, 1943
		Clint Smith	Chicago Blackhawks *v.* Montreal Canadiens	March 4, 1945
		Red Berenson	St. Louis Blues *v.* Philadelphia Flyers	November 7, 1968
		Wayne Gretzky	Edmonton Oilers *v.* St. Louis Blues	February 18, 1981
		Grant Mulvey	Chicago Blackhawks *v.* St. Louis Blues	February 3, 1982
		Bryan Trottier	New York Islanders *v.* Philadelphia Flyers	February 13, 1982
		Al Secord	Chicago Blackhawks *v.* Toronto Maple Leafs	January 7, 1987
		Joe Nieuwendyk	Calgary Flames *v.* Winnipeg Jets	January 11, 1989
Game	7	Joe Malone	Quebec Bulldogs *v.* Toronto St. Patricks	January 31, 1920
Season	92	Wayne Gretzky	Edmonton Oilers	1981–82
Career	803	Wayne Gretzky	Edmonton Oilers, Los Angeles Kings	1979–88, 1988–94*

Assists

Period	5	Dale Hawerchuk	Winnipeg Jets *v.* Los Angeles Kings	March 6, 1984
Game	7	Billy Taylor	Detroit Red Wings *v.* Chicago Blackhawks	March 16, 1947
		Wayne Gretzky	Edmonton Oilers *v.* Washington Capitals	February 15, 1980
		Wayne Gretzky	Edmonton Oilers *v.* Chicago Blackhawks	December 11, 1985
		Wayne Gretzky	Edmonton Oilers *v.* Quebec Nordiques	February 14, 1986
Season	163	Wayne Gretzky	Edmonton Oilers	1985–86
Career	1,655	Wayne Gretzky	Edmonton Oilers, Los Angeles Kings	1979–94*

Points

Period	6	Bryan Trottier	New York Islanders *v.* New York Rangers	December 23, 1978
Game	10	Darryl Sittler	Toronto Maple Leafs *v.* Boston Bruins	February 7, 1976
Season	215	Wayne Gretzky	Edmonton Oilers	1985–86
Career	2,658	Wayne Gretzky	Edmonton Oilers, Los Angeles Kings	1979–94*

Goaltenders
Shutouts

Season	22	George Hainsworth	Montreal Canadiens	1928–29
Career	103	Terry Sawchuk	Detroit Red Wings, Boston Bruins, Toronto Maple Leafs, Los Angeles Kings, New York Rangers	1949–70

Wins

Season	47	Bernie Parent	Philadelphia Flyers	1973–74
Career	435	Terry Sawchuk	Detroit Red Wings, Boston Bruins, Toronto Maple Leafs, Los Angeles Kings, New York Rangers	1949–70

* As of January 11, 1995
Source: NHL

1975 to October 10, 1987. During the streak, Jarvis played for three teams: the Montreal Canadiens, Washington Capitals and Hartford Whalers.

Fastest goal The fastest goal from the start of a game is 5 seconds, a feat performed by three players: Doug Smail (Winnipeg Jets) *v.* St. Louis Blues at Winnipeg on December 20, 1981; Bryan Trottier (New York Islanders) *v.* Boston Bruins at Boston on March 22, 1984; and Alexander Mogilny (Buffalo Sabres) *v.* Toronto Maple Leafs at Toronto on December 21, 1991. The fastest goal from the start of any period was after 4 seconds, achieved by two players: Claude Provost (Montreal Canadiens) *v.* Boston Bruins in the second period at Montreal on November 9, 1957, and by Denis Savard (Chicago Blackhawks) *v.* Hartford Whalers in the third period at Chicago on January 12, 1986.

Most hat tricks The most hat tricks (three or more goals in a game) in a career is 49, by Wayne Gretzky for the Edmonton Oilers and Los Angeles Kings in 13 seasons (1979–92). "The Great One" has recorded 36 three-goal games, nine four-goal games and four five-goal games. Gretzky also holds the record for most hat tricks in a season, 10, in both the 1981–82 and 1983–84 seasons for the Edmonton Oilers.

Longest consecutive goal-scoring streak The most consecutive games scoring at least one goal in a game is 16, by Harry (Punch) Broadbent

Record Quotable

"Some guys are pure goal scorers. . . . I don't know if I was a pure goal scorer. I don't have a very hard shot. I *still* don't have a very hard shot."

—Wayne Gretzky, quoted in *Sports Illustrated*, on having set the record for career goals in 1994

MEET THE PRESS ■ WAYNE GRETZKY BOMBARDED BY REPORTERS AFTER HE SCORED HIS RECORD-BREAKING 803RD GOAL ON MARCH 24, 1994. (ALLSPORT/AL BELLOW)

HART MEMORIAL TROPHY WINNERS (1924–1994)

The Hart Trophy has been awarded annually since the 1923–24 season by the Professional Hockey Writers Association to the Most Valuable Player of the NHL. Wayne Gretzky has won the award a record nine times, 1980–87 and 1989.

Year	Player	Team	Year	Player	Team
1924	Frank Nighbor	Ottawa Senators	1960	Gordie Howe	Detroit Red Wings
1925	Billy Burch	Hamilton Tigers	1961	Bernie Geoffrion	Montreal Canadiens
1926	Nels Stewart	Montreal Maroons	1962	Jacques Plante	Montreal Canadiens
1927	Herb Gardiner	Montreal Canadiens	1963	Gordie Howe	Detroit Red Wings
1928	Howie Morenz	Montreal Canadiens	1964	Jean Beliveau	Montreal Canadiens
1929	Roy Worters	New York Americans	1965	Bobby Hull	Chicago Blackhawks
1930	Nels Stewart	Montreal Maroons	1966	Bobby Hull	Chicago Blackhawks
1931	Howie Morenz	Montreal Canadiens	1967	Stan Mikita	Chicago Blackhawks
1932	Howie Morenz	Montreal Canadiens	1968	Stan Mikita	Chicago Blackhawks
1933	Eddie Shore	Boston Bruins	1969	Phil Esposito	Boston Bruins
1934	Aurel Joliat	Montreal Canadiens	1970	Bobby Orr	Boston Bruins
1935	Eddie Shore	Boston Bruins	1971	Bobby Orr	Boston Bruins
1936	Eddie Shore	Boston Bruins	1972	Bobby Orr	Boston Bruins
1937	Babe Siebert	Montreal Canadiens	1973	Bobby Clarke	Philadelphia Flyers
1938	Eddie Shore	Boston Bruins	1974	Phil Esposito	Boston Bruins
1939	Toe Blake	Montreal Canadiens	1975	Bobby Clarke	Philadelphia Flyers
1940	Ebbie Goodfellow	Detroit Red Wings	1976	Bobby Clarke	Philadelphia Flyers
1941	Bill Cowley	Boston Bruins	1977	Guy Lafleur	Montreal Canadiens
1942	Tom Anderson	Brooklyn Americans	1978	Guy Lafleur	Montreal Canadiens
1943	Bill Cowley	Boston Bruins	1979	Bryan Trottier	New York Islanders
1944	Babe Pratt	Toronto Maple Leafs	1980	Wayne Gretzky	Edmonton Oilers
1945	Elmer Lach	Montreal Canadiens	1981	Wayne Gretzky	Edmonton Oilers
1946	Max Bentley	Chicago Blackhawks	1982	Wayne Gretzky	Edmonton Oilers
1947	Maurice Richard	Montreal Canadiens	1983	Wayne Gretzky	Edmonton Oilers
1948	Buddy O'Connor	New York Rangers	1984	Wayne Gretzky	Edmonton Oilers
1949	Sid Abel	Detroit Red Wings	1985	Wayne Gretzky	Edmonton Oilers
1950	Charlie Rayner	New York Rangers	1986	Wayne Gretzky	Edmonton Oilers
1951	Milt Schmidt	Boston Bruins	1987	Wayne Gretzky	Edmonton Oilers
1952	Gordie Howe	Detroit Red Wings	1988	Mario Lemieux	Pittsburgh Penguins
1953	Gordie Howe	Detroit Red Wings	1989	Wayne Gretzky	Los Angeles Kings
1954	Al Rollins	Chicago Blackhawks	1990	Mark Messier	Edmonton Oilers
1955	Ted Kennedy	Toronto Maple Leafs	1991	Brett Hull	St. Louis Blues
1956	Jean Beliveau	Montreal Canadiens	1992	Mark Messier	New York Rangers
1957	Gordie Howe	Detroit Red Wings	1993	Mario Lemieux	Pittsburgh Penguins
1958	Gordie Howe	Detroit Red Wings	1994	Sergei Fedorov	Detroit Red Wings
1959	Andy Bathgate	New York Rangers			

(Ottawa Senators) in the 1921–22 season. Broadbent scored 25 goals during the streak.

Longest consecutive assist-scoring streak The record for most consecutive games recording at least one assist is 23 games, by Wayne Gretzky (Los Angeles Kings) in 1990–91. Gretzky was credited with 48 assists during the streak.

Most consecutive 50-or-more-goal seasons Mike Bossy (New York Islanders) scored at least 50 goals in nine consecutive seasons from 1977–78 through 1985–86.

Longest consecutive point-scoring streak The most consecutive games scoring at least one point is 51, by Wayne Gretzky (Edmonton Oilers) between October 5, 1983 and January 27, 1984. During the streak, Gretzky scored 61 goals, 92 assists for 153 points.

Longest shutout sequence by a goaltender Alex Connell (Ottawa Senators) played 461 minutes, 29 seconds without conceding a goal in the 1927–28 season.

Longest undefeated streak by a goaltender Gerry Cheevers (Boston Bruins) went 32 games (24 wins, 8 ties) undefeated during the 1971–72 season.

Defensemen Paul Coffey (Edmonton Oilers, 1980–87; Pittsburgh Penguins, 1987–91; Los Angeles Kings, 1991–93; Detroit Red Wings, 1993) holds the all-time records for goals, assists and points by a defenseman. As of January 11, 1995, Coffey's career marks were 344 goals, 914 assists and 1,278 points. Coffey also holds the single-season record for goals scored by a defenseman, 48, which he scored in 1985–86 when he played for the Edmonton Oilers. Bobby Orr (Boston Bruins) holds the single-season marks for assists (102) and points (139), both of which were set in 1970–71.

COACHES

Most wins As of February 6, 1995, Scotty Bowman has coached his teams to 880 victories (110 wins, St. Louis Blues, 1967–71; 419 wins, Montreal Canadiens, 1971–79; 210 wins, Buffalo Sabres, 1979–87, 95 wins, Pittsburgh Penguins, 1991–93; 46 wins, Detroit Red Wings, 1993–94).

Most games coached As of January 11, 1995, Al Arbour has coached a record 1,573 games with two teams: St. Louis Blues, 1970–73; New York Islanders, 1973–86, 1988–94. Arbour's career record is 764 wins, 567 losses, 242 ties.

STANLEY CUP

The Stanley Cup is currently the oldest competition in North American professional sports. The cup was donated to the Canadian Amateur Hockey Association (AHA) by Sir Frederick Arthur Stanley, Lord Stanley of Preston in 1893. The inaugural championship was presented to the AHA champion, but since 1894 there has always been a playoff. The playoff format underwent several changes until 1926, when the National Hockey League (NHL) playoffs became the permanent forum to decide the Stanley Cup champion.

Most championships The Montreal Canadiens have won the Stanley Cup a record 24 times: 1916, 1924, 1930–31, 1944, 1946, 1953, 1956–60, 1965–66, 1968–69, 1971, 1973, 1976–79, 1986, 1993.

Most consecutive wins The Montreal Canadiens won the Stanley Cup for five consecutive years, 1956–60.

Most games played Larry Robinson has played in 227 Stanley Cup playoff games for the Montreal Canadiens (1973–89, 203 games) and the Los Angeles Kings (1990–92, 24 games).

GOAL SCORING RECORDS

Fastest goal The fastest goal from the start of any playoff game was scored by Don Kozak (Los Angeles Kings) past Gerry Cheevers (Boston Bruins) with 6 seconds elapsed. The Kings went on to win 7–4; the game was played on April 17, 1977. Kozak's goal shares the mark for fastest goal from the start of any period with one scored by Pelle Eklund (Philadelphia Flyers). Eklund scored in the second period of a game against the Pittsburgh Penguins in Pittsburgh on April 25, 1989; his effort was in vain, however, as the Penguins won 10–7.

SHORTHANDED GOALS SCORED

Period The most shorthanded goals scored in a single period is two, shared by three players. Bryan Trottier was the first player to perform this feat, on April 8, 1990 for the New York Islanders v. the Los Angeles Kings. His goals came in the second period of an 8–1 Islanders victory. Bobby Lalonde (Boston Bruins) matched Trottier on April 11, 1981. His double came in the third period of a Bruins 6–3 loss to the Minnesota North Stars. Jari Kurri (Edmonton Oilers) joined this club on April 24, 1983. His goals came in the third period of an Oilers 8–4 win over the Chicago Blackhawks.

Series The record for most shorthanded goals in a playoff series is three, shared by two players: Bill Barber (Philadelphia Flyers) in a Flyers 4–1 series victory over the Minnesota North Stars in 1980; and Wayne Presley (Chicago Blackhawks) in a series v. the Detroit Red Wings in 1989.

Season The record for shorthanded goals in one season is three, shared by five players: Derek Sanderson (Boston Bruins) in 1969; Bill Barber (Philadelphia Flyers) in 1980; Lorne Henning (New York Islanders) in 1980; Wayne Gretzky (Edmonton Oilers) in 1983; and Wayne Presley (Chicago Blackhawks) in 1989.

Career Mark Messier (Edmonton Oilers, New York Rangers) holds the mark for career playoff goals at 14 in 179 games (1979–94).

DON'T MESS WITH MESSIER ■ **IN 1994 MARK MESSIER EXTENDED HIS CAREER RECORD FOR SHORTHANDED PLAYOFF GOALS.** (NEW YORK RANGERS)

DEFENSEMEN RECORDS

GOAL SCORING

Game The most goals scored by a defenseman in a playoff game is three, by eight players: Bobby Orr, Boston Bruins v. Montreal Canadiens, April 11, 1971; Dick Redmond, Chicago Blackhawks v. St. Louis Blues, April 4, 1973; Denis Potvin, New York Islanders v. Edmonton Oilers, April 17, 1981; Paul Reinhart, Calgary Flames, who performed the feat twice, v. Edmonton Oilers, April 14, 1983; v. Vancouver Canucks, April 8, 1984; Doug Halward, Vancouver Canucks v. Calgary Flames, April 7, 1984; Al Ioufrate, Washington Capitals v. New York Islanders, April 26, 1993; Eric DesJardins, Montreal Canadiens v. Los Angeles Kings, June 3, 1993; and Gary Suter, Chicago Black Hawks v. Toronto Maple Leafs, April 24, 1994.

Season Paul Coffey (Edmonton Oilers) scored 12 goals in 18 games during the 1985 playoffs.

Career Denis Potvin (New York Islanders, 1973–88) has scored a playoff record 56 goals.

ASSISTS

Game The most assists in a game is five, by two players: Paul Coffey, Edmonton Oilers v. Chicago Blackhawks on May 14, 1985; and Risto Siltanen, Quebec Nordiques v. Hartford Whalers on April 14, 1987.

Season The most assists in one playoff year is 25, by Paul Coffey, Edmonton Oilers in 1985. Coffey played in 18 games.

Career The most assists by a defenseman in a career is 108, by Denis Potvin (New York Islanders, 1983–88). Potvin played in 185 games.

POINT SCORING

Game Paul Coffey earned a record six points on one goal and five assists, for the Edmonton Oilers v. the Chicago Blackhawks on May 14, 1985.

Season Paul Coffey also holds the record for most points by a defenseman in a season, with 37 in 1985 for the Edmonton Oilers. Coffey's total comprised 12 goals and 25 assists in 18 games.

Career Denis Potvin (New York Islanders, 1973–88) has scored a playoff record 164 points. Potvin scored 56 goals and 108 assists in 185 games.

CONSECUTIVE RECORDS

Point-scoring streak Bryan Trottier (New York Islanders) scored a point in 27 consecutive playoff games over three seasons (1980–82), scoring 16 goals and 26 assists for 42 points.

Goal-scoring streak Reggie Leach (Philadelphia Flyers) scored at least one goal in nine consecutive playoff games in 1976. The streak started on April 17 *v.* the Toronto Maple Leafs, and ended on May 9 when he was shut out by the Montreal Canadiens. Overall, Leach scored 14 goals during his record-setting run.

Consecutive wins by a goaltender Two goalies have won 11 straight playoff games: Ed Belfour (Chickago Blackhawks), and Tom Barrasso (Pittsburgh Penguins), both in 1992.

Longest shutout sequence In the 1936 semifinal contest between the Detroit Red Wings and the Montreal Maroons, Norm Smith, the Red Wings goaltender, shut out the Maroons for 248 minutes, 32 seconds. The Maroons failed to score in the first two games (the second game lasted 116 minutes, 30 seconds, the longest overtime game in playoff history), and finally breached Smith's defenses at 12:02 of the first period in game three. After such a stellar performance, it is no surprise that the Red Wings swept the series 3–0.

STANLEY CUP CHAMPIONS (1893–1904)

Year	Champion	Loser	Series
1893	Montreal A.A.A.	(no challenger)	——
1894	Montreal A.A.A.	Ottawa Generals	3–1*
1895	Montreal Victorias	(no challenger)	——
1896	Winnipeg Victorias (February)	Montreal Victorias	2–0*
	Montreal Victorias (December)	Winnipeg Victorias	6–5*
1897	Montreal Victorias	Ottawa Capitals	15–2*
1898	Montreal Victorias	(no challenger)	——
1899	Montreal Victorias (February)	Winnipeg Victorias	2–0
	Montreal Shamrocks (March)	Queen's University	6–2*
1900	Montreal Shamrocks	Halifax Crescents	**
		Winnipeg Victorias	
1901	Winnipeg Victorias	Montreal Shamrocks	2–0
1902	Winnipeg Victorias (January)	Toronto Wellingtons	2–0
	Montreal A.A.A. (March)	Winnipeg Victorias	2–1
1903	Montreal A.A.A. (February)	Winnipeg Victorias	2–1
	Ottawa Silver Seven (March)	Rat Portage Thistles	**
		Montreal Victorias	
1904	Ottawa Silver Seven	Brandon Wheat Kings	**
		Montreal Wanderers	
		Toronto Marlboros	
		Winnipeg Rowing Club	

* Final score of single challenge game.

** Multiple challenger series.

STANLEY CUP CHAMPIONS (1905–1926)

Year	Champion	Loser	Series
1905	Ottawa Silver Seven	Rat Portage Thistles Dawson City Nuggets	**
1906	Ottawa Silver Seven (February)	Queen's Unversity Smith's Falls	**
	Montreal Wanderers (March)	New Glasgow Clubs Ottawa Silver Seven	**
1907	Kenora Thistles (January)	Montreal Wanderers	2–0
	Montreal Wanderers (March)	Kenora Thistles	1–1†
1908	Montreal Wanderers	Edmonton Eskimos Toronto Maple Leafs Winnipeg Maple Leafs Ottawa Victorias	**
1909	Ottawa Senators	(no challenger)	
1910	Ottawa Senators (January)	Galt Edmonton Eskimos	**
	Montreal Wanderers (March)	Berlin (Kitchener)	7–3*
1911	Ottawa Senators	Galt Port Arthur	**
1912	Quebec Bulldogs	Moncton Victorias	2–0
1913	Quebec Bulldogs	Sydney Miners	2–0
1914	Toronto Blueshirts	Victoria Cougars Montreal Canadiens	**
1915	Vancouver Millionaires	Ottawa Senators	3–0
1916	Montreal Canadiens	Portland Rosebuds	3–2
1917	Seattle Metropolitans	Montreal Canadiens	3–1
1918	Toronto Arenas	Vancouver Millionaires	3–2
1919	no decision		‡
1920	Ottawa Senators	Seattle Metropolitans	3–2
1921	Ottawa Senators	Vancouver Millionaires	3–2
1922	Toronto St. Patricks	Vancouver Millionaires	3–2
1923	Ottawa Senators	Vancouver Maroons Edmonton Eskimos	**
1924	Montreal Canadiens	Vancouver Maroons Calgary Tigers	**
1925	Victoria Cougars	Montreal Canadiens	3–1
1926	Montreal Maroons	Victoria Cougars	3–1

* Final score of single challenge game.

** Multiple challenger series.

† Series decided on total goals scored.

‡ Due to an influenza epidemic in Seattle the final series between the Montreal Canadiens and the Seattle Metropolitans was canceled. The series was tied 2–2–1 in games.

STANLEY CUP CHAMPIONS (1927–1964)

Year	Champion	Loser	Series
1927	Ottawa Senators	Boston Bruins	2–0
1928	New York Rangers	Montreal Maroons	3–2
1929	Boston Bruins	New York Rangers	2–0
1930	Montreal Canadiens	Boston Bruins	2–0
1931	Montreal Canadiens	Chicago Blackhawks	3–2
1932	Toronto Maple Leafs	New York Rangers	3–0
1933	New York Rangers	Toronto Maple Leafs	3–1
1934	Chicago Blackhawks	Detroit Red Wings	3–1
1935	Montreal Maroons	Toronto Maple Leafs	3–0
1936	Detroit Red Wings	Toronto Maple Leafs	3–1
1937	Detroit Red Wings	New York Rangers	3–2
1938	Chicago Blackhawks	Toronto Maple Leafs	3–1
1939	Boston Bruins	Toronto Maple Leafs	4–1
1940	New York Rangers	Toronto Maple Leafs	4–2
1941	Boston Bruins	Detroit Red Wings	4–0
1942	Toronto Maple Leafs	Detroit Red Wings	4–3
1943	Detroit Red Wings	Boston Bruins	4–0
1944	Montreal Canadiens	Chicago Blackhawks	4–0
1945	Toronto Maple Leafs	Detroit Red Wings	4–3
1946	Montreal Canadiens	Boston Bruins	4–1
1947	Toronto Maple Leafs	Montreal Canadiens	4–2
1948	Toronto Maple Leafs	Detroit Red Wings	4–0
1949	Toronto Maple Leafs	Detroit Red Wings	4–0
1950	Detroit Red Wings	New York Rangers	4–3
1951	Toronto Maple Leafs	Montreal Canadiens	4–1
1952	Detroit Red Wings	Montreal Canadiens	4–0
1953	Montreal Canadiens	Boston Bruins	4–1
1954	Detroit Red Wings	Montreal Canadiens	4–3
1955	Detroit Red Wings	Montreal Canadiens	4–3
1956	Montreal Canadiens	Detroit Red Wings	4–1
1957	Montreal Canadiens	Boston Bruins	4–1
1958	Montreal Canadiens	Boston Bruins	4–2
1959	Montreal Canadiens	Toronto Maple Leafs	4–1
1960	Montreal Canadiens	Toronto Maple Leafs	4–0
1961	Chicago Blackhawks	Detroit Red Wings	4–2
1962	Toronto Maple Leafs	Chicago Blackhawks	4–2
1963	Toronto Maple Leafs	Detroit Red Wings	4–1
1964	Toronto Maple Leafs	Detroit Red Wings	4–3

STANLEY CUP CHAMPIONS (1965–1994)

Year	Champion	Loser	Series
1965	Montreal Canadiens	Chicago Blackhawks	4–3
1966	Montreal Canadiens	Detroit Red Wings	4–2
1967	Toronto Maple Leafs	Montreal Canadiens	4–2
1968	Montreal Canadiens	St. Louis Blues	4–0
1969	Montreal Canadiens	St. Louis Blues	4–0
1970	Boston Bruins	St. Louis Blues	4–0
1971	Montreal Canadiens	Chicago Blackhawks	4–3
1972	Boston Bruins	New York Rangers	4–2
1973	Montreal Canadiens	Chicago Blackhawks	4–2
1974	Philadelphia Flyers	Boston Bruins	4–2
1975	Philadelphia Flyers	Buffalo Sabres	4–2
1976	Montreal Canadiens	Philadelphia Flyers	4–0
1977	Montreal Canadiens	Boston Bruins	4–0
1978	Montreal Canadiens	Boston Bruins	4–2
1979	Montreal Canadiens	New York Rangers	4–1
1980	New York Islanders	Philadelphia Flyers	4–2
1981	New York Islanders	Minnesota North Stars	4–1
1982	New York Islanders	Vancouver Canucks	4–0
1983	New York Islanders	Edmonton Oilers	4–0
1984	Edmonton Oilers	New York Islanders	4–1
1985	Edmonton Oilers	Philadelphia Flyers	4–1
1986	Montreal Canadiens	Calgary Flames	4–1
1987	Edmonton Oilers	Philadelphia Flyers	4–3
1988	Edmonton Oilers	Boston Bruins	4–0
1989	Calgary Flames	Montreal Canadiens	4–2
1990	Edmonton Oilers	Boston Bruins	4–1
1991	Pittsburgh Penguins	Minnesota North Stars	4–2
1992	Pittsburgh Penguins	Chicago Blackhawks	4–0
1993	Montreal Canadiens	Los Angeles Kings	4–1
1994	New York Rangers	Vancouver Canucks	4–3

COACHES

Most championships Toe Blake coached the Montreal Canadiens to eight Stanley Cups, 1956–60, 1965–66, 1968.

Most playoff wins Through the 1992–93 season the record for playoff wins is 137 games, by Scotty Bowman, St. Louis Blues, 1967–71 (26 wins), Montreal Canadiens, 1971–79 (70 wins), Buffalo Sabres, 1979–87 (18 wins), Pittsburgh Penguins, 1992–93 (23 wins).

Most games Scotty Bowman holds the mark for most games coached, at 219 with four teams: St. Louis Blues, 1967–71; Montreal Canadiens, 1971–79; Buffalo Sabres, 1979–87; Pittsburgh Penguins, 1992–93.

STANLEY CUP INDIVIDUAL RECORDS

Records in this section are listed only from the formation of the National Hockey League in 1917.

Goals Scored

		Player(s)	Team(s)	Date(s)
Period	4	Tim Kerr	Philadelphia Flyers v. New York Rangers	April 13, 1985
		Mario Lemieux	Pittsburgh Penguins v. New York Rangers	April 25, 1989
Game	5	Newsy Lalonde	Montreal Canadiens v. Ottawa Senators	March 1, 1919
		Maurice Richard	Montreal Canadiens v. Toronto Maple Leafs	March 23, 1944
		Darryl Sittler	Toronto Maple Leafs v. Philadelphia Flyers	April 22, 1976
		Reggie Leach	Philadelphia Flyers v. Boston Bruins	May 6, 1976
		Mario Lemieux	Pittsburgh Penguins v. Philadelphia Flyers	April 25, 1989
Series (any round)	12	Jari Kurri	Edmonton Oilers v. Chicago Blackhawks	1985
Series (final)	9	Babe Dye	Toronto St. Patricks v. Vancouver Millionaires	1922
Season	19	Reggie Leach	Philadelphia Flyers	1976
		Jari Kurri	Edmonton Oilers	1985
Career	110	Wayne Gretzky	Edmonton Oilers, Los Angeles Kings	1979–93

Power-Play Goals Scored

Period	3	Tim Kerr	Philadelphia Flyers v. New York Rangers	April 13, 1985
Series	6	Chris Kontos	Los Angeles Kings v. Edmonton Oilers	1989
Season	9	Mike Bossy	New York Islanders	1981
		Cam Neely	Boston Bruins	1991
Career	35	Mike Bossy	New York Islanders	1977–87

Points Scored

Period	4	Maurice Richard	Montreal Canadiens v. Toronto Maple Leafs	March 29, 1945
		Dickie Moore	Montreal Canadiens v. Boston Bruins	March 25, 1954
		Barry Pederson	Boston Bruins v. Buffalo Sabres	April 8, 1982
		Peter McNab	Boston Bruins v. Buffalo Sabres	April 11, 1982
		Tim Kerr	Philadelphia Flyers v. New York Rangers	April 13, 1985
		Ken Linseman	Boston Bruins v. Montreal Canadiens	April 14, 1985
		Wayne Gretzky	Edmonton Oilers v. Los Angeles Kings	April 12, 1987
		Glenn Anderson	Edmonton Oilers v. Winnipeg Jets	April 6, 1988
		Mario Lemieux	Pittsburgh Penguins v. Philadelphia Flyers	April 25, 1989
		Dave Gagner	Minnesota North Stars v. Chicago Blackhawks	April 8, 1991
		Mario Lemieux	Pittsburgh Penguins v. Washington Capitals	April 23, 1992
Game	8	Patrik Sundstrom	New Jersey Devils v. Washington Capitals	April 22, 1988
		Mario Lemieux	Pittsburgh Penguins v. Philadelphia Flyers	April 25, 1989
Series (any round)	19	Rick Middleton	Boston Bruins v. Buffalo Sabres	1983
Series (final)	13	Wayne Gretzky	Edmonton Oilers v. Boston Bruins	1988
Season	47	Wayne Gretzky	Edmonton Oilers	1985
Career	346	Wayne Gretzky	Edmonton Oilers, Los Angeles Kings	1979–93

STANLEY CUP INDIVIDUAL RECORDS

Assists

		Player(s)	Team(s)	Date(s)
Period	3	This feat has been achieved 58 times.		
Game	6	Mikko Leinonen	New York Rangers v. Philadelphia Flyers	April 8, 1982
		Wayne Gretzky	Edmonton Oilers v. Los Angeles Kings	April 9, 1987
Series (any round)	14	Rick Middleton	Boston Bruins v. Buffalo Sabres	1983
		Wayne Gretzky	Edmonton Oilers v. Chicago Blackhawks	1985
Series (final)	10	Wayne Gretzky	Edmonton Oilers v. Boston Bruins	1988
Season	31	Wayne Gretzky	Edmonton Oilers	1988
Career	236	Wayne Gretzky	Edmonton Oilers, Los Angeles Kings	1979–93

Goaltenders

Shutouts

Season	4	Clint Benedict	Montreal Maroons	1926
		Clint Benedict	Montreal Maroons	1928
		Dave Kerr	New York Rangers	1937
		Frank McCool	Toronto Maple Leafs	1945
		Terry Sawchuk	Detroit Tigers	1952
		Bernie Parent	Philadelphia Flyers	1975
		Ken Dyrden	Montreal Canadiens	1977
Career	15	Clint Benedict	Ottawa Senators, Montreal Maroons	1917–30

Minutes Played

Season	1,540	Ron Hextall	Philadelphia Flyers	1987
Career	7,645	Billy Smith	New York Islanders	1971–89

Wins

Season	16	Grant Fuhr	Edmonton Oilers	1988
		Mike Vernon	Calgary Flames	1989
		Bill Ranford	Edmonton Oilers	1990
		Tom Barrasso	Pittsburgh Penguins	1992
Career	88	Billy Smith	New York Islanders	1975–88

Penalty Minutes

Game	42	Dave Schultz	Philadelphia Flyers v. Toronto Maple Leafs	April 22, 1976
Career	599	Dale Hunter	Quebec Nordiques, Washington Capitals	1980–93

Source: NHL

OLYMPIC GAMES

Hockey was included in the 1920 Summer Olympics in Antwerp, Belgium, and has been an integral part of the Winter Olympics since its introduction in 1924.

Most gold medals (country) The USSR/Unified Team has won eight Olympic titles, in 1956, 1964, 1968, 1972, 1976, 1984, 1988 and 1992.

WORLD CHAMPIONSHIPS (MEN) The world championships were first held in 1920 in conjunction with the Olympic Games. Since 1930, the world championships have been held annually. Through the 1964 Olympics, the Games were considered the world championships, and records for those Games are included in this section. Since 1977, the championships have been open to professionals.

Most titles The USSR has won the world championship 22 times: 1954, 1956, 1963–71, 1973–75, 1978–79, 1981–83, 1986, 1989–90.

Most consecutive titles The USSR won nine consecutive championships from 1963–71.

WORLD CHAMPIONSHIPS (WOMEN) The inaugural tournament was held in 1990. Canada won the inaugural event, defeating the United States 5–2 in the final, staged in Ottawa, Canada on March 24, 1990.

NCAA CHAMPIONSHIPS A men's Division I hockey championship was first staged in 1948, and has been held annually since.

Most wins Michigan has won the title seven times: 1948, 1951–53, 1955–56 and 1964.

HORSE RACING

ORIGINS Horsemanship was an important part of the Hittite culture of Anatolia, Turkey, dating from 1400 B.C. The 33rd ancient Olympic Games of 648 B.C. in Greece featured horse racing. Horse races can be traced in England from the 3rd century. The first sweepstakes race was originated by the 12th Earl of Derby at his estate in Epsom in 1780. The Epsom Derby is still run today and is the classic race of the English flat racing season.

United States Horses were introduced to the North American continent from Spain by Cortéz in 1519. In colonial America, horse racing was common. Colonel Richard Nicholls, commander of English forces in New York, is believed to have staged the first organized race at Salisbury Plain, Long Island, N.Y. in 1665. The first jockey club to be founded was at Charleston, S.C. in 1734. Thoroughbred racing was first staged at Saratoga Springs, N.Y. in 1863.

TRIPLE CROWN WINNERS

Year	Horse	Jockey	Trainer	Owner
1919	Sir Barton	Johnny Loftus	H. Guy Bedwell	J. K. L. Ross
1930	Gallant Fox	Earl Sande	J. E. Fitzsimmons	Belair Stud
1935	Omaha	Willie Saunders	J. E. Fitzsimmons	Belair Stud
1937	War Admiral	Chas. Kurtsinger	George Conway	Samuel Riddle
1941	Whirlaway	Eddie Arcaro	Ben A. Jones	Calumet Farm
1943	Count Fleet	Johnny Longden	Don Cameron	Mrs. J. D. Hertz
1946	Assault	Warren Mehrtens	Max Hirsch	King Ranch
1948	Citation	Eddie Arcaro	Ben A. Jones	Calumet Farm
1973	Secretariat	Ron Turcotte	Lucien Laurin	Meadow Stable
1977	Seattle Slew	Jean Cruguet	Billy Turner	Karen Taylor
1978	Affirmed	Steve Cauthen	Laz Barrera	Harbor View Farm

Jim Fitzsimmons and Ben Jones are the only trainers to have trained two Triple Crown winners. Eddie Arcaro is the only jockey to have ridden two Triple Crown winners.

RACING RECORDS (UNITED STATES)

HORSES

CAREER RECORDS

Most wins The most wins in a racing career is 89, by Kingston, from 138 starts, 1986–94.

Most wins (graded stakes races) John Henry won 25 graded stakes races, including 16 Grade I races, 1978–84.

HIGHEST EARNINGS

Career The career record for earnings is $6,679,242, by Alysheba, 1986–88. Alysheba's career record was 11 wins, eight seconds and two thirds from 26 races.

BUSY '93 ■ JOCKEY MIKE SMITH WON 62 RACES IN 1993. (DAILY RACING FORM)

Season The single-season earnings record is $4,578,454, by Sunday Silence, in 1989, from nine starts (seven wins and two seconds).

Single race The richest race in the United States is the Breeders' Cup Classic, which carries a purse of $3 million, with first-place prize money of $1,560,000 to the winner.

JOCKEYS

CAREER RECORDS

Most wins Bill Shoemaker rode a record 8,833 winners from 40,350 mounts. "The Shoe" made his debut aboard Waxahachie on March 19, 1949, and raced for the last time on Patchy Groundfog on February 3, 1990. His first victory came on April 20, 1949 aboard Shafter V, his last on January 20, 1990 aboard Beau Genius at Gulfstream Park, Fla.

SEASON RECORDS

Most wins Kent Desormeaux rode a season record 598 winners, from 2,312 mounts, in 1989.

Most wins (stakes races) Mike Smith rode a season record 62 stakes race winners in 1993.

DAILY RECORDS

Most wins (single day) The most winners ridden in one day is nine, by Chris Antley on October 31, 1987. Antley rode four winners in the afternoon at Aqueduct, N.Y. and five in the evening at The Meadowlands, N.J.

Most wins (one card) The most winners ridden on one card is eight, achieved by four jockeys: Hubert Jones, from 13 rides, at Caliente, Calif., on June 11, 1944; Dave Gall, from 10 rides, at Cahokia Downs, East St. Louis, Ill., on October 18, 1978; Robert Williams, from 10 rides, at Lincoln, Neb., on September 29, 1984; and Pat Day, from nine rides, at Arlington, Ill., on September 13, 1989.

Consecutive wins The longest consecutive winning streak by a jockey is nine races, by two jockeys. Albert Adams won nine races at Marlboro Racetrack, Md., over three days, September 10–12, 1930. He won the last two races on September 10, all six races on September 11, and the first race on September 12. Tony Black won nine races on July 30–31, 1993. He won three races at Atlantic City Racecourse on July 30, two at Philadelphia Park on July 31 and four at Atlantic City on July 31.

KENTUCKY DERBY WINNERS (1875–1994)

This event is held on the first Saturday in May at Churchill Downs, Louisville, Ky. The first race was run in 1875 over 1½ miles; the distance was shortened to 1¼ miles in 1896 and is still run at that length.

Most Wins

Jockey Five, by two jockeys: Eddie Arcaro (1938, 1941, 1945, 1948, 1952); Bill Hartack (1957, 1960, 1962, 1964, 1969).

Trainer Six, by Ben Jones (1938, 1941, 1944, 1948–49, 1952).

Owner Eight, by Calumet Farm (1941, 1944, 1948–49, 1952, 1957–58, 1968).

Fastest time 1 minute 59⅖ seconds, by Secretariat, 1973.

Largest field 23 horses in 1974.

Year	Horse	Year	Horse	Year	Horse	Year	Horse
1875	Aristides	1905	Agile	1935	Omaha	1965	Lucky Debonair
1876	Vagrant	1906	Sir Huon	1936	Bold Venture	1966	Kauai King
1877	Baden-Baden	1907	Pink Star	1937	War Admiral	1967	Proud Clarion
1878	Day Star	1908	Stone Street	1938	Lawrin	1968	Forward Pass
1879	Lord Murphy	1909	Wintergreen	1939	Johnstown	1969	Majestic Prince
1880	Fonso	1910	Donau	1940	Giallahadian	1970	Dust Commander
1881	Hindoo	1911	Meridian	1941	Whirlaway	1971	Canonero II
1882	Apollo	1912	Worth	1942	Shut Out	1972	Riva Ridge
1883	Leonatus	1913	Donerail	1943	Count Fleet	1973	Secretariat
1884	Buchanan	1914	Old Rosebud	1944	Pensive	1974	Cannonade
1885	Joe Cotton	1915	Regret	1945	Hoop Jr.	1975	Foolish Pleasure
1886	Ben Ali	1916	George Smith	1946	Assault	1976	Bold Forbes
1887	Montrose	1917	Omar Khayyam	1947	Jet Pilot	1977	Seattle Slew
1888	Macbeth II	1918	Exterminator	1948	Citation	1978	Affirmed
1889	Spokane	1919	Sir Barton	1949	Ponder	1979	Spectacular Bid
1890	Riley	1920	Paul Jones	1950	Middleground	1980	Genuine Risk
1891	Kingman	1921	Behave Yourself	1951	Count Turf	1981	Pleasant Colony
1892	Azra	1922	Morvich	1952	Hill Gail	1982	Gato Del Sol
1893	Lookout	1923	Zev	1953	Dark Star	1983	Sunny's Halo
1894	Chant	1924	Black Gold	1954	Determine	1984	Swale
1895	Halma	1925	Flying Ebony	1955	Swaps	1985	Spend a Buck
1896	Ben Brush	1926	Bubbling Over	1956	Needles	1986	Ferdinand
1897	Typhoon II	1927	Whiskery	1957	Iron Liege	1987	Alysheba
1898	Plaudit	1928	Reigh Count	1958	Tim Tam	1988	Winning Colors
1899	Manuel	1929	Clyde Van Dusen	1959	Tomy Lee	1989	Sunday Silence
1900	Lieut. Gibson	1930	Gallant Fox	1960	Venetian Way	1990	Unbridled
1901	His Eminence	1931	Twenty Grand	1961	Carry Back	1991	Strike the Gold
1902	Alan-a-Dale	1932	Burgoo King	1962	Decidedly	1992	Lil E. Tee
1903	Judge Himes	1933	Brokers Tip	1963	Chateaugay	1993	Sea Hero
1904	Elwood	1934	Cavalcade	1964	Northern Dancer	1994	Go for Gin

PREAKNESS STAKES WINNERS (1873–1994)

Inaugurated in 1873, this event is held annually at Pimlico Race Course, Baltimore, Md. Originally run at 1½ miles, the distance was changed several times before being settled at the current length of 1 3/16 miles in 1925.

Most Wins
Jockey Six, by Eddie Arcaro (1941, 1948, 1950–51, 1955, 1957).

Trainer Seven, by Robert Wyndham Walden (1875, 1878–82, 1888).

Owner Five, by George Lorillard (1878–82).

Fastest time 1 minute 53⅕ seconds, by Tank's Prospect, 1985.

Largest field 18 horses in 1928.

Year	Horse	Year	Horse	Year	Horse	Year	Horse
1873	Survivor	1903	Flocarline	1933	Head Play	1964	Northern Dancer
1874	Culpepper	1904	Bryn Mawr	1934	High Quest	1965	Tom Rolfe
1875	Tom Ochiltree	1905	Cairngorm	1935	Omaha	1966	Kauai King
1876	Shirley	1906	Whimsical	1936	Bold Venture	1967	Damascus
1877	Cloverbrook	1907	Don Enrique	1937	War Admiral	1968	Forward Pass
1878	Duke of Magenta	1908	Royal Tourist	1938	Dauber	1969	Majestic Prince
1879	Harold	1909	Effendi	1939	Challedon	1970	Personality
1880	Grenada	1910	Layminister	1940	Bimelech	1971	Canonero II
1881	Saunterer	1911	Watervale	1941	Whirlaway	1972	Bee Bee Bee
1882	Vanguard	1912	Colonel Holloway	1942	Alsab	1973	Secretariat
1883	Jacobus	1913	Buskin	1943	Count Fleet	1974	Little Current
1884	Knight of Ellerslie	1914	Holiday	1944	Pensive	1975	Master Derby
1885	Tecumseh	1915	Rhine Maiden	1945	Polynesian	1976	Elocutionist
1886	The Bard	1916	Damrosch	1946	Assault	1977	Seattle Slew
1887	Dunboyne	1917	Kalitan	1947	Faultless	1978	Affirmed
1888	Refund	1918	War Cloud*	1948	Citation	1979	Spectacular Bid
1889	Buddhist	1918	Jack Hare Jr.*	1949	Capot	1980	Codex
1890	Montague	1919	Sir Barton	1950	Hill Prince	1981	Pleasant Colony
1891	not held	1920	Man o'War	1951	Bold	1982	Aloma's Ruler
1892	not held	1921	Broomspun	1952	Blue Man	1983	Deputed Testamony
1893	not held	1922	Pillory	1953	Native Dancer	1984	Gate Dancer
1894	Assignee	1923	Vigil	1954	Hasty Road	1985	Tank's Prospect
1895	Belmar	1924	Nellie Morse	1955	Nashua	1986	Snow Chief
1896	Margrave	1925	Coventry	1956	Fabius	1987	Alysheba
1897	Paul Kauvar	1926	Display	1957	Bold Ruler	1988	Risen Star
1898	Sly Fox	1927	Bostonian	1958	Tim Tam	1989	Sunday Silence
1899	Half Time	1928	Victorian	1959	Royal Orbit	1990	Summer Squall
1900	Hindus	1929	Dr. Freeland	1960	Bally Ache	1991	Hansel
1901	The Parader	1930	Gallant Fox	1961	Carry Back	1992	Pine Bluff
1902	Old England	1931	Mate	1962	Greek Money	1993	Prairie Bayou
		1932	Burgoo King	1963	Candy Spots	1994	Tabasco Cat

* The 1918 race was run in two divisions.

BELMONT STAKES WINNERS (1867-1994)

This race is the third leg of the Triple Crown, first run in 1867 at Jerome Park, N.Y. Since 1905 the race has been staged at Belmont Park, N.Y. Originally run over 1 mile 5 furlongs, the current distance of 1½ miles has been set since 1926.

Most Wins

Jockey Six, by two jockeys: Jim McLaughlin (1882–84, 1886–88); Eddie Arcaro (1941–42, 1945, 1948, 1952, 1955).

Trainer Eight, by James Rowe Sr. (1883–84, 1901, 1904, 1907–08, 1910, 1913).

Owner Six, by three owners: Belmont Family (1869, 1896, 1902, 1916–17, 1983); James R. Keene (1879, 1901, 1904, 1907–08, 1910); Belair Stud (1930, 1932, 1935–36, 1939, 1955).

Fastest time 2 minutes 24 seconds, by Secretariat, 1973.

Largest field 15 horses, in 1983.

Year	Horse	Year	Horse	Year	Horse	Year	Horse
1867	Ruthless	1899	Jean Bereaud	1931	Twenty Grand	1963	Chateaugay
1868	General Duke	1900	Ildrim	1932	Faireno	1964	Quadrangle
1869	Fenian	1901	Commando	1933	Hurryoff	1965	Hail to All
1870	Kingfisher	1902	Masterman	1934	Peace Chance	1966	Amberoid
1871	Harry Bassett	1903	Africander	1935	Omaha	1967	Damascus
1872	Joe Daniels	1904	Delhi	1936	Granville	1968	Stage Door Johnny
1873	Springbok	1905	Tanya	1937	War Admiral	1969	Arts and Letters
1874	Saxon	1906	Burgomaster	1938	Pasteurized	1970	High Echelon
1875	Calvin	1907	Peter Pan	1939	Johnstown	1971	Pass Catcher
1876	Algerine	1908	Colin	1940	Bimelech	1972	Riva Ridge
1877	Cloverbrook	1909	Joe Madden	1941	Whirlaway	1973	Secretariat
1878	Duke of Magenta	1910	Sweep	1942	Shut Out	1974	Little Current
1879	Spendthrift	1911	not held	1943	Count Fleet	1975	Avatar
1880	Grenada	1912	not held	1944	Bounding Home	1976	Bold Forbes
1881	Saunterer	1913	Prince Eugene	1945	Pavot	1977	Seattle Slew
1882	Forester	1914	Luke McLuke	1946	Assault	1978	Affirmed
1883	George Kinney	1915	The Finn	1947	Phalanx	1979	Coastal
1884	Panique	1916	Friar Rock	1948	Citation	1980	Temperence Hill
1885	Tyrant	1917	Hourless	1949	Capot	1981	Summing
1886	Inspector B.	1918	Johren	1950	Middleground	1982	Conquistador Cielo
1887	Hanover	1919	Sir Barton	1951	Counterpoint	1983	Caveat
1888	Sir Dixon	1920	Man o'War	1952	One Count	1984	Swale
1889	Eric	1921	Grey Lag	1953	Native Dancer	1985	Creme Fraiche
1890	Burlington	1922	Pillory	1954	High Gun	1986	Danzig Connection
1891	Foxford	1923	Zev	1955	Nashua	1987	Bet Twice
1892	Patron	1924	Mad Play	1956	Needles	1988	Risen Star
1893	Commanche	1925	American Flag	1957	Gallant Man	1989	Easy Goer
1894	Henry of Navarre	1926	Crusader	1958	Cavan	1990	Go and Go
1895	Belmar	1927	Chance Shot	1959	Sword Dancer	1991	Hansel
1896	Hastings	1928	Vito	1960	Celtic Ash	1992	A.P. Indy
1897	Scottish Chieftain	1929	Blue Larkspur	1961	Sherluck	1993	Colonial Affair
1898	Bowling Brook	1930	Gallant Fox	1962	Jaipur	1994	Tabasco Cat

HIGHEST EARNINGS

Career Laffit Pincay Jr. has won a career record $184,008,559 from 1964 through January 18, 1995.

Season The greatest prize money earned in a single season is $14,877,298, by Jose Santos in 1988.

JOCKEYS (WOMEN)

Most wins Julie Krone has won a record 2,872 races from 1980 through 1994.

Highest earnings Julie Krone has won a record $58,044,321 from 1980 through January 18, 1995.

THE TRIPLE CROWN The races that make up the Triple Crown are the Kentucky Derby, the Preakness Stakes and the Belmont Stakes. The Triple Crown is for three-year-olds only and has been achieved by 11 horses.

BREEDERS' CUP CHAMPIONSHIP

The Breeders' Cup Championship has been staged annually since 1984. It was devised by John R. Gaines, a leading thoroughbred owner and breeder, to provide a season-ending championship for each division of thoroughbred racing. The Breeders' Cup Championship consists of seven races: Juvenile, Juvenile Fillies, Sprint, Mile, Distaff, Turf and the Classic, with a record purse of $10 million.

CHAMPIONSHIP RECORDS

HORSES

Most wins Three horses have won two Breeders' Cup races: Bayakoa, which won the Distaff in 1989 and 1990; Miesque, which won the Mile in 1987 and 1988; and Lure, which won the Mile in 1992 and 1993.

CAREER MAN ■ LAFFIT PINCAY JR.'S CAREER EARNINGS HAVE GIVEN THE JOCKEY A LOT TO SMILE ABOUT. (DAILY RACING FORM)

Highest earnings Alysheba has won a record $2,133,000 in Breeders' Cup races, from three starts, 1986–88.

JOCKEYS

Most wins Two jockeys have ridden seven winners in the Breeders' Cup Championship: Laffit Pincay Jr., Juvenile (1985, 1986, 1988), Classic (1986), Distaff (1989, 1990), Juvenile Fillies (1993); and Eddie Delahoussaye, Distaff (1984, 1993), Turf (1989), Juvenile Fillies (1991), Sprint (1992, 1993).

Highest earnings Pat Day has won a record $11,631,000 in Breeders' Cup racing, 1984–94.

BREEDERS' CUP CLASSIC This race, the principal event of the Breeders' Cup Championship, is run over 1¼ miles. The Classic offers a single-race record $3 million purse, with $1,560,000 to the winner.

Record Quotable

"I know how crazy I made myself in 1979. I know these titles are not worth making yourself crazy for. I am not that same person I was then. But I want it, the title. How can I stop now?"

—Laffit Pincay Jr., quoted in *Sports Quotes*, by Bob Abel and Michael Valenti.

Most wins (horse) The Classic has been won by a different horse on each occasion.

Most wins (jockey) Three jockeys have won the Classic twice: Pat Day, 1984 and 1990; Chris Mc-Carron, 1988 and 1989; and Jerry Bailey, 1991 and 1993.

INTERNATIONAL RACES

VRC Melbourne Cup This contest, Australia's most prestigious classic race, has been staged annually since 1861. The race is run almost two miles at the Flemington Racetrack, Victoria.

Fastest time The fastest time is 3 minutes 16.3 seconds, by Kingston Rule, ridden by Darren Beadman in 1990.

Most wins (jockeys) Two jockeys have won the race four times: Bobby Lewis, 1902, 1915, 1919 and 1927; Harry White, 1974–75 and 1978–79.

DAY TIME ■ PAT DAY, THE HIGHEST EARNER IN THE BREEDERS' CUP CHAMPIONSHIP. (DAILY RACING FORM)

Derby England's most prestigious classic race has been staged annually since 1780. The race is contested over 1 mile 4 furlongs at Epsom Downs, Surrey.

Fastest time The fastest time is 2 minutes 33.8 seconds, by Mahmoud, ridden by Charlie Smirke, in 1936. Kahyasi, ridden by Ray Cochrane, won the 1988 Derby in an electronically timed 2 minutes 33.84 seconds.

Most wins (jockey) Lester Piggott has won the Derby a record nine times: 1954, 1957, 1960, 1968, 1970, 1972, 1976–77 and 1983.

Grand National England's most famous steeple-chase race, and most beloved sporting event, has been staged annually since 1839. The race is contested over a 4½ mile course of 30 fences at Aintree, Liverpool.

Fastest time The fastest time is 8 minutes 47.8 seconds, by Mr. Frisk, ridden by Marcus Army-tage, in 1990.

Most wins (jockey) George Stevens won the National five times: 1856, 1863–64 and 1869–70.

Prix de l'Arc de Triomphe France's most prestigious classic race, and Europe's richest thoroughbred race, has been staged annually since 1920. The race is contested over 1 mile 864 yards at Longchamps, Paris.

Fastest time The fastest time is 2 minutes 26.3 seconds, by Trempolino, ridden by Pat Eddery, in 1987.

Most wins (jockeys) Four jockeys have won the Arc four times: Jacques Doyasbere, 1942, 1944, 1950–51; Freddy Head, 1966, 1972, 1976, 1979; Yves Saint-Martin, 1970, 1974, 1982, 1984; Pat Eddery, 1980, 1985–87.

Irish Derby Ireland's most prestigious classic race has been staged annually since 1866. The race is contested over 1½ miles at The Curragh, County Kildare.

Fastest time The fastest time is 2 minutes 25.6 seconds, by St. Jovite, ridden by Christie Roche in 1992.

Most wins (jockey) Morny Wing has won the Irish Derby a record six times: 1921, 1923, 1930, 1938, 1942 and 1946.

HORSESHOE PITCHING

The object of the game of horseshoes is to toss a horseshoe over an iron stake so that it "comes to rest encircling the stake." The playing area, the horseshoe court, requires two stakes to be securely grounded 40 feet apart within a six-foot-square pitcher's box. Each contestant pitches two shoes in succession from the pitcher's box to the stake at the opposite end of the court. The pitching distance is 40 feet for men, and 30 feet for women. The winner is determined by a point system based on the shoe that is pitched closest to the stake. The pitcher with the most points wins the contest.

ORIGINS Historians claim that a variation of horseshoe pitching was first played by Roman soldiers to relieve the monotony of guard duty. Horseshoes was introduced to North America by the first settlers, and every town had its own horseshoe courts and competitions. The game was a popular pastime for soldiers during the Revolutionary War, and the famed British officer the Duke of Wellington wrote in his memoirs that "The War was won by pitchers of horse hardware!" The modern sport of horseshoes dates to the formation of the National Horseshoe Pitcher's Association (NHPA) in 1914.

WORLD CHAMPIONSHIPS First staged in 1909, the tournament was staged intermittently until 1946; since then it has been an annual event.

Most titles (men) Ted Allen (U.S.) has won 10 world titles: 1933–35, 1940, 1946, 1953, 1955–57 and 1959.

Most titles (women) Vicki Winston (née Chappelle) has won a record 10 women's titles: 1956, 1958–59, 1961, 1963, 1966–67, 1969, 1975 and 1981.

Perfect game A perfect game consists of amassing 40 points throwing only ringers. In world championship play only three pitchers have thrown perfect games: Guy Zimmerman (U.S.) in 1948; Elmer Hohl (Canada) in 1968; and Jim Walters (U.S.) in 1993. Hohl extended past his perfect game for a total of 56 consecutive ringers, a championship record.

INLINE SKATING (ROLLERBLADING)

See also ROLLER SKATING.

ORIGINS The roots of inline skating (sometimes hyphenated "in-line," and often referred to as "rollerblading" or the slang "blading") can be traced to Belgian Joseph Merlin's 18th century invention, the roller skate. In 1823, 40 years prior to James Plimpton's patent of the four-wheeled roller skate, Englishman Robert John Tyers created the first inline skate—then called a "rolite"—by positioning five wheels in a row on the bottom of the skate. The idea was ridiculed until 1980, when Scott and Brennan Olsen took the concept of the five-wheel skate and applied it to an ice hockey boot, thereby creating the modern inline skate (then called the "Ultimate Street Skate"). In 1986, five-wheel skates called "skeelers" began to see usage in the Netherlands. Today, inline skates have revolutionized the sport of speed skating because they are dramatically faster than conventional skates; they are now preferred by millions of professional and amateur rollerbladers worldwide. Related sports such as roller hockey and roller basketball continue to increase in popularity.

In the United States, the leading organization for roller blading is the Atlanta-based International Inline Skating Association (IISA). The United States Amateur Confederation of Roller Skating (USACRS) also governs amateur competitions. Inline skates were first allowed in international competition in 1992.

WORLD CHAMPIONSHIPS The United States has dominated the sport thus far. Derek Parra (Dover, Del.) was the overall world track champion in 1993 and the overall individual road champion for 1994. Heather Laufer (Kansas City, Mo.) was the 1994 women's world champion.

Record Quotable

"If you can find anybody in the world that can do this, I'll kiss your fanny in Macy's window on a Saturday night."

—Chuck Tamagni, age 71, in a letter to Guinness, in reference to having rollerbladed 104 miles in 10 hours.

INLINE SKATING WORLD RECORDS (Men and Women)			
One Hour			
Skater (Country)	**Distance**	**Place**	**Date**
Halco Bauma (Netherlands)	22.11 miles	Groningen, Netherlands	August 16, 1994
Six Hours			
Jonathan Seutter (U.S.)	91.35 miles	Long Beach, California	February 2, 1991
Twelve Hours			
Jonathan Seutter (U.S.)	177.63 miles	Long Beach, California	February 2, 1991
Twenty-four Hours			
Kimberly Ames (U.S.)	283.07 miles	Long Beach, California	October 31, 1994

Source: International Inline Skating Association

Speed records In the 1994 Championships in Gujan Mestras, France, Derek Parra (Dover, Del.) broke two records: the 1,500 meter, 2 minutes 6.42 seconds; and the 42k marathon, 1 hour 4 minutes 27.986 seconds.

INCLINING AWAY ■ 71-YEAR-OLD CHUCK TAMAGNI ON THE ROLLERBLADING WARPATH. (CHUCK TAMAGNI)

FANTASTIC FEATS

Chuck Tamagni, 71, of Lakeside, Calif., rollerbladed 104 miles in 10 hours on September 5, 1994.

JUDO

ORIGINS Judo is a modern combat sport that developed from an amalgam of several old Japanese martial arts, the most popular of which was ju-jitsu (jiujitsu), which is thought to be of Chinese origin. Judo has developed greatly since 1882, when it was first devised by Dr. Jigoro Kano. The International Judo Federation was founded in 1951.

Highest grades The efficiency grades in judo are divided into pupil (*kyu*) and master (*dan*) grades. The highest grade awarded is the extremely rare red belt *judan* (10th dan), given to only 13 men so far. The judo protocol provides for an 11th dan

BLADE OF GLORY ■ KIMBERLY AMES, THE WORLD'S FASTEST RECORDED 24-HOUR INLINE SKATER. (JERRY BROWN)

(*juichidan*) who also would wear a red belt, a 12th dan (*junidan*) who would wear a white belt twice as wide as an ordinary belt, and the highest of all, *shihan* (doctor), but these have never been bestowed, save for the 12th dan, to the founder of the sport, Dr. Jigoro Kano.

OLYMPIC GAMES Judo was first included in the Games in 1964 in Tokyo, Japan, and has been included in every Games since 1972. Women's events were first included as official events at the Barcelona Games in 1992.

Most gold medals Four men have won two gold medals: Willem Ruska (Netherlands), open class and over 93 kilograms class, in 1972; Hiroshi Saito (Japan), over 95 kilograms class, in 1984 and 1988; Peter Seisenbacher (Austria), up to 86 kilograms class, in 1984 and 1988; and Waldemar Legien (Poland), up to 78 kilograms class, in 1988 and up to 86 kilograms class, in 1992.

Most medals (individual) Angelo Parisi has won a record four Olympic medals, while representing two countries. In 1972 Parisi won a bronze medal in the open class, representing Great Britain. In 1980 Parisi represented France and won a gold, over 95 kilograms class, and a silver, open class; and won a second silver in the open class in 1984.

WORLD CHAMPIONSHIPS The first men's world championships were held in Tokyo, Japan in 1956. The event has been staged biennially since 1965. A world championship for women was first staged in New York City in 1980.

Most titles (men) Three men have won four world titles: Yasuhiro Yamashita (Japan), open class, 1981; over 95 kilograms class, 1979, 1981, 1983; Shozo Fujii (Japan), under 80 kilograms class, 1971, 1973, 1975; under 78 kilograms class, 1979; and Naoya Ogawa (Japan), open class, 1987, 1989, 1991 and over 95 kilograms class, 1989.

Most titles (women) Ingrid Berghmans (Belgium) has won a record six world titles: open class, 1980, 1982, 1984 and 1986; under 72 kilograms class, 1984 and 1989.

FANTASTIC FEATS

Judo throws Lee Finney and Gary Foster (both Great Britain) completed 27,803 throwing moves in 10 hours at the Forest Judo Club, Leicester, England on September 25, 1993.

KARATE

ORIGINS Karate is a martial art developed in Japan. Karate (empty hand) techniques evolved from the Chinese art of shoalin boxing, known as kempo, which was popularized in Okinawa in the 16th century as a means of self-defense, and became known as Tang Hand. Tang Hand was introduced to Japan by Funakoshi Gichin in the 1920s, and the name karate was coined in the 1930s. Gichin's style of karate, known as shotokan, is one of five major styles adapted for competition, the others being wado-ryu, gojuryu, shito-ryu and kyokushinkai. Each style places different emphasis on the elements of technique, speed and power. Karate's popularity grew in the West in the late 1950s.

WORLD CHAMPIONSHIPS The first men's world championships were staged in Tokyo, Japan in 1970; a women's competition was first staged in 1980. Both tournaments are now staged biennially. The competition consists of two types: kumite, in which combatants fight each other, and kata events, in which contestants perform routines.

KUMITE CHAMPIONSHIPS (MEN)

Most titles (team) Great Britain has won six kumite world team titles, in 1975, 1982, 1984, 1986, 1988 and 1990.

Most titles (individual) Four men have won two individual world titles: Pat McKay (Great Britain) in the under 80 kilograms class, 1982, 1984; Emmanuel Pinda (France), in the open class, 1984, and the over 80 kilograms class, 1988; Thierry Masci (France), in the under 70 kilograms class, 1986, 1988; Jose Manuel Egea (Spain), in the under 80 kilograms class, 1990, 1992.

KATA CHAMPIONSHIPS (MEN)

Most titles (team) Japan has won two kata world team titles, in 1986 and 1988.

Most titles (individual) Tsuguo Sakumoto (Japan) has won three world titles, in 1984, 1986 and 1988.

KUMITE CHAMPIONSHIPS (WOMEN)

Most titles (individual) Guus van Mourik (Netherlands) has won four world titles in the over 60 kilograms class, in 1982, 1984, 1986 and 1988.

KATA CHAMPIONSHIPS (WOMEN)

Most titles (individual) Mie Nakayama (Japan) has won three world titles, in 1982, 1984 and 1986.

LACROSSE

LACROSSE (MEN)

ORIGINS The sport is of Native American origin, derived from the intertribal game of *baggataway*, which has been recorded as being played by Iroquois tribes as early as 1492. French settlers in North America coined the name "La Crosse" (the French word for a crozier or staff). The National Lacrosse Association was formed in Canada in 1867. The United States Amateur Lacrosse Association was founded in 1879. The International Federation of Amateur Lacrosse (IFAL) was founded in 1928.

WORLD CHAMPIONSHIPS The men's world championships were first staged in Toronto, Canada in 1967.

Most titles The United States has won six world titles, in 1967, 1974, 1982, 1986, 1990 and 1994.

NCAA CHAMPIONSHIPS (DIVISION I) The men's NCAA championship was first staged in 1971.

Most titles Johns Hopkins has won seven lacrosse titles, in 1974, 1978–80, 1984–85 and 1987.

NCAA CHAMPIONSHIPS (DIVISION III) The men's division started in 1980.

Most titles Hobart College has won 13 titles, 1980–91 and 1993.

LACROSSE (WOMEN)

ORIGINS Women were first reported to have played lacrosse in 1886. The women's game evolved separately from the men's, developing different rules; thus two distinct games were created: the women's game features 12-a-side and six-a-side games, while men's games field 10-a-side teams.

WORLD CHAMPIONSHIPS A women's world championship was first held in 1969. Since 1982 the world championships have been known as the World Cup.

Most titles The United States has won four world titles, in 1974, 1982, 1989, and 1993.

NCAA CHAMPIONSHIPS (DIVISION I) The NCAA first staged a women's national championship in 1982.

Most titles Three teams have won two titles: Temple, 1984 and 1988; Penn State, 1987 and 1989; and Maryland, 1986 and 1992.

NCAA CHAMPIONSHIPS (DIVISION III) The women's division began play in 1985.

Most titles Trenton State has won six titles, 1985, 1987–88, 1991, 1993–94.

MODERN PENTATHLON

ORIGINS The modern pentathlon is made up of five activities: fencing, horseback riding, pistol shooting, swimming and cross-country running. The sport derives from military training in the 19th century, which was based on a messenger's being able to travel across country on horseback, fighting his way through with sword and pistol, and being prepared to swim across rivers and complete his journey on foot. Each event is scored

AGAIN IN '94 ■ **THE U.S. MEN'S LACROSSE** TEAM ONCE AGAIN DOMINATED THE SPORT, WINNING ITS SIXTH TITLE IN **1994.** (U.S. MEN'S LACROSSE TEAM/MIKE WELSH)

on points, determined either against other contestants or against scoring tables. There is no standard course; therefore, point totals are not comparable. *L'Union Internationale de Pentathlon Moderne* (UIPM) was formed in 1948 and expanded to include the administration of the biathlon in 1957. (For further information on the biathlon, see page 60.)

United States The United States Modern Pentathlon and Biathlon Association was established in 1971, but this body was split to create the U.S. Modern Pentathlon Association in 1978.

OLYMPIC GAMES Modern pentathlon was first included in the 1912 Games held in Stockholm, Sweden, and has been part of every Olympic program since.

Most gold medals Andras Balczo (Hungary) has won three gold medals in Olympic competition: team event, 1960 and 1968; individual title, 1972.

Most gold medals (team event) Two countries have won the team event four times: Hungary, 1952, 1960, 1968 and 1988; USSR, 1956, 1964, 1972 and 1980.

Most medals (individual) Pavel Lednev (USSR) has won a record seven medals in Olympic competition: two gold—team event, 1972 and 1980; two silver—team event, 1968; individual event, 1976; and three bronze—individual event, 1968, 1972 and 1980.

WORLD CHAMPIONSHIPS An official men's world championship was first staged in 1949, and has been held annually since. In Olympic years the Games are considered the world championships, and results from those events are included in world championship statistics. A women's world championship was inaugurated in 1981.

MEN'S CHAMPIONSHIP

Most titles (overall) Andras Balczo (Hungary) has won a record 13 world titles, including a record six individual titles: seven team, 1960, 1963, 1965–68 and 1970; six individual, 1963, 1965–67, 1969 and 1972.

Most titles (team event) The USSR has won 17 world championships: 1956–59, 1961–62, 1964, 1969, 1971–74, 1980, 1982–83, 1985 and 1991.

United States The United States won its only team world title in 1979, when Bob Nieman became the first American athlete, and so far the only man, to win an individual world championship.

WOMEN'S CHAMPIONSHIP

Most titles (individual event) Eva Fjellerup (Denmark) is the only woman to win the individual title four times, in 1990, 1991, 1993 and 1994.

Most titles (team event) Poland has won five world titles: 1985, 1988–91.

United States The best result for the U.S. in the team event is second place, which has been achieved twice, in 1981 and 1989. Lori Norwood won the individual championship in 1989.

UNITED STATES NATIONAL CHAMPIONSHIPS The men's championship was inaugurated in 1955, and the women's in 1977.

Most titles (men) Mike Burley has won four men's titles, in 1977, 1979, 1981 and 1985.

Most titles (women) Kim Arata (née Dunlop) has won nine titles, in 1979–80, 1984–89 and 1991.

MOTORCYCLE RACING

ORIGINS The first recorded motorcycle race took place in France on September 20, 1896, when eight riders took part in a 139-mile race from Paris to Nantes and back. The winner was M. Chevalier on a Michelin-Dion tricycle; he covered the course in 4 hours 10 minutes 37 seconds. The first race for two-wheeled motorcycles was held on a one-mile oval track at Sheen House, Richmond, England on November 29, 1897. The *Fédération Internationale Motorcycliste* (FIM) was founded in 1904 and is the world governing body.

WORLD CHAMPIONSHIPS The FIM instituted world championships in 1949 for 125, 250, 350 and 500cc classes. In 1962, a 50cc class was introduced, which was upgraded to 80cc in 1983. In 1982, the 350cc class was discontinued.

Most Championships

Overall 15, by Giacomo Agostini (Italy): 7—350cc (1968–74); 8—500cc (1966–72, 1975).

50cc 6, by Angel Nieto (Spain), 1969–70, 1972, 1975–77.

80cc 3, by Jorge Martinez (Spain), 1986–88.

125cc 7, by Angel Nieto (Spain), 1971–72, 1979, 1981–84.

250cc 4, by Phil Read (Great Britain), 1964–65, 1968, 1971.

350cc 7, by Giacomo Agostini (Italy), 1968–74.

500cc 8, by Giacomo Agostini (Italy), 1966–72, 1975.

Multiple titles The only rider to win more than one world championship in one year is Freddie Spencer (U.S.), who won the 250cc and 500cc titles in 1985.

United States The most world titles won by an American rider is four, by Eddie Lawson at 500cc in 1984, 1986, 1988–89.

Most Grand Prix Wins

Overall 122, by Giacomo Agostini (Italy): 54—350cc; 68—500cc.

50cc 27, by Angel Nieto (Spain).

80cc 21, by Jorge Martinez (Spain).

125cc 62, by Angel Nieto (Spain).

250cc 33, by Anton Mang (West Germany).

350cc 54, by Giacomo Agostini (Italy).

500cc 68, by Giacomo Agostini (Italy).

Most successful machines Japanese Yamaha machines won 45 world championships between 1964 and 1993.

Fastest circuits The highest average lap speed attained on any closed circuit is 160.288 mph, by Yvon du Hamel (Canada) on a modified 903cc four-cylinder Kawasaki Z1 at the 31-degree banked 2.5 mile Daytona International Speedway, Fla. in March 1973. His lap time was 56.149 seconds.

The fastest road circuit was the Francorchamps circuit near Spa, Belgium, then 8.74 miles long. It was lapped in 3 minutes 50.3 seconds (average speed 137.150 mph) by Barry Sheene (Great Britain) on a 495cc four-cylinder Suzuki during the Belgian Grand Prix on July 3, 1977. On that occasion he set a record time for this 10-lap (87.74-mile) race of 38 minutes 58.5 seconds (average speed 135.068 mph).

MOTO-CROSS RACING

WORLD CHAMPIONSHIPS Joel Robert (Belgium) won six 250cc Moto-cross World Championships (1964, 1968–72). Between April 25, 1964 and June 18, 1972 he won a record fifty 250cc Grand Prix. Eric Geboers (Belgium) has uniquely won all three

categories of the Moto-cross World Championships, at 125cc in 1982 and 1983, 250cc in 1987 and 500cc in 1988 and 1991.

Youngest champion The youngest moto-cross world champion was Dave Strijbos (Netherlands), who won the 125cc title at the age of 18 years 296 days on August 31, 1986.

OLYMPIC GAMES

Records in this section include results from the Intercalated Games staged in 1906.

ORIGINS The exact date of the first Olympic Games is uncertain. The earliest date for which there is documented evidence is July 776 B.C. By order of Theodosius I, emperor of Rome, the Games were prohibited in A.D. 394. The revival of the Olympic Games is credited to Pierre de Fredi, Baron de Coubertin, a French aristocrat, who was commissioned by his government to form a universal sports association in 1889. Coubertin presented his proposals for a modern Games on November 25, 1892 in Paris; this led to the formation of the International Olympic Committee (IOC) in 1894 and thence to the staging of the first modern Olympic Games, which were opened in Athens, Greece on April 6, 1896. In 1906, the IOC organized the Intercalated Games in Athens, to celebrate the 10th anniversary of the revival of the Games. In 1924, the first Winter Olympics were held in Chamonix, France.

OLYMPIC GAMES MEDAL RECORDS

INDIVIDUAL RECORDS

Most gold medals Ray Ewry (U.S.) has won 10 gold medals in Olympic competition: standing high jump, 1900, 1904, 1906 and 1908; standing long jump, 1900, 1904, 1906 and 1908; standing triple jump, 1900 and 1904. The most gold medals won by a woman is nine, by gymnast Larissa Latynina (USSR): all-around, 1956 and 1960; vault, 1956; floor exercise, 1956, 1960 and 1964; team title, 1956, 1960 and 1964.

Most medals Gymnast Larissa Latynina (USSR) has won 18 medals (nine gold, five silver and four bronze), 1956–64. The most medals won by a man is 15 (seven gold, five silver and three bronze), by gymnast Nikolai Andrianov (USSR), 1972–80.

Most gold medals at one Olympics Swimmer Mark Spitz (U.S.) won a record seven gold medals at Munich in 1972. His victories came in the 100-meter freestyle, 200-meter freestyle, 100-meter butterfly, 200-meter butterfly, and three relay events. The most gold medals won at one Games by a woman athlete is six, by swimmer Kristin Otto (East Germany), who won six gold medals at the 1988 Games. Her victories came in the 50-meter freestyle, 100-meter freestyle, 100-meter backstroke, 100-meter butterfly, and two relay events.

The most individual events won at one Games is five, by speed skater Eric Heiden (U.S.) in 1980. Heiden won the 500 meters, 1,000 meters, 1,500 meters, 5,000 meters, and 10,000 meters.

Most medals at one Olympics Gymnast Aleksandr Dityatin (USSR) won eight medals (three gold, four silver and one bronze) at Moscow, USSR in 1980. The most medals won by a woman athlete is seven (two gold and five silver), by gymnast Maria Gorokhovskaya (USSR) in 1952.

SUMMER OLYMPIC GAMES MEDAL WINNERS (1896–1992)

Country	Gold	Silver	Bronze	Total	Country	Gold	Silver	Bronze	Total
United States	789	603	518	1,910	Greece	24	40	39	103
USSR[1]	442	361	333	1,136	South Korea	31	27	41	99
Germany[2]	186	227	236	649	Yugoslavia[5]	26	30	30	86
Great Britain	177	224	218	619	Cuba	36	25	23	84
France	161	175	191	527	Austria	19	29	33	81
Sweden	133	149	171	453	New Zealand	27	10	28	65
East Germany[3]	154	131	126	411	South Africa	16	17	20	53
Italy	153	126	131	410	Turkey	26	15	12	53
Hungary	136	124	144	404	Argentina	13	19	15	47
Finland	98	77	112	287	Spain	17	19	10	46
Japan	90	83	93	266	Mexico	9	13	18	40
Australia	78	76	98	252	Brazil	9	10	21	40
Romania	59	70	90	219	Kenya	13	13	13	39
Poland	43	62	105	210	Iran	4	12	17	33
Canada	45	67	80	192	Jamaica	4	13	9	26
Netherlands	45	52	72	169	Estonia[6]	7	6	10	23
Switzerland	42	63	58	163	North Korea[7]	6	5	10	21
Bulgaria	38	69	55	162	Egypt	6	6	6	18
Czechoslovakia[4]	49	50	49	148	Ireland	5	5	5	15
Denmark	26	51	53	130	India	8	3	3	14
Belgium	35	47	44	126	Portugal	2	4	7	13
China	36	41	37	114	Mongolia	0	5	8	13
Norway	43	37	34	114	Ethiopia	6	1	6	13

[1] Includes Czarist Russia; Unified Team (1992)
[2] Germany 1896–1964, 1992; West Germany 1968–88
[3] 1968–88
[4] Includes Bohemia
[5] Includes I.O.P. (1992)
[6] Estonia and Latvia up to 1936
[7] North Korea from 1964

Most consecutive gold medals (same event) Al Oerter (U.S.) is the only athlete to win the same event, the discus, at four consecutive Games, 1956–68. Yachtsman Paul Elvstrom (Denmark) won four successive golds at monotype events, 1948–60, but there was a class change: Firefly in 1948; Finn class, 1952–60. Including the Intercalated Games of 1906, Ray Ewry (U.S.) won four consecutive gold medals in two events: standing high jump, 1900–1908; standing long jump, 1900–1908.

Oldest gold medalist Oscar Swahn (Sweden) was aged 64 years 258 days when he won an Olympic gold medal in 1912 as a member of the team that won the running deer shooting single-shot title. The oldest woman to win a gold medal was Queenie Newall (Great Britain), who won the 1908 national round archery event at age 53 years 275 days.

Youngest gold medalist The youngest-ever winner was an unnamed French boy who coxed the Netherlands pair to victory in the 1900 rowing

SUMMER OLYMPIC GAMES MEDAL WINNERS (1896–1992) (cont.)

Country	Gold	Silver	Bronze	Total	Country	Gold	Silver	Bronze	Total
Pakistan	3	3	4	10	Tanzania	0	2	0	2
Morocco	4	2	3	9	Cameroon	0	1	1	2
Uruguay	2	1	6	9	Haiti	0	1	1	2
Venezuela	1	2	5	8	Iceland	0	1	1	2
Chile	0	6	2	8	Israel	0	1	1	2
Nigeria	0	4	4	8	Panama	0	0	2	2
Philippines	0	1	7	8	Slovenia	0	0	2	2
Trinidad	1	2	4	7	Zimbabwe	1	0	0	1
Indonesia	2	3	1	6	Costa Rica	0	1	0	1
Latvia[8]	0	4	2	6	Ivory Coast	0	1	0	1
Colombia	0	2	4	6	Netherlands Antilles	0	1	0	1
Uganda	1	3	1	5	Senegal	0	1	0	1
Puerto Rico	0	1	4	5	Singapore	0	1	0	1
Tunisia	1	2	2	5	Sri Lanka	0	1	0	1
Peru	1	3	0	4	Syria	0	1	0	1
Algeria	1	0	3	4	Virgin Islands	0	1	0	1
Lebanon	0	2	2	4	Barbados	0	0	1	1
Taipei (Taiwan)	0	2	2	4	Bermuda	0	0	1	1
Ghana	0	1	3	4	Djibouti	0	0	1	1
Thailand	0	1	3	4	Dominican Republic	0	0	1	1
Bahamas	1	0	2	3	Guyana	0	0	1	1
Croatia	0	1	2	3	Iraq	0	0	1	1
Luxembourg	1	1	0	2	Malaysia	0	0	1	1
Lithuania	1	0	1	2	Niger	0	0	1	1
Suriname	1	0	1	2	Qatar	0	0	1	1
Namibia	0	2	0	2	Zambia	0	0	1	1

[8] Estonia and Latvia up to 1936

event. He was believed to be 7–10 years old. The youngest-ever woman champion was Marjorie Gestring (U.S.), who at age 13 years 268 days won the 1936 women's springboard diving event.

Most Games Three Olympians have competed in eight Games: show jumper Raimondo d'Inzeo (Italy), 1948–76; yachtsman Paul Elvstrom (Denmark), 1948–60, 1968–72, 1984–88; yachtsman Durwood Knowles (Great Britain/Bahamas), 1948–72, 1988. The most appearances by a woman is seven, by fencer Kerstin Palm (Sweden), 1964–88.

Summer/Winter Games gold medalist The only person to have won gold medals in both Summer and Winter Olympiads is Edward Eagan (U.S.), who won the 1920 light-heavyweight boxing title and was a member of the 1932 winning four-man bobsled team.

Summer/Winter Games medalist (same year) The only athlete to have won medals at both the Winter and Summer Games held in the same year is Christa Rothenburger-Luding (East Germany). At the 1988 Winter Games in Calgary, Canada, Rothenburger-Luding won two speed skating medals: gold medal, 1,000 meters, and silver medal, 500 meters; and at the Seoul Games that summer she won a silver medal in the women's sprint cycling event.

UNITED STATES RECORDS

Most gold medals The records for most gold medals overall and at one Games are both held by American athletes (see above). The most gold medals won by an American woman is five, by Bonnie Blair, speed skating 1988–94.

Most medals The most medals won by an American Olympian is 11, by three athletes: Carl Osburn, shooting—five gold, four silver and two bronze (1912–24); Mark Spitz, swimming—nine gold, one silver and one bronze (1968–72); Matt Biondi, swimming—eight golds, two silver and one bronze (1984–92). The most medals won by an American woman is eight, by Shirley Babashoff, swimming—two gold and six silver (1972–76).

Oldest gold medalist The oldest U.S. Olympic champion was Galen Spencer, who won a gold medal in the Team Round archery event in 1904, at age 64 years 2 days.

Youngest gold medalist The youngest gold medalist was Jackie Fields, who won the 1924 featherweight boxing title at age 16 years 162 days.

Oldest medalist The oldest U.S. medalist was Samuel Duvall, who was a member of the 1904 silver-medal-winning team in the team round archery event, at age 68 years 194 days.

Youngest medalist The youngest American medal winner, and the youngest-ever participant, was Dorothy Poynton, who won a silver medal in springboard diving at the 1928 Games at age 13 years 23 days. The youngest men's medalist was Donald Douglas Jr., who won a silver medal at six-meter yachting in 1932, at age 15 years 40 days.

Most games Equestrian Michael Plumb has participated in seven Olympics, 1960–76, 1984 and 1992. He was selected for the 1980 team, but the Moscow Games were boycotted by the U.S. Fencer Janice Romary has appeared in six Games, 1948–68, the most for an American woman.

WINTER GAMES MEDAL RECORDS

INDIVIDUAL RECORDS

Most gold medals Speed skater Lydia Skoblikova (USSR) has won six gold medals in Winter Games competition: 500 meters, 1964; 1,000 meters, 1964; 1,500 meters, 1960–64; 3,000 meters, 1960–64. The most gold medals won by a man is five, by two speed skaters: Clas Thunberg (Finland), 500 meters, 1928; 1,500 meters, 1924–28; 5,000 meters, 1924; all-around title, 1924; Eric Heiden (U.S.), 500, 1,000, 1,500, 5,000 and 10,000 meters, all in 1980.

Most medals Cross-country skier Raisa Smetanina (USSR/Unified Team) has won 10 medals (four gold, five silver and one bronze), 1976–92. The most medals won by a man is nine (four gold, three silver and two bronze), by cross-country skier Sixten Jernberg (Sweden), 1956–64.

Oldest gold medalist Jay O'Brien (U.S.) was aged 48 years 359 days when he won an Olympic gold medal in 1932 in the four-man bobsled event. The oldest woman to win a gold medal was Raisa Smetanina (Unified Team), who was a member of the 1992 4 x 5 km relay team at age 39 years 352 days.

Youngest gold medalist Maxi Herber (Germany) was aged 15 years 128 days when she won the 1936 figure skating title. The youngest-ever men's champion was Toni Neiminen (Finland), who at age 16 years 259 days was a member of the winning ski jumping team in 1992.

WINTER OLYMPIC GAMES MEDAL WINNERS (1924–1994)

Country	Gold	Silver	Bronze	Total
USSR[1]	99	71	71	241
Norway	73	77	65	215
United States	53	55	39	147
Austria	36	48	44	128
Germany[2]	45	43	37	125
Finland	36	45	42	123
East Germany[3]	39	36	35	110
Sweden	39	26	34	99
Switzerland	27	29	29	85
Italy	25	21	21	67
Canada	19	21	24	64
France	16	16	21	53
Netherlands	14	19	17	50
Czechoslovakia[4]	2	8	16	26
Great Britain	7	4	12	23
Japan	3	8	8	19
South Korea	6	2	2	10
Liechtenstein	2	2	5	9
Hungary	0	2	4	6
China	0	4	2	6
Belgium	1	1	2	4
Poland	1	1	2	4
Yugoslavia	0	3	1	4
Kazakhstan	1	2	0	3
Slovenia	0	0	3	3
Spain	1	0	1	2
Luxembourg	0	2	0	2
North Korea[5]	0	1	1	2
Ukraine	1	0	1	2
Belarus	0	2	0	2
New Zealand	0	1	0	1
Bulgaria	0	0	1	1
Romania	0	0	1	1
Uzbekistan	0	0	0	1
Australia	0	0	1	1

[1] Includes Unified Team (1992)

[2] Germany 1924–64, 1992, 1994; West Germany from 1968–88

[3] 1968–82

[4] Includes Bohemia

[5] North Korea from 1964

ORIENTEERING

Orienteering combines cross-country running with compass and map navigation. The object of the sport is for the competitor to navigate across a set course in the fastest time possible using a topographical map and a compass. The course contains designated locations called controls, identified by orange and white markers, which the runner must find and identify on a punch card that is handed to the official timer at the end of the race.

REPEAT PERFORMANCES ■ IN 1994 NORWAY RE-CAPTURED THE MEN'S ORIENTEERING RELAY TITLE AND SWEDEN THE WOMEN'S. TOP: VIDAR BENJAMIN-SEN LIFTS HIS ARM UP IN TRIUMPH OVER NORWAY'S EIGHTH GOLD. BOTTOM: LENA HASSLESTROM BRINGS IN SWEDEN'S TENTH GOLD, TO THE DELIGHT OF TEAMMATES ANNIKA ZELL AND ANNE-CHAR-LOTTE CARLSSON. (ORIENTEERING NORTH AMERICA)

ORIGINS Orienteering can be traced to Scandinavia at the turn of the 20th century. Major Ernst Killander (Sweden) is regarded as the father of the sport, having organized the first large race in Saltsjobaden, Sweden in 1919. The Swedish federation, *Svenska Orienteringsforbundet*, was founded in 1936. The International Orienteering Federation was established in 1961.

United States Orienteering was introduced to the U.S. in the 1940s. The first U.S. Orienteering Championships were held on October 17, 1970. The U.S. Orienteering Federation (USOF) was founded on August 1, 1971.

WORLD CHAMPIONSHIPS The world championships were first held in 1966 in Fiskars, Finland, and are held biennially.

Most titles (relay) The men's relay has been won a record eight times by Norway—1970, 1978, 1981, 1983, 1985, 1987, 1989 and 1994. Sweden has won the women's relay 11 times—1966, 1970, 1974, 1976, 1981, 1983, 1985, 1989, 1991, 1993 and 1994.

Most titles (individual) Three women's individual titles have been won by Annichen Kringstad (Sweden), in 1981, 1983 and 1985. The men's title has been won twice by three men: Age Hadler (Norway), in 1966 and 1972; Egil Johansen (Norway), in 1976 and 1978; and Oyvin Thon (Norway), in 1979 and 1981.

UNITED STATES NATIONAL CHAMPIONSHIPS First held on October 17, 1970, the nationals are held annually.

Most titles Sharon Crawford, New England Orienteering Club, has won a record 11 overall women's titles: 1977–82, 1984–87, and 1989. The men's title has been won six times by Mikell Platt, Blue Star Komplex Orienteering Club, 1986, 1988–92.

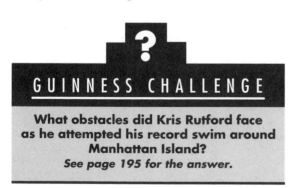

? GUINNESS CHALLENGE

What obstacles did Kris Rutford face as he attempted his record swim around Manhattan Island?
See page 195 for the answer.

PARACHUTING

ORIGINS The sport of parachuting traces its origins to the early 20th century, when daredevils performed parachute stunts at fairs and carnivals across the United States. Target jumping contests were first organized in the 1930s. In 1952 the sport was organized internationally by the *Fédération Aeronautique Internationale*. The sport is now contested in two main formats: target jumping and display formation.

WORLD CHAMPIONSHIPS

Most wins (team) The USSR won seven men's world titles, 1954, 1958, 1960, 1966, 1972, 1976 and 1980; and six women's world titles, 1956, 1958, 1966, 1968, 1972, 1976.

Most wins (individual) Nikolay Ushamyev (USSR) is the only jumper to have won two world titles, 1974 and 1980.

FANTASTIC FEATS

Total descents (men) Don Kellner (U.S.) parachuted 20,000 times at various locations up through November 14, 1993.

Total descents (women) Valentina Zakoretskaya (USSR) made 8,000 jumps between 1964 and September 1980.

Total descents—24 hours (men) Dale Nelson (U.S.) jumped 301 times on May 26–27, 1988.

Total descents—24 hours (women) Cheryl Stearns (U.S.) parachuted 255 times on November 26–27, 1987.

Oldest (men) Edwin Townsend (U.S.), 89 years of age, jumped on February 5, 1986.

Oldest (women) Mrs. Sylvia Brett (Great Britain), 80 years, 166 days, completed her jump on August 23, 1986.

Oldest tandem parachutist (men) Edward Royds-Jones, 95 years, 170 days, made a tandem parachute jump at Dunkeswell, Great Britain on July 2, 1994.

Oldest tandem parachutist (women) Corena Leslie (U.S.), 89 years, 326 days, completed her tandem parachute jump on June 11, 1992.

POLO

The object of the game is to score in the opponent's goals, the goalposts being eight yards wide, with the team scoring the most goals winning the game. Each side fields a team of four players; the game is played over six periods of seven minutes' duration each. A period is known as a chukka, and players must change their mount after each chukka.

ORIGINS Polo originated in Central Asia, possibly as early as 3100 B.C., in the state of Manipur. The name is derived from the Tibetan word *pulu*. The modern era began in India in the 1850s when British army officers were introduced to the game. The Cachar Club, Assam, India was founded in 1859, and is believed to be the first polo club of the modern era. The game was introduced in England in 1869. The world governing body, the Hurlingham Polo Association, was founded in London, England in 1874 and drew up the laws of the game in 1875.

United States Polo was introduced to the U.S. by James Gordon Bennett in 1876, when he arranged for the first indoor game at Dickel's Riding Academy, N.Y. The first game played outdoors was held on May 13, 1876 at the Jerome Park Racetrack in Westchester County, N.Y. The oldest existing polo club in the United States is Meadowbrook Polo Club, Jericho, N.Y., founded in 1879. The United States Polo Association was formed on March 21, 1890.

UNITED STATES OPEN POLO CHAMPIONSHIP The U.S. Open was first staged in 1904 and is an annual event.

Most wins The Meadow Brook Club, Westbury, N.Y. has won the U.S. Open 28 times: 1916, 1920, 1923–41, 1946–51, and 1953.

Highest score The highest aggregate number of goals scored in an international match is 30, when Argentina beat the U.S. 21–9 at the Meadow Brook Club, Westbury, N.Y. in September 1936.

Highest handicap Polo players are assigned handicaps based on their skill, with a 10 handicap being the highest level of play. Only 56 players have been awarded the 10-goal handicap.

40-goal games There have only been three games staged between two 40-goal handicap teams. These games were staged in Argentina in 1975, United States in 1990 and Australia in 1991.

POOL

ORIGINS Pool traces its ancestry to billiards, an English game introduced in Virginia in the late 17th century. During the 19th century the game evolved from one in which a mace was used to push balls around a table, to a game of precise skill using a cue, with the aim of pocketing numbered balls. The original form of pool in the United States was known as pyramid pool, with the object being to pocket eight out of the 15 balls on the table. From this game, "61-pool" evolved: each of the 15 balls was worth points equal to its numerical value; the first player to score 61 points was the winner. In 1878 the first world championship was staged under the rules of 61-pool. In 1910, Jerome Keogh suggested that the rules be adjusted to make the game faster and more attractive; he proposed that the last ball be left free on the table to be used as a target on the next rack; the result was 14.1 continuous pool (also known as American straight pool). The game of 14.1 was adopted as the championship form of pool from 1912 onwards. In the last 20 years, nine-ball pool and eight-ball pool have surpassed 14.1 in popularity. In 1990 the World Pool Billiard Association inaugurated the nine-ball world championship.

14.1 CONTINUOUS POOL (ALSO KNOWN AS AMERICAN STRAIGHT POOL)

WORLD CHAMPIONSHIPS The first official world championship was held in April 1912 and was won by Edward Ralph (U.S.).

Most titles Two players have won the world title six times: Ralph Greenleaf (U.S.) and Willie Mosconi (U.S.). From 1919–37, Greenleaf won the title six times and defended it 13 times. Between 1941 and 1956, Mosconi also won the title six times and defended it 13 times.

Longest consecutive run The longest consecutive run in 14.1 recognized by the Billiard Congress of America (BCA) is 526 balls, by Willie Mosconi in March 1954 during an exhibition in Springfield, Ohio. Michael Eufemia is reported to have pocketed 625 balls at Logan's Billiard Academy in Brooklyn, N.Y. on February 2, 1960; however, this run has never been ratified by the BCA.

NINE-BALL POOL

WORLD CHAMPIONSHIP In this competition, inaugurated in 1990, Earl Strickland (U.S.) has won the

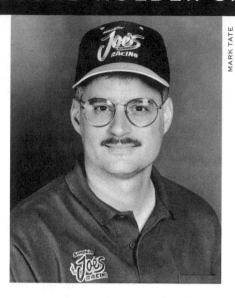

MARK TATE

MARK TATE

Holy smokes! Or is it holy *Smokin' Joe's*? That's the name of the famed hydroplane that shot through the water at a record elapsed average time of 146.269 mph over five heats in the American Power Boat Association (APBA) Gold Cup race in Detroit, Michigan in June 1994. "The record was second to the boat race. I just wanted to win. Anything above that was a bonus," 34-year-old driver Mark Tate says. "But being in *Guinness* is neat because there's so much prestige."

Owned by Steve Woomer, *Smokin' Joe's* is 30 ft. in length, 15 ft. in width and weighs approximately 6,000 lbs. It was designed by crew chief/team manager Jim Lucero and is maintained by eight crew members. Although Mark Tate is the lone driver in the boat, he is emphatic that the team's role is paramount: "Before the race I get together with the crew and we examine the race conditions. We take great pains to test the water, learn the set-ups and make adjustments to the boat."

But the danger of the sport remains the driver's alone. If the hydroplane, which travels on a cushion of air above the water, catches wind it could "blowover" and plunge the driver and craft into the water. Tate had one such spill in August 1993, from which he received a series of injuries including a concussion, bruised kidneys, two broken fingers and compressed vertebrae. "When I recovered, I got right back up and started racing again," Tate said.

How does it feel to rocket over 145 mph through the water? "It's a hard sensation to explain. You go so fast—the length of a football field in a second—you have no time to lay back. It's not like a roller coaster where you can enjoy the tummy-drop and jostling."

men's title twice, 1990–91. Robin Bell (U.S.) has won the women's title twice, 1990–91.

POWERBOAT RACING

ORIGINS A gasoline engine was first installed in a boat by Jean Lenoir on the River Seine, Paris, France in 1865. Organized powerboat races were first run at the turn of the 20th century. The first major international competition was the Harnsworth Trophy, launched in 1903. Modern powerboat racing is broken down into two main types: circuit racing in sheltered waterways, and offshore racing. Offshore events were initially for displacement (nonplaning) cruisers, but in 1958 the 170-mile Miami, Fla.–to–Nassau, Bahamas race was staged for planing cruisers.

United States The American Power Boat Association (APBA) was founded on April 22, 1903 in New York City. In 1913 the APBA issued the "Racing Commission" rules, which created its powers for governing the sport in North America. In 1924 the APBA set rules for boats propelled by outboard detachable motors and became the governing body for both inboard and outboard racing in North America. The APBA is currently based in Eastpointe, Mich.

APBA GOLD CUP The APBA held its first Gold Cup race at the Columbia Yacht Club on the Hudson River, N.Y. in 1904, when the winner was *Standard*, piloted by C. C. Riotto at an average speed of 23.6 mph.

Most wins (driver) The most wins is nine, by Chip Hanauer, 1982–88 and 1992–93.

Most wins (boat) The most successful boat has been *Miss Budweiser* with nine wins, driven by Bill

---

POWERBOAT SPEED RECORDS

The following is a selection of speed records recognized by the APBA as of January 1, 1995.

Distance: One Kilometer

Type	Class	Speed (mph)	Driver	Location	Year
Inboard	GP	170.024	Kent MacPhail	Decatur, Ill.	1989
Inboard	KRR	146.649	Gordon Jennings	Lincoln City, Ore.	1989
Offshore	Super Boat	148.238	Thomas Gentry	New Orleans, La.	1987
Offshore	Open	138.512	Al Copeland	New Orleans, La.	1987
PR Outboard	500ccH	121.940	Daniel Kirts	Moore Haven, Fla.	1987
PR Outboard	700ccH	118.769	Billy Rucker Jr.	Waterford, Calif.	1992
Performance	Champ Boat	131.963	Jim Merten	Kaukauna, Wis.	1978
Performance	Mod U	142.968	Bob Wartinger	Moore Haven, Fla.	1989
Special Event	Formula 1	165.338	Robert Hering	Parker, Ariz.	1986
Special Event	Jet	317.600	Ken Warby	Tumut, Australia	1976

Unlimited in Competition

Type	Distance	Speed (mph)	Driver	Location	Year
Qual. Lap	2 miles	165.975	Chip Hanauer	Evansville, Ind.	1992
Lap	2 miles	156.713	Chip Hanauer	Evansville, Ind.	1992
Qual. Lap	2.5 miles	168.935	Chip Hanauer	Evansville, Ind.	1992
Lap	2.5 miles	166.296	Steve David	Honolulu, Hawaii	1992
Lap	3 miles	155.682	Mark Tate	San Diego, Calif.	1991

Source: APBA

GO JOE! ■ SMOKIN' JOE'S, THE POWERBOAT THAT CATAPULTED MARK TATE INTO THE RECORD BOOKS. (MARK'S PHOTO)

Sterett Sr. in 1969; by Dean Chenoweth in 1970, 1973 and 1980–81; by Tom D'Eath in 1989–90; and by Chip Hanauer in 1992–93.

Consecutive wins Chip Hanauer has won a record seven successive victories, 1982–88.

Fastest winner The highest average speed for the race is 146.269 mph by Mark Tate, piloting *Smokin' Joe's* in June 1994.

RACQUETBALL

ORIGINS Racquetball, using a 40-foot x 20-foot court, was invented in 1950 by Joe Sobek at the Greenwich YMCA, Greenwich, Conn. Sobek designed a "strung paddle racquet" and combined the rules of squash and handball to form the game of "paddle rackets." The International Racquetball Association (IRA) was founded in 1960 by Bob Kendler, and was renamed the American Amateur Racquetball Association (AARA) in 1979. The International Amateur Racquetball Federation (IARF) was founded in 1979 and staged its first world championship in 1981.

WORLD CHAMPIONSHIPS First held in 1981, the IARF world championships have been held biennially since 1984.

Most titles (team) The United States has won all six team titles, in 1981, 1984, 1986 (tie with Canada), 1988, 1990 and 1992.

Most titles (men) Egan Inoue (U.S.) has won two singles titles, in 1986 and 1990.

Most titles (women) Two women have won two world titles: Cindy Baxter (U.S.), 1981 and 1986; and Heather Stupp (Canada), 1988 and 1990.

UNITED STATES NATIONAL CHAMPIONSHIPS The first championships were held in 1968.

Most titles Michelle Gilman-Gould of Idaho has won a record five women's titles, 1989–93. Four men's open titles have been won by Ed Andrews of California, 1980–81 and 1985–86.

RODEO

ORIGINS Rodeo originated in Mexico, developing from 18th century fiestas, and moved north to the United States and Canada with the expansion of the North American cattle industry in the 18th and 19th centuries. There are several claims to the earliest organized rodeo. The Professional Rodeo Cowboys Association (PRCA) sanctions the West of the Pecos Rodeo, Pecos, Tex. as the oldest; it was first held in 1883. The development of rodeo as a regulated national sport can be traced to the formation of the Cowboys' Turtle Association in 1936. In 1945 the Turtles became the Rodeo Cowboy Association, which in 1975 was renamed the Professional Rodeo Cowboys Association (PRCA). The PRCA is recognized as the oldest and largest rodeo-governing body in the world.

Rodeo events are divided into two groups: roughstock and timed.

Roughstock The roughstock events are saddle bronc riding, bareback riding, and bull riding. In these events the cowboy is required to ride the mount for eight seconds to receive a score. The cowboy must use only one hand to grip the "rigging" (a handhold secured to the animal), and is disqualified if the free hand touches the animal or equipment during the round. The performance is judged on the cowboy's technique and the animal's bucking efforts.

Timed The timed events are calf roping, steer roping, team roping, and steer wrestling. In these events the cowboy chases the calf or steer, riding a registered quarter horse, catches up to the animal, and then captures the animal performing the required feat. The cowboy's performance is timed, with the fastest time winning the event.

Record Quotable

"Asking me if I was scared is like asking a kid who plays football if he was scared of getting tackled. It didn't matter. . . ."

—Ty Murray, youngest rodeo champion, quoted in *The Guinness Book of Records 1995.*

WORLD CHAMPIONSHIPS The Rodeo Association of America organized the first world championships in 1929. The championship has been organized under several different formats and sponsored by several different groups throughout its existence. The current championship is a season-long competition based on PRCA earnings. The PRCA has organized the championship since 1945 (as the Rodeo Cowboy Association through 1975).

Most titles (overall) Jim Shoulders has won 16 rodeo world championship events: all-around, 1949, 1956–59; bareback riding, 1950, 1956–58; bull riding, 1951, 1954–59.

INDIVIDUAL EVENTS

All-around Three cowboys have won six all-around titles: Larry Mahan, 1966–70, 1973; Tom Ferguson, 1974–79; and Ty Murray, 1989–94.

RIDE 'EM COWBOY! ■ TY MURRAY, A YOUNG RODEO RIDER ALREADY IN THE SAME LEAGUE WITH LEGENDS LARRY MAHAN AND TOM FERGUSON. (PROFESSIONAL RODEO COWBOYS ASSOCIATION)

Saddle bronc riding Casey Tibbs won six saddle bronc titles, in 1949, 1951–54 and 1959.

Bareback riding Two cowboys have won five titles: Joe Alexander, 1971–75; Bruce Ford, 1979–80, 1982–83, 1987.

Bull riding Don Gay has won eight bullriding titles: 1975–81 and 1984.

Calf roping Dean Oliver has won eight titles: 1955, 1958, 1960–64 and 1969.

Steer roping Guy Allen has won nine titles: 1977, 1980, 1982, 1984, 1989, 1991–94.

Steer wrestling Homer Pettigrew has won six titles: 1940, 1942–45 and 1948.

Team roping The team of Jake Barnes and Clay O'Brien Cooper has won seven titles, 1985–89, 1992 and 1994.

Women's barrel racing Charmayne Rodman has won 10 titles, 1984–93.

Oldest world champion Ike Rude won the 1953 steer roping title at age 59 to became the oldest rodeo titleholder.

Youngest champions The youngest winner of a world title is Anne Lewis, who won the WPRA barrel racing title in 1968 at 10 years of age. Ty Murray, 20, became the youngest cowboy to win the PRCA All-Around Champion title in 1989.

RIDING RECORDS

HIGHEST SCORES (MAXIMUM POSSIBLE: 100 POINTS)

Bull riding Wade Leslie scored 100 points riding Wolfman Skoal at Central Point, Ore. in 1991.

Saddle bronc riding Doug Vold scored 95 points riding Transport at Meadow Lake, Saskatchewan, Canada in 1979.

Bareback riding Joe Alexander scored 93 points riding Marlboro at Cheyenne, Wyo. in 1974.

FASTEST TIMES

Calf roping The fastest time in this event is 5.7 seconds, by Lee Phillips at Assinobia, Saskatchewan, Canada in 1978.

Steer wrestling Without a barrier, the fastest time is reported to have been 2.2 seconds by Oral Zumwalt in the 1930s. With a barrier, the record time is 2.4 seconds, achieved by three cowboys: Jim Bynum at Marietta, Okla. in 1955; Gene Melton at Pecatonia, Ill. in 1976; and Carl Deaton at Tulsa, Okla. in 1976.

MYSTERIOUS LADY ■ CHARMAYNE (JAMES) RODMAN, PARTIALLY CONCEALED BY A HAT, DISPLAYING HER BARREL RACING PROWESS. (WOMEN'S PROFESSIONAL RODEO ASSOCIATION)

Team roping The team of Bob Harris and Tee Woolman performed this feat in a record 3.7 seconds at Spanish Fork, Utah in 1986.

Steer roping The fastest time in this event is 8.4 seconds, by Guy Allen at Garden City, Kan. in 1991.

HIGHEST EARNINGS

Career Roy Cooper holds the career PRCA earnings mark at $1,489,698, 1976–94.

Season The single-season PRCA mark is $297,896 by Ty Murray in 1993.

FANTASTIC FEATS

Texas skips Vince Bruce (U.S.) performed 4,001 Texas skips (jumping back and forth through a large, vertical spun hoop) on July 22, 1991 in New York City.

Largest loop Kalvin Cook spun a 95-foot loop in Las, Vegas, Nev. on March 27, 1994.

ROLLER SKATING

See also INLINE SKATING (ROLLERBLADING.)

ORIGINS Roller skates were invented by Joseph Merlin of Belgium. He demonstrated his new mode of transport at a masquerade party in London in 1760, with disastrous consequences—he was unable to stop and crashed into a large mirror, receiving near-fatal wounds. In 1863, James L. Plimpton of Medfield, Mass. patented the modern four-wheeled roller skate. In 1866, he opened the first public roller-skating rink in the United States in Newport, R.I. The *Fédération Internationale de Roller Skating* was founded in 1924 and is now headquartered in Spain. The Roller Skating Rink Operators' Association staged the first U.S. National Championship in 1937. Since 1973 the United States Amateur Confederation of Roller Skating has been the governing body of the sport in the United States. Three distinct sports have derived from roller skating: speed skating, artistic skating, and roller hockey.

SPEED SKATING

International speed skating events are divided into two categories: road racing and track racing. World championships are staged in alternate years for each discipline.

GREAT SCOTT! ■ SCOTT COHEN, FORMER WORLD CHAMPION ARTISTIC ROLLER SKATER. (U.S. AMATEUR CONFEDERATION OF ROLLER SKATING)

WORLD CHAMPIONSHIPS The first world championships were held in Monza, Italy in 1937. A women's championship was first staged in 1953.

Most titles Alberta Vianello (Italy) has won a record 19 world titles—eight track and 11 road—1953–65. Marco Cantarella (Italy) has won 15 men's titles—seven track and eight road—1964–80.

UNITED STATES NATIONAL CHAMPIONSHIPS The first U.S. championships were staged in 1937 for indoor competition, and contests have been held annually since. In 1985 a separate outdoor championship was initiated, and this is also staged annually.

Most titles Dante Muse has won seven men's overall titles—four indoors, 1986, 1990, 1992–93; three outdoors, 1987, 1989 and 1990. Mary Merrell has won a record six overall champion titles, 1959–61, 1964, and 1966–67 (all indoors).

ARTISTIC SKATING

WORLD CHAMPIONSHIPS The first world championships were held in Washington D.C. in 1947. The championships have been held annually since 1970.

Most titles Scott Cohen (U.S.) has won five men's free-skating titles, 1985–86 and 1989–91. Sandro

Guerra (Italy) has won five men's combined titles, 1987–89, 1991–92. Rafaella del Vinaccio (Italy) has won five free-skating and five combined women's titles, 1988–92.

UNITED STATES NATIONAL CHAMPIONSHIPS The first U.S. championships were staged in 1939, and contests are now held annually.

Most titles Michael Jacques has won seven free-skating titles, 1966–72. Laurene Anselmi has won seven women's titles—three figure skating, 1951, 1953–54; four free-skating, 1951–54.

ROLLER HOCKEY

Roller hockey is played by two five-man teams over two 20-minute periods.

WORLD CHAMPIONSHIPS First held in Stuttgart, Germany in 1936, the world championships have been held under several formats, both annual and biennial. Currently the tournament is an annual event.

Most titles Portugal has won 14 world titles: 1947–50, 1952, 1956, 1958, 1960, 1962, 1968, 1974, 1982, 1991 and 1993.

ROWING

ORIGINS Forms of rowing can be traced back to ancient Egypt; however, the modern sport of rowing dates to 1715, when the Doggett's Coat and Badge scull race was established in London, England. Types of regattas are believed to have taken place in Venice, Italy in 1300, but the modern regatta can also be traced to England, where races were staged in 1775 on the River Thames at Ranleigh Gardens, Putney. The world governing body is the *Fédération Internationale des Sociétés d'Aviron* (FISA), founded in 1892. Rowing has been part of the Olympic Games since 1900.

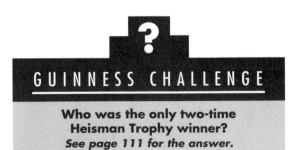

?
GUINNESS CHALLENGE

Who was the only two-time Heisman Trophy winner?
See page 111 for the answer.

HEAVE HO ■ **STEVEN REDGRAVE, ONE OF SEVEN OARSMEN TO WIN THREE GOLD MEDALS.** (ALLSPORT/ B. MARTIN)

United States The first organized boat races in the United States were reportedly races staged between boatmen in New York harbor in the late 18th century. The first rowing club formed in the United States was the Castle Garden Amateur Boat Club Association, New York City, in 1834. The oldest active boat club is the Detroit Boat Club, founded in 1839. The first and oldest collegiate boat club was formed at Yale University in 1843. The National Association of Amateur Oarsmen (NAAO) was formed in 1872. The NAAO merged with the National Women's Rowing Association in 1982 to form the United States Rowing Association.

OLYMPIC GAMES Men's rowing events have been included in the Olympic Games since 1900. In 1976 women's events were included.

Most gold medals Seven oarsmen have won three gold medals: John Kelly (U.S.), single sculls,

1920, double sculls, 1920 and 1924; Paul Costello (U.S.), double sculls, 1920, 1924 and 1928; Jack Beresford (Great Britain), single sculls, 1924, coxless fours, 1932, double sculls, 1936; Vyacheslav Ivanov (USSR), single sculls, 1956, 1960 and 1964; Siegfried Brietzke (East Germany), coxless pairs, 1972, coxless fours, 1976 and 1980; Pertti Karppinen (Finland), single sculls, 1976, 1980 and 1984; Steven Redgrave (Great Britain), coxed fours, 1984, coxless pairs, 1988 and 1992.

Most medals Jack Beresford (Great Britain) won five medals in rowing competition: three gold (see above) and two silver (single sculls, 1920, and eights, 1928).

WORLD CHAMPIONSHIPS World rowing championships staged separately from the Olympic Games were first held in 1962. Since 1974 the championships have been staged annually. In Olympic years the Games are considered the world championships, and results from the Olympics are included in this section.

Most titles Giuseppe and Carmine Abbagnale (both Italy) have won nine coxed pairs titles, 1981–82, 1984–85 and 1987–91. Jutta Behrendt (née Hampe; East Germany) has won six titles: three single sculls, 1983, 1986 and 1988; three quadruple sculls, 1985, 1987 and 1989.

Single sculls Three oarsmen have won five single sculls titles: Peter-Michael Kolbe (West Germany), 1975, 1978, 1981, 1983 and 1986; Pertti Karppinen (Finland), 1976, 1979–80 and 1984–85; and Thomas Lange (Germany), 1988–92. Christine Hahn (née Scheiblich; East Germany) has won five women's titles, 1974–78.

Eights Since 1962, East German crews have won seven men's eights titles—1970, 1975–80. In women's competition the USSR has won seven titles—1978–79, 1981–83, 1985–86.

COLLEGIATE CHAMPIONSHIPS Harvard and Yale staged the first intercollegiate boat race in 1852. The Intercollegiate Rowing Association (IRA) was formed in 1895, and in 1898 inaugurated the Varsity Challenge Cup, which was recognized as the premier event in college racing. In 1979, a women's national championship was inaugurated, followed by an official men's event in 1982.

The University of Washington has won the women's title a record seven times: 1981–85 and 1987–88. Since 1982 Harvard University has won the most men's titles, with five: 1983, 1985 and 1987–89.

Most wins (men) Cornell has won 24 titles: 1896–97 (includes two wins in 1897), 1901–03, 1905–07, 1909–12, 1915, 1930, 1955–58, 1962–63, 1971, 1977, and 1981. Since 1982, Harvard has won six titles, 1983, 1985, 1987–89, and 1992.

Most wins (women) Washington has won seven titles—1981–85, 1987–88.

Fastest speed The fastest recorded speed on non-tidal water for 2,000 meters is by an American eight, in 5 minutes 27.14 seconds (13.68 mph) at Lucerne, Switzerland on June 17, 1984. A crew from Penn AC was timed in 5 minutes 18.8 seconds (14.03 mph) in the FISA Championships on the River Meuse, Liège, Belgium on August 17, 1930.

RUGBY

ORIGINS As with baseball in the United States, the origins of rugby are obscure—but a traditional "history" has become so embedded in the national psyche, in this case that of Great Britain, that any historical revision is either ignored or derided. The tradition is that the game began when William Webb Ellis picked up the ball during a soccer game at Rugby School in November 1823 and ran with it. Whether or not there is any truth to this legend, the "new" handling code of soccer developed, and the game was played at Cambridge University in 1839. The first rugby club was formed at Guy's Hospital, London, England in 1843, and the Rugby Football Union (RFU) was founded in January 1871. The International Rugby Football Board (IRFB) was founded in 1886.

OLYMPIC GAMES Rugby was played at four Games from 1900 to 1924. The only double gold medalist was the U.S., which won in 1920 and 1924.

WORLD CUP The World Cup is staged every four years and is the world championship for rugby. The first World Cup was hosted by Australia and New Zealand in 1987.

Most wins New Zealand won the first World Cup in 1987, and Australia won the second tournament in 1991.

WORLD CUP SCORING RECORDS

TEAM RECORDS

Most points (game) The most points in World Cup play is 74, scored by New Zealand against Fiji (13 points) at Christchurch, New Zealand on May 27, 1987.

Most points (game, aggregate score) The highest aggregate score in World Cup competition is 87 points, New Zealand defeating Fiji 74–13 (see above).

INDIVIDUAL RECORDS

Most points (game) Didier Camberabero (France) scored 30 points (three tries and nine conversions) *v.* Zimbabwe at Auckland, New Zealand on June 2, 1987.

Most points (tournament) Grant Fox (New Zealand) scored 126 points in 1987.

Most points (career) Grant Fox (New Zealand) scored 170 points in 1987 and 1991.

INTERNATIONAL RUGBY RECORDS

Highest score The highest score by a team in a full international game is 164, by Hong Kong aginst Singapore at Kuala Lumpur, Malaysia on October 27, 1994.

INDIVIDUAL RECORDS

Game

Most points Ashley Billington scored 50 points (10 tries) on October 27, 1994.

Most tries Ashley Billington scored 10 tries on October 27, 1994.

Most penalty goals 8, tied by two: Mark Wyatt (Canada) kicked eight *v.* Scotland at St. John, New Brunswick on May 25, 1991; Neil Jenkins (Wales) kicked eight on November 10, 1993.

Career

Most points Michael Lynagh (Australia) has scored a record 821 points in international rugby competition, 1984–94.

Most tries David Campese (Australia) is the leading try scorer in international competition with 60 tries, 1982–94.

Most internationals Philippe Sella (France) has played a record 101 international matches, 1982–94.

Consecutive internationals Two players played in 53 consecutive games: Gareth Edwards (Wales), 1967–78; Willie John McBride (Ireland), 1962–75.

SHOOTING

The National Rifle Association recognizes four categories of shooting competition: conventional, international, silhouette, and action pistol. This section reports records only for international style shooting—the shooting discipline used at the Olympic Games.

ORIGINS The earliest recorded shooting club is the Lucerne Shooting Guild (Switzerland), formed *c.* 1466. The first known shooting competition was held at Zurich, Switzerland in 1472. The international governing body, the *Union International de Tir* (UIT), was formed in Zurich in 1907.

United States The National Rifle Association (NRA) was founded in 1871, and is designated as the national governing body for shooting sports in the United States by the U.S. Olympic Committee.

INTERNATIONAL STYLE SHOOTING

International or Olympic-style shooting is comprised of four disciplines: rifle, pistol, running target, and shotgun. Running target events are limited to male competitors. Shotgun shooting (also known as trap and skeet) requires the competitor to hit clay targets released from a skeet.

OLYMPIC GAMES Shooting has been part of the Olympic program since the first modern Games in 1896. Women were allowed to compete against men at the 1968 Games, and separate women's events were included in 1984.

Most gold medals Seven marksmen have won five gold medals: Konrad Staheli (Switzerland), 1900–1906; Louis Richardet (Switzerland), 1900–06; Alfred Lane (U.S.), 1912–20; Carl Osburn (U.S.), 1912–24; Ole Lilloe-Olsen (Norway), 1920–24; Morris Fisher (U.S.), 1920–24; and Willis Lee (U.S.), 1920. Marina Logvinenko (Unified Team)

SHOOTING—INDIVIDUAL WORLD RECORDS

In 1986 the International Shooting Union introduced new regulations for determining major championships and world records. Now the leading competitors undertake an additional round with a target subdivided to tenths of a point for rifle and pistol shooting and an extra 25 shots for trap and skeet. The table below shows the world records for the 13 Olympic shooting disciplines, giving in parentheses the score for the number of shots specified plus the score in the additional round.

Men

Event	Points	Marksman (Country)	Date
Free rifle 50 m 3 x 40 shots	1,287.9 (1,186 + 101.9)	Rajmond Debevec (Slovenia)	August 29,1992
Free rifle 50 m 60 shots prone	703.5 (599 + 104.5)	Jens Harskov (Denmark)	June 6, 1991
Air rifle 10 m 60 shots	699.4 (596 + 103.4)	Rajmond Debevec (Yugoslavia)	June 7, 1990
Free pistol 50 m 60 shots	672.5 (575 + 97.5)	Sergey Pyzhyanov (USSR)	June 15, 1993
Rapid-fire pistol 25 m 60 shots	689 (593 +96)	Vladimir Vokhmianin (Kazakhstan)	June 2, 1993
Air pistol 10 m 60 shots	695.1 (593 + 102.1)	Sergey Pyzhyanov (USSR)	October 3, 1989
Running target 10 m 30 + 30 shots	679 (582 + 97)	Lubos Racansky (Czechoslovakia)	May 30, 1991
Trap 150 targets	148 (124 + 24)	Giovanni Pellielo (Italy)	June 9, 1993
	149 (124 + 25)	Marco Venturini (Italy)	June 15, 1993
Skeet 150 targets	149 (124 + 25)	Dean Clark (U.S.)	June 20, 1993

Women

Event	Points	Markswoman (Country)	Date
Standard rifle 50 m 3 x 20 shots	689.3 (590 + 99.3)	Vessela Letcheva (Bulgaria)	August 28, 1992
Air rifle 10 m 40 shots	500.8 (399 + 101.8)	Valentina Cherkasova (Georgia)	May 8, 1993
Sport pistol 25 m 60 shots	693.8 (591 + 102.8)	Nino Salukvadse (USSR)	July 13, 1989
Air pistol 10 m 40 shots	492.4 (392 + 100.4)	Lieselotte Breker (West Germany)	May 18, 1989

The first world record by a woman at any sport for a category in direct and measurable competition with men was by Margaret Murdock (née Thompson; U.S.), who set a world record for smallbore rifle (kneeling position) of 391 in 1967.

is the only woman to win two gold medals: sport pistol and air pistol, both in 1992.

Most medals Carl Osburn (U.S.) has won 11 medals: five gold, four silver and two bronze. The greatest tally by a woman competitor is three medals, by Jasna Sekaric (Yugoslavia/Independent Olympic Participant). She won one gold and one bronze in 1988, and one silver in 1992.

NCAA CHAMPIONSHIPS A combined NCAA rifle championship was inaugurated in 1980, and the contest is now held annually.

Most titles (team) West Virginia has won nine NCAA team titles, 1983–84, 1986, and 1988–93.

Most titles (individual) Seven competitors have won two individual titles: Rod Fitz-Randolph, Tennessee Tech, smallbore and air rifle, 1980; Kurt Fitz-Randolph, Tennessee Tech, smallbore, 1981–82; John Rost, West Virginia, air rifle, 1981–82; Pat Spurgin, Murray State, air rifle, 1984, smallbore, 1985; Web Wright, West Virginia, smallbore, 1987–88; Michelle Scarborough, South Florida, air rifle, 1989, smallbore, 1990; Ann-Marie Pfiffner, West Virginia, air rifle, 1991–92.

SKIING

ORIGINS Skiing traces its history to Scandinavia; *ski* is the Norwegian word for snowshoe. A ski discovered in a peat bog in Hoting, Sweden dates to *c.* 2500 B.C., and records note the use of skis at the Battle of Isen, Norway in A.D. 1200. The first ski races were held in Norway and Australia in the 1850s and 1860s. Two men stand out as pioneers of the development of skiing in the 19th century: Sondre Nordheim, a Norwegian, who designed equipment and developed skiing techniques; and Mathias Zdarsky, an Austrian, who pioneered Alpine skiing. The first national governing body was that of Norway, formed in 1833. The International Ski Commission was founded in 1910 and was succeeded as the world governing body in 1924 by the International Ski Federation (FIS).

United States The first ski club in the United States was formed at Berlin, N.H. in January 1872. The United States Ski Association was originally founded as the National Ski Association in 1905; in 1962, it was renamed the United States Ski Association, and in 1990 it was renamed U.S. Skiing.

In the modern era, skiing has evolved into two main categories, Alpine and Nordic. Alpine skiing encompasses downhill and slalom racing. Nordic skiing covers ski jumping events and cross-country racing.

ALPINE SKIING

OLYMPIC GAMES Downhill and slalom events were first included at the 1936 Olympic Games.

Most gold medals In men's competition, the most gold medals won is three, by three skiers: Anton Sailer (Austria), who won all three events, downhill, slalom and giant slalom, in 1956; Jean-Claude Killy (France), who matched Sailer's feat in 1968; and Alberto Tomba (Italy), who won the slalom and giant slalom in 1988 and the giant slalom in 1992. For women the record is two golds, achieved by seven skiers: Andrea Mead-Lawrence (U.S.), slalom, giant slalom, 1952; Marielle Goitschel (France), giant slalom 1964, slalom, 1968; Marie-Therese Nadig (Switzerland), downhill, giant slalom, 1972; Rosi Mittermaier (West Germany), downhill, slalom, 1976; Hanni Wenzel (Liechtenstein),

giant slalom, slalom, 1980; Vreni Schneider (Switzerland), giant slalom, slalom, 1988; and Petra Kronberger (Austria), giant slalom and combined, 1992.

Most medals Hanni Wenzel (Liechtenstein) has won four Olympic medals: two gold, one silver and one bronze, 1976–80. The most medals won by a male skier is also four, by Alberto Tomba (Italy)— three golds and one silver, 1988–92.

WORLD CHAMPIONSHIPS This competition was inaugurated in 1931 at Murren, Switzerland. From 1931–39 the championships were held annually; from 1950 they were held biennially. Up to 1980, the Olympic Games were considered the world championships, except in 1936. In 1985, the championship schedule was changed so as not to coincide with an Olympic year.

Most gold medals Christel Cranz (Germany) won a record 12 titles: four slalom, 1934, 1937–39; three downhill, 1935, 1937, 1939; five combined, 1934–35, 1937–39. Anton Sailer (Austria) holds the men's record with seven titles: one slalom, 1956; two giant slalom, 1956, 1958; two downhill, 1956, 1958; two combined, 1956, 1958.

WORLD CUP Contested annually since 1967, the World Cup is a circuit of races where points are earned during the season, with the champion being the skier with the most points at the end of the season.

INDIVIDUAL RACING RECORDS

Most wins (men) Ingemar Stenmark (Sweden) won a record 86 races (46 giant slalom, 40 slalom) from 287 contested, 1974–89.

Most wins (women) Annemarie Moser-Pröll (Austria) won a record 62 races, 1970–79.

Most wins (season) Ingemar Stenmark (Sweden) won 13 races in 1978–79 to set the men's mark. Vreni Schneider (Switzerland) won 13 races in 1988–89 to set the women's mark.

Consecutive wins Ingemar Stenmark (Sweden) won 14 successive giant slalom races from March 18, 1978 to January 21, 1980. The women's record is 11 wins by Annemarie Moser-Pröll (Austria) in the downhill from December 1972 to January 1974.

UNITED STATES NATIONAL CHAMPIONSHIPS

Most titles Tamara McKinney won seven slalom titles, 1982–84, 1986–89—the most by any skier in one discipline. Phil Mahre won five giant slalom titles, 1975, 1977–79, 1981—the most by a male skier in one event.

NCAA CHAMPIONSHIPS The NCAA skiing championship was introduced in 1954. Teams compete in both Alpine and cross-country events, with cumulative point totals determining the national champion. Teams are comprised of both men and women.

Most titles (team) Denver has won 14 titles, 1954–57, 1961–67, and 1969–71.

Most titles (individual) Chiharu Igaya of Dartmouth won a record six NCAA titles: Alpine, 1955–56; downhill, 1955; slalom, 1955–57.

NORDIC SKIING

CROSS-COUNTRY SKIING

OLYMPIC GAMES Cross-country racing has been included in every Winter Olympic Games.

Most gold medals In men's competition, three skiers have each won four gold medals: Sixten Jernberg (Sweden), 50 km, 1956; 30 km, 1960; 50 km and 4 x 10 km relay, 1964; Gunde Svan (Sweden), 15 km and 4 x 10 km relay, 1984; 50 km and 4 x 10 km relay, 1988; Thomas Wassberg (Sweden), 15 km, 1980; 50 km and 4 x 10 km relay, 1984; 4 x 10 km relay, 1988. The women's record is also four golds, won by two skiers: Galina Kulakova (USSR), 5 km, 10 km and 3 x 5 km relay, 1972; 4 x 5 km relay, 1976; Raisa Smetanina (USSR/Unified Team), 10 km and 4 x 5 km relay, 1976; 5 km, 1980; 4 x 5 km, 1992.

Most medals The most medals won in Nordic events is 10, by Raisa Smetanina (four gold, five silver and one bronze, 1976–92). Sixten Jernberg (Sweden) holds the men's record with nine (four gold, three silver, two bronze, 1956–64).

WORLD CUP A season series of World Cup races was instituted in 1981.

Most titles Gunde Svan (Sweden) has won five overall cross-country skiing titles, 1984–86 and 1988–89. Two women have won three overall titles: Marjo Matikainen (Finland), 1986–88; Yelena Vialbe (USSR/Russia), 1989, 1991–92.

UNITED STATES NATIONAL CHAMPIONSHIPS

Most titles Martha Rockwell has won a record 14 national titles, 1969–75. The record in men's competition is 12, by Audun Endestad, 1984–90.

SKI JUMPING

OLYMPIC GAMES Ski jumping has been included in every Winter Games.

Most gold medals Matti Nykanen (Finland) has won four gold medals: 70-meter hill, 1988; 90-meter hill, 1984 and 1988; 90-meter team, 1988.

Most medals Matti Nykanen has won five medals in Olympic competition: four gold (see above) and one silver, 70-meter hill, 1984.

WORLD CUP A season series of ski jumping events was instituted in 1981.

Most titles Matti Nykanen (Finland) has won four World Cup titles, 1983, 1985–86 and 1988.

UNITED STATES NATIONAL CHAMPIONSHIPS

Most titles Lars Haugen has won seven ski jumping titles, 1912–28.

FREESTYLE SKIING

Freestyle skiing is composed of three skiing disciplines: moguls, aerials and ballet. Moguls was included as an Olympic event for the first time at the 1992 Games.

MOGULS

Skiers race down a slope marked with small snow hills (moguls). The skiers are required to perform two jumps during the run. The score is calculated by combining the speed of the run and marks awarded for performance.

OLYMPIC GAMES Moguls was a full medal sport for the first time at the 1992 Games. Edgar Grospiron (France) won the men's event; Donna Weinbrecht (U.S.) won the women's event.

WORLD CHAMPIONSHIP First staged in 1986, the event has been staged biennially since 1989.

Most wins (men) Edgar Grospiron (France) has won the event twice, 1989 and 1991.

Most wins (women) Raphaelle Monod (France) has won the event twice, 1989 and 1991.

AERIALS

WORLD CHAMPIONSHIP

Most wins (men) Lloyd Langlois (Canada) has won the title twice, 1986 and 1989.

Most wins (women) No skier has won this event more than once.

WORLD CHAMPIONSHIP

Most wins (men) No skier has won the event more than once.

Most wins (women) Jan Bucher (U.S.) has won the event twice, 1986 and 1989.

SPEED AND DISTANCE RECORDS

Fastest speed (men) The official world record is 145.161 mph by Philippe Goitschel (France) on April 21, 1993.

Fastest speed (women) The fastest speed by a woman is 136.232 mph, by Tarja Mulari (Finland).

Fastest speed—one-legged On April 16, 1988 Patrick Knaff set a one-legged speed record at 115.306 mph.

Fastest speed—cross-country The world record time for a 50 km race is 1 hour 54 minutes 46 seconds by Aleksey Prokurorov (Russia) at Thunder Bay on March 19, 1994 at an average speed of 16.24 mph.

Distance—24 hours cross-country Seppo-Juhani Savolainen skied 258.2 miles at Saariselka, Finland on April 8–9, 1988.

SLED DOG RACING

ORIGINS Racing between harnessed dog teams (usually huskies) is believed to have been practiced by Inuits in North America, and also by the peoples of Scandinavia, long before the first recorded formal race, the All-America Sweepstakes, which took place in 1908. Sled dog racing was a demonstration sport at the 1932 Olympic Games. The best known race is the Iditarod Trail Sled Dog Race, first run in 1973.

IDITAROD TRAIL SLED DOG RACE

The annual race from Anchorage to Nome, Alaska commemorates the 1925 midwinter emergency mission to get medical supplies to Nome during a diphtheria epidemic. Raced over alternate courses, the northern and southern trails, the Iditarod was first run in 1973.

CRUISIN' ■ PHILIPPE GOITSCHEL TRAVELING AT RECORD SPEED. (ALLSPORT)

FEEDING THE DOGS ■ MARTIN BUSER, 1994 RE-CORD BREAKER, HOT ON THE FROZEN IDITAROD TRAIL. (ALLSPORT/PAUL SOLDERS)

IDITAROD WINNERS (1973–1994)

Year	Musher	Elapsed Time
1973	Dick Wilmarth	20 days, 00:49:41
1974	Carl Huntington	20 days, 15:02:07
1975	Emmitt Peters	14 days, 14:43:45
1976	Gerald Riley	18 days, 22:58:17
1977	Rick Swenson	16 days, 16:27:13
1978	Rick Mackey	14 days, 18:52:24
1979	Rick Swenson	15 days, 10:37:47
1980	Joe May	14 days, 07:11:51
1981	Rick Swenson	12 days, 08:45:02
1982	Rick Swenson	16 days, 04:40:10
1983	Rick Mackey	12 days, 14:10:44
1984	Dean Osmar	12 days, 15:07:33
1985	Libby Riddles	18 days, 00:20:17
1986	Susan Butcher	11 days, 15:06:00
1987	Susan Butcher	11 days, 02:05:13
1988	Susan Butcher	11 days, 11:41:40
1989	Joe Runyan	11 days, 05:24:34
1990	Susan Butcher	11 days, 01:53:23
1991	Rick Swenson	12 days, 16:34:39
1992	Martin Buser	10 days, 19:36:17
1993	Jeff King	10 days, 15:38:17
1994	Martin Buser	10 days, 13:02:39

Most wins Rick Swenson has won the event five times: 1977, 1979, 1981–82, 1991.

Record time The fastest recorded time is 10 days, 13 hours, 2 minutes, 39 seconds, by Martin Buser (U.S.) in 1994.

SNOOKER

ORIGINS Neville Chamberlain, a British army officer, is credited with inventing the game in Jubbulpore, India in 1875. Snooker is a hybrid of pool and pyramids. Chamberlain added a set of colored balls to the 15 red ones used in pyramids and devised a scoring system based on pocketing the balls in sequence: red, color, red, color until all the reds have been cleared, leaving the colored balls to be pocketed in numerical order. The modern scoring system (a red ball is worth one point, yellow—2, green—3, brown—4, blue—5, pink—6 and black—7) was adopted in England in 1891. The sequence of pocketing the balls is called a break, the maximum possible being 147. The name *snooker* comes from the term coined for new recruits at the Woolwich Military Academy and was Chamberlain's label for anyone who lost at his game.

LUCKY SEVEN ■ ALLISON FISHER, SEVEN-TIME SNOOKER CHAMP. (ALLISON FISHER)

WORLD PROFESSIONAL CHAMPIONSHIPS This competition was first organized in 1927.

Most titles Joe Davis (England) won the world title on the first 15 occasions it was contested, and this still stands as the all-time record for victories. In the Amateur Championships, the most wins is two—by Gary Owen (England), 1963 and 1966; Ray Edmonds (England), 1972 and 1974; and Paul Mifsud (Malta), 1985–86. Allison Fisher (Great Britain) has won seven World Championships, 1985–86, 1988–89, 1991 and 1993–94. Maureen Bayton (née Barrett) won a record eight Women's Amateur Championships between 1954 and 1958, as well as seven at billiards.

Maximum break More than 200 male players have scored the 147 "maximum break." The highest break by a woman is 137, by Stacey Hilliard (Great Britain), in Aylesbury, Great Britain on February 23, 1992.

SOARING

See also HANG GLIDING.

ORIGINS Research by Isadore William Deiches has shown evidence of the use of gliders in ancient Egypt *c.* 2500–1500 B.C. Emanuel Swedenborg of Sweden made sketches of gliders *c.* 1714. The earliest human-carrying glider was designed by Sir George Cayley and carried his coachman (possibly John Appleby) about 500 yards across a valley in Brompton Dale, North Yorkshire, England in the summer of 1853.

WORLD CHAMPIONSHIPS World championships were instituted in 1937.

Most individual titles The most individual titles won is four, by Ingo Renner (Australia) in 1976 (Standard class), 1983, 1985 and 1987 (Open).

United States The most titles won by an American pilot is two, by George Moffat, in the Open category, 1970 and 1974.

SOARING WORLD RECORDS (SINGLE-SEATERS)

DISTANCE AND HEIGHT

Straight distance 907.7 miles, Hans-Werner Grosse (Germany), Lubeck, Germany to Biarritz, France, April 25, 1972.

Declared goal distance 779.4 miles, by three pilots: Bruce Drake, David Speight and Dick Georgeson (all New Zealand), who each flew from Te Anau to Te Araroa, New Zealand, January 14, 1978.

Goal and return 1,023.2 miles, Tom Knauff (U.S.), Williamsport, Pa. to Knoxville, Tenn., April 25, 1983.

Absolute altitude 49,009 feet, Robert R. Harris (U.S.), over California, February 17, 1986. The women's record is 41,449 feet, by Sabrina Jackintell (U.S.) on February 14, 1979.

Height gain 42,303 feet, Paul Bikle (U.S.), Mojave, Calif., February 25, 1961. The women's record is 33,506 feet, by Yvonne Loader (New Zealand) at Omarama, New Zealand on January 12, 1988.

SPEED OVER TRIANGULAR COURSE

100 km 121.35 mph, Ingo Renner (Australia), December 14, 1982.

300 km 105.32 mph, Jean-Paul Castel (France), November 15, 1986.

500 km 105.67 mph, Beat Bunzli (Switzerland), January 9, 1988.

750 km 98.43 mph, Hans-Werner Grosse (Germany), January 8, 1985.

1,000 km 90.32 mph, Hans-Werner Grosse (Germany), January 3, 1979.

1,250 km 82.79 mph, Hans-Werner Grosse (Germany), January 9, 1980.

SOCCER

ORIGINS A game called *tsu chu* ("to kick a ball of stuffed leather") was played in China more than 2,500 years ago. However, the ancestry of the modern game is traced to England. In 1314, King Edward II prohibited the game because of excessive noise. Three subsequent monarchs also banned the game. Nevertheless, soccer continued its development in England. In 1848, the first rules were drawn up at Cambridge University; in 1863, the Football Association (FA) was founded in England. The sport grew in popularity worldwide, and the *Fédération Internationale de Football Association* (FIFA), the world governing body, was formed in Paris, France in 1904. FIFA currently has more than 160 members.

WORLD CUP World Cup USA '94 (June 17–July 17, 1994) was a milestone championship event for records. In addition to the team and individual records listed below, the following were also set:

- *Most watched television event:* Over one billion people worldwide watched the World Cup Final between Brazil and Italy, at the Rose Bowl, Pasadena, Calif., on July 17, 1994. Brazil defeated Italy by a penalty kick, marking the first time the championship had been decided in that manner.

- *Largest attendance:* 3,567,994 people attended the 52 games of the tournament. The 68,615 average attendance was also a record.

- *Most yellow and red cards (penalties):* 227 yellow cards (an average of 4.36 per game) and 15 red cards were handed out.

TEAM RECORDS

Most appearances and wins Brazil, the only country to qualify for all 15 World Cup tournaments, has won the World Cup a record four times, 1958, 1962, 1970 and 1994.

Longest winning streak 17, by Bulgaria, ended by a 4–0 loss to Greece in 1994.

Most goals 10, by Hungary in a 10–1 defeat of El Salvador at Elche, Spain on June 15, 1982. The most total goals is 148 (in 66 games) by Brazil.

INDIVIDUAL RECORDS

Most wins Pelé (Brazil) played on three winning teams, 1958, 1962 and 1970. (He played during the

HEADBANGER ■ IN 1994 WORLD CUP SOCCER, DIEGO MARADONA PLAYED HIS 21ST FINALS GAME, TYING THREE OTHERS FOR THE RECORD. (ALLSPORT/SIMON BRUTY)

DYNAMIC DEFENDER ■ MARCELLO BALBOA, A KEY FIGURE ON THE U.S. TEAM IN '94 WORLD CUP GAMES. (ALLSPORT/SHAUN BOTTERILL)

1962 Finals but was unable to play in the final match due to injury.)

Most goals (game) In the Finals the record is three, by Geoff Hurst, England *v*. West Germany on July 30, 1966. In other championship games, the record is five, set in 1994 by Oleg Salenko (Russia).

Most goals (tournament) 13, by Just Fontaine (France), in 1958, in six games.

Most goals (career) 14, by Gerd Müller (West Germany), 10 in 1970 and four in 1974.

Most games played (Finals) 21, by four players: Uwe Seeler (West Germany), 1958–70; Wladyslaw Zmuda (Poland), 1974–86; Diego Maradona (Argentina), 1982–94; and Lothar Matthaus (West Germany/Germany), 1982–94. In other championship games, defender Marcello Balboa has appeared a record 94 times for the United States team.

Oldest player In 1994, 42-year-old Cameroonian Roger Milla became the oldest World Cup player and the oldest to score a goal.

EUROPEAN CHAMPIONSHIP Staged every four years, the European Championships were the brainchild of Frenchman Henri Delaunay. First held in 1960, the competition was known as the European Nations Cup. In 1968 the tournament was renamed the European Championship.

Most wins West Germany has won the tournament twice, 1972 and 1980.

SOUTH AMERICAN CHAMPIONSHIP The South American Championship was first staged in 1916. By the mid-1960s the tournament had lost popularity, and it was abandoned in 1967. In 1975 the tournament was revived as the Copa America. Since 1987 the tournament has been staged every two years.

Most wins Argentina has won the tournament 14 times, 1921, 1925, 1927, 1929, 1937, 1941, 1945–47, 1955, 1957, 1959, 1991 and 1993.

AFRICAN NATIONS CUP First staged in 1957, the tournament is played biennially.

Most wins Ghana has won the tournament four times, 1963, 1965, 1978 and 1982.

WORLD CLUB CHAMPIONSHIP Originally designed as a two-game home-and-away series between the European and South American champions, the first World Club Championship was held in 1960. Violence marred many of the games, and European teams often refused invitations to play. In 1980 the format was changed to a one-match playoff staged in Tokyo, Japan, between the winner of the European Champions Cup and the Copa Libertadores.

Most wins Three teams have won the title three times: Penarol (Uruguay), 1961, 1966, 1982;

Nacional (Uruguay), 1971, 1980, 1988; A.C. Milan (Italy), 1969, 1989–90.

EUROPEAN CHAMPIONS CUP Known as the European Cup, the competition is an annual playoff competition for the league champions of all UEFA-affiliated countries. The competition was devised by French newspaperman Gabriel Hanot and was first staged in 1956.

Most wins Real Madrid (Spain) has won the competition six times, 1956–60, 1966.

SOUTH AMERICAN CUP First contested in 1960 as the South American Champion Clubs' Cup, the tournament was expanded in 1965 to include two teams from each South American country. At that time the competition was renamed the Copa Libertadores de America.

Most wins Independiente (Argentina) has won the competition seven times, 1964–65, 1972–75, 1984.

INDIVIDUAL SCORING RECORDS

Most goals (game) 16, by Stephan Stanis for Racing Club Lens (*v.* Aubry-Asturies) on December 13, 1942.

Most goals (game, international) 10, by two players: Sofus Nielsen for Denmark (*v.* France) in 1908; Gottfried Fuchs for Germany (*v.* Russia) in 1912.

Most goals (career) 1,329, by Artur Friedenreich, who played for six teams (Germania, CA Ipiranga, Americano, CA Paulistano, Sao Paulo, Flamengo) from 1909–35.

Most goals (career, internationals) 97, by Pelé for Brazil in 111 internationals, 1957–70.

Most hat-tricks (career) 92, by Pelé, 1956–77.

NCAA DIVISION I CHAMPIONSHIPS The NCAA Division I men's championship was first staged in 1959. A women's tournament was introduced in 1982.

Most titles (men) The University of St. Louis has won the most Division I titles with 10 victories, which includes one tie: 1959–60, 1962–63, 1965, 1967, 1969–70, 1972–73.

Most titles (women) The University of North Carolina has won a record 13 Division I titles. Its victories came in 1982–84 and 1986–94.

Record Quotable

"I was born for soccer, just as Beethoven was born for music."

—Pelé, quoted in *The Sports Curmudgeon* by George Sullivan.

FANTASTIC FEATS

Juggling Volkhart Caro (Canada) juggled a regulation soccer ball for 18 hours nonstop with his feat, legs and head, without the ball ever touching the ground, at Edmonton, Canada, on June 26–27, 1983. Tomas Lundman (Sweden) "headed" a ball for 7 hours 5 minutes 5 seconds at Nöjeskäallan, Märsta, Sweden on September 5, 1992.

SOFTBALL

ORIGINS Softball, a derivative of baseball, was invented by George Hancock at the Farragut Boat Club, Chicago, Ill. in 1887. Rules were first codified in Minneapolis, Minn. in 1895 under the name kitten ball. The name *softball* was introduced by Walter Hakanson at a meeting of the National Recreation Congress in 1926. The name was adopted throughout the United States in 1930. Rules were formalized in 1933 by the International Joint Rules Committee for Softball and adopted by the Amateur Softball Association of America (ASA). Located in Oklahoma City, the ASA is also home to the Softball Hall of Fame. A competing organization, the United States Slo-Pitch Softball Association (U.S.S.S.A.), was formed in 1968 and is concerned exclusively with slow pitch. The International Softball Federation (ISF) was formed in 1950 as governing body for both fast pitch and slow pitch.

FAST PITCH SOFTBALL

WORLD CHAMPIONSHIPS A women's fast pitch world championship was first staged in 1965, and a men's tournament in 1966. Both tournaments are held quadrennially.

Most titles (men) The United States has won five world titles: 1966, 1968, 1976 (tied), 1980 and 1988.

Most titles (women) The United States has won four world titles: 1974, 1978, 1986, and 1990.

AMATEUR SOFTBALL ASSOCIATION NATIONAL CHAMPIONSHIP The first ASA national championship was staged in 1933 for both men's and women's teams.

Most titles (men) The Clearwater Bombers (Florida) won 10 championships between 1950 and 1973.

Most titles (women) The Raybestos Brakettes (Stratford, Conn.) have won 23 women's fast pitch titles from 1958 through 1992.

STRIKEOUT QUEEN ■ SOUTHPAW FLAMETHROWER MICHELE GRANGER BLEW AWAY 18 FEMALE BATTERS IN A ROW IN 1988. MALE SOFTBALL POWERHOUSES CAN'T CONNECT WITH HER PITCHES EITHER.
(RUSSELL MOTT)

RUSSELL MOTT

CARL ROSE

He averages a home run every 2.2 times at bat. He once blasted a softball 480 feet. He has hit nine home runs in a single game five times and once hit 15 home runs in a row. In 1990 he tied the record for highest batting average in a super slow pitch tournament at .900.

Who is this remarkable slugger? Barry Bonds? Jose Conseco? Not even close. The phenomenon in question is not even a baseball star—he's Carl Rose, home-run-hitting powerhouse for the Lighthouse–Worth softball team. "I never get bored doing home run trots," he says with Ruthian self-assurance. "I always try to outdo myself for distance and height."

In addition to playing softball, Rose is athletic director at Westbrook High School in Dixie, Georgia. He also serves as spokesman for the Worth softball company, the nation's leading manufacturer of softball equipment. At 28, Rose feels his softball career has just begun. "I've been told softball players reach their peak between 30–32 years of age, so I've got some years to look forward to."

Rose, a former minor league player in the Pirates organization, began playing slow pitch softball in 1988. He's emphatic that softball and baseball defy comparison. "There's no similarity between baseball and softball, except they both have bases and foul lines. . . . Baseball is America's pastime, you can't deny that. But 45 million people *play* softball. It's not a spectator sport. It's a game people play."

Rose sees another distinct advantage to softball: "At least softball players don't have to worry about going on strike."

SOFTBALL CHAMPIONSHIP RECORDS (MEN)

Individual Batting Records

	Fast Pitch	Super Slow Pitch	Major Slow Pitch
Batting Average	.632, Ted Hicks, CMI, Springfield, Mo., 1978	.900, tied by two: Carl Rose, Lighthouse/Sunbelt, 1990; and Wes Lord, Budweiser, San Francisco, Calif., 1990	.947, David Bear, Reece Astros, Indianapolis, Ind., 1994
Home runs	5, tied by two: Jody Hennigan, Farm Tavern, Madison, Wis., 1990; and Bob McClish, Springfield, Mo., 1973	20, tied by two: Doug Roberson, Superior/Apollo, Windsor Locks, Conn., 1990; and Rick Scherr, Howard's-Western Steer, Denver, NC, 1984	23, Stan Harvey, Howard's-Western Steer, Denver, NC, 1978
RBI	13, Bob McClish, Springfield, Mo., 1973	35, Doug Roberson, Superior/Apollo, Windsor Locks, Conn., 1990	54, Russ Earnest, Back Porch, Niceville, Fla., 1994

Pitching Records (Fast Pitch)

Wins	8, tied by four: Peter Meredith, Tran-Aire, Elkhart, Ind., 1988; Grame Robertson, Pay 'n Pak, Seattle, Wash., 1987; Harvey Sterkel, Aurora, Ill., 1959; and Bonnie Jones, Butch Grinders, Detroit, Mich., 1959
Strikeouts (total)	140, Mike Piechnik, Farm Tavern, Madison, Wis., 1988
Strikeouts (game)	55 in 21 innings, Herb Dudley, Bombers, Clearwater, Fla., 1949

SOFTBALL CHAMPIONSHIP RECORDS (WOMEN)

Individual Batting Records

	Fast Pitch	Major Slow Pitch
Batting Average	Not available	.857, Princess Carpenter, Rutenschroer Floral, Cincinnati, Ohio, 1973
Home runs	5, Kim Maher, Redding, Calif., 1994	5, tied by two: Patsy Danson, Carter's Rebel, Jacksonville, Fla., 1970; and Sue Taylor, Huntington YMCA, N.Y., 1970
RBI	12, Kim Maher, Redding, Calif., 1994	Not available

Pitching (Fast Pitch)

Wins	8, Joan Joyce, Stratford, Conn., 1973
Strikeouts (total)	134, Joan Joyce, Stratford, Conn., 1973
Strikeouts (game)	40 in 19 innings, Joan Joyce, Stratford, Conn., 1961
Strikeouts (consecutive)	18, Michele Granger, Orange County Majestics, Calif., 1988

Source: Amateur Softball Association

NCAA Championships The first NCAA Division I women's championship was staged in 1982.

Most titles UCLA has won seven titles: 1982, 1984–85, 1988–90, and 1992.

SLOW PITCH SOFTBALL

World Championships A slow pitch world championship was staged for men's teams in 1987. The United States team won this event. So far a second tournament has not been scheduled. No world championship has been staged for women's teams.

Amateur Softball Association National Championship The first men's ASA national championship was staged in 1953. The first women's event was staged in 1962.

Most titles (men—major slow pitch) Two teams have won three major slow pitch championships: Skip Hogan A.C. (Pittsburgh, Pa.), 1962, 1964–65; Joe Gatliff Auto Sales (Newport, Ky.), 1956–57, 1963.

Most titles (men—super slow pitch) Two teams have won three super slow pitch titles: Howard's Western Steer (Denver, Colo.), 1981, 1983–84; Steele's Silver Bullets (Grafton, Ohio), 1985–87.

Most titles (women) The Dots of Miami (Fla.) have won five major slow pitch titles, 1969, 1974–75, 1978–79.

SPEED SKATING

Origins The world's longest skating race, the 124-mile "Elfstedentocht" ("Tour of the Eleven Towns"), is said to commemorate a similar race staged in the Netherlands in the 17th century. The first recorded skating race was staged in 1763, from Wisbech to Whittlesey, England. The International Skating Union (ISU) was founded at Scheveningen, Netherlands in 1892 and is the governing body for both speed skating and figure skating.

Olympic Games Men's speed skating events have been included in the Olympic Games since 1924. Women's events were first staged in 1960.

Most gold medals Lydia Skoblikova (USSR) has won six gold medals: 500-meter, 1964; 1,000-meter, 1964; 1,500-meter, 1960, 1964; 3,000-meter, 1960, 1964. The men's record is five, shared by two skaters: Clas Thunberg (Finland), 500-meter, 1928; 1,500-meter, 1924, 1928; 5,000-meter, 1924; all-around title, 1924; and Eric Heiden (U.S.), 500-meter, 1,000-meter, 1,500-meter, 5,000-meter, and 10,000-meter, all in 1980.

World Championships Speed skating world championships were first staged in 1893.

Most titles Oscar Mathisen (Norway) and Clas Thunberg (Finland) have won a record five overall world titles. Mathisen won titles in 1908–09 and 1912–14; Thunberg won in 1923, 1925, 1928–29 and 1931. Karin Enke-Kania (East Germany) holds the women's mark, also at five. She won in 1982, 1984 and 1986–88.

United States Eric Heiden won three overall world titles, 1977–79, the most by any U.S. skater. His sister Beth became the only American woman to win an overall championship in 1979.

SHORT TRACK SPEED SKATING

Origins An indoor version of the more familiar outdoor speed skating races, short track speed skating was developed in North America in the 1960s. Besides being held indoors and on a shorter circuit, short track racing also differs from the longer version in that there are usually a pack of four skaters in a race, and a certain amount of bumping between the competitors is allowed. World championships were first staged unofficially in 1978, and the sport gained offical Olympic status at the 1992 Games.

World Championship Unofficial world championships were first staged in 1978. Since 1981 the championships have been recognized by the ISU. The event is staged annually. Two championships were staged in 1987.

Most wins (men) Three skaters have won two titles: Guy Daignault (Canada), 1982 and 1984; Toshinobu Kawai (Japan), 1985 and 1987; Michel Daignault (Canada), 1987, 1989.

BRUCE BENNETT STUDIOS

BONNIE BLAIR

"**W**hy Bonnie Blair?" That's the question this skater asks herself when she discusses the question of speed. And she falters over the answer. "Some people look at me in awe. That's very flattering to me, but I don't want to think I'm different from everyone else. I feel fortunate, but I don't really know. Why me, and not someone else?"

Known as one of speed skating's best technicians, Blair is all too able to see flaws. "I'm not perfect. There are still things I need to work on. Because of that, there is a possibility of going faster. As long as there's that possibility, I want to try." But what's the point of beating your own records? Is it, as some climbers say of Mount Everest, just because it's there? "I hope that people with high goals do it for the love of it, so they can say, 'Hey, I did that.' That's my feeling. Back in Calgary in 1988 when I won the world

record and the gold, people said 'Why do you keep doing this? You've already done the ultimate.' I love to compete. There's a passion inside me for it, a fire that keeps burning bright."

For Blair, there's always just one more goal. "At Lillehammer I crossed the 39-second mark in the 500 meters. If I hadn't kept going I wouldn't have done that. I think especially in our sport, where everything is related to the clock, time is a point of self-satisfaction. In the 1,500 meters (at the 1994 Olympics) I came in fourth. I missed the bronze by .03 seconds. But it was my personal best by half a second. That was great for me. I felt like I had won."

What gives Bonnie Blair her greatest joy? "Competition, yes. But I also love speed. The satisfaction of beating myself just puts me on top of the world."

SPEED SKATING WORLD RECORDS

Meters	min:sec	Name and Country	Date
MEN			
500	35.76	Dan Jansen (U.S.)	January 30, 1994
1,000	1:12.37	Yas Unori Miyabe (Japan)	March 26, 1994
1,500	1:51.29	Johann Olav Koss (Norway)	February 16, 1994
3,000	3:56.16	Thomas Bos (Netherlands)	March 3, 1992
5,000	6:34.96	Johann Olav Koss (Norway)	February 13, 1994
10,000	13:43.54	Johann Olav Koss (Norway)	February 20, 1994
WOMEN			
500	38.99	Bonnie Blair (U.S.)	March 26, 1994
1,000	1:17.65	Christa Rothenburger (now Luding) (East Germany)	February 26, 1988
1,500	1:59.30†	Karin Kania (East Germany)	March 22, 1986
3,000	4:09.32	Gunda Niemann (née Kleeman) (Germany)	March 25, 1994
5,000	7:03.26	Gunda Niemann	March 26, 1994

†Set at high altitude

Short Track

Meters	min:sec	Name and Country	Date
MEN			
500	43.08	Mirko Vuillermin (Italy)	March 27, 1993
1,000	1:28.47	Mike McMillen (New Zealand)	April 4, 1992
1,500	2:22.36	Eric Flaim (U.S.)	March 21, 1993
3,000	5:00.83	Chae Ji-hoon (South Korea)	January 16, 1993
5,000 relay	7:10.95	New Zealand	March 28, 1993
WOMEN			
500	45.60	Zhang Yanmei (China)	March 27, 1993
1,000	1:35.83	Chun Lee-kyung (South Korea)	December 6, 1993
1,500	2:28.26	Eden Donatelli (Canada)	March 31, 1991
3,000	5:17.59	Won Hye-kyung (South Korea)	December 6, 1993
3,000 relay	4:26.56	Canada	March 28, 1993

Record Quotable

"To look up and see 35 was something I'd dreamed of for a long time."

—Dan Jansen, quoted in *Sports Illustrated*, referring to his having broken the 36-second barrier in the 500 meters.

Most wins (women)   Sylvie Daigle (Canada) has won four world titles, 1979, 1983, 1989–90.

Olympic Games   Short track speed skating was included as a demonstration sport at the 1988 Calgary Games, and gained official status at the 1992 Games in Albertville.

Most gold medals   Kim Ki-hoon (South Korea) won two gold medals at the 1992 Games: 1,000 meters and 5,000 meter relay.

SQUASH

ORIGINS Squash is an offshoot of rackets and is believed to have been first played at Harrow School, London, England in 1817. The International Squash Rackets Federation (ISRF) was founded in 1967. The Women's International Squash Rackets Federation was formed in 1976.

United States The U.S. Squash Racquets Association was formed in 1907, and staged the first U.S. amateur championships that year.

WORLD OPEN CHAMPIONSHIPS Both the men's and women's events were first held in 1976. The men's competition is an annual event, but the women's tournament was biennial until 1989, when it switched to the same system as the men's event. There was no championship in 1978.

Most titles Jahangir Khan (Pakistan) has won six titles, 1981–85 and 1988. Susan Devoy (New Zealand) holds the mark in the women's event with five victories, 1985, 1987, 1990–92.

UNITED STATES AMATEUR CHAMPIONSHIPS The U.S. Amateur Championships were first held for men in 1907, and for women in 1928.

Most titles G. Diehl Mateer won 11 men's doubles titles between 1949 and 1966 with five different partners. Joyce Davenport won eight women's doubles titles between 1969 and 1990 with two different partners.

Most titles (singles) Alicia McConnell has won seven women's singles titles, 1982–88. Stanley Pearson won a record six men's titles, 1915–17, 1921–23.

SURFING

ORIGINS The Polynesian sport of surfing in a canoe (*ehorooe*) was first recorded by the British explorer Captain James Cook in December 1771 during his exploration of Tahiti. The modern sport developed in Hawaii, California and Australia in the mid-1950s. Although Hawaii is one of the 50 states, it is allowed to compete sepa-

BOY WONDER ■ THE YOUNGEST MEN'S SURFING WORLD CHAMPION, KELLY SLATER. (ALLSPORT/ROBERT BROWN)

rately from the U.S. in international surfing competition.

WORLD AMATEUR CHAMPIONSHIPS First held in May 1964 in Sydney, Australia, the open championship is the most prestigious event in both men's and women's competition.

Most titles In the women's division the title has been won twice by two surfers: Joyce Hoffman (U.S.), 1965–66; and Sharon Weber (Hawaii), 1970 and 1972. The men's title has been won by different surfers on each occasion.

WORLD PROFESSIONAL CHAMPIONSHIPS First held in 1970, the World Championship has been organized by the Association of Surfing Professionals (ASP) since 1976. The World Championship is a circuit of events held throughout the year; the winning surfer is the one who gains the most points over the course of the year.

Most titles The most titles won by a professional surfer is four, by Mark Richards (Australia), 1979–82. The women's record is also four, by two surfers: Frieda Zamba (U.S.), 1984–86, 1988; Wendy Botha (Australia), 1987, 1989, 1991–92.

FANTASTIC FEATS

Youngest champion The youngest surfing world champion was Frieda Zamba, who was 19 years old when she won in 1984. The youngest men's champion was Kelly Slater, who won the 1992 crown at age 20.

Career earnings Barton Lynch (Australia) has the highest career earnings with $504,187. The women's leader is Pam Burridge (Australia) with $206,235.

CRAMP FREE ZONE ■ PAM BURRIDGE, WOMEN'S EARNINGS LEADER, STRETCHING BEFORE A CHAMPIONSHIP SURFING MATCH. (ALLSPORT/TONY DUFFY)

SWIMMING

ORIGINS The earliest references to swimming races were in Japan in 36 B.C. The first national swimming association, the Metropolitan Swimming Clubs Association, was founded in England in 1791. The international governing body for swimming, diving and water polo—the *Fédération Internationale de Natation Amateur* (FINA)—was founded in 1908.

OLYMPIC GAMES Swimming events were included in the first modern Games in 1896 and have been included in every Games since.

Most gold medals The greatest number of Olympic gold medals won is nine, by Mark Spitz (U.S.): 100-meter and 200-meter freestyle, 1972; 100-meter and 200-meter butterfly, 1972; 4 x 100-meter freestyle, 1968 and 1972; 4 x 200-meter freestyle, 1968 and 1972; 4 x 100-meter medley, 1972. The record number of gold medals won by a woman is six, by Kristin Otto (East Germany) at Seoul, South Korea in 1988: 100-meter freestyle, backstroke and butterfly, 50-meter freestyle, 4 x 100-meter freestyle and 4 x 100-meter medley.

Most medals The most medals won by a swimmer is 11, by two competitors: Mark Spitz (U.S.): nine gold (see above), one silver and one bronze, 1968–72; and Matt Biondi (U.S.), eight gold, two silver and one bronze, 1984–92. The most medals won by a woman is eight, by three swimmers: Dawn Fraser (Australia), four gold, four silver, 1956–64; Kornelia Ender (East Germany), four gold, four silver, 1972–76; Shirley Babashoff (U.S.), two gold, six silver, 1972–76.

Most medals (one Games) The most medals won at one Games is seven, by two swimmers: Mark Spitz (U.S.), seven golds in 1972; and Matt Biondi (U.S.), five gold, one silver and one bronze in 1988. Kristin Otto (East Germany) won six gold medals at the 1988 Games, the most for a woman swimmer.

WORLD CHAMPIONSHIPS The first world swimming championships were held in Belgrade, Yugoslavia in 1973. The championships have been held quadrennially since 1978.

Most gold medals Kornelia Ender (East Germany) won eight gold medals, 1973–75. Jim Mont-

SWIMMING—MEN'S WORLD RECORDS (set in 50-meter pools)

Freestyle

Event	Time	Swimmer (Country)	Date
50 meters	21.81	Tom Jager (U.S.)	March 24, 1990
100 meters	48.21	Alexander Popou (Russia)	June 18, 1994
200 meters	1:46.69	Giorgio Lamberti (Italy)	August 15, 1989
400 meters	3:43.80	Kieren Perkins (Australia)	September 9, 1994
800 meters	7:46.00	Kieren Perkins (Australia)	August 24, 1994
1,500 meters	14:41.66	Kieren Perkins (Australia)	August 24, 1994
4 x 100-meter relay	3:16.53	U.S. (Chris Jacobs, Troy Dalbey, Tom Jager, Matt Biondi)	September 25, 1988
4 x 200-meter relay	7:11.95	Unified Team (Dmitri Lepikov, Vladimir Pychenko, Veniamin Taianovitch, Yevgeni Sadovyi)	July 27, 1992

Breaststroke

Event	Time	Swimmer (Country)	Date
100 meters	1:00.95	Karoly Guttler (Hungary)	August 5, 1993
200 meters	2:10.16	Michael Barrowman (U.S.)	July 29, 1992

Butterfly

Event	Time	Swimmer (Country)	Date
100 meters	52.84	Pablo Morales (U.S.)	June 23, 1986
200 meters	1:55.69	Melvin Stewart (U.S.)	January 12, 1991

Backstroke

Event	Time	Swimmer (Country)	Date
100 meters	53.86	Jeff Rouse (U.S.)	July 31, 1992
200 meters	1:56.57	Martin Zubero (Spain)	November 23, 1991

Individual Medley

Event	Time	Swimmer (Country)	Date
200 meters	1:58.16	Jani Sievinen (Finland)	September 11, 1994
400 meters	4:12.30	Tom Dolan (U.S.)	September 6, 1994
4 x 100-meter relay	3:36.93	U.S. (David Berkoff, Rich Schroeder, Matt Biondi, Chris Jacobs)	September 23, 1988
	3.36.93	U.S. (Jeff Rouse, Nelson Diebel, Pablo Morales, Jon Olsen)	July 31, 1992

Source: USA Swimming

gomery (U.S.) won six gold medals, 1973–75, the most by a male swimmer.

Most medals Michael Gross (West Germany) has won 13 medals: five gold, five silver and three bronze, 1982–90. The most medals won by a female swimmer is 10, by Kornelia Ender, who won eight gold and two silver, 1973–75.

Most medals (one championship) Matt Biondi (U.S.) won seven medals—three gold, one silver and three bronze—in 1986 at Madrid, Spain. Three swimmers share the women's record of six medals: Tracy Caulkins (U.S.), five gold, one silver in 1978; Kristin Otto (East Germany), four gold, two silver in 1986; Mary T. Meagher (U.S.), one gold, three silver, two bronze in 1986.

UNITED STATES NATIONAL CHAMPIONSHIPS The first United States swimming championships were staged by the Amateur Athletic Union on August 25, 1888.

Most titles Tracy Caulkins has won a record 48 national swimming titles, 1977–84. The most titles for a male swimmer is 36, by Johnny Weissmuller, 1921–28.

STEVE PINETTI

ANDREW PINETTI

"**M**y Dad swims in San Francisco Bay," Andrew Pinetti says. "That's how I first got interested in swimming across Golden Gate Bridge. He said I could do it—but that I'd have to practice a lot first. And I did."

When he was 10 years old, Andrew became the youngest male to swim across the 1.25-mile Golden Gate, from San Francisco to Marin. At 11 years of age, Andrew swam 1½ miles from Alcatraz to San Francisco in a time of 31 minutes 26 seconds. So what's next for the athletic prodigy? "Next summer I think I'm gonna swim from bridge to bridge," he says. "That's from Golden Gate Bridge to Bay Bridge . . . I think it's five and a half miles."

It shouldn't be surprising that Andrew's idol is not a baseball or football player, but a swimmer—Pablo Morales. Morales is currently a record holder for the 100-meter butterfly. "Pablo has good technique and speed," Andrew observes. "And I like to swim both freestyle and butterfly, just like him."

Andrew always tries to follow the advice of his swimming coach: "He tells me not to think about my time, just keep going and swimming. . . . And also to keep warm."

MID-MANHATTAN SWIMMING ASSOCIATION

KRIS RUTFORD

When attempting an outdoor swimming record, a swimmer typically faces obstacles such as the weather, the water temperature and the height of the tide. In the case of swimming around Manhattan Island, however, the first thing one has to overcome is the cliché image of New York's polluted waters. "I had a lot of curiosity about the cleanliness of Manhattan water," record holder Kris Rutford said. "You hear a lot about the garbage and medical waste. It wasn't nearly as bad as I expected, though."

Still, as Rutford describes it, there are lots of "floating things" in the waters surrounding Manhattan Island (the East River, the Harlem River and the Hudson River), ranging from two-liter soda bottles to plastic garbage bags. Rutford says his least-liked body of water is the Harlem River because it "has an iron, oily taste and feel." The Hudson River is somewhat better, though it contains "squishy things" that he prefers not to attempt to identify.

So how did Rutford, a CPA and a resident of Lincoln, Nebraska, end up swimming around Manhattan Island? "In 1988 I was over in England to swim the English Channel. When I was there someone suggested I do the Manhattan Island swim. I first did it in 1988 and did it every year from then through 1993. . . . It's a great way to see New York."

Rutford accomplished his record-breaking swim around Manhattan Island in 5 hours, 53 minutes and 57 seconds back on August 29, 1992. That day he had another rather unusual obstacle to face: "The Staten Island Ferry was pulling out and blocking my way. I had to tread water for a few minutes while they decided if they'd let me go or not . . . which they finally did."

SWIMMING—WOMEN'S WORLD RECORDS (set in 50-meter pools)
Freestyle

Event	Time	Swimmer (Country)	Date
50 meters	24.51	Jingyi Le (China)	September 11, 1994
100 meters	54.01	Jingyi Le (China)	September 5, 1994
200 meters	1:56.78	Franziska Van Almsick (Germany)	September 6, 1994
400 meters	4:03.85	Janet Evans (U.S.)	September 22, 1988
800 meters	8:16.22	Janet Evans (U.S.)	August 20, 1989
1,500 meters	15:52.10	Janet Evans (U.S.)	March 26, 1988
4 x 100-meter relay	3:37.91	China (Jingyi Le, Shan Ying, Ying Le, Lu Bin)	September 10, 1994
4 x 200-meter relay	7:55.47	East Germany (Manuella Stellmach, Astrid Strauss, Anke Möhring, Heike Freidrich)	August 18, 1987

Breaststroke

100 meters	1:07.69	Samantha Riley (Australia)	September 9, 1994
200 meters	2:24.76	Rebecca Brown (Australia)	March 16, 1994

Butterfly

100 meters	57.93	Mary T. Meagher (U.S.)	August 16, 1981
200 meters	2:05.96	Mary T. Meagher (U.S.)	August 13, 1981

Backstroke

100 meters	1:00.16	Cihong He (China)	September 10, 1994
200 meters	2:06.82	Kristina Egerszegi (Hungary)	August 26, 1991

Individual Medley

200 meters	2:11.65	Lin Li (China)*	July 30, 1992
400 meters	4:36.10	Petra Schneider (East Germany)	August 1, 1982
4 x 100-meter relay	4:01.67	China (Cihong He, Guohong Dai, Limin Liu, Jingyi Le)	September 10, 1994

Source: USA Swimming
*Bin Lu (China) swam 2:11:57 on October 7, 1994, but she was disqualified for drugs.

Fastest swimmer In a 25-yard pool, Tom Jager (U.S.) achieved an average speed of 5.37 mph, swimming 50 yards in 19.05 seconds at Nashville, Tenn. on March 23, 1990. The women's fastest average speed is by Jingyi Le (China) in her 50-meter world record (see World Records table, this page).

FANTASTIC FEATS

Manhattan swim The fastest swim around Manhattan Island in New York City is 5 hours 53 minutes 57 seconds, achieved by Kris Rutford (U.S.), on August 29, 1992.

English Channel swim Chad Hundeby (Irvine, Calif.) swam the English Channel in a record time of 7 hours 17 minutes on September 27, 1994.

Youngest Golden Gate swim Andrew Pinetti, 10, swam across the 1.25-mile Golden Gate, from San Francisco to Marin, in a time of 31 minutes 26 seconds on August 11, 1993.

SYNCHRONIZED SWIMMING

In international competition, synchronized swimmers compete in three disciplines: solo, duet and team. In all three disciplines the swimmers perform to music a series of moves that are judged for technical merit and artistic interpretation. In solo events the swimmer has to be synchronized with the music; in duet and team events the swimmers have to be synchronized with each other as well as with the music.

ORIGINS Annette Kellerman and Kay Curtis are considered the pioneers of synchronized swimming in the United States. Kellerman's water ballet performances drew widespread attention throughout the U.S. at the beginning of the 20th century. Curtis was responsible for establishing synchronized swimming as part of the physical education program at the University of Wisconsin. In the 1940s, film star Esther Williams again drew attention to the sport, and in 1945 the Amateur Athletic Union recognized the sport. In 1973 the first world championship was staged, and in 1984 synchronized swimming was recognized as an official Olympic sport. The governing body for the sport in this country is United States Synchronized Swimming, formed in 1978.

OLYMPIC GAMES Synchronized swimming was first staged as an official sport at the 1984 Games.

Most gold medals Two swimmers have won two gold medals: Tracie Ruiz-Conforto (U.S.), solo and duet, 1984; Carolyn Waldo (Canada), solo and duet, 1988.

Most medals Two swimmers have won three medals: Tracie Ruiz-Conforto (U.S.), two gold and one silver, 1984–88; Carolyn Waldo (Canada), two gold and one silver, 1984–88.

WORLD CHAMPIONSHIPS The world championships were first held in 1973, and have been held quadrennially since 1978.

Most titles The solo title has been won by a different swimmer on each occasion.

GUINNESS CHALLENGE

Who was the shortest player in baseball history?
See page 28 for the answer.

Most titles (team) The United States has won five team titles, 1973, 1975, 1978, 1991 and 1994.

UNITED STATES NATIONAL CHAMPIONSHIPS The first national championships were staged in 1946, and the competition is now an annual event.

Most titles Gail Johnson has won 11 national titles: six solo (two indoors, four outdoors), 1972–75; and five duet (two indoors, three outdoors), 1972–74.

Most titles (duet) The team of Karen and Sarah Josephson has won seven national duet titles, 1985–88, and 1990–92.

TABLE TENNIS

ORIGINS The earliest evidence relating to a game resembling table tennis (also commonly known as Ping-Pong) has been found in the catalogs of London sporting goods manufacturers in the 1880s. The International Table Tennis Federation (ITTF) was founded in 1926.

United States The United States Table Tennis Association was established in 1933. In 1971, a U.S. table tennis team was invited to play in the People's Republic of China, thereby initiating the first officially sanctioned Chinese–American cultural exchange in almost 20 years.

OLYMPIC GAMES Table tennis was included in the Olympic Games in 1988 for the first time.

Most medals Yoo Nam-Kyu (South Korea) has won three medals in Olympic competition: one gold, two bronze, 1988–92. Chin Jing (China) is the only woman to win two medals, one gold, one silver, in 1988.

WORLD CHAMPIONSHIPS The ITTF instituted European championships in 1926 and later designated this event the world championship. The tournament was staged annually until 1957, when the event became biennial.

SWAYTHLING CUP The men's team championship is named after Lady Swaythling, who donated the trophy in 1926.

Most titles The most wins is 12, by Hungary (1926, 1928–31, 1933 [two events were held that year, with Hungary winning both times], 1935, 1938, 1949, 1952, 1979).

CORBILLON CUP The women's team championship is named after M. Marcel Corbillon, president of the French Table Tennis Association, who donated the trophy in 1934.

Most titles China has won the most titles, with 10 wins (1965, 1975, 1977, 1979, 1981, 1983, 1985, 1987, 1989 and 1993).

Men's singles The most victories in singles is five, by Viktor Barna (Hungary), 1931, 1932–35.

Women's singles The most victories is six, by Angelica Rozeanu (Romania), 1950–55.

Men's doubles The most victories is eight, by Viktor Barna (Hungary), 1929–35, 1939. The partnership that won the most titles is Viktor Barna and Miklos Szabados (Hungary), 1929–33, 1935.

Women's doubles The most victories is seven, by Maria Mednyanszky (Hungary), 1928, 1930–35. The team that won the most titles is Maria Mednyanszky and Anna Sipos (Hungary), 1930–35.

Mixed doubles Maria Mednyanszky (Hungary) won a record six mixed doubles titles: 1927–28, 1930–31, 1933 (twice). The pairing of Miklos Szabados and Maria Mednyanszky (Hungary) won the title a record three times: 1930–31, 1933.

UNITED STATES NATIONAL CHAMPIONSHIPS U.S. national championships were first held in 1931.

Most titles Leah Neuberger (née Thall) won a record 21 titles between 1941 and 1961: nine women's singles, 12 women's doubles. Richard Mills won a record 10 men's singles titles between 1945 and 1962.

FANTASTIC FEATS

Most hits The record number of hits in 60 seconds is 173, by Jackie Bellinger and Lisa Lomas (née Bellinger) in Great Britain on February 7, 1993. With a paddle in each hand, Gary D. Fisher

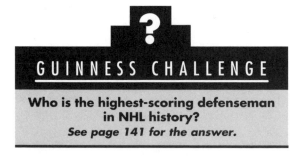

GUINNESS CHALLENGE

Who is the highest-scoring defenseman in NHL history?
See page 141 for the answer.

of Olympia, Wash. completed 5,000 consecutive volleys over the net in 44 minutes 28 seconds on June 25, 1975.

Youngest championship player Joy Foster (Jamaica) was eight years old when she played at the West Indies Championships at Port of Spain, Trinidad in August 1988.

TAEKWONDO

ORIGINS Taekwondo is a martial art, with all activities based on defensive spirit, developed over 20 centuries in Korea. It was officially recognized as part of Korean tradition and culture on April 11, 1955. The first World Taekwondo Championships were organized by the Korean Taekwondo Association and were held at Seoul, South Korea in 1973. The World Taekwondo Federation was then formed and has organized biennial championships.

United States The United States Taekwondo Union was founded in 1974.

OLYMPIC GAMES Taekwondo was included as a demonstration sport at the 1988 and 1992 Games.

WORLD CHAMPIONSHIPS These biennial championships were first held in Seoul, South Korea in 1973, when they were staged by the Korean Taekwondo Association. Women's events were first staged unofficially in 1983 and have been officially recognized since 1987.

Most titles Chung Kook-hyun (South Korea) has won a record four world titles: light middleweight, 1982–83; welterweight 1985, 1987. The women's record is three titles, achieved by Lynette Love (U.S.), 1985, 1987 and 1991.

TEAM HANDBALL

ORIGINS Team handball developed around the turn of the 20th century. It evolved from a game devised by soccer players in northern Germany and Denmark designed to keep them fit during the winter months. An outdoors version of the game was included in the 1936 Olympic Games as a demonstration sport. In 1946 the International Handball Federation (IHF) was formed. The growth of team handball has been rapid since its reintroduction into the Olympic Games in 1972 as an indoor game with seven players on each side. The IHF claims 4.2 million members from 88 countries, second only to soccer in terms of world-wide membership.

United States Team handball was first introduced to the United States in the 1920s, and a national team entered the 1936 Olympic demonstration competition. In 1959 the United States Team Handball Federation (USTHF) was formed, and it still governs the sport in this country.

OLYMPIC GAMES

Most wins In men's competition the USSR/Unified Team has won the Olympic gold medal three times—1976, 1988 and 1992. In women's competition, introduced in 1976, two countries have won the gold medal twice: the USSR in 1976 and 1980; and South Korea in 1988 and 1992.

WORLD CHAMPIONSHIP This competition was instituted in 1938.

Most titles (country) Romania has won four men's and three women's titles (two outdoor, one indoor) from 1956 to 1974. East Germany has also won three women's titles, in 1971, 1975 and 1978.

TENNIS

ORIGINS The modern game evolved from the indoor sport of real tennis. There is an account of a game called "field tennis" in an English sports periodical dated September 29, 1793; however, the "father" of lawn tennis is considered to be Major Walter Wingfield, who patented a type of tennis called "sphairistike" in 1874. The Marylebone Cricket Club, England revised Wingfield's initial rules in 1877, and the famed All-England Croquet Club (home of the Wimbledon Championships) added the name Lawn Tennis to its title in 1877. The "open" era of tennis, when amateurs were permitted to play with and against professionals, was introduced in 1968.

GRAND SLAM

The grand slam is achieved by winning all four grand slam events—the Australian Open, French Open, Wimbledon and U.S. Open—in one calendar year.

GRAND SLAM WINNERS

Singles Don Budge (U.S.) was the first player to achieve the grand slam when he won all four events in 1938. The only player to have won the grand slam twice is Rod Laver (Australia), who accomplished this in 1962 and 1969. Three women have completed the grand slam: Maureen Connolly (U.S.), in 1953; Margaret Court (née Smith; Australia), in 1970; and Steffi Graf (West Germany), in 1988.

Doubles The only men to win the grand slam for doubles were Frank Sedgman and Ken McGregor (Australia) in 1951. Three women have won the grand slam: Maria Bueno (Brazil) in 1960; Martina Navratilova and Pam Shriver (U.S.) in 1984. Navratilova and Shriver won eight consecutive doubles titles from 1983–85.

Mixed doubles Ken Fletcher and Margaret Court (Australia) won all four legs of the grand slam in 1963. Owen Davidson (Australia) won all four events, with two partners, in 1967.

MOST GRAND SLAM TITLES

Singles The most singles championships won in grand slam tournaments is 24, by Margaret Court (née Smith; Australia): 11 Australian, five French, three Wimbledon, five U.S. Open between 1960 and 1973. The men's record is 12, by Roy Emerson (Australia): six Australian, two French, two Wimbledon, two U.S. Open between 1961 and 1967.

Doubles The most wins by a doubles partnership is 20, by two teams: Louise Brough (U.S.) and Margaret Du Pont (U.S.), who won three French, five Wimbledon and 12 U.S. Opens, 1942–57; and by Martina Navratilova (U.S.) and Pam Shriver (U.S.). They won seven Australian, four French, five Wimbledon, four U.S. Opens, 1981–89.

AUSTRALIAN OPEN CHAMPIONSHIPS

The first Australasian championships were held in 1905, with New Zealand hosting the event in 1906 and 1912. A women's championship was not introduced until 1922. The tournament was changed to the Australian Open in 1925 and is counted as a grand slam event from that year. There were two championships in 1977 because the event was moved from early season (January) to December. It reverted to a January date in 1987, which meant there was no championship in 1986. Currently the tournament is held at the Australian Tennis Center in Melbourne and is the first leg of the grand slam.

Most wins (men) The most wins is six, by Roy Emerson (Australia), 1961, 1963–67.

Most wins (women) The most wins is 11, by Margaret Court (née Smith) of Australia, 1960–66, 1969–71, 1973.

Men's doubles The most wins by one pair is eight, by John Bromwich and Adrian Quist (Australia), 1938–40, 1946–50. In addition, Quist holds the record for most wins by one player with 10,

winning in 1936–37 with Don Turnbull, to add to his triumphs with Bromwich.

Women's doubles The most wins by one pair is 10, by Nancye Bolton (née Wynne) and Thelma Long (née Coyne), both Australian. Their victories came in 1936–40, 1947–49, 1951–52. Long also holds the record for most wins with 12, winning in 1956 and 1958 with Mary Hawton.

Mixed doubles The most wins by one pair is four, by two teams: Harry Hopman and Nell Hopman

AUSTRALIAN OPEN CHAMPIONS (1905–1952)

Men's Singles

Year	Player	Year	Player
1905	Rodney Heath	1929	John Gregory
1906	Tony Wilding	1930	Gar Moon
1907	Horace Rice	1931	Jack Crawford
1908	Fred Alexander	1932	Jack Crawford
1909	Tony Wilding	1933	Jack Crawford
1910	Rodney Heath	1934	Fred Perry
1911	Norman Brookes	1935	Jack Crawford
1912	J. Cecil Parke	1936	Adrian Quist
1913	E. F. Parker	1937	V. B. McGrath
1914	Pat O'Hara Wood	1938	Don Budge
1915	Francis Lowe	1939	John Bromwich
1916	not held	1940	Adrian Quist
1917	not held	1941	not held
1918	not held	1942	not held
1919	A. Kingscote	1943	not held
1920	Pat O'Hara Wood	1944	not held
1921	Rhys Gemmell	1945	not held
1922	Pat O'Hara Wood	1946	John Bromwich
1923	Pat O'Hara Wood	1947	Dinny Pails
1924	James Anderson	1948	Adrian Quist
1925	James Anderson	1949	Frank Sedgman
1926	John Hawkes	1950	Frank Sedgman
1927	Gerald Patterson	1951	Dick Savitt
1928	Jean Borotra	1952	Ken McGregor

Women's Singles

Year	Player	Year	Player
1905	no event	1929	Daphne Akhurst
1906	no event	1930	Daphne Akhurst
1907	no event	1931	Coral Buttsworth
1908	no event	1932	Coral Buttsworth
1909	no event	1933	Joan Hartigan
1910	no event	1934	Joan Hartigan
1911	no event	1935	Dorothy Round
1912	no event	1936	Joan Hartigan
1913	no event	1937	Nancye Wynne
1914	no event	1938	Dorothy M. Bundy
1915	no event	1939	Emily Westacott
1916	not held	1940	Nancye Wynne
1917	not held	1941	not held
1918	not held	1942	not held
1919	no event	1943	not held
1920	no event	1944	not held
1921	no event	1945	not held
1922	Margaret Molesworth	1946	Nancye Bolton[1]
1923	Margaret Molesworth	1947	Nancye Bolton
1924	Sylvia Lance	1948	Nancye Bolton
1925	Daphne Akhurst	1949	Doris Hart
1926	Daphne Akhurst	1950	Louise Brough
1927	Esna Boyd	1951	Nancye Bolton
1928	Daphne Akhurst	1952	Thelma Long

1– Nancye Bolton (née Wynne)

(née Hall; Australia), 1930, 1936–37, 1939; Colin Long and Nancye Bolton (née Wynne; Australia), 1940, 1946–48.

Most titles (overall) Margaret Court (née Smith) has won a record 21 Australian Open titles between 1960 and 1973—11 singles, eight doubles and two mixed doubles.

BACKHAND ■ STEFFI GRAF'S BACKHAND HELPED ENSURE VICTORY IN THE 1994 AUSTRALIAN OPEN CHAMPIONSHIP. (ALLSPORT/CLIVE BRUNSKILL)

AUSTRALIAN OPEN CHAMPIONS (1953–1994)

Men's Singles

Year	Player	Year	Player
1953	Ken Rosewall	1975	John Newcombe
1954	Mervyn Rose	1976	Mark Edmondson
1955	Ken Rosewall	1977	Roscoe Tanner*
1956	Lew Hoad	1977	Vitas Gerulaitis*
1957	Ashley Cooper	1978	Guillermo Vilas
1958	Ashley Cooper	1979	Guillermo Vilas
1959	Alex Olmedo	1980	Brian Teacher
1960	Rod Laver	1981	Johan Kriek
1961	Roy Emerson	1982	Johan Kriek
1962	Rod Laver	1983	Mats Wilander
1963	Roy Emerson	1984	Mats Wilander
1964	Roy Emerson	1985	Stefan Edberg
1965	Roy Emerson	1986	not held
1966	Roy Emerson	1987	Stefan Edberg
1967	Roy Emerson	1988	Mats Wilander
1968	Bill Bowrey	1989	Ivan Lendl
1969	Rod Laver	1990	Ivan Lendl
1970	Arthur Ashe	1991	Boris Becker
1971	Ken Rosewall	1992	Jim Courier
1972	Ken Rosewall	1993	Jim Courier
1973	John Newcombe	1994	Pete Sampras
1974	Jimmy Connors	1995	Andre Agassi

Women's Singles

Year	Player	Year	Player
1953	Maureen Connolly	1975	Evonne Goolagong
1954	Thelma Long	1976	Evonne Cawley[3]
1955	Beryl Penrose	1977	Kerry Reid*
1956	Mary Carter	1977	Evonne Cawley*
1957	Shirley Fry	1978	Christine O'Neill
1958	Angela Mortimer	1979	Barbara Jordan
1959	Mary Reitano[1]	1980	Hana Mandlikova
1960	Margaret Smith	1981	Martina Navratilova
1961	Margaret Smith	1982	Chris Evert
1962	Margaret Smith	1983	Martina Navratilova
1963	Margaret Smith	1984	Chris Evert
1964	Margaret Smith	1985	Martina Navratilova
1965	Margaret Smith	1986	not held
1966	Margaret Smith	1987	Hana Mandlikova
1967	Nancy Richey	1988	Steffi Graf
1968	Billie Jean King	1989	Steffi Graf
1969	Margaret Court[2]	1990	Steffi Graf
1970	Margaret Court[2]	1991	Monica Seles
1971	Margaret Court[2]	1992	Monica Seles
1972	Virginia Wade	1993	Monica Seles
1973	Margaret Court[2]	1994	Steffi Graf
1974	Evonne Goolagong	1995	Mary Pierce

1–Mary Reitano (née Carter)   2–Margaret Court (née Smith)   3–Evonne Cawley (née Goolagong)
* There were two championships in 1977 because the event was moved from early season (January) to December.

FRENCH OPEN CHAMPIONS (1925–1994)

Men's Singles

Year	Player	Year	Player
1925	Rene Lacoste	1960	Nicola Pietrangeli
1926	Henri Cochet	1961	Manuel Santana
1927	Rene Lacoste	1962	Rod Laver
1928	Henri Cochet	1963	Roy Emerson
1929	Rene Lacoste	1964	Manuel Santana
1930	Henri Cochet	1965	Fred Stolle
1931	Jean Borotra	1966	Tony Roche
1932	Henri Cochet	1967	Roy Emerson
1933	Jack Crawford	1968	Ken Rosewall
1934	Gottfried Von Cramm	1969	Rod Laver
1935	Fred Perry	1970	Jan Kodes
1936	Gottfried Von Cramm	1971	Jan Kodes
1937	Henner Henkel	1972	Andres Gimeno
1938	Don Budge	1973	Ilie Nastase
1939	Donald McNeil	1974	Bjorn Borg
1940	not held	1975	Bjorn Borg
1941	Bernard Destremau*	1976	Adriano Panatta
1942	Bernard Destremau*	1977	Guillermo Vilas
1943	Yvon Petra*	1978	Bjorn Borg
1944	Yvon Petra*	1979	Bjorn Borg
1945	Yvon Petra*	1980	Bjorn Borg
1946	Marcel Bernard	1981	Bjorn Borg
1947	Jozsef Asboth	1982	Mats Wilander
1948	Frank Parker	1983	Yannick Noah
1949	Frank Parker	1984	Ivan Lendl
1950	Budge Patty	1985	Mats Wilander
1951	Jaroslav Drobny	1986	Ivan Lendl
1952	Jaroslav Drobny	1987	Ivan Lendl
1953	Ken Rosewall	1988	Mats Wilander
1954	Tony Trabert	1989	Michael Chang
1955	Tony Trabert	1990	Andres Gomez
1956	Lew Hoad	1991	Jim Courier
1957	Sven Davidson	1992	Jim Courier
1958	Mervyn Rose	1993	Sergei Bruguera
1959	Nicola Pietrangeli	1994	Sergei Bruguera

Women's Singles

Year	Player	Year	Player
1925	Suzanne Lenglen	1960	Darlene Hard
1926	Suzanne Lenglen	1961	Ann Haydon
1927	Kea Bouman	1962	Margaret Smith
1928	Helen Moody[1]	1963	Lesley Turner
1929	Helen Moody	1964	Margaret Smith
1930	Helen Moody	1965	Lesley Turner
1931	Cilly Aussem	1966	Ann Jones[3]
1932	Helen Moody	1967	Francoise Durr
1933	Margaret Scriven	1968	Nancy Richey
1934	Margaret Scriven	1969	Margaret Court[4]
1935	Hilde Sperling	1970	Margaret Court
1936	Hilde Sperling	1971	Evonne Goolagong
1937	Hilde Sperling	1972	Billie Jean King
1938	Simone Mathieu	1973	Margaret Court
1939	Simone Mathieu	1974	Chris Evert
1940	not held	1975	Chris Evert
1941	not held	1976	Sue Barker
1942	not held	1977	Mima Jausovec
1943	not held	1978	Virginia Ruzici
1944	not held	1979	Chris Evert
1945	not held	1980	Chris Evert
1946	Margaret Osborne	1981	Hana Mandlikova
1947	Pat Todd	1982	Martina Navratilova
1948	Nelly Landry	1983	Chris Evert
1949	Margaret Du Pont[2]	1984	Martina Navratilova
1950	Doris Hart	1985	Chris Evert
1951	Shirley Fry	1986	Chris Evert
1952	Doris Hart	1987	Steffi Graf
1953	Maureen Connolly	1988	Steffi Graf
1954	Maureen Connolly	1989	Arantxa Sánchez Vicario
1955	Angela Mortimer	1990	Monica Seles
1956	Althea Gibson	1991	Monica Seles
1957	Shirley Bloomer	1992	Monica Seles
1958	Zsuzsi Kormoczy	1993	Steffi Graf
1959	Christine Truman	1994	Arantxa Sánchez Vicario

1 – Helen Moody (née Wills)   2 – Margaret Du Pont (née Osborne)   3 – Ann Jones (née Haydon)   4 – Margaret Court (née Smith)
* From 1941–45 the event was called Tournoi de France and was open only to French citizens.

Youngest champions The youngest women's singles champion was Monica Seles (Yugoslavia), who won the 1991 event at age 17 years 55 days.

FRENCH OPEN CHAMPIONSHIPS

The first French championships were held in 1891; however, entry was restricted to members of French clubs until 1925. Grand slam records include the French Open only from 1925. This event has been staged at the Stade Roland Garros since 1928 and currently is the second leg of the grand slam.

Most wins (men) Bjorn Borg (Sweden) has won the French title a record six times: 1974–75, 1978–81.

Most wins (women) Chris Evert has won a record seven French titles: 1974–75, 1979–80, 1983, 1985–86.

Men's doubles Roy Emerson (Australia) has won the men's doubles a record six times, 1960–65, with five different partners.

Women's doubles The pair of Martina Navratilova and Pam Shriver (both U.S.) have won the doubles title a record four times, 1984–85, 1987–88. The most wins by an individual player is seven, by Martina Navratilova—four times with Pam Shriver, 1984–85, 1987–88; and with three other players, in 1975, 1982 and 1986.

Mixed doubles Two teams have won the mixed title three times: Ken Fletcher and Margaret Smith (Australia), 1963–65; Jean-Claude Barclay and Francoise Durr (France), 1968, 1971, 1973. Margaret Court (née

FOND FAREWELL ■ **MARTINA NAVRATILOVA IN THE FINAL MATCH OF HER GLORIOUS CAREER.** (ALLSPORT/ SIMON BRUTY)

Smith) has won the title the most times, with four wins, winning with Marty Riessen (U.S.) in 1969, in addition to her three wins with Fletcher. Fletcher and Barclay share the men's record of three wins.

Most titles (overall) Margaret Court (née Smith) has won a record 13 French Open titles, 1962–73: five singles, four doubles and four mixed doubles.

Youngest champions The youngest singles champion at the French Open was Monica Seles (Yugoslavia) in 1990, at 16 years 169 days. The youngest men's winner is Michael Chang (U.S.), who was 17 years 109 days when he won the 1989 title.

WIMBLEDON CHAMPIONSHIPS

The "Lawn Tennis Championships" at the All-England Club, Wimbledon are generally regarded as the most prestigious in tennis and currently form the third leg of the grand slam events. They were first held in 1877 and, until 1922, were organized on a challenge round system (the defending cham-

WIMBLEDON CHAMPIONS (1877–1933)

Men's Singles

Year	Player	Year	Player
1877	Spencer Gore	1907	Norman Brookes
1878	Frank Hadlow	1908	Arthur Gore
1879	Rev. John Hartley	1909	Arthur Gore
1880	Rev. John Hartley	1910	Tony Wilding
1881	William Renshaw		
1882	William Renshaw	1911	Tony Wilding
1883	William Renshaw		
1884	William Renshaw	1912	Tony Wilding
1885	William Renshaw	1913	Tony Wilding
1886	William Renshaw	1914	Norman Brookes
1887	Herbert Lawford		
1888	Ernest Renshaw	1915	not held
1889	William Renshaw	1916	not held
1890	Willoughby Hamilton	1917	not held
1891	Wilfred Baddeley	1918	not held
1892	Wilfred Baddeley	1919	Gerald Patterson
1893	Joshua Pim	1920	Bill Tilden
1894	Joshua Pim	1921	Bill Tilden
1895	Wilfred Baddeley	1922	Gerald Patterson
1896	Harold Mahoney	1923	William Johnston
1897	Reginald Doherty	1924	Jean Borotra
1898	Reginald Doherty	1925	Rene Lacoste
1899	Reginald Doherty	1926	Jean Borotra
1900	Reginald Doherty	1927	Henri Cochet
1901	Arthur Gore	1928	Rene Lacoste
1902	Lawrence Doherty	1929	Henri Cochet
1903	Lawrence Doherty	1930	Bill Tilden
1904	Lawrence Doherty	1931	Sidney Wood
1905	Lawrence Doherty	1932	Ellsworth Vines
1906	Lawrence Doherty	1933	Jack Crawford

Women's Singles

Year	Player	Year	Player
1877	no event	1907	May Sutton
1878	no event	1908	Charlotte Sterry
1879	no event	1909	Dora Boothby
1880	no event	1910	Dorothea Lambert-Chambers[3]
1881	no event		
1882	no event	1911	Dorothea Lambert-Chambers
1883	no event		
1884	Maud Watson	1912	Ethel Larcombe
1885	Maud Watson	1913	Dorothea Lambert-Chambers
1886	Blanche Bingley		
1887	Lottie Dod	1914	Dorothea Lambert-Chambers
1888	Lottie Dod		
1889	Blanche Hillyard[1]	1915	not held
1890	Helene Rice	1916	not held
1891	Lottie Dod	1917	not held
1892	Lottie Dod	1918	not held
1893	Lottie Dod	1919	Suzanne Lenglen
1894	Blanche Hillyard	1920	Suzanne Lenglen
1895	Charlotte Cooper	1921	Suzanne Lenglen
1896	Charlotte Cooper	1922	Suzanne Lenglen
1897	Blanche Hillyard	1923	Suzanne Lenglen
1898	Charlotte Cooper	1924	Kathleen McKane
1899	Blanche Hillyard	1925	Suzanne Lenglen
1900	Blanche Hillyard	1926	Kathleen Godfree[4]
1901	Charlotte Sterry[2]	1927	Helen Wills
1902	Muriel Robb	1928	Helen Wills
1903	Dorothea Douglass	1929	Helen Wills
1904	Dorothea Douglass	1930	Helen Moody[5]
1905	May Sutton	1931	Cilly Aussem
1906	Dorothea Douglass	1932	Helen Moody
		1933	Helen Moody

1–Blanche Hillyard (née Bingley) 2–Charlotte Sterry (née Cooper) 3–Dorothea Lambert-Chambers (née Douglass) 4–Kathleen Godfree (née McKane) 5–Helen Moody (née Wills)

WIMBLEDON CHAMPIONS (1934–1994)

Men's Singles

Year	Player	Year	Player
1934	Fred Perry	1965	Roy Emerson
1935	Fred Perry	1966	Manuel Santana
1936	Fred Perry	1967	John Newcombe
1937	Don Budge	1968	Rod Laver
1938	Don Budge	1969	Rod Laver
1939	Bobby Riggs	1970	John Newcombe
1940	not held	1971	John Newcombe
1941	not held	1972	Stan Smith
1942	not held	1973	Jan Kodes
1943	not held	1974	Jimmy Connors
1944	not held	1975	Arthur Ashe
1945	not held	1976	Bjorn Borg
1946	Yvon Petra	1977	Bjorn Borg
1947	Jack Kramer	1978	Bjorn Borg
1948	Bob Falkenburg	1979	Bjorn Borg
1949	Ted Schroeder	1980	Bjorn Borg
1950	Budge Patty	1981	John McEnroe
1951	Dick Savitt	1982	Jimmy Connors
1952	Frank Sedgman	1983	John McEnroe
1953	Vic Seixas	1984	John McEnroe
1954	Jaroslav Drobny	1985	Boris Becker
1955	Tony Trabert	1986	Boris Becker
1956	Lew Hoad	1987	Pat Cash
1957	Lew Hoad	1988	Stefan Edberg
1958	Ashley Cooper	1989	Boris Becker
1959	Alex Olmedo	1990	Stefan Edberg
1960	Neale Fraser	1991	Michael Stich
1961	Rod Laver	1992	Andre Agassi
1962	Rod Laver	1993	Pete Sampras
1963	Chuck McKinley	1994	Pete Sampras
1964	Roy Emerson		

Women's Singles

Year	Player	Year	Player
1934	Dorothy Round	1965	Margaret Smith
1935	Helen Moody[5]	1966	Billie Jean King
1936	Helen Jacobs	1967	Billie Jean King
1937	Dorothy Round	1968	Billie Jean King
1938	Helen Moody	1969	Ann Jones
1939	Alice Marble	1970	Margaret Court[6]
1940	not held	1971	Evonne Goolagong
1941	not held	1972	Billie Jean King
1942	not held	1973	Billie Jean King
1943	not held	1974	Chris Evert
1944	not held	1975	Billie Jean King
1945	not held	1976	Chris Evert
1946	Pauline Betz	1977	Virginia Wade
1947	Margaret Osborne	1978	Martina Navratilova
1948	Louise Brough	1979	Martina Navratilova
1949	Louise Brough	1980	Evonne Cawley[7]
1950	Louise Brough	1981	Chris Evert
1951	Doris Hart	1982	Martina Navratilova
1952	Maureen Connolly	1983	Martina Navratilova
1953	Maureen Connolly	1984	Martina Navratilova
1954	Maureen Connolly	1985	Martina Navratilova
1955	Louise Brough	1986	Martina Navratilova
1956	Shirley Fry	1987	Martina Navratilova
1957	Althea Gibson	1988	Steffi Graf
1958	Althea Gibson	1989	Steffi Graf
1959	Maria Bueno	1990	Martina Navratilova
1960	Maria Bueno	1991	Steffi Graf
1961	Angela Mortimer	1992	Steffi Graf
1962	Karen Susman	1993	Steffi Graf
1963	Margaret Smith	1994	Conchita Martinez
1964	Maria Bueno		

5 – Helen Moody (née Wills)   6 – Margaret Court (née Smith)
7 – Evonne Cawley (née Goolagong)

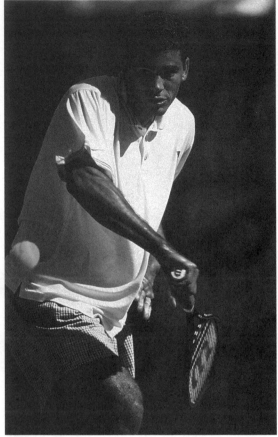

TWO-TIMER ■ 1993–94 WIMBLEDON CHAMPION PETE SAMPRAS. (ALLSPORT/ CLIVE BRUNSKILL)

pion automatically qualifies for the following year's final and plays the winner of the challenger event). Wimbledon became an open championship (professionals could compete) in 1968.

Most titles (men) Overall, the most titles is seven, by William Renshaw (Great Britain), 1881–86, 1889. Since the abolition of the Challenge Round in 1922, the most wins is five, by Bjorn Borg (Sweden), 1976–80.

Most titles (women) Martina Navratilova has won a record nine titles: 1978–79, 1982–87, 1990.

Men's doubles Lawrence and Reginald Doherty (Great Britain) won the doubles title a record eight times: 1897–1901, 1903–05.

Women's doubles Suzanne Lenglen (France) and Elizabeth Ryan (U.S.) won the doubles a record six times: 1919–23, 1925. Elizabeth Ryan was

a winning partner on a record 12 occasions: 1914, 1919–23, 1925–27, 1930, 1933–34.

Mixed doubles The team of Ken Fletcher and Margaret Court (née Smith), both of Australia, won the mixed doubles a record four times: 1963, 1965–66, 1968. Fletcher's four victories tie him for the men's record for wins, which is shared by two other players: Vic Seixas (U.S.), 1953–56; Owen Davidson (Australia), 1967, 1971, 1973–74. Elizabeth Ryan (U.S.) holds the women's record with seven wins: 1919, 1921, 1923, 1927–28, 1930, 1932.

Most titles (overall) Billie Jean King (U.S.) won a record 20 Wimbledon titles from 1961–79: six singles, 10 doubles and four mixed doubles.

Youngest champions The youngest champion was Lottie Dod (Great Britain), who was 15 years 285 days when she won in 1887. The youngest men's champion was Boris Becker (Germany), who was 17 years 227 days when he won in 1985.

UNITED STATES OPEN CHAMPIONSHIPS

The first official U.S. championships were staged in 1881. From 1884 to 1911, the contest was based on a challenger format. In 1968 and 1969, separate amateur and professional events were held. Since 1970, there has been only an Open competition. On the current schedule the U.S. Open is the fourth and final leg of the grand slam and is played at the U.S. National Tennis Center, Flushing Meadows, N.Y.

Most titles (men) The most wins is seven, by three players: Richard Sears (U.S.), 1881–87; William Larned (U.S.), 1901–02, 1907–11; Bill Tilden (U.S.), 1920–25, 1929.

Most titles (women) Molla Mallory (née Bjurstedt; U.S.) won a record eight titles: 1915–18, 1920–22, 1926.

Men's doubles The most wins by one pair is five, by Richard Sears and James Dwight (U.S.), 1882–84, 1886–87. The most wins by an individual player is six, by two players: Richard Sears, 1882–84, 1886–87 (with Dwight) and 1885 (with Joseph Clark); Holcombe Ward, 1899–1901 (with Dwight Davis), 1904–06 (with Beals Wright).

Women's doubles The most wins by a pair is 12, by Louise Brough and Margaret Du Pont (née

Osborne), both of the U.S.. They won in 1942–50 and in 1955–57. Margaret Du Pont holds the record for an individual player with 13 wins; adding to her victories with Brough was the 1941 title with Sarah Cooke.

Mixed doubles The most wins by one pair is four, by William Talbert and Margaret Osborne (U.S.), who won in 1943–46. The most titles won by any individual is nine, by Margaret Du Pont (née Osborne). She won in 1943–46, 1950, 1956, 1958–60.

U.S. OPEN CHAMPIONS (1881–1938)

Men's Singles

Year	Player	Year	Player
1881	Richard Sears	1910	William Larned
1882	Richard Sears	1911	William Larned
1883	Richard Sears	1912	Maurice McLoughlin
1884	Richard Sears	1913	Maurice McLoughlin
1885	Richard Sears	1914	Richard Williams
1886	Richard Sears	1915	William Johnston
1887	Richard Sears	1916	Richard Williams
1888	Henry Slocum Jr.	1917	Lindley Murray
1889	Henry Slocum Jr.	1918	Lindley Murray
1890	Oliver Campbell	1919	William Johnston
1891	Oliver Campbell	1920	Bill Tilden
1892	Oliver Campbell	1921	Bill Tilden
1893	Robert Wrenn	1922	Bill Tilden
1894	Robert Wrenn	1923	Bill Tilden
1895	Fred Hovey	1924	Bill Tilden
1896	Robert Wrenn	1925	Bill Tilden
1897	Robert Wrenn	1926	Rene Lacoste
1898	Malcolm Whitman	1927	Rene Lacoste
1899	Malcolm Whitman	1928	Henri Cochet
1900	Malcolm Whitman	1929	Bill Tilden
1901	William Larned	1930	John Doeg
1902	William Larned	1931	Ellsworth Vines
1903	Lawrence Doherty	1932	Ellsworth Vines
1904	Holcombe Ward	1933	Fred Perry
1905	Beals Wright	1934	Fred Perry
1906	William Clothier	1935	Wilmer Allison
1907	William Larned	1936	Fred Perry
1908	William Larned	1937	Don Budge
1909	William Larned	1938	Don Budge

Women's Singles

Year	Player	Year	Player
1881	no event	1910	Hazel Hotchkiss
1882	no event	1911	Hazel Hotchkiss
1883	no event	1912	Mary Browne
1884	no event	1913	Mary Browne
1885	no event	1914	Mary Browne
1886	no event	1915	Molla Bjurstedt
1887	Ellen Hansell	1916	Molla Bjurstedt
1888	Bertha Townsend	1917	Molla Bjurstedt
1889	Bertha Townsend	1918	Molla Bjurstedt
1890	Ellen Roosevelt	1919	Hazel Wightman[1]
1891	Mabel Cahill	1920	Molla Mallory[2]
1892	Mabel Cahill	1921	Molla Mallory
1893	Aline Terry	1922	Molla Mallory
1894	Helen Helwig	1923	Helen Wills
1895	Juliette Atkinson	1924	Helen Wills
1896	Elisabeth Moore	1925	Helen Wills
1897	Juliette Atkinson	1926	Molla Mallory
1898	Juliette Atkinson	1927	Helen Wills
1899	Marion Jones	1928	Helen Wills
1900	Myrtle McAteer	1929	Helen Wills
1901	Elisabeth Moore	1930	Betty Nuthall
1902	Marion Jones	1931	Helen Moody[3]
1903	Elisabeth Moore	1932	Helen Jacobs
1904	May Sutton	1933	Helen Jacobs
1905	Elisabeth Moore	1934	Helen Jacobs
1906	Helen Homans	1935	Helen Jacobs
1907	Evelyn Sears	1936	Alice Marble
1908	Maud Bargar-Wallach	1937	Anita Lizana
1909	Hazel Hotchkiss	1938	Alice Marble

1 – Hazel Wightman (née Hotchkiss) 2 – Molla Mallory (née Bjurstedt) 3 – Helen Moody (née Wills)

The most titles won by a man is four, accomplished by six players: Edwin Fischer (U.S.), 1894–96, 1898; Wallace Johnson (U.S.), 1907, 1909, 1911, 1920; Bill Tilden (U.S.), 1913–14, 1922–23; William Talbert (U.S.), 1943–46; Owen Davidson (Australia), 1966–67, 1971, 1973; and Marty Riessen (U.S.), 1969–70, 1972, 1980.

Most titles (overall) Margaret Du Pont (née Osborne) won a record 25 U.S. Open titles from 1941–60—three singles, 13 doubles, and nine mixed doubles.

U.S. OPEN CHAMPIONS (1939–1994)

Men's Singles

Year	Player	Year	Player
1939	Bobby Riggs	1968	Arthur Ashe*
1940	Donald McNeil	1968	Arthur Ashe†
1941	Bobby Riggs	1969	Stan Smith*
1942	Ted Schroeder	1969	Rod Laver†
1943	Joseph Hunt	1970	Ken Rosewall
1944	Frank Parker	1971	Stan Smith
1945	Frank Parker	1972	Ilie Nastase
1946	Jack Kramer	1973	John Newcombe
1947	Jack Kramer	1974	Jimmy Connors
1948	Pancho Gonzalez	1975	Manuel Orantes
1949	Pancho Gonzalez	1976	Jimmy Connors
1950	Arthur Larsen	1977	Guillermo Vilas
1951	Frank Sedgman	1978	Jimmy Connors
1952	Frank Sedgman	1979	John McEnroe
1953	Tony Trabert	1980	John McEnroe
1954	Vic Seixas	1981	John McEnroe
1955	Tony Trabert	1982	Jimmy Connors
1956	Ken Rosewall	1983	Jimmy Connors
1957	Malcolm Anderson	1984	John McEnroe
1958	Ashley Cooper	1985	Ivan Lendl
1959	Neale Fraser	1986	Ivan Lendl
1960	Neale Fraser	1987	Ivan Lendl
1961	Roy Emerson	1988	Mats Wilander
1962	Rod Laver	1989	Boris Becker
1963	Raphael Osuna	1990	Pete Sampras
1964	Roy Emerson	1991	Stefan Edberg
1965	Manuel Santana	1992	Stefan Edberg
1966	Fred Stolle	1993	Pete Sampras
1967	John Newcombe	1994	Andre Agassi

Women's Singles

Year	Player	Year	Player
1939	Alice Marble	1968	Margaret Court*4
1940	Alice Marble	1968	Virginia Wade†
1941	Sarah Cooke	1969	Margaret Court*
1942	Pauline Betz	1969	Margaret Court†
1943	Pauline Betz	1970	Margaret Court
1944	Pauline Betz	1971	Billie Jean King
1945	Sarah Cooke	1972	Billie Jean King
1946	Pauline Betz	1973	Margaret Court
1947	Louise Brough	1974	Billie Jean King
1948	Margaret Du Pont	1975	Chris Evert
1949	Margaret Du Pont	1976	Chris Evert
1950	Margaret Du Pont	1977	Chris Evert
1951	Maureen Connolly	1978	Chris Evert
1952	Maureen Connolly	1979	Tracy Austin
1953	Maureen Connolly	1980	Chris Evert
1954	Doris Hart	1981	Tracy Austin
1955	Doris Hart	1982	Chris Evert
1956	Shirley Fry	1983	Martina Navratilova
1957	Althea Gibson	1984	Martina Navratilova
1958	Althea Gibson	1985	Hanna Mandlikova
1959	Maria Bueno	1986	Martina Navratilova
1960	Darlene Hard	1987	Martina Navratilova
1961	Darlene Hard	1988	Steffi Graf
1962	Margaret Smith	1989	Steffi Graf
1963	Maria Bueno	1990	Gabriela Sabatini
1964	Maria Bueno	1991	Monica Seles
1965	Margaret Smith	1992	Monica Seles
1966	Maria Bueno	1993	Steffi Graf
1967	Billie Jean King	1994	Arantxa Sánchez Vicario

4– Margaret Court (née Smith)   * Amateur championship   † Open championship

Youngest champions The youngest singles champion was Tracy Austin (U.S.), who was 16 years 271 days when she won the women's singles in 1979. The youngest men's champion was Pete Sampras (U.S.), who was 19 years 28 days when he won the 1990 title.

OLYMPIC GAMES Tennis was reintroduced to the Olympic Games in 1988, having originally been included at the Games from 1896 to 1924. It was also a demonstration sport in 1968 and 1984.

Most gold medals Max Decugis (France) won four gold medals: men's singles, 1906; men's doubles, 1906; mixed doubles, 1906 and 1920.

Most medals Max Decugis (France) won a record six medals in Olympic competition: four gold (see above), one silver and one bronze, 1900–20. Kitty McKane (Great Britain) won a women's record five medals: one gold, two silver and two bronze, 1920–24.

DAVIS CUP The Davis Cup, the men's international team championship, was first held in 1900, and is held annually.

Most wins The U.S. team has won the Davis Cup a record 30 times, 1900–92.

Most matches (career) Nicola Pietrangeli (Italy) played a record 163 matches (66 ties), 1954 to 1972, winning 120. He played 109 singles (winning 78) and 54 doubles (winning 42).

Most matches (season) Ilie Nastase (Romania) set a singles season mark of 18 wins (with 2 losses) in 1971.

UNITED STATES TEAM RECORDS

Most selections John McEnroe has played for the U.S. team on 31 occasions, 1978–92.

TRIUMPH ■ ANDRE AGASSI AND ARANTXA-SÁNCHEZ VICARIO, 1994 MEN'S AND WOMEN'S U.S. OPEN WINNERS.
(ALLSPORT/CLIVE BRUNSKILL)

Most wins John McEnroe has won 60 matches in Davis Cup competition—41 singles and 19 doubles.

FEDERATION CUP The Federation Cup, the women's international team championship, was first held in 1963 and is an annual event.

Most wins The United States has won the Federation Cup a record 14 times.

MEN'S PROFESSIONAL TOUR RECORDS

Most singles titles (career) Jimmy Connors (U.S.) has won 109 singles titles, 1972–89.

Most singles titles (season) Three players have won 15 titles in one season: Jimmy Connors (U.S.), 1977; Guillermo Vilas (Argentina), 1977; Ivan Lendl (Czechoslovakia), 1982.

Most doubles titles (career) Tom Okker (Netherlands) has won 78 doubles titles, 1968–79.

Most doubles titles (season) John McEnroe (U.S.) won 17 doubles titles in 1979.

Most consecutive match wins Guillermo Vilas (Argentina) won 46 consecutive matches, 1977–78.

Most weeks ranked number one Jimmy Connors (U.S.) held the number one ranking on the ATP computer from July 29, 1974 to August 16, 1977, a total of 159 weeks—the longest streak in tour history.

Highest earnings (career) Ivan Lendl (Czechoslovakia, now U.S.) has won a career record $20,512,417 in prize money, 1978–94.

Highest earnings (season) Pete Sampras (U.S.) earned a season record $3,648,075 in 1993.

WOMEN'S PROFESSIONAL TOUR RECORDS

Most singles titles (career) Martina Navratilova (U.S.) has won 167 titles, 1975–94.

Most singles titles (season) Martina Navratilova won 16 titles in 1983.

Most consecutive matches won Martina Navratilova won 74 consecutive matches in 1984.

Most consecutive weeks ranked number one Steffi Graf (Germany) held the number one computer ranking from August 17, 1987 to March 11, 1991, a total of 186 weeks.

Highest earnings (career) Martina Navratilova (U.S.) has won a career record $20,283,727 in prize money, 1972–94.

Highest earnings (season) Arantxa Sánchez Vicario (Spain) won a season record $2,943,665 in 1994.

FANTASTIC FEATS

Fastest serve Steve Denton (U.S.) completed a serve of 138 mph at Beaver Creek, Colo. on July 29, 1984. The women's record is tied by two players at 115 mph: Brenda Schultz (Netherlands) and Jana Novotna (Czechoslavakia), both at the 1993 Wimbledon Championships.

TRACK AND FIELD

ORIGINS Competition in running, jumping and throwing must have occurred from the earliest days of humankind. The earliest evidence of organized running is from 3800 B.C. in Egypt. The ancient Olympic Games were cultural festivals that highlighted the ancient Greek ideal of perfection of mind and body. The first modern Olympic Games, staged in 1896, focused on athletic achievement and the spirit of competition, and the Games have provided the focus for track and field as a sport ever since. In 1983, a separate world championship was introduced.

OLYMPIC GAMES The first modern Olympic Games were staged in Athens, Greece, April 6–15, 1896. Fifty-nine athletes from 10 nations competed; women's events were not added until 1928.

Most gold medals Ray Ewry (U.S.) holds the all-time record for most appearances atop the winners'

HURDLING INTO THE FUTURE ■ **RECORD HOLDER COLIN JACKSON (RIGHT) COMPETING AGAINST MARK McKOY IN THE 1993 GRAND PRIX CHAMPIONSHIP.**
(ALL-SPORT/GRAY MORTIMORE)

WORLD RECORDS—MEN

World records are for the men's events scheduled by the International Amateur Athletic Federation. Full automatic electronic timing is mandatory for events up to 400 meters.

Event	Time	Athlete (Country)	Place	Date
100 meters	9.85	Leroy Burrell (U.S.)	Lausanne, Switzerland	Aug. 25, 1991
200 meters	19.72	Pietro Mennea (Italy)	Mexico City, Mexico	Sept. 12, 1979
400 meters	43.29	Butch Reynolds (U.S.)	Zürich, Switzerland	Aug. 17, 1988
800 meters	1:41.73	Sebastian Coe (Great Britain)	Florence, Italy	June 10, 1981
1,500 meters	3:28.86	Noureddine Morceli (Algeria)	Rieti, Italy	Sept. 6, 1992
1 mile	3:44.39	Noureddine Morcelli (Algeria)	Rietti, Italy	Sept. 5, 1993
2,000 meters	4:50:81	Said Aouita (Morocco)	Paris, France	July 16, 1987
5,000 meters	12:56.96	Haile Gebreselasie (Ethiopia)	Hengelo, Holland	June 4, 1994
10,000 meters	26:52.23	William Sigei (Kenya)	Oslo, Norway	July 22, 1994
110 meter hurdles	12.91	Colin Jackson (Great Britain)	Stuttgart, Germany	Aug. 20, 1993
400 meter hurdles	46.78	Kevin Young (U.S.)	Barcelona, Spain	Aug. 6, 1992
3,000-meter steeplechase	8:02.08	Moses Kiptanui (Kenya)	Zürich, Switzerland	Aug. 19, 1992
4 x 100 meters	37.40	United States (Mike Marsh, Leroy Burrell, Dennis Mitchell, Carl Lewis)	Barcelona, Spain	Aug. 8, 1992
	37.40	United States (John Drummond, Andre Cason, Dennis Mitchell, Leroy Burrell)	Stuttgart, Germany	Aug. 21, 1993
4 x 400 meters	2:54.29	United States (Andrew Valmon, Quincy Watts, Butch Reynolds, Michael Johnson)	Stuttgart, Germany	Aug. 22, 1993

Distance

Event	Time	Athlete (Country)	Place	Date
High jump	8' ½"	Javier Sotomayor (Cuba)	Salamanca, Spain	July 27, 1993
Pole vault	20' 1¾"	Sergei Bubka (Ukraine)	Sestriere, Italy	July 31, 1994
Long jump	29' 4½"	Mike Powell (U.S.)	Tokyo, Japan	Aug. 30, 1991
Triple jump	58' 11½"	Willie Banks (U.S.)	Indianapolis, Ind.	June 16, 1985
Shot	75' 10¼"	Randy Barnes (U.S.)	Los Angeles, Calif.	May 20, 1990
Discus	243' 0"	Jürgen Schult (East Germany)	Neubrandenburg, Germany	June 6, 1986
Hammer	284' 7"	Yuriy Sedykh (USSR)	Stuttgart, Germany	Aug. 30, 1986
Javelin	313' 10"	Jan Zelezny (Czech Republic)	Sheffield, England	Aug. 29, 1993

Decathlon

8,891 points	Dan O'Brien (U.S.) (1st day: 100m 10.43 sec, Long jump 26' 6¼", Shot put 54' 9¼", High jump 6' 9½", 400 m 48.51 sec), (2nd day: 110 m hurdles 13.98 sec, Discus 159' 4", Pole vault 16' 4¾", Javelin 205' 4", 1,500 m 4:42.10 sec), Talence, France, Sept. 4–5, 1992

Walking

Event	Time	Athlete (Country)	Place	Date
20 km	1:18.35.2	Stefan Johansson (Sweden)	Fana, Norway	May 15, 1992
50 km	3:41.38.4	Raul Gonzales (Mexico)	Bergen, Norway	May 27, 1979

ALLSPORT

JACKIE JOYNER-KERSEE

"The record is the dessert," Jackie Joyner-Kersee says; "I gotta do the main course first." As a multiple record holder, Joyner-Kersee is eating cheesecake these days. "I'm not conscious all the time of my records; your mark [e.g., points in the heptathlon] is your target—the standard to shoot for."

Considered by many to be the world's greatest female athlete, Jackie Joyner-Kersee holds the world record in the heptathlon and the national record in the long jump. Although all her accomplishments are important to her, "Being the first woman to score 7,000 points in the heptathlon is definitely my favorite."

Also close to her heart is making people realize that multi-events are not just men's domain anymore. "I hope that in the future, I can help educate people so that young girls can do this event without being looked upon strangely by their peers."

Joyner-Kersee's education never ends. She continues to strive for greater challenges and accomplishments. "Track teaches me a lot—I have to go up against myself, there's no one else to look to."

What does Jackie Joyner-Kersee foresee in the future? The 1996 Olympics in Atlanta, of course. "Discipline and hard work . . . and always believing in the total being. It's the philosophy I live by."

WORLD RECORDS—WOMEN

World records are for the women's events scheduled by the International Amateur Athletic Federation. The same stipulation about automatically timed events applies in the six events up to 400 meters as in the men's list.

Event	Time	Athlete (Country)	Place	Date
100 meters	10.49	Florence Griffith-Joyner (U.S.)	Indianapolis, Ind.	July 16, 1988
200 meters	21.34	Florence Griffith-Joyner (U.S.)	Seoul, South Korea	Sept. 29, 1988
400 meters	47.60	Marita Koch (East Germany)	Canberra, Australia	Oct. 6, 1985
800 meters	1:53.28	Jarmila Kratochvilová (Czechoslovakia)	Münich, Germany	July 26, 1983
1,500 meters	3:50.46	Qu Yunxia (China)	Beijing, China	Sept. 11, 1993
1 mile	4:15.61	Paula Ivan (Romania)	Nice, France	July 10, 1989
2,000 meters	5:25.36	Sonia O'Sullivan (Ireland)	Edinburgh, Scotland	July 8, 1994
3,000 meters	8:06.11	Wang Junxia (China)	Beijing, China	Sept. 13, 1993
5,000 meters	14:37.33	Ingrid Kristiansen (Norway)	Stockholm, Sweden	Aug. 5, 1986
10,000 meters	29:31.78	Wang Junxia (China)	Beijing, China	Sept. 8, 1993
100 meter hurdles	12.21	Yordanka Donkova (Bulgaria)	Stara Zagora, Bulgaria	Aug. 20, 1988
400 meter hurdles	52.74	Sally Gunnell (Great Britain)	Stuttgart, Germany	Aug. 19, 1993
4 x 100 meters	41.37	East Germany (Silke Gladisch, Sabine Rieger, Ingrid Auerswald, Marlies Göhr)	Canberra, Australia	Oct. 6, 1985
4 x 400 meters	3:15.17	USSR (Tatyana Ledovskaya, Olga Nazarova, Maria Pinigina, Olga Bryzgina)	Seoul, South Korea	Oct. 1, 1988

Distance

Event	Distance	Athlete (Country)	Place	Date
High jump	6' 10¼"	Stefka Kostadinova (Bulgaria)	Rome, Italy	Aug. 30, 1987
Long jump	24' 8¼"	Galina Chistyakova (USSR)	Leningrad, USSR	June 11, 1988
Triple jump	49' 6¼"	Ana Biryukova (Russia)	Stuttgart, Germany	Aug. 19, 1993
Shot	74' 3"	Natalya Lisovskaya (USSR)	Moscow, USSR	June 7, 1987
Discus	252' 0"	Gabriele Reinsch (East Germany)	Neubrandenburg, Germany	July 9, 1988
Javelin	262' 5"	Petra Felke (East Germany)	Potsdam, Germany	Sept. 9, 1988

Heptathlon

7,291 points Jacqueline Joyner-Kersee (U.S.) (100 m hurdles 12.69 sec; High jump 6' 1¼"; Shot put 51' 10"; 200 m 22.56 sec; Long jump 23' 10"; Javelin 149' 9"; 800 m 2:08.51 sec), Seoul, South Korea, Sept. 23–24, 1988

Walking

Event	Time	Athlete (Country)	Place	Date
5 km	20:07.52	Beate Anders (East Germany)	Rostock, Germany	June 23, 1990
10 km	41:56.21	Nadezhda Ryashkina (USSR)	Seattle, Wash.	July 24, 1990

podium, with 10 gold medals: standing high jump (1900, 1904, 1906, 1908); standing long jump (1900, 1904, 1906, 1908); standing triple jump (1900, 1904). The women's record is four, shared by four athletes: Fanny Blankers-Koen (Netherlands): 100 m, 200 m, 80 m hurdles and 4 x 100 m relay in 1948; Betty Cuthbert (Australia): 100 m, 200 m, 4 x 100 m relay in 1956, and 400 m in 1964; Barbel Wockel (née Eckert; East Germany): 200 m and 4 x 100 m relay in both 1976 and 1980; Evelyn Ashford (U.S.): 100 m and 4 x 100 m relay in 1984, 4 x 100 m relay in 1988, 4 x 100 m relay in 1992.

Most gold medals (one Games) Paavo Nurmi (Finland) won five gold medals at the 1924 Games. His victories came in the 1,500 m, 5,000 m, 10,000 m cross-country, 3,000 m team, and cross-country team. The most wins at individual events (not including relay or other team races) is four, by Alvin Kraenzlein (U.S.) in 1900 at 60 m, 110 m hurdles, 200 m hurdles and the long jump.

UP AND OVER ■ SERGEI BUBKA SURPASSED HIS OWN POLE-VAULTING RECORD BY ¼ IN. IN 1994. (ALLSPORT/MIKE POWELL)

Most medals won Paavo Nurmi (Finland) won a record 12 medals (nine gold, three silver) in the Games of 1920, 1924 and 1928. The women's record is seven, shared by two athletes: Shirley de la Hunty (Australia), three gold, one silver, three bronze in the 1948, 1952 and 1956 Games; Irena Szewinska (Poland), three gold, two silver, two bronze in the 1964, 1968, 1972 and 1976 Games.

INDIVIDUAL RECORDS (U.S. ATHLETES)

Most medals Ray Ewry's 10 gold medals are the most won by any U.S. athlete (see above). Florence Griffith-Joyner has won a women's record five medals in track and field—three golds, two silver in the 1984 and 1988 Games.

Most gold medals Ray Ewry holds the Olympic mark for most golds (see above). The women's record for gold medals is four, by Evelyn Ashford—100m and 4 x 100 m relay in 1984, 4 x 100 m relay in 1988, 4 x 100 m relay in 1992.

RUNNING FOR JOY ■ SONIA O'SULLIVAN COMPETING IN THE NEW YORK GAMES IN 1992. TWO YEARS LATER, O'SULLIVAN BROKE THE MARK IN THE 2,000 METER RACE. (ALLSPORT)

Most gold medals (one Games) The most gold medals won at one Olympics is four, by three men: Alvin Kraenzlein (see above); Jesse Owens, 100 m, 200 m, long jump and 4 x 100 m relay in 1936; Carl Lewis, 100 m, 200 m, long jump and 4 x 100 m relay in 1984. The women's record is three golds, held by Wilma Rudolph, Valerie Brisco and Florence Griffith-Joyner (see above).

WORLD CHAMPIONSHIPS Quadriennial world championships distinct from the Olympic Games were first held in 1983 at Helsinki, Finland.

Most medals The most medals won is 10, by two athletes: seven gold, two silver, one bronze by Carl Lewis (U.S.), 1983–93; and two gold, two silver, six bronze by Merlene Ottey (Jamaica), 1983–93.

Most consecutive titles Sergei Bubka (USSR/Ukraine) is the only athlete to win four consecutive world titles, winning the pole vault, 1983, 1987, 1991 and 1993.

UNITED STATES NATIONAL CHAMPIONSHIPS

Most titles The most American national titles won at all events, indoors and out, is 65, by Ronald Owen Laird at various walking events between 1958 and 1976. Excluding the walks, the record is 41, by Stella Walsh (née Walasiewicz), who won 41 women's events between 1930 and 1954: 33 outdoors and eight indoors.

Longest winning sequence Iolanda Balas (Romania) won a record 140 consecutive competitions at high jump from 1956 to 1967. The record at a track event was 122, at 400 meter hurdles, by Edwin Moses (U.S.) between his loss to Harald Schmid (West Germany) at Berlin, Germany on August 26, 1977 and that to Danny Harris (U.S.) at Madrid, Spain on June 4, 1987.

ROAD RUNNING

MARATHON

The marathon is run over a distance of 26 miles 385 yards. This distance was the one used for the race at the 1908 Olympic Games, run from Windsor to the White City stadium, London, England, and it became standard from 1924 on. The marathon was introduced at the 1896 Olympic Games to commemorate the legendary run of Pheidippides (or Philippides) from the battlefield of Marathon to Athens in 490 B.C. The 1896 Olympic marathon was preceded by trial races that year.

The first Boston Marathon, the world's oldest annual marathon race, was held on April 19, 1897 at 24 miles 1,232 yards, and the first national marathon championship was that of Norway in 1897.

The first championship marathon for women was organized by the Road Runners Club of America on September 27, 1970.

Most marathons run Norm Frank (U.S.) ran 525 marathons of 26 miles or more as of May 1, 1994.

WORLD RECORDS There are as yet no official records for the marathon, and it should be noted that courses may vary in severity. The following are the best times recorded, all on courses with verified distances: for men, 2 hours 6 minutes 50 seconds, by Belayneh Dinsamo (Ethiopia) at Rotterdam, Netherlands on April 17, 1988; for women, 2 hours 21 minutes 6 seconds, by Ingrid Kristiansen (née Christensen; Norway) at London, England on April 21, 1985.

United States The Athletics Congress recognizes the following U.S. records: for men, Pat Peterson, 2 hours 10 minutes 4 seconds, at London, England on April 23, 1989; for women, Joan Benoit Samuelson, 2 hours 21 minutes 21 seconds, at Chicago, Ill., on October 20, 1985.

OLYMPIC GAMES The marathon has been run at every Olympic Games of the modern era; however, a women's race wasn't included in the Games until 1984.

Most gold medals The record for most wins in the men's race is two, by two marathoners: Abebe Bikila (Ethiopia), 1960 and 1964; Waldemar Cierpinski (East Germany), 1976 and 1980. The women's event has been run twice, with different winners.

WORLD CHAMPIONSHIP The marathon has been included as part of both the men's and women's programs at every World Track and Field championship.

Most wins No athlete in either the men's or women's division has won the world title more than once.

BOSTON MARATHON The world's oldest annual running race, the Boston Marathon was first staged on April 19, 1897.

Most wins (men) Clarence De Mar (U.S.) has won the race seven times—1911, 1922–24, 1927–28, 1930.

Most wins (women) Rosa Mota (Portugal) has won the women's division three times—1987–88, 1990. Prior to 1972, when the marathon was opened to women, two women "unofficially" won the women's division three times each: Roberta Gibb (U.S.) 1966–68; and Sarah Mae Berman (U.S.) in 1969–71.

Fastest time The course record for men is 2 hours 7 minutes 15 seconds, by Cosmas Ndeti (Kenya) in 1994. The women's record is 2 hours 21 minutes 45 seconds, by Uta Pippig (Germany) in 1984.

NEW YORK CITY MARATHON The race was run in Central Park each year from 1970 to 1976, when, to celebrate the U.S. Bicentennial, the course was changed to a route through all five boroughs of the city. From that year, when there were 2,090 runners, the race has become one of the world's great sporting occasions; in 1992 there were a record 27,797 finishers.

Most wins Grete Waitz (Norway) has won nine times—1978–80, 1982–86 and 1988. Bill Rodgers has a men's record four wins—1976–79.

Fastest time The course record for men is 2 hours 8 minutes 1 second, by Juma Ikangaa (Tanzania), and for women, 2 hours 24 minutes 40 seconds, by Lisa Ondieki (Australia), both set in 1992.

LONG-DISTANCE RUNNING RECORDS

Longest race (distance) The longest races ever staged were the 1928 (3,422 miles) and 1929 (3,665 miles) transcontinental races from New York City to Los Angeles, Calif. Johnny Salo (U.S.) was the winner in 1929 in 79 days, from March 31 to June 18. His elapsed time of 525 hours 57 minutes 20 seconds (averaging 6.97 mph) left him only 2 minutes 47 seconds ahead of Englishman Peter Gavuzzi.

The longest race staged annually is Australia's Westfield Run from Paramatta, New South Wales to Doncaster, Victoria (Sydney to Melbourne). The distance run has varied slightly, but the record is by Yiannis Kouros (Greece) in 5 days 2 hours 27 minutes 27 seconds in 1989, when the distance was 658 miles.

Longest runs The longest run by an individual is one of 11,134 miles around the United States, by Sarah Covington-Fulcher (U.S.), starting and finishing in Los Angeles, Calif., between July 21, 1987 and October 2, 1988. Robert J. Sweetgall (U.S.) ran 10,608 miles around the perimeter of the United States, starting and finishing in Washington D.C., between October 1982 and July 15, 1983.

WALKING

OLYMPIC GAMES Walking races have been included in the Olympic events since 1906.

Most gold medals The only walker to win three gold medals has been Ugo Frigerio (Italy), with the 3,000 meter in 1920, and the 10,000 meter in 1920 and 1924.

Most medals The record for most medals is four, by two walkers: Ugo Frigerio (Italy), three gold, one bronze, 1920–32; Vladimir Golubnichiy (USSR), two gold medals, one silver and one bronze, 1960–68.

WORLD CHAMPIONSHIP Walking races have been included in every World Track and Field championship.

Most medals Maurizio Damilano (Italy) is the only walker to win two world titles, for the 20 km walk in 1987 and 1991.

FANTASTIC FEATS

Backwards 100 meter 12.7 seconds by Ferdie Adoboe on July 25, 1991.

Backwards marathon Timothy "Bud" Badyna (U.S.) ran a marathon backwards in 4 hours 15 seconds at Columbus, Ohio, November 10, 1991.

Walking on hands Mark Kenny (U.S.) completed a 50 meter inverted sprint in 16.93 seconds at Norwood, Mass. on February 16, 1994.

BACKTRACKING ■ TIMOTHY "BACKWARDS BUD" BADYNA BACKWARDS MARATHONING IN RECORD TIME. (DAVIDYA BADYNA)

HEAD RUSH ■ WALKING ON HIS HANDS IN DOUBLE-TIME IS MARK KENNY'S SPECIALTY. (DAVID A. BREEN)

TRAMPOLINING

ORIGINS Trampolining has been part of circus acts for many years. The sport of trampolining dates from 1936, when the prototype "T" model trampoline was designed by George Nissen of the United States. The first official tournament took place in 1947.

WORLD CHAMPIONSHIPS Instituted in 1964, championships have been staged biennially since 1968. The world championships recognize champions, both men and women, in four events: individual, synchronized pairs, tumbling, and double mini trampoline.

Most titles Judy Wills (U.S.) has won a record five individual world titles, 1964–68. The men's record is two, shared by six trampolinists: Wayne Miller (U.S.), 1966 and 1970; Dave Jacobs (U.S.), 1967–68; Richard Tisson (France), 1974 and 1976; Yevgeniy Yanes (USSR), 1976 and 1978; Lionel Pioline (France), 1984 and 1986; and Alexander Maskalenko (USSR/Russia), 1990 and 1992.

UNITED STATES NATIONAL CHAMPIONSHIPS The American Trampoline & Tumbling Association staged the first national championship in 1947. The inaugural event was open only to men; a women's event was introduced in 1961.

Most titles Two people have won a record 12 national titles: Stuart Ransom—six individual, 1975–76, 1978–80, 1982; three synchronized, 1975, 1979–80; and three double mini-tramp, 1979–80 and 1982; and Karl Heger—four individual, 1991–94; two synchronized, 1982 and 1986; and six double mini-tramp, 1986–87, 1991–94. Leigh Hennessy has won a record 10 women's titles: one individual, 1978; eight synchronized, 1972–73, 1976–78, 1980–82; one double mini-tramp, 1978.

DEFYING GRAVITY ■ LEIGH HENNESSY BOUNCING UP AND INTO THE RECORD BOOKS. (JEFF HENNESSY)

IRONMAN ■ MARK ALLEN HAS WON THE MOST
WORLD TRIATHLON CHAMPIONSHIPS AND HOLDS THE
COURSE SPEED RECORD FOR THE HAWAII IRONMAN
TRIATHLON. (ALLSPORT/GARY NEWKIRK)

TRIATHLON

ORIGINS The triathlon combines long distance
swimming, cycling, and running. The sport was
developed by a group of dedicated athletes who
founded the Hawaii "Ironman" in 1974. After a
series of unsuccessful attempts to create a world
governing body, *L'Union Internationale de
Triathlon* (UIT) was founded in Avignon, France in
1989. The UIT staged the first official world championships in Avignon on August 6, 1989.

WORLD CHAMPIONSHIPS An unofficial world
championship has been held in Nice, France since
1982. The three legs comprise a 3,200 meter swim
(4,000 meter since 1988), 120 kilometer bike ride,
and 32 kilometer run.

Most titles Mark Allen (U.S.) has won a record
eight times, 1982–86, 1989–91. Paula Newby-Fraser (Zimbabwe) has won a record three women's
titles, 1989–91.

Fastest times The men's record is 5 hours 46
minutes 10 seconds, by Mark Allen (U.S.) in 1988.

The women's record is 6 hours 27 minutes 6 seconds, by Erin Baker (New Zealand) in 1988.

HAWAII IRONMAN This is the first, and best known,
of the triathlons. Instituted on February 18, 1978,
the first race was contested by 15 athletes. The
Ironman grew rapidly in popularity, and 1,000
athletes entered the 1984 race. Contestants must
first swim 2.4 miles, then cycle 112 miles, and
finally run a full marathon of 26 miles 385 yards.

Most titles Dave Scott (U.S.) has won the Ironman a record six times, 1980, 1982–84, 1986–87.
The women's event has been won a record six
times by Paula Newby-Fraser (Zimbabwe) in 1986,
1988–89, and 1991–93.

Fastest times Mark Allen (U.S.) holds the course
record at 8 hours 7 minutes 45 seconds in 1993.
Paula Newby-Fraser holds the women's record at
8 hours 55 seconds in 1992.

Fastest time The fastest time ever recorded over
the Ironman distances is 8 hours 1 minute 32
seconds, by Dave Scott (U.S.) at Lake Biwas, Japan
on July 30, 1989.

Largest field The most competitors to finish a
triathlon race were the 3,888 who completed the
1987 Bud Lite U.S. Triathlon in Chicago, Ill.

TUG-OF-WAR

ORIGINS Tug-of-War, a trial of strength and skill
involving two teams of eight pulling against each
other on opposite ends of a long, thick rope, gained
its name in England in the 19th century. The
actual test of strength that the sport is based on
dates to antiquity.

OLYMPIC GAMES Tug-of-War was an Olympic
event from 1900–20.

GUINNESS CHALLENGE

**What country is generally credited
as being "home of the modern game"
of golf?**
See page 118 for the answer.

Most wins Great Britain won the event twice, 1908 and 1920.

WORLD CHAMPIONSHIPS A men's tournament was first staged in 1975 and a women's was added in 1986.

Most wins (men) England has won 15 titles in all weight categories, 1975–90.

Most wins (women) Sweden has won five titles: 520 kg, 1986, 1988; 560 kg, 1986, 1988, 1990.

VOLLEYBALL

ORIGINS The game was invented as *mintonette* in 1895 by William G. Morgan at the YMCA gymnasium at Holyoke, Mass. The International Volleyball Association (IVA) was formed in Paris, France in April 1947. The United States Volleyball Association was founded in 1922 and is the governing body for the sport in this country. The United States National Championships were inaugurated for men in 1928, and for women in 1949.

OLYMPIC GAMES Volleyball became an official Olympic sport in 1964, when both men's and women's tournaments were staged in Tokyo, Japan.

Most gold medals (country) The USSR has won three men's titles, 1964, 1968 and 1980; and four women's titles, 1968, 1972, 1980 and 1988.

Most medals (individual) Inna Ryskal (USSR) has won four medals in Olympic competition: two gold, 1968, 1972; and two silver, 1964, 1976. The men's record is three, won by three players: Yuriy Poyarkov (USSR), two golds, 1964 and 1968, one bronze, 1972; Katsutoshi Nekoda (Japan), one gold, 1972, one silver, 1968, and one bronze, 1964; and Steve Timmons (U.S.), two gold, 1984 and 1988, and one bronze, 1992.

WORLD CHAMPIONSHIPS World championships were instituted in 1949 for men and in 1952 for women.

Most titles The USSR has won six men's titles, 1949, 1952, 1960, 1962, 1978 and 1982, and five women's titles, 1952, 1956, 1960, 1970 and 1990.

BEACH VOLLEYBALL

In professional beach volleyball the court dimensions are the same as in the indoor game: 30 feet x 60 feet, or 30 feet x 30 feet on each side, with the net set at a height of eight feet. In beach volleyball,

BLOCKING ■ **KARCH KIRALY BRACING FOR A BLOCK AT THE 1992 SAN DIEGO AVP TOURNAMENT.** (ALLSPORT/KEN LEVINE)

teams play two-a-side, as opposed to six-a-side for the indoor game.

ORIGINS Beach volleyball originated in California in the 1940s. The sport grew rapidly in the 1960s, and the first world championships were staged in 1976. In 1981 the Association of Volleyball Professionals was founded, and the AVP/Miller Lite Tour was formed that year.

UNITED STATES CHAMPIONSHIPS

Most titles Three players are tied with five: Sinjin Smith (U.S.), 1979 and 1981 (with Karch Kiraly), 1982, 1988 and 1990 (with Randy Stoklos); and

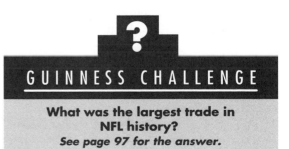

?

GUINNESS CHALLENGE

What was the largest trade in NFL history?
See page 97 for the answer.

KEEP IT UP ■ INCREDIBLE RESCUES SUCH AS THIS ONE EXPLAIN WHY SINJIN SMITH HAS WON MORE TITLES THAN ANY OTHER BEACH PLAYER. (ALLSPORT/KEN LEVINE)

Mike Dodd (U.S.) and Tim Hovland (U.S.), 1983, 1985–87 and 1989.

AVP/Miller Lite Tour Records

Most tour wins Sinjin Smith has won 135 tour events, 1977–94.

Highest earnings Karch Kiraly has earned a career record $1,683,149 as of January 18, 1995.

WATER POLO

Origins This game was originally played in England as "water soccer" in 1869. The first rules were drafted in 1876. Water polo has been an Olympic event since 1900. In 1908, FINA (see Swimming) became the governing body for water polo. The first world championships were held in 1973.

Olympic Games Water polo was first included at the 1900 Games, and has been included in every Games since.

Most gold medals (country) Hungary has won six Olympic titles, 1932, 1936, 1952, 1956, 1964 and 1976.

Most gold medals (players) Five players have won three gold medals: George Wilkinson (Great Britain), 1900, 1908, 1912; Paul Radmilovic (Great Britain), 1908, 1912, 1920; Charles Smith (Great Britain), 1908, 1912, 1920; Deszo Gyarmati (Hungary), 1952, 1956, 1964; Gyorgy Karpati (Hungary), 1952, 1956, 1964.

World Championships A competition was first held at the World Swimming Championships in 1973. A women's event was included from 1986.

Most titles Two countries have won two men's titles: USSR, 1975 and 1982; Yugoslavia, 1986 and 1991. The women's competition was won by Australia in 1986, and by the Netherlands in 1991.

United States National Championships The first men's national championship was held in 1891. A women's tournament was first held in 1926.

Most titles The New York Athletic Club has won 25 men's titles: 1892–96, 1903–04, 1906–08, 1922, 1929–31, 1933–35, 1937–39, 1954, 1956, 1960–61, and 1971. The Industry Hills Athletic Club (Calif.) has won nine women's titles: 1980–81 and 1984–88 (outdoors), 1987–88 (indoors).

WATERSKIING

Origins Modern waterskiing was pioneered in the 1920s. Ralph Samuelson, who skied on Lake Pepin, Minn. in 1922 using two curved pine boards, is credited as being the father of the sport. Forms of skiing on water can be traced back centuries to people attempting to walk on water with planks. The development of the motorboat to tow skiers was the largest factor in the sport's growth. The world governing body is the International Water Ski Federation (IWSF), which replaced the World Water Ski Union (WWSU) in 1988. WWSU had succeeded the *Union Internationale de Ski Nautique,* which had been formed in Geneva, Switzerland in 1946. The American Water Ski Association was founded in 1939 and held the first national championships that year.

World Championships The first world championships were held in 1949.

Most titles Sammy Duvall (U.S.) has won four overall titles, in 1981, 1983, 1985 and 1987. Two women have won three overall titles: Willa McGuire (née Worthington; U.S.), 1949–50 and 1955; Liz Allan-Shetter (U.S.), 1965, 1969 and 1975.

Most individual titles Liz Allan-Shetter has won a record eight individual championship events and is the only person to win all four titles—slalom, jumping, tricks, and overall in one year, at Copenhagen, Denmark in 1969. Patrice Martin (France) has won a men's record seven titles: three overall,

1989, 1991, 1993, and four tricks, 1979, 1985, 1987 and 1991.

UNITED STATES NATIONAL CHAMPIONSHIPS National championships were first held at Marine Stadium, Jones Beach State Park, Long Island, N.Y. on July 22, 1939.

THUMBS UP ■ IN 1993 SUSI GRAHAM SHATTERED THE WOMEN'S SLALOM RECORD, WHICH HAD PREVIOUSLY BEEN TIED BY THREE ATHLETES. (ALLSPORT/ SCOTT HALLERAN)

Most titles The most overall titles is nine, tied by two individuals: Carl Roberge, 1980–83, 1985–88 and 1990; and Willa McGuire, 1946–51 and 1953–55.

WEIGHTLIFTING

There are two standard lifts in weightlifting: the "snatch" and the "clean and jerk." Totals of the two lifts determine competition results. The "press," which had been a standard lift, was abolished in 1972.

ORIGINS Competitions for lifting weights of stone were held at the ancient Olympic Games. In the 19th century, weightlifting consisted of professional exhibitions in which some of the advertised poundages were open to doubt. The *Fédération Internationale Haltérophile et Culturiste*, now the International Weightlifting Federation (IWF), was established in 1905, and its first official championships were held in Tallinn, Estonia on April 29–30, 1922.

WORLD WEIGHTLIFTING RECORDS

From January 1, 1993, the International Weightlifting Federation (IWF) introduced modified weight categories, thereby making the then world records redundant. In February, the IWF announced that "the results of major IWF-controlled competitions and championships will be collected until September 30, 1993 and the best results be declared as basic performances, with world records to be broken for the first time at the Melbourne World Championships (November 12–21)." This is the current list, with world standards yet to be set and records set as of November 25, 1994 for men and November 18, 1994 for women.

Men

Bodyweight	Lift	kg	lb	Name and Country	Place	Date
54 kg *119 lb*	Snatch	130	286.52	Halil Mutlu (Turkey)	Istanbul, Turkey	Nov. 18, 1994
	Jerk	160	352.64	Halil Mutlu (Turkey)	Istanbul, Turkey	Nov. 18, 1994
	Total	290	639.16	Halil Mutlu (Turkey)	Istanbul, Turkey	Nov. 18, 1994
59 kg *130 lb*	Snatch	137.5	303	*World Standard*		
	Jerk	167.5	369¼	Nikolai Pershalov (Bulgaria)	Melbourne, Australia	Nov. 13, 1993
	Total	305	672¼	Nikolai Pershalov (Bulgaria)	Melbourne, Australia	Nov. 13, 1993
64 kg *141 lb*	Snatch	145	319¾	Naim Suleymanoglu (Turkey)*	Sokolov, Czech Republic	May 5, 1994
	Jerk	180	396¾	Naim Suleymanoglu (Turkey)*	Sokolov, Czech Republic	May 5, 1994
	Total	325	716½	Naim Suleymanoglu (Turkey)*	Sokolov, Czech Republic	May 5, 1994
70 kg *154¼ lb*	Snatch	157.5	347¼	Israil Militosyan (Armenia)	Sokolov, Czech Republic	May 5, 1994
	Jerk	192.5	424¼	Yotov Yoto (Bulgaria)	Sokolov, Czech Republic	May 5, 1994
	Total	345	760½	Yotov Yoto (Bulgaria)	Sokolov, Czech Republic	May 5, 1994
76 kg *167½ lb*	Snatch	170	374¾	Ruslan Savchenko (Ukraine)	Melbourne, Australia	Nov. 16, 1993
	Jerk	205	452	Pablo Lara (Cuba)	Ponce, Puerto Rico	Nov. 25, 1993
	Total	370	815¾	Ruslan Savchenko (Ukraine)	Melbourne, Australia	Nov. 16, 1993
83 kg *183 lb*	Snatch	175	385¾	*World Standard*		
	Jerk	210	463	Marc Huster (Germany)	Melbourne, Australia	Nov. 17, 1993
	Total	380	837¾	*World Standard*		
91 kg *200½ lb*	Snatch	185	407¾	Ivan Chakarov (Australia)	Melbourne, Australia	Nov. 18, 1993
	Jerk	227.5	501½	Alexey Petrov (Russia)	Sokolov, Czech Republic	May 7, 1994
	Total	412.5	909¼	Alexey Petrov (Russia)	Sokolov, Czech Republic	July 23, 1994
99 kg *218½ lb*	Snatch	191	421	Sergey Syrtsov (Russia)	Sokolov, Czech Republic	July 23, 1994
	Jerk	217.5	920¼	Sergey Syrtsov (Russia)	Sokolov, Czech Republic	May 7, 1994
	Total	415	915	Sergey Syrtsov (Russia)	Sokolov, Czech Republic	May 7, 1994
108 kg *238 lb*	Snatch	201	443	Andrew Chemerkin (Russia)	St. Petersburg, Russia	July 23, 1994
	Jerk	235	518	Timour Taimazov (Ukraine)	Sokolov, Czech Republic	May 8, 1994
	Total	430	948	Timour Taimazov (Ukraine)	Sokolov, Czech Republic	May 8, 1994
Over 108 kg	Snatch	200.5	442	Andrey Chermkin (Russia)	Sokolov, Czech Republic	May 8, 1994
	Jerk	250	551	Andrey Chermkin (Russia)	Sokolov, Czech Republic	May 8, 1994
	Total	450	992	Andrey Chermkin (Russia)	Sokolov, Czech Republic	May 8, 1994

*Formerly Naim Suleimanov or Neum Shalamanov of Bulgaria

WORLD WEIGHTLIFTING RECORDS

Women

Bodyweight	Lift	kg	lb	Name and Country	Place	Date
46 kg 101¼ lb	Snatch	80.5	177.42	Yanhong (China)	Istanbul, Turkey	Nov. 18, 1994
	Jerk	92.5	204	Luo Hongwei (China)	Shilong, China	Dec. 15, 1993
	Total	165	363¾	Luo Hongwei (China)	Shilong, China	Dec. 15, 1993
50 kg 110¼ lb	Snatch	77.5	170¾	Liu Xiuhia (China)	Melbourne, Australia	Nov. 13, 1993
	Jerk	110	242½	Liu Xiuhia (China)	Melbourne, Australia	Nov. 13, 1993
	Total	187.5	413¼	Liu Xiuhia (China)	Melbourne, Australia	Nov. 13, 1993
54 kg 119 lb	Snatch	90	198	Chen Xiaoming (China)	Melbourne, Australia	Nov. 14, 1993
	Jerk	112.5	248	Long Yuiling (China)	Shilong, China	Dec. 16, 1993
	Total	200	441	Chen Xiaoming (China)	Melbourne, Australia	Nov. 14, 1993
59 kg 130 lb	Snatch	97.5	215	Sun Caiyan (China)	Melbourne, Australia	Nov. 15, 1993
	Jerk	120.5	265½	Zuo Feie (China)	Shilong, China	Dec. 16, 1993
	Total	217.5	479½	Sun Caiyan (China)	Melbourne, Australia	Nov. 15, 1993
64 kg 141 lb	Snatch	103	227	Li Hongyun (China)	Shilong, China	Dec. 17, 1993
	Jerk	125	275½	Lei Li (China)	Shilong, China	Dec. 17, 1993
	Total	227.5	501½	Lei Li (China)	Shilong, China	Dec. 17, 1993
70 kg 154¼ lb	Snatch	100	220½	Milena Trendafilova (Bulgaria)	Melbourne, Australia	Nov. 17, 1993
	Jerk	120	264½	Milena Trendafilova (Bulgaria)	Melbourne, Australia	Nov. 17, 1993
	Total	220	485	Milena Trendafilova (Bulgaria)	Melbourne, Australia	Nov. 17, 1993
76 kg 167¼ lb	Snatch	105	231½	Hua Ji (China)	Melbourne, Australia	Nov. 18, 1993
	Jerk	140	308½	Zhang Guimei (China)	Shilong, China	Dec. 18, 1993
	Total	235	518	Zhang Guimei (China)	Shilong, China	Dec. 18, 1993
83 kg 183 lb	Snatch	107.5	237	Xing Shiwen (China)	Melbourne, Australia	Nov. 19, 1993
	Jerk	127.5	281	Chen Shu-chih (Taipei)	Melbourne, Australia	Nov. 19, 1993
	Total	230	507	Chen Shu-chih (Taipei)	Melbourne, Australia	Nov. 19, 1993
+83 kg	Snatch	105	231½	Li Yahuan (China)	Melbourne, Australia	Nov. 20, 1993
	Jerk	155	341½	Li Yahuan (China)	Melbourne, Australia	Nov. 20, 1993
	Total	260	573	Li Yahuan (China)	Melbourne, Australia	Nov. 20, 1993

OLYMPIC GAMES Weightlifting events were included in the first modern Games in 1896.

Most gold medals Four lifters won two gold medals: John Davis Jr. (U.S.), heavyweight, 1948 and 1952; Tommy Kono (U.S.), lightweight, 1952, light heavyweight, 1956; Chuck Vinci Jr. (U.S.), bantamweight, 1956 and 1960; and Naim Suleymanoglu (Turkey), featherweight, 1988 and 1992.

Most medals Norbert Schemansky (U.S.) won four medals: one gold, one silver and two bronze, 1960–64.

WORLD CHAMPIONSHIPS The IWF held its first world championships at Tallinn, Estonia in 1922, but has subsequently recognized 20 championships held in Vienna, Austria and London, England between 1898 and 1920. The championships have been held annually since 1946, with the Olympic Games recognized as world championships in the year of the Games until 1988, when a championship separate from the Olympics was staged. A women's championship was introduced in 1987.

THE SULEYMANOGLU LIFT ■ ON MAY 5, 1994, THREE WEIGHTLIFTING RECORDS WERE SHATTERED IN ONE DAY BY NAIM SULEYMANOGLU. (ALLSPORT/ SIMON BRUTY)

Most titles The record for most titles is eight, held by three lifters: John Davis (U.S.), 1938, 1946–52; Tommy Kono (U.S.), 1952–59; and Vasiliy Alekseyev (USSR), 1970–77. Two American women won world titles: Karyn Marshall, at 82 kg in 1987; and Robyn Byrd, at 77.5 kg in 1994.

UNITED STATES NATIONAL CHAMPIONSHIPS

Most titles The most titles won is 13, by Anthony Terlazzo at 137 pounds, 1932 and 1936, and at 148 pounds, 1933, 1935, 1937–45.

WRESTLING

ORIGINS Wrestling was the most popular sport in the ancient Olympic Games; wall drawings dating to *c.* 2600 B.C. show that the sport was popular long before the Greeks. Wrestling was included in the first modern Games. The International Amateur Wrestling Association (FILA) was founded in 1912. There are two forms of wrestling at the international level: freestyle and Greco-Roman. The use of the legs and holds below the waist are prohibited in Greco-Roman.

OLYMPIC GAMES Wrestling events have been included in all the Games since 1896.

Most gold medals Three wrestlers won three Olympic titles: Carl Westergren (Sweden) in 1920, 1924 and 1932; Ivar Johansson (Sweden) in 1932 (two) and 1936; and Aleksandr Medved (USSR) in 1964, 1968 and 1972.

Most medals (individual) Wilfried Dietrich (Germany) won five medals in Olympic competition: one gold, two silver and two bronze, 1956–68. The most Olympic medals won by a U.S. wrestler is three, by freestyler Bruce Baumgartner: two gold and one silver, 1984–92.

WORLD CHAMPIONSHIPS The United States has competed in the freestyle World Women's Championships since 1989.

Most titles (men's individual) The freestyler Aleksandr Medved (USSR) won a record seven world championships, 1962–63, 1966–67 and 1969–71, in three weight categories. The most world titles won by any U.S. wrestler is four, by the freestyler John Smith, 1987 and 1989–91.

Most titles (women's individual) Yayoi Urano (Japan) has won four titles, 1990–91, 1993–94.

Most titles (women's team) Japan has won all six women's world titles (1989–94) since 1989, when women first competed.

U.S. NATIONAL TITLES

Most titles (men's) 15, tied by two. Bruce Baumgartner (Cambridge Springs, Pa.) won all of his titles in freestyle events, 1980 and 1982 in AAU Championships and 1981, 1983–94 in USA Wrestling Championships. Bill Berslake (Cleveland, Ohio) won eight freestyle, 1953–60 in AAU Championships, and seven Greco-Roman titles 1953–59 in USA Wrestling Championships.

Most titles (women's) Five, by Tricia Sanders, Phoenix, Az., 1990–94.

BAUM GOT HIM ■ BRUCE BAUMGARTNER, WINNER OF THREE OLYMPIC MEDALS, DEFEATING DAN PAYNE AT THE 1987 PAN AM GAMES. (ALLSPORT/D. STROHMEYER)

NCAA Division I Championship Oklahoma State University was the first unofficial national champion, in 1928.

Most titles (team) Including five unofficial titles, Oklahoma State has won a record 30 NCAA titles, in 1928–31, 1933–35, 1937–42, 1946, 1948–49, 1954–56, 1958–59, 1961–62, 1964, 1966, 1968, 1971, 1989–90 and 1994.

Most titles (individual) Pat Smith of Oklahoma State is the only wrestler to win four NCAA Division I individual national titles, claiming the 158-pound weight class in 1990, 1991, 1992 and 1994.

Consecutive titles The University of Iowa has won the most consecutive titles, with nine championships from 1978–86.

SUMO WRESTLING

Sumo bouts are fought between two wrestlers (*rikishi*) inside a 14.9-foot-diameter earthen circle (*dohyo*), covered by a roof, symbolizing a Shinto shrine. The wrestlers try to knock each other out of the ring or to the ground. The wrestler who steps out of the dohyo or touches the ground with any part of his body except the soles of his feet loses the contest. Sumo wrestlers are ranked according to their skills; the highest rank is *Yokozuna* (Grand Champion).

ORIGINS Sumo wrestling traces its origins to the development of the Shinto religion in Japan in the eighth century A.D. Sumo matches were staged at Shinto shrines to honor the divine spirits (known as *kami*) during planting and harvesting ceremonies. During the Edo era (1600–1868) sumo wresling became a professional sport. Currently, sumo wrestling is governed by Nihon Sumo Kyokai (Japan Sumo Association), which stages six 15-day tournaments (*basho*) throughout the year.

Most wins (bouts) Kenji Hatano, known as Oshio, won a record 1,107 bouts in 1,891 contests, 1962–88.

Highest winning percentage Tameemon Torokichi, known as Raiden, compiled a .961 winning percentage—244 wins in 154 bouts—from 1789 to 1810.

Heaviest sumo The heaviest *rikishi* of all time is Samoan-American Salevaa Fuali Atisnoe, alias Konishiki, who weighed 580 pounds as of January 4, 1993.

YACHTING

ORIGINS Sailing as a sport dates from the 17th century. Originating in the Netherlands, it was introduced to England by Charles II, who participated in a 23-mile race along the River Thames in 1661. The oldest yacht club in the world is the Royal Cork Yacht Club, which claims descent from the Cork Harbor Water Club, founded in Ireland in 1720. The oldest continuously existing yacht club in the United States is the New York Yacht Club, founded in 1844.

Fastest circumnavigation *Enza New Zealand*, skippered by Peter Blake and Robin Knox-Johnston, completed the fastest nonstop circumnavigation at Ushart, France on April 1, 1994.

AMERICA'S CUP The America's Cup was originally won as an outright prize by the schooner *America* on August 22, 1851 at Cowes, England and was later offered by the New York Yacht Club as a challenge trophy. On August 8, 1870, J. Ashbury's *Cambria* (Great Britain) failed to capture the trophy from *Magic*, owned by F. Osgood (U.S.). The Cup has been challenged 27 times. The U.S. was undefeated until 1983, when *Australia II*, skippered by John Bertrand and owned by a Perth syndicate headed by Alan Bond, beat *Liberty* 4–3, the narrowest series victory, at Newport, R.I.

Most wins (skipper) Three skippers have won the cup three times: Charlie Barr (U.S.), who defended in 1899, 1901 and 1903; Harold S. Vanderbilt (U.S.), who defended in 1930, 1934 and

THE WEATHER STARTED GETTING ROUGH ■ **THE ENZA NEW ZEALAND** OVERCOMING OBSTACLES IN ITS QUEST FOR THE NONSTOP CIRCUMNAVIGATION RECORD IN 1994. (PPL LIMITED/MARK PEPPER)

AMERICA'S CUP WINNERS (1851–1992)

Year	Cup Winner	Skipper	Challenger	Series
1851	America	Richard Brown	—	—
1870	Magic	Andrew Comstock	Cambria (England)	—
1871	Columbia	Nelson Comstock	Livonia (England)	4–1
1876	Madeleine	Josephus Williams	Countess of Dufferin (Canada)	2–0
1881	Mischief	Nathaniel Cook	Atalanta (Canada)	2–0
1885	Puritan	Aubrey Crocker	Genesta (England)	2–0
1886	Mayflower	Martin Stone	Galatea (England)	2–0
1887	Volunteer	Henry Haff	Thistle (Scotland)	2–0
1893	Vigilant	William Hansen	Valkyrie II (England)	3–0
1895	Defender	Henry Haff	Valkyrie III (England)	3–0
1899	Columbia	Charlie Barr	Shamrock I (England)	3–0
1901	Columbia	Charlie Barr	Shamrock II (England)	3–0
1903	Reliance	Charlie Barr	Shamrock III (England)	3–0
1920	Resolute	Charles Adams	Shamrock IV (England)	3–2
1930	Enterprise	Harold Vanderbilt	Shamrock V (England)	4–0
1934	Rainbow	Harold Vanderbilt	Endeavour (England)	4–2
1937	Ranger	Harold Vanderbilt	Endeavour II (England)	4–0
1958	Columbia	Briggs Cunningham	Sceptre (England)	4–0
1962	Weatherly	Emil Mosbacher Jr.	Gretel (Australia)	4–1
1964	Constellation	Bob Bavier Jr.	Sovereign (England)	4–0
1967	Intrepid	Emil Mosbacher Jr.	Dame Pattie (Australia)	4–0
1970	Intrepid	Bill Fricker	Gretel II (Australia)	4–1
1974	Courageous	Ted Hood	Southern Cross (Australia)	4–0
1977	Courageous	Ted Turner	Australia (Australia)	4–0
1980	Freedom	Dennis Conner	Australia (Australia)	4–1
1983	Australia II	John Bertrand	Liberty (U.S.)	4–3
1987	Stars & Stripes	Dennis Conner	Kookaburra III (Australia)	4–0
1988	Stars & Stripes	Dennis Conner	New Zealand (New Zealand)	2–0
1992	America[3]	Bill Koch	Il Moro di Venezia (Italy)	4–1

1937; and Dennis Conner (U.S.), who defended in 1980, challenged in 1987, and defended in 1988.

Largest yacht The largest yacht to have competed in the America's Cup was the 1903 defender, the gaff-rigged cutter *Reliance*, with an overall length of 144 feet, a record sail area of 16,160 square feet and a rig 175 feet high.

OLYMPIC GAMES Bad weather caused the abandonment of yachting events at the first modern Games in 1896. However, the weather has stayed "fair" ever since, and yachting has been part of every Games.

Most gold medals Paul Elvstrom (Denmark) won a record four gold medals in yachting, and in the process became the first competitor in Olympic history to win individual gold medals in four successive Games. Elvstrom's titles came in the Firefly class in 1948, and in the Finn class in 1952, 1956 and 1960.

Most medals Paul Elvstrom's four gold medals are also the most medals won by any Olympic yachtsman.

ROUND-THE-WORLD RACING

Longest race (nonstop) The world's longest nonstop sailing race is the Vendée Globe Challenge, the first of which started from Les Sables d'Olonne, France on November 26, 1989. The distance circumnavigated without stopping was 22,500 nautical miles. The race is for boats between 50–60 feet, sailed single-handed. The record time on the course is 109 days 8 hours 48 minutes 50 seconds, by Titouan Lamazou (France) in the sloop *Ecureuil d'Aquitaine*, which finished at Les Sables on March 19, 1990.

Longest race (total distance) The longest and oldest regular sailing race around the world is the quadrennial Whitbread Round the World race (instituted August 1973), organized by the Royal Naval Sailing Association (Great Britain). It starts in England, and the course around the world and

the number of legs with stops at specified ports are varied from race to race. The distance for 1993–94 was 32,000 nautical miles. The record time for the race is 120 days 5 hours 9 minutes, by *New Zealand Endeavour*, skippered by Grant Dalton (New Zealand) on June 3, 1994.

BOC racing French sailor Isabelle Autissier, on her sailboat *Ecureuil Poitou-Charentes 2*, set a record in the first leg of this round-the-world yacht race (Charleston to Cape Town), sailing 6,800 miles in 35 days 8 hours 52 minutes in October 1994.

Boldface page numbers indicate special features. *Italic* page numbers indicate illustrations or captions. Page numbers followed by t indicate tables. Page numbers followed by q indicate quotations.

skiing **178–180** *see also* biathlon
ski jumping 179
skydiving *see* parachuting
sledding *see* bobsled and luge
sled dog racing 180–181
snooker 181–182
soaring 182
soccer 182–185
softball 185–188
somersaults 131t
speed skating
 ice skating **188–190**
 roller skating 173
spinning (basketball) 59
squash 191
squats (gymnastics) 131t
Stanley Cup (NHL championship)
 champions 143t–146
 coaches 146
 records 141–143, 147t, 148t
steer roping 172, 173
steer wrestling 172
stunt flying *see* aerobatics
Sugar Bowl 111
sumo wrestling 225
Super Bowl (NFL championship)
 coaches 97, 102
 individual records 100–101t,
  102
  MVP awards 97
 team records 97
 winners 99t
surfing 191–192
swimming 192–196 *see also* modern pentathlon; triathlon; water polo
 world records (men) 193t

world records (women) 196t
synchronized swimming 196–197